W9-DIP-029

Regional Conflicts: The Challenge to US–Russian Co-operation

Stockholm International Peace Research Institute

SIPRI is an independent international institute for research into problems of peace and conflict, especially those of arms control and disarmament. It was established in 1966 to commemorate Sweden's 150 years of unbroken peace.

The Institute is financed mainly by the Swedish Parliament. The staff and the Governing Board are international. The Institute also has an Advisory Committee as an international consultative body.

The Governing Board is not responsible for the views expressed in the publications of the Institute.

Governing Board

Professor Daniel Tarschys, Chairman (Sweden)
Sir Brian Urquhart, Vice Chairman (United Kingdom)
Dr Oscar Arias Sánchez (Costa Rica)
Dr Gyula Horn (Hungary)
Dr Ryukichi Imai (Japan)
Professor Catherine Kelleher (United States)
Dr Marjatta Rautio (Finland)
Dr Lothar Rühl (Germany)
The Director

Director

Dr Adam Daniel Rotfeld (Poland)

sipri

Stockholm International Peace Research Institute
Pipers väg 28, S-170 73 Solna, Sweden
Cable: SIPRI
Telephone: 46 8/655 97 00
Telefax: 46 8/655 97 33
E-mail: sipri@sipri.se
Internet URL: http://www.sipri.se

Regional Conflicts: The Challenge to US–Russian Co-operation

Edited by
James E. Goodby

sipri

OXFORD UNIVERSITY PRESS
1995

Oxford University Press, Walton Street, Oxford OX2 6DP
Oxford New York
Athens Auckland Bangkok Bombay
Calcutta Cape Town Dar es Salaam Delhi
Florence Hong Kong Istanbul Karachi
Kuala Lumpur Madras Madrid Melbourne
Mexico City Nairobi Paris Singapore
Taipei Tokyo Toronto
and associated companies in
Berlin Ibadan

Oxford is a trade mark of Oxford University Press

Published in the United States
by Oxford University Press Inc., New York

British Library Cataloguing in Publication Data
Data available

Library of Congress Cataloging in Publication Data
Regional conflicts: the challenge to US–Russian co-operation /
edited by James E. Goodby .
Includes index.
1. United States—Foreign relations—Russia (Federation)
2. Russia (Federation)—Foreign relations—United States.
3. World politics —1985–1995.
I. Goodby, James E.   II. Stockholm International Peace Research Institute.
E183.8.R9R28 1994 327.73047'09'049—dc20 94–38331
ISBN 0–19–829171–X

Typeset and originated by Stockholm International Peace Research Institute
Printed in Great Britain
on acid-free paper by
Biddles Ltd, Guildford and King's Lynn

Contents

5. Controlling the high-technology militarization of the developing world   75

M. Granger Morgan and Mitchel B. Wallerstein

Part III. Where interests diverge: dilemmas of US–Russian security co-operation

6. Global co-operation and regional conflict: problems in co-ordinating the US and Russian security agendas   95

Russell Leigh Moses

7. Post-independence decolonization: a framework for analysing Russia's relations with neighbouring states   119

John J. Maresca

Preface

The end of the cold war has closed one chapter in history—the global struggle between the United States and the Soviet Union. It has not brought an end to regional conflicts. There was never any reason to suppose that these conflicts were purely the result of the bipolar struggle, although many of them became caught up in the global competition. The frequency of regional conflicts, in fact, may be rising.

It was tempting to think as the cold war wound down that the 'international community' would confront regional conflicts and prevent, contain or end them. In the early 1990s, the United Nations was thought to be fulfilling its original promise when the members of the Security Council began to work together co-operatively for practically the first time in the history of the Security Council. Euphoria soon gave way to scepticism. The conflicts in the former Yugoslavia showed that the international community was not truly ready for heroic efforts in collective security. By the autumn of 1993 President Bill Clinton was warning the United Nations to be more discriminating in undertaking peacekeeping operations.

Virulent nationalism and ethnic and cultural chauvinism are the antitheses of pluralistic democracies. This is the latest global ideological threat to liberal democracy and makes regional security a more important issue for the democracies than it was during the cold war. The old democracies have been slow to recognize this. The 'end-of-history' conception of international relations seems to have caught on, and with it an indifference bordering on complacency.

Whether Russia and the USA, each warily evaluating the other's performance, can find it possible to co-operate in dealing with regional conflict is still very uncertain. This is the major challenge to the still limited partnership. Post-cold war conflicts in Yugoslavia and in the Caucasus have been difficult passages for the two former adversaries. Russian technology transfers to India and Iran also have severely tested the evolving relationship. These cases illustrate two different types of regional problems that, if not handled well, can block the possibilities for a growing partnership between Moscow and Washington.

Co-operation between these two countries might take the form of tolerating each other's intervention in areas of special concern to one or the other on condition that certain internationally approved ground rules are followed. In the Caucasus and the Caribbean the faltering first steps towards this type of regime already have been taken. The two countries also might co-operate by agreeing tacitly that neither will intervene on a significant scale as so far has been the case in the former Yugoslavia. However, rivalry, more than partnership, has been the hallmark of these types of co-operation in sensitive regions.

Although the prospects for effective Russian–US co-operation in containing future regional conflicts may not be bright, their stakes in many of these conflicts will be so high that the two nations and other great powers are almost duty-bound to consider how they might jointly conduct a form of preventive diplomacy. Even minimal co-operation can be significant: think what the situation would have been had Moscow and Washington taken opposite sides in regional conflicts in recent years. At least, there may now be hope that Russian–US diplomacy could prevent the worst effects of such conflicts—those that might be caused by weapons of mass destruction.

Controlling arms and technology transfers will be a major test of whether Moscow and Washington can co-operate in regional security matters after the cold war. Issues of this type already have arisen in North-east Asia, South Asia and the Middle East. Arms and technology transfers are important to Russia's military–industrial complex as its leaders struggle to keep this sector of the Russian economy in the vanguard of technological developments and competitive with other demands for Russia's resources. Because arms sales and technology transfers are important hard-currency earners for Russia there will be powerful incentives to develop markets for them. However, US–Russian co-operation can be placed in jeopardy by the drive for contracts in developing countries, as the Russian–Iranian nuclear reactor deal has shown.

Russia and the USA may find it easier to co-operate in regional security matters in some instances within the framework of an international organization or an international regime. This will most likely be the case when neither country perceives that it has much at stake in a regional problem except for humanitarian concerns or a general preference for order over anarchy. Situations like this already have occurred in Rwanda and Somalia. A characteristic of conflicts in the post-cold war world, illustrated by these two cases, is that they are conflicts *within* a country rather than *between* countries. A potentially fruitful area for co-operation between Russia and the USA lies in developing the ability of the United Nations to deal with such conflicts, rather than becoming involved directly themselves.

In 1995, 50 years after the founding of the United Nations, the organization faces a crisis of confidence, generated in large part by conflicts *within* national frontiers. The Secretary-General wrote with a haunting sense of tragedies yet to come in his report *Supplement to An Agenda for Peace*: 'hard decisions, if postponed, will appear in retrospect as having been relatively easy when measured against the magnitude of tomorrow's trouble'.[1]

Political figures and others seeking non-involvement in the responsibilities for promoting peace sometimes say, or imply, that the transactions of the great powers can proceed without being much troubled by a world rife with regional conflicts. The experience of the post-cold war world suggests otherwise.

---

[1] United Nations Security Council, *Supplement to An Agenda for Peace: Position Paper of the Secretary General on the Occasion of the Fiftieth Anniversary of the United Nations*, Report of the Secretary-General on the work of the Organization, UN document A/50/60 (S/1995/1), 3 Jan. 1995, para. 104 (reproduced in appendix 10A in this volume).

Regional conflicts can impose serious strains on the fabric of international peace and security, including Russian–US relations. There are many forms of co-operation between these two great powers that could alleviate these strains. This book suggests a few of them, but its primary purpose is to point out the types of problems that must be confronted if co-operation is to have any hope of being effective. Rough spots in the relationship are inevitable. Losing sight of the long-term interest of Russia and the USA in co-operation is not.

***

This is the second volume of a two-part study on international security issues in the post-cold war era undertaken collaboratively by the Program on International Peace and Security at Carnegie Mellon University and the Stockholm International Peace Research Institute (SIPRI). The first volume, published in 1993 and entitled *The Limited Partnership: Building a Russian–US Security Community*, described the incredibly difficult and dangerous passage from Soviet state to Russian Federation. It addressed the nature of Russian–US interaction in the security field and suggested how Russian–US military co-operation could contribute to the building of a security community. In this second book, the contributing authors were asked to consider regional conflicts, how relations among the great powers could be affected by such conflicts and how co-operation among the leading nations, especially Russia and the United States, might influence the course of regional strife. Conflicts around the periphery of Russia, especially in what Moscow calls 'the near abroad', will be the subject of a further study by SIPRI and Carnegie Mellon.

Readers of this study may find the forthcoming SIPRI volume, *Russia and Europe: The Emerging Security Agenda*, edited by Vladimir Baranovsky, of interest. It examines Russia's foreign and security policy options with respect to Europe, explores the domestic context of Russian policy making, analyses Russia's changing relations with its European neighbours and speculates on Russia's role in the building of a new European security architecture. Authors from Russia and other countries offer analyses from both a Russian and non-Russian perspective.

***

The research and writing of this volume and its predecessor, *The Limited Partnership*, was a collaborative effort between SIPRI and the Program on International Peace and Security at Carnegie Mellon University. The entire project was made possible through the generous support of the Ford Foundation. For this, SIPRI and Carnegie Mellon University are profoundly grateful. We wish to thank, in particular, Dr Enid Shoettle Okun and Dr Shepard Forman, past and present directors of the Ford Foundation's International Affairs Program.

Special homage is due the authors of these chapters for their courage, as well as their insights in writing about a field that is so unsettled. Contemporaneous interpretations of historical shifts of the magnitude the world is now witnessing are bound to be approximations of the truth. None the less, policies are made and decisions executed in such an environment; scholars and analysts, it seems, have an obligation to try to understand and explain what they think is happening even though time may prove them wrong. It is in that spirit that the points of view expressed in this book are offered.

The initial review and organizing of the material for this book was undertaken by Judyth Twigg and William Newmann. Few people could have been better qualified for such a mission. The discipline and dedication which they brought to this task, as well as their success in helping to craft a coherent product was, typically, of the very highest order.

For the editor, the constant support and encouragement of Professor M. Granger Morgan, Head of the Department of Engineering and Public Policy at Carnegie Mellon University, was an indispensable element throughout the process of completing this book. Special thanks are owed him.

Once again, we are indebted to Patty Currie of the Program on International Peace and Security at Carnegie Mellon University for all she has done to bring this ship into port. As usual she has assumed more than her fair share of responsibility for the outcome. Her oversight of the work on the manuscript and her involvement in every one of the endless details that go into the creation of a book made it possible for this voyage to be successfully completed.

The SIPRI editor, Jetta Gilligan Borg, deserves special honours for her patience and perseverance in preparing final camera-ready copy of the text. She has done a superb job. Her enthusiasm, skill and devotion made this volume a better product. For this, the editor gives her his heartfelt thanks.

James E. Goodby   Adam Daniel Rotfeld
The Program on International   Director
Peace and Security   SIPRI
Carnegie Mellon University

March 1995

Acronyms

ABM	Anti-ballistic missile
AFV	Armoured fighting vehicle
AICV	Armoured infantry combat vehicle
AIDS	Acquired immune deficiency syndrome
APEC	Asia–Pacific Economic Cooperation
ARF	ASEAN Regional Forum
ASEAN	Association of South-East Asian Nations
AWACS	Airborne warning and control system
BW	Biological weapons
CENTCOM	Central Command
CFE	Conventional Armed Forces in Europe
CIA	Central Intelligence Agency
CIS	Commonwealth of Independent States
CMCA	Commission of Mediation, Conciliation and Arbitration
COCOM	Coordinating Committee (on Multilateral Export Controls)
CPC	Conflict Prevention Centre
CSBM	Confidence- and security-building measure
CSCE	Conference on Security and Co-operation in Europe
CW	Chemical weapons
CWC	Chemical Weapons Convention
DEA	Drug Enforcement Agency
EC	European Community
ECOWAS	Economic Community of West African States
EPCI	Enhanced Proliferation Control Initiative
EU	European Union
GATT	Global Agreement on Tariffs and Trade
GCC	Gulf Co-operation Council
HACV	Heavy armoured combat vehicles
IADB	Inter-American Defense Board
IAEA	International Atomic Energy Agency
IAPC	Inter-American Committee on Peaceful Settlement
INF	Intermediate-range nuclear forces
JCS	Joint Chiefs of Staff
JNA	Yugoslav National Army
MLRS	Multiple launcher rocket system
MSC	Military Staff Committee (UN Security Council)
MTCR	Missile Technology Control Regime
NAC	North Atlantic Council
NACC	North Atlantic Co-operation Council
NATO	North Atlantic Treaty Organization
NBC	Nuclear, biological and chemical
NJM	New Jewel Movement

NPFL	National Patriotic Forces of Liberia
NPT	Non-Proliferation Treaty
NSC	National Security Council
OAS	Organization of American States
OAU	Organization of African Unity
PDD	Presidential Decision Directive
PDF	Panama Defense Forces
PFP	Partnership for Peace
PLO	Palestine Liberation Organization
R&D	Research and development
RDJTF	Rapid Deployment Joint Task Force
SAARC	South Asian Association for Regional Cooperation
SHAPE	Supreme Headquarters Allied Powers Europe
SOUTHCOM	Southern Command
SSG	Special Situations Group
START	Strategic Arms Reduction Talks/Treaty
UNPROFOR	United Nations Protection Force
WEU	Western European Union
WTO	Warsaw Treaty Organization

Part I
Introduction

1. Introductory remarks

James E. Goodby

I. The theses of the study

With the end of the cold war Russia and the United States should find it possible to co-operate rather than compete in preventing, stopping or containing conflict. It will not be easy to do this. Distrust remains a commonplace reaction to each other's behaviour: Russian peacekeeping efforts in the Caucasus are seen in the West as neo-imperialism while US objections to Russian technology transfers are seen in Moscow as attempts to deny Russia legitimate markets for its goods.

This being the situation, it should be asked whether US–Russian co-operation in managing regional conflict is a useful policy to pursue either in Moscow or in Washington. It is to this question that this book is primarily addressed. There is no single answer, but the question itself has not been posed in ways that might yield even general guidance for policy makers.

Regional conflicts have become a challenge to the limited partnership between Russia and the USA in both a positive and a negative sense. In the positive sense, US–Russian co-operation in preventing the worst manifestations of regional conflict can reinforce the partnership between the two countries. In the negative sense, regional conflict can become an irritant, or worse, in US–Russian relations. Many post-cold war regional conflicts, perhaps most, have contained elements that have had both positive and negative effects. This seems to have been the case in Iran, Iraq, Nagorno-Karabakh and Yugoslavia, to cite a few recent cases.

How can the two countries maximize the positive impact of their interaction in regional conflicts while reducing the negative? The advice offered in this book is that Moscow and Washington need to take a more strategic view of three types of regional conflicts and, to the extent their differing national interests permit, adopt positions which are supportive of common goals. The three types of regional conflict considered in this book are : (*a*) cases where weapons of mass destruction might come into play; (*b*) cases where one or both countries have strong interests—strategic, historical or economic—in the progress or outcome of a regional conflict; (*c*) cases where neither Russia nor the USA have much at stake aside, perhaps, from shared humanitarian concerns.

The common goals of Russia and the USA in such conflicts, at the most basic level, are: (*a*) to contain the proliferation of weapons of mass destruction and to make their use in war less likely; (*b*) to manage regional conflict in a way that contributes to a predictable international order and does not undercut each other's fundamental interests; and (*c*) to strengthen the ability of international organizations to prevent, contain or stop regional conflict and to provide humanitarian assistance.

Diplomacy aimed at forestalling armed conflict and resolving disputes needs greater emphasis in building a US–Russian partnership. Typically, the opportunity costs of not engaging in timely preventive diplomacy are discounted by national governments, with the result that regional conflicts are allowed to develop into crises before diplomatic efforts become seriously engaged. This book is intended to illuminate the possibilities for US–Russian preventive diplomacy. It does this by discussing the problems and opportunities presented in various types of conflict situations. By examining the challenges the two countries face, as well as the means currently available to them in dealing with these challenges, a more strategic or conceptual approach may be possible. Instead of dealing with each new regional conflict as though it were a special situation with no wider meaning, Russia and the USA could view conflicts more generically and consider how their responses could more effectively serve their common goals.

II. The structure of the study

Three broad categories of regional conflicts—potential or actual—are plainly visible in the post-cold war landscape, as seen from the perspective of US and Russian engagement with the parties to a conflict. The first involves those countries that can be identified as among the most advanced, economically and technologically, of the developing world and where, in many cases, US and Russian interests are more or less equally engaged. Typical of this category are the countries of the Middle East and South Asia. What makes this category special and distinct is that conflicts among these countries present the risk that weapons of mass destruction might be used and that war might spread, out of control, through vast regions of the developing world.

The second category of regional conflict is defined primarily by the fact that the country or countries involved are of special interest to one or more of the great powers. 'Sphere of interest' politics is another way of identifying this category, with an implication that the interests of Russia and the USA are heavily engaged in the fate of these countries. In this category are the newly independent states along the southern borders of the Russian Federation. The nations of the Caribbean and Central America also may be placed in this category. So too may the nations of Europe in the special sense that both Russia and the USA are deeply involved in the affairs of the European continent, and conflicts there are likely to have major effects on their security.

The third category is defined by the absence of any overriding Russian or US national security interest. Rwanda and Somalia are illustrative of this category. Internal chaos leading to human catastrophes cries out for intervention, but in such situations only the flimsy support structure of international organizations is typically available.

As in any attempt to categorize, certain countries may fit in both these types of conflict situations. In the Middle East, for example, are several instances of developing countries that are not only economically and technologically advanced but that also, because of special ties, proximity or oil resources, are of concern to Russia or the USA, or to both. From the point of view of US–Russian co-operation in dealing with regional conflict, the typology here has the advantage of highlighting the differing ways in which regional conflicts present opportunities and dangers for US–Russian relations. Despite the inevitable difficulties in forcing messy real-world situations into neat categories, therefore the editor has chosen to organize this book along these lines.

Part II contains four chapters that discuss US–Russian co-operation in a world where the parties to a dispute are relatively advanced technologically and where Russian and US interests are not asymmetrically engaged, as in a sphere of interest situation. In such a world US–Russian diplomacy should be aimed at preventing the outbreak of hostilities or at limiting the effects of a conflict should it occur. Methods which were used to good effect in Europe, and also in the Middle East, might be helpful in such situations. However, the most distinctive feature of US–Russian co-operation in the circumstances envisaged in Part II is that it calls for a high degree of co-ordinated interaction—both between Russia and the USA and among the countries of a region.

Regional conflicts are much more dangerous than in the past because of the possibility that one or more parties to a dispute may be equipped with some version of weapons of mass destruction. The outlook for effective intervention by the great powers in preventing conflict or resolving disputes is not promising, to judge by the experiences described in this book. Especially where conflicts have internal origins, the international community has not been prone to intervene at early stages when conflict could conceivably have been avoided. Russian–US partnership in dealing with regional conflicts does not seem to be heading towards unqualified co-operation. Instead it appears to be developing more in the direction of a tacit or acquiescent form of co-operation, based on a geographic division of labour. This would be an improvement over the cold war but it is a weak form of co-operation, not one that holds great promise in stopping regional conflicts in their tracks. Perhaps, then, US–Russian partnership should emphasize those elements designed to limit the damage that regional conflicts could cause. Foremost among these would be co-operation in preventing the proliferation of arms and advanced weapon technologies, conventional as well as nuclear, biological and chemical.

The idea of co-operation is open to many interpretations and approaches, as Professor Phil Williams points out in chapter 2. He distinguishes between tacit, acquiescent and unqualified co-operation as methods by which Russia and the United States might jointly deal with problems of preventing or managing crises in the developing world. Examples of each type of co-operation can be identified and may be models for future Russian–US relations even though the bipolar pattern of the past no longer exists. As to the salience of regional conflicts as a possible focus of Russian–US co-operation, Professor Williams suggests that such conflicts may be more prevalent and more dangerous than ever before because of the proliferation of modern weapon technology. In opposition to the notion that despite the increasing danger of regional conflicts Russia is not an appropriate partner for the United States in dealing with them, Professor Williams explains why US and Russian interests would be well served by such co-operation. One example is nuclear weapon proliferation where Professor Williams suggests that if proliferation cannot be prevented in particular cases, Russia and the United States could act jointly or in parallel to mitigate its worst effects.

In chapter 3 a distinguished Russian analyst, Dr Sergey Rogov, writes that regional security should be based on co-operation among the regional countries themselves. The nations of a region should establish, for example, an agency to control arms transfers into the region, refrain from purchasing some types of offensive weapons and co-operate in international regimes to renounce weapons of mass destruction. However, for such regional systems to be fully effective, external weapon suppliers should also join together to limit arms transfers into the region. In Dr Rogov's opinion, Russia and the United States should work closely together to promote arms control and that form of co-operative security usually known as confidence- and security-building measures (CSBMs) in the developing world. What he proposes amounts to the elements of a North–South security system.

CSBMs no doubt deserve a special place in regional efforts to deal with the proliferation of weapons of mass destruction and advanced weapon technology. Russia and the United States have jointly participated in several confidence-building regimes, both bilaterally and in company with other nations. The experience was beneficial, particularly in fostering military-to-military contacts. In chapter 4 James Macintosh, a leading expert on CSBMs, subjects the problem of destabilizing military technologies to a vigorous theoretical treatment. He draws on the considerable experience of the Conference on Security and Co-operation in Europe (CSCE)[1] to describe an array of confidence-building techniques that are available for application in other contexts. Macintosh believes that qualitative arms control—measures that deal with technological improvements—must come to grips with the subjective nature of decision making and of perceptions of stability. For this purpose, he argues, confidence building, with its stress on transparency and on inducing changes in threat perception, is an ideal mechanism to constrain and manage the destabilizing impact of changes in military capability.

Chapter 5, written by Professor M. Granger Morgan and Dr Mitchel B. Wallerstein, argues the case for collective action by the great powers to limit

---

[1] In December 1994 the participants in the CSCE decided to rename this institution. They dropped the word 'Conference' and substituted the word 'Organization', to signify a more permanent and operational role for what is now the OSCE. The editor has elected to retain the older title since most readers are more likely to be familiar with it than with the new one.

the spread of high-technology weapons and weapons of mass destruction in the developing world. While supporting efforts to reduce demand, they stress the element of supply. They believe the great powers should, if necessary, impose a system of limitations on the developing world, including *in extremis* joint military action to destroy proliferation-related facilities in developing countries. Evidently this option was considered and discarded by the Clinton Administration in the case of North Korea. More than likely this would have been a unilateral US action.

Morgan and Wallerstein emphasize the need for a dual-use export control regime narrowly focused on selected technologies and destinations and widely multilateral in nature. They also believe that governments and universities should do a better job of impeding the flow of assistance to developing world military programmes provided by individual technical experts.

Part III addresses cases where potential conflicts hit close to home, almost literally, in the countries that Russia likes to call the 'near abroad' and that US journalists and politicians like to call 'America's backyard'. However, it also discusses cases like Afghanistan and the Persian Gulf where Russia (or the Soviet Union) and the USA had special interests that each perceived to be so important as to require unilateral intervention if necessary. It also contains a chapter on Yugoslavia where the conflict was of special concern both to Russia and the USA but where, for much of the time, inaction by both powers was generally considered to be preferable to unilateral action by either of them, or to joint military action.

In chapter 6 Professor Russell Leigh Moses writes that the possibilities for US–Russian co-operation in regional conflicts are limited because Russian leaders must focus much of their attention on their most critical security issues resulting from the breakup of the Soviet Union. Disputes in the developing world and the proliferation of advanced weapon technologies do not rank as high on Russia's security agenda as instability in the 'near abroad', those new independent states that once were part of the Soviet Union. Therefore, Professor Moses argues, if the attention of the top Russian leaders is to be fully engaged in Russian–US security co-operation, such co-operation must come to grips with the problems Russia is facing along its southern flank. Paradoxically, while peacekeeping in those areas is where Russian–US co-operation is most needed, this is also where it will be most difficult to achieve.

Building on studies of the Soviet Government's decisions to intervene in Afghanistan and co-operate up to a point with the USA in the 1991 Persian Gulf War, Professor Moses stresses that there is a very fine line between intervention and co-operation. Co-operation, he believes, benefits from predictability and trust. Neither is likely to be readily available in crisis situations of the type that have arisen in the past to the south of Russia. Moses concludes that an effective Western strategy to deal with this problem should link Western economic assistance to Moscow's decisions regarding the use of Russian peacekeeping forces in neighbouring states and also should envisage the use in these areas of non-Russian peacekeeping forces supplied under United Nations auspices.

Is US–Russian co-operation likely to be productive in that part of the world? Ambassador John Maresca addresses that question in chapter 7, after first analysing the decolonization process that is proceeding fitfully, sometimes violently, across the southern tier of what used to be the Soviet Union. He highlights the importance, both for Russia and the USA, of a better understanding of the nature of this decolonization process and the sensitivities it entails. He argues that it will be better for Russia and the USA to co-operate in encouraging international involvement to ensure stability in this region, rather than for Russia to simply try to manage the area's problems by itself. Thus far it has been difficult to find agreement on how to do this, although the encouraging agreement at the Budapest CSCE summit meeting in December 1994 may have set a valuable precedent.

The asymmetry between the post-cold war situations of Russia and the USA cannot be disregarded in considering whether or how the two countries can co-operate in dealing with conflicts in the developing world. Their relative power status measured by almost any standard has shifted dramatically in favour of the United States. Professor Moses and Ambassador Maresca write convincingly in chapters 6 and 7 of how the West might influence Russia's peacekeeping operations in Russia's bordering states, either through the UN or the CSCE; in chapter 8, however, William W. Newmann sees Russian co-operation as relevant to interventions in Latin America only if Washington opts for a UN mandate there, as in the case of Haiti, but not a necessary condition even for a truly multilateral operation.

A more meaningful measure of change may be the radically altered strategic framework for decision making that has emerged as the cold war has ended. US influence in Latin America far outreaches Russian interests there, but, for that matter, Russian influence in much of the former Soviet Union outweighs the interests and influence of the USA. Newmann points out that US calculations concerning intervention in Latin America are no longer based on a reading of benefits or losses to a global competitor. Rather, the assessment is based on whether internal developments in these neighbouring countries have led to a provocative and inescapable confrontation with the United States. This is shown by the two Latin American cases described in his chapter: Grenada, a cold war intervention, and Panama, a post-cold war case. Is the situation the same in what Russia sees as its near abroad?

The change in the strategic framework is even more striking on examining the two Persian Gulf cases Newmann presents. The flagging of Kuwaiti tankers was undertaken by the USA with the intention of denying Moscow any security role in the Gulf. In the war with Iraq three years later the United States looked to the UN Security Council to legitimize its own role in the Gulf and actively sought Moscow's co-operation to force Saddam Hussein out of Kuwait.

It is not necessary to argue that these are prototypical cases to see that the judgements of Washington policy makers are already based on a different set of factors than those that motivated US leaders during the cold war. Newmann concludes that the shared security interests of Washington and Moscow are likely to strengthen the limited Russian–US partnership that has developed in the post-cold war period.

Chapter 9 is a case study of regional conflict in Europe. The editor's essay on the former Yugoslavia reveals a case of missed opportunities. The year 1990 was probably the last in which the war in the Balkans could have been headed off altogether but there were opportunities to block the extension of the Serbian–Croatian conflict to Bosnia and Herzegovina. These opportunities were not only missed but the situation was handled in a way that made matters worse. Self-determination and the rights of minorities were high on the list of complex issues that defied solution. The fact that the conflict could be described as a civil war made many countries hesitant to intervene. None the less, from mid-1991 onwards the European Community (EC)—later the European Union (EU)—engaged intensively in efforts to negotiate cease-fires and broker a political solution. The Community publicly rejected proposals to interfere using military force.

The United Nations came on the scene in late 1991. Former US Secretary of State Cyrus Vance, the representative of the Secretary-General, was instrumental in negotiating a cease-fire between Serbia and Croatia. Efforts by the EC and the UN jointly to negotiate a political settlement failed to produce results. Partnership between Moscow and Washington in the crisis was largely absent until the situation became too dangerous for them not to co-operate. This did not happen until February 1994 when a combination of events forced them to make common cause in order to protect their own interests. The experience may be salutary but its relevance outside the Balkans remains to be seen.

Part IV addresses the question of how effectively international organizations might deal with regional conflicts, including conflicts within states, in those situations where perceived national interests do not evoke a direct response either by Russia or the USA. Should the nations put more reliance on regional organizations, since the UN clearly is overburdened and inadequately funded? This review provides little room for encouragement. Outside of Europe, regional security organizations where they exist at all are not geared to collective security operations. The editor and the co-author of chapter 10, Daniel B. O'Connor, see few alternatives to the UN in the near term. One of the more important challenges to US–Russian co-operation lies in rebuilding the UN's peacekeeping and peacemaking functions and strengthening preventive diplomacy through use of the UN's multilateral mediation and monitoring services. This could be one of the most productive and cost-effective areas for US–Russian co-operation. To the many tragedies associated with the fate of disintegrating societies can be added the dim prospects for this kind of co-operation between Russia and the USA.

Part II
Preventive diplomacy in an era of high technology

2. The potential for US–Russian security co-operation in the developing world

Phil Williams

I. Introduction

The end of the cold war, the disintegration of the Soviet Union, the transition from a bipolar to a multilayered international system in which power is more diffuse, the proliferation of weapons of mass destruction and the growing aspirations for the creation of a 'new world order', all these developments compel new and imaginative efforts to think about the problems of regional conflict and how they might be contained. Unless this is done successfully, the much-vaunted new world order will become a new world disorder in which the diffusion of power is followed by a diffusion of regional conflict. The danger is that the removal of past constraints will not be accompanied by the imposition of new security arrangements, new institutions or new mechanisms that can ameliorate or contain emerging challenges to regional security.

In responding to this potential problem, much will depend upon the degree to which there is great power co-operation. Accordingly, this chapter focuses on future regional conflicts with particular attention to the likelihood of co-operation between Washington and Moscow in efforts at both conflict prevention and conflict management. Initially, the chapter looks at the notion of co-operation in relation to regional conflict and makes some general observations about the co-operative process. This is followed by an analysis of the kinds of co-operation which characterized US–Soviet relations during the cold war. Although the roles of Moscow and Washington are likely to be very different in future regional conflicts, the historical experience may have continued relevance. Delineating the forms that superpower co-operation took during the cold war and identifying both the incentives for and the obstacles to such co-operation will provide a basis for considering what has changed and what remains the same. The third section of the chapter looks at the impact of the end of the cold war on the prospects for regional conflict and instability. In view of the changes that have taken place in what used to be the superpower relationship, attention is then focused on the question of whether co-operation between Moscow and Washington has much relevance to future regional conflicts. The conclusion is that it does, although within a broader and rather different framework than in the past. Finally, the chapter examines the issue of nuclear proliferation and considers the kinds of co-operation which may be most useful in relation to nuclear conflict prevention and conflict management in the future.

II. Forms of co-operation

Co-operation can take many forms and be analysed in many different ways. For present purposes, however, it is particularly useful to distinguish between tacit, asymmetrical and fully fledged co-operation.

By its very nature, tacit co-operation lacks formality and explicitness, yet it may be one of the most important forms of co-operation. Its purpose is to avoid conflict getting out of hand, and, as will be argued below, this was one of the most prevalent forms of superpower co-operation during the cold war. Although the primary motive for tacit co-operation may be negative in the sense that it is concerned with avoiding or reducing dangers, its consequences can be very positive. Under certain circumstances, forms of tacit co-operation can provide a basis for the development of a formal or informal regime.

The essence of asymmetrical, or 'acquiescent', co-operation is that one side is heavily involved and the other gives it tacit or overt support, acting in what is essentially a facilitating or enabling role. In some respects this was the pattern of the crisis and war in the Persian Gulf in 1990–91, when the United States took the lead and the USSR provided minimum direct support and, by and large, refrained from any actions which could have derailed US efforts to mobilize international support against Saddam Hussein.

A third form is 'unqualified' or 'fully fledged' co-operation: in this, the great powers have a joint or mutual interest in a particular outcome and explicitly work together in order to achieve it. This might be the case, for example, if they decided that the peace process in the Middle East required joint support and therefore made systematic efforts to facilitate the process. One of the potential problems with this kind of co-operation is that it could very easily raise the spectre of great power condominium. Not surprisingly, during the cold war there were times when states resisted the idea of superpower collaboration by taking disruptive or precipitate action. Egypt's decision to resort to war against Israel in October 1973 had elements of this and was, in part at least, a protest against the fact that superpower *détente* was relegating the Arab–Israeli conflict to the back burner.

In addition to the manner and extent of co-operation, it is necessary to consider the range of issues that co-operation can encompass. There are two major areas of co-operation that are most relevant to regional conflicts: co-operation in crisis prevention, and co-operation in crisis management to ensure that regional conflicts do not become a source of wider confrontation. In both cases, the mechanisms, procedures and institutions that are available to facilitate co-operation can have a major impact. Indeed, there may well be occasions when bilateral efforts can best be achieved, sustained and legitimized by being part of a wider process undertaken through a multinational forum such as the United Nations or the CSCE Conflict Prevention Centre (CPC) in Vienna.

In thinking about co-operation in any particular instance it is also necessary to consider the incentives for co-operation on the one side and the penalties or potential risks that will be incurred through co-operative rather than unilateral responses on the other. There will be occasions when the impediments to co-operation, either domestic or international, will be greater than the pressures or incentives in favour of the adoption of a co-operative approach to regional conflicts. There must be a gradual increase in mutual trust if there is to be progress from tacit and acquiescent co-operation to more ambitious co-operative ventures. The greater the experience of successful and beneficial co-operation, the less concern there will be about the possibility of defection and the less likely it will be that each side would be preoccupied with relative benefits as opposed to the absolute benefits resulting from co-operation. At the same time, there has to be some equity: co-operation cannot afford one side a permanent advantage and the other a permanent disability or disadvantage. Moreover, there must be penalties for defection from a co-operative approach, if only in terms of the impact on the overall relationship of those involved.

With these issues in mind, it is now necessary to examine the evolution of superpower co-operation during the cold war.

III. Superpower co-operation: a historical perspective

The cold war can be understood either as a prolonged period of confrontation in which the USA and the USSR were very lucky to avoid major and highly destructive conflict or as an exercise in evolutionary co-operation.[1] Yet it is perhaps one of the most distinguishing features of the cold war that it was both of these things simultaneously. The USA and the USSR co-operated in several ways as part of a relationship which was appropriately described as an 'adversary partnership'.[2] Although the superpowers were adversaries, they were also partners in the task of 'disaster avoidance'.[3] This led them to develop certain norms and conventions and to accept the need for constraints on their behaviour.

Indeed, the cold war exhibited the paradox that the more intense the confrontation, the greater the need for co-operation. This was not surprising, as the calculation was a very simple one: in situations in which the penalties for mistakes, miscalculations or transgression of some very basic 'rules of prudence' were both obvious and unmistakable, the incentives for co-operation between enemies and observance of these rules were very real. One of the most impor-

---

[1] For the latter approach see Kanet, R. A. and Kolodziej, E. A. (eds), *The Cold War as Cooperation* (Johns Hopkins University Press: Baltimore, 1991).

[2] The nature of this relationship is discussed more fully in Aron, R., *Peace and War* (Praeger: New York, 1968).

[3] This term is used by G. Snyder in 'Crisis bargaining', ed. C. F. Hermann, *International Crises: Insights from Behavioral Research* (Free Press: New York, 1972).

tant facets of co-operation resulted from the mutual recognition by Moscow and Washington of the need to contain, and even defuse, regional conflicts. The superpowers found it necessary to co-operate, at least tacitly and sometimes explicitly, to ensure that they were not dragged into conflicts between regional powers on opposing sides, that local powers were not able to precipitate superpower confrontations, and that they did not allow regional concerns to override their central preoccupation with avoiding nuclear war.

Although superpower arms control ventures had the greatest visibility, the most important and certainly the most urgent form of superpower co-operation emerged in relation to crisis management. From the early years of the cold war the superpowers engaged in tacit co-operation to manage their crises. They agreed on certain 'rules of the game' or codes of conduct which each of them observed even when it was not clearly in its self-interest (as opposed to their mutual interest in war avoidance) to do so in a particular situation or crisis. Among the most important of these was the need to avoid crossing the threshold between coercion and violence as well as taking other escalatory steps, the need to give the adversary a path of retreat without humiliation, the need to limit objectives and avoid trespassing on the adversary's vital interests, and the need to maintain open communication channels. The superpowers also took great care to maintain control over events and allies so that escalation did not occur inadvertently. Although there were several occasions when these 'rules of prudence' were jeopardized, major transgressions were avoided. Indeed, one of the most important features of the cold war was that Soviet and US forces never met in combat. Despite the fact that there were crises in which the local balance of conventional power greatly favoured one superpower or the other, the dangers of crossing the line between coercion and violence greatly outweighed any possible gains that might be made by efforts to exploit this local advantage—especially since there was great nervousness about the ability of either side to maintain control over the escalation process.[4] Moreover, the benefits from continued maintenance of the rules outweighed the benefits that might be gained by non-observance in a particular instance.

The imperatives for crisis management were overriding. Critics, though, contended that the very term 'crisis management' was a misnomer—and a rather dangerous one—since it encouraged governments to believe that they had greater control over the situation than was actually the case. Ken Booth, for example, has written that those who live by crisis management could also die by crisis management.[5] However, as the only real alternative was crisis mismanagement, it is not surprising that the superpowers were willing to co-operate at precisely those junctures where their relationship was most dangerous.

---

[4] For an excellent discussion of the role of perceptions of escalation in superpower crises see Rogers, P., 'Crisis bargaining codes and crisis management', ed. A. L. George, *Avoiding War: Problems of Crisis Management* (Westview Press: Boulder, Colo., 1991), pp. 413–42.

[5] For a useful critique of crisis management, see Booth, K., *Strategy and Ethnocentrism* (Croom Helm: London, 1979), pp. 58–60.

At the same time, the superpowers recognized that crisis management was an inherently dangerous undertaking. Indeed, throughout much of the cold war their predominant concern was crisis prevention. Like co-operation in crisis management, co-operation in avoiding crises was accomplished largely through tacit agreement on codes of conduct. These rules of the game enabled them to avoid transforming regional crises and conflicts into direct superpower confrontations. Regional crises frequently added to the acrimony and the general level of tension in superpower relations, but they rarely precipitated direct confrontation. One reason for this was that there was what might be termed 'decoupling through spheres of influence'. Although tacit agreement on spheres of influence was often criticized in the West as giving the USSR a free hand in Eastern Europe, in fact it ensured that any upheaval in the eastern part of the continent was not transformed into a major military confrontation between the North Atlantic Treaty Organization (NATO) and the Warsaw Treaty Organization (WTO). The Brezhnev Doctrine (the term given to Soviet justification of the August 1968 intervention in Czechoslovakia) formalized this decoupling, but the USA had tacitly accepted Soviet domination of Eastern Europe from the early 1950s onwards. In effect, this decoupled events in Eastern Europe from the overall military relationship between the superpowers. Soviet interventions in Eastern Europe became a source of contention between the superpowers but did not provoke confrontation. In this sense there was a ritualistic element to US denunciations of such Soviet actions as the 1968 invasion of Czechoslovakia.

There was also an element of reciprocity in the understanding about spheres of influence. The USSR accepted that in Latin America the USA had an equally free hand and could engage in military intervention with impunity. This reciprocity led Franck and Weisband to refer to superpower spheres of influence as a 'dual ghetto system'.[6] They also contended that the justifications that were provided for superpower military interventions in Eastern Europe and Latin America were remarkably similar. Yet, although it is clear that there were enormous costs, especially to the East Europeans, associated with superpower regional domination, the main advantage of the clear delineation of spheres of influence was that it helped to minimize the prospects for miscalculation in US–Soviet relations.

Not all regions, of course, were clearly within the sphere of influence of one or other superpower. The decoupling principle, however, was tacitly extended beyond regions where one or the other was clearly dominant. If one of them was involved in a regional conflict, the other generally stayed on the sidelines, giving moral and material support to its proxy but avoiding direct involvement. This norm of 'asymmetrical intervention' was crucial in ensuring that limited wars in which one of the superpowers was involved did not escalate into a direct conflict between them.

[6] Franck, T. and Weisband, E., *Word Politics* (Oxford University Press: New York, 1971).

One of the most interesting characteristics of the development of superpower co-operation in relation to regional conflict was the progression from tacit co-operation in crisis management and crisis prevention to more explicit and formal efforts to co-operate not only in preventing regional crises but also in defusing or ending them. The *détente* of the 1970s saw an effort by the superpowers to establish a crisis prevention regime. This failed partly because Washington was interested in imposing restraint on the USSR, while Moscow was interested in obtaining equality with the USA—an equality which was expressed largely in terms of power projection and involvement in Third World conflicts.[7] The US interest in preventing all regional crises was undercut by the Soviet desire to prevent only those crises likely to lead to direct superpower confrontation. Indeed, the divergent expectations led to allegations of duplicity and bad faith, which contributed to the demise of *détente* in the late 1970s.

As part of the new *détente* of the mid-1980s, superpower co-operation once again moved on to the agenda. On this occasion, however, such co-operation was more pragmatic in form: the USA and the USSR did not attempt to establish another global regime for crisis prevention—instead they used quiet, low-key diplomacy in an effort to bring to an end existing military conflicts throughout the Third World. Their efforts were both collaborative and complementary. A large part of the reason for this was the shift in Soviet calculations—a shift which began in the early 1980s as Moscow gradually came to realize that its actions in the Third World during the 1970s had helped erode support for *détente* in the USA. This reassessment was encouraged by the fact that the geopolitical gains made by Moscow during the 1970s looked far less impressive from the perspective of the 1980s.

All this provided an important foundation on which Mikhail Gorbachev was to build. The growing recognition of the limits of Soviet power, combined with Gorbachev's belief that reforming the Soviet economy required a much more relaxed relationship with the West and especially the USA, encouraged the development of Soviet 'new thinking' in foreign policy and security. Although there is a tendency to see this exclusively as a function of Soviet weakness, it also reflected Gorbachev's awareness that Soviet actions did affect Western threat assessments and his desire to break out of the dynamics of the security dilemma in which each side's defensive actions were interpreted by the adversary as threatening. As Robert Legvold has argued, 'Gorbachev's foreign policy revolution redid the superpower relationship before the Soviet Union ceased to be a superpower'.[8] Moreover, Soviet disengagement from Afghanistan helped to break the log-jam between the superpowers and provided a precedent which Gorbachev saw as having application elsewhere. Legvold notes: 'The pattern was an accretionary one, with expediencies and concepts slowly accumulating

---

7 See George, A. L. *et al.*, *Managing US–Soviet Rivalry* (Westview Press: Boulder, Colo., 1983). See also Bowker, M. and Williams, P., *Superpower Détente* (Sage: London, 1988).

8 Legvold, R., 'The Third World and the superpowers in a different era', eds T. G. Weiss and M. A. Kessler, *Third World Security in the Post-Cold War Era* (Lynne Reinner: Boulder, Colo., 1991), p. 97.

until they became more substantial and coherent. To give these notions practical content and begin the process of shedding the Soviet burden, Moscow had to draw Washington in and persuade it that it wanted to end the local turmoil, or at least the Soviet part in it, not simply to prosecute the interest of its clients by other means'.[9]

Increasingly, the USA was persuaded of the seriousness of Soviet intent and displayed greater flexibility in its own approach to regional conflicts.

This pattern was evident in both Angola and Cambodia. The situation in Cambodia was particularly complex. The initial impetus to break the impasse came from Gorbachev's desire for a thaw in Sino-Soviet relations, a desire which encouraged Moscow to put pressure on Viet Nam to withdraw from Cambodia.[10] Although this offered considerable promise, a final settlement remained a distant prospect, with the USA still supporting the non-communist rebels in spite of their links to the Khmer Rouge. On 18 July 1990, however, the Bush Administration announced that it was abandoning support for the rebels, was willing to enter into dialogue with Hanoi about a peace settlement in Cambodia, and would provide humanitarian assistance to Cambodia. This shift, which was announced after a two-hour meeting between Secretary of State James Baker and Soviet Foreign Minister Eduard Shevardnadze, reflected the abandonment of the traditional geopolitical imperatives in which the USA and the USSR backed opposing sides in local or regional conflicts.[11] The willingness of the superpowers to adopt a more co-operative approach to these issues provided a solid basis for United Nations involvement and facilitated the process whereby a peace treaty was eventually signed on 23 October 1991. As part of this settlement it was accepted by all parties that the United Nations would play a central role not only in supervising the implementation of the treaty but also in the reconstruction of Cambodia.

The new role of the United Nations in international politics was also evident in the crisis and subsequent war in the Persian Gulf in 1990–91. Indeed, this episode provided an excellent example of acquiescent co-operation between Washington and Moscow. The crisis did not lead to fully fledged co-operation with the two superpowers playing equally important roles: the USA was clearly the dominant actor, and for much of the time the USSR simply seemed to be a bystander. Nevertheless, the Persian Gulf War highlighted what Robbin Laird has described as the enabling or facilitating role of the USSR—even though it was not militarily involved in the crisis.[12] Had it wanted to, the USSR could have played a crucial spoiling role and made it much more difficult for the USA to mobilize and maintain the international coalition against Iraq; as well as direct interference, the USSR could have made it much more difficult for the USA to move forces from other areas, especially Western Europe. Yet it did

[9] Legvold (note 8), p. 100.

[10] Rodman, P. W., 'Supping with devils', *National Interest*, no. 25 (fall 1991), pp. 44–50.

[11] See Friedman. T. L., 'US shifts Cambodia policy, ends recognition of rebels, agrees to talk with Hanoi', *New York Times,* 19 July 1990, p. 1.

[12] The author would like to express his appreciation to Dr Laird for this point.

not. One of the reasons that the USA was able to deploy forces from Europe to the Persian Gulf and create a very effective offensive military option was because of diminished fears about the Soviet military threat to Western Europe. In so far as this resulted from diminished capability, it was not simply a matter of the USA placing its trust in the USSR. There was also a variety of concrete indicators which confirmed that it was relatively safe for the USA to reduce its forces in Europe. Nevertheless, the sense of confidence that the resulting weakness in Europe would not be exploited underlined not only the impact of the revolution in Eastern Europe in 1989 but also the changes in superpower relations during the latter half of the 1980s.

This is not to deny that there were questions about Soviet behaviour during the crisis. As one Congressional Research Service paper noted, 'The Gulf crisis began with very close US–Soviet collaboration, but ended with lingering questions about the role the Soviets tried to play and the overall state of the relationship'.[13] However, it is clear that without Soviet acquiescence the USA would have faced far greater problems than it did. Moscow could have obstructed US policy simply through using its veto in the United Nations Security Council. This would not only have challenged the legitimacy of the embargo and the subsequent use of force but also made it much more difficult for Washington to maintain the anti-Saddam coalition. Although the Soviet record of co-operation in the crisis was mixed, the constructive steps that the USSR did take were significant, even though some of these stemmed from Shevardnadze's penchant for co-operation with the USA, and some stemmed from the fact that Shevardnadze and Secretary of State Baker were meeting when the crisis broke. On 2 August 1990 the USSR not only condemned the Iraqi invasion of Kuwait but also announced that it was suspending arms shipments to Iraq. The next day Baker and Shevardnadze issued a joint statement condemning Iraq's actions. The USSR also voted for all 12 Security Council resolutions establishing the demand for an unconditional withdrawal of Iraqi forces from Kuwait and authorizing the use of force if necessary to expel Iraqi forces. In addition, Moscow not only accepted US military deployments to Saudi Arabia but also recognized that the USA was taking the lead in the crisis and that the USSR had, at best, only a supporting role.

On the other hand, there were some facets of Soviet behaviour which were rather less constructive. It is not clear, for example, that the USSR withdrew all its military technicians from Iraq even after the war had started. Moreover, throughout the crisis the USSR always seemed sympathetic to Saddam Hussein's efforts to link the Kuwait issue to the Palestinian issue—a linkage that was consistently rejected by the USA. From the US perspective, however, the most unhelpful episode was the Soviet diplomatic initiative designed to pre-empt a ground offensive by bringing about a negotiated Iraqi withdrawal. Yet, even though this was regarded in Washington with considerable irritation, it

---

[13] Lowenthal, M. M., *The Persian Gulf War: Preliminary Foreign Policy 'Lessons' and Perceptions*, Congressional Research Service Report for Congress (Congressional Research Service: Washington, DC, 18 Mar. 1991), p. 5.

was something on which George Bush and Gorbachev communicated very fully. Moreover, Gorbachev consistently attempted to move towards the US position of placing more stringent demands upon Iraq. Even so, the initiative would have been even more troublesome had Saddam Hussein been more responsive and had Bush not issued an ultimatum for Iraqi withdrawal that effectively ended the mediation effort.

There has been much speculation as to why Gorbachev should intrude or 'meddle' in the diplomatic process at this late stage. One interpretation is that he was anxious to avoid a ground war in which Soviet equipped and trained forces were likely to be humiliated. Another is that he was concerned about large-scale fighting and the presence of US forces close to Soviet territory. It has also been claimed that the war became an issue 'in the struggle between pro-democracy reformers and reactionaries in the Soviet Union', that the military leadership in particular was unhappy at the abandonment of an old ally and was exerting pressure for action to save Iraq from total defeat.[14] Another possible interpretation is that the USSR was simply attempting to position itself as a moderating influence for the post-war settlement and was anxious to obtain the public relations benefits of the mediator role.

Although Soviet actions were sometimes interpreted as a defection from a co-operative approach to the crisis by Moscow, this argument is not persuasive. Involvement in the crisis over Kuwait was never symmetrical, and co-operation was never complete. Moreover, while Soviet and US interests converged at several junctures, they were certainly not identical. The USSR played a role which was essentially permissive but with which it was not entirely comfortable—this was most evident in the last-minute diplomatic efforts to avoid the ground war. Rather than attempting to disrupt US policy, Moscow was signalling that there were limits to its acquiescence, and that the USA should continue to limit its objectives to those outlined in the UN resolutions. Such behaviour was not inconsistent with acquiescent co-operation.

Perhaps as remarkable as the extent to which US–Soviet co-operation was achieved was the extent of the reliance on the United Nations. Yet this had been something that Gorbachev had been advocating and was clearly part of Soviet 'new thinking' on foreign policy and international security. As Robert Legvold has written, 'the sudden effectiveness of the UN Security Council in the Gulf crisis not only owed to Soviet cooperation, but it also conformed to Soviet concept'.[15] In part, of course, this reflected a natural tendency for the weaker of the two superpowers to place greater emphasis on rules or on due process when it could no longer compete effectively in an unrestrained competition. The UN had considerable appeal to Soviet policy makers because it 'relies not on power

---

[14] *Soviet–US Relations: A Briefing Book*, Congressional Research Service Report for Congress (Congressional Research Service: Washington, DC, Mar. 1991), p. 90.
[15] Legvold (note 8), p. 100.

to prevail but on a process of negotiation in which legitimate perspectives and interests can be expressed and common ground negotiated'.[16]

If there was a convergence of self-interest rather than a true common interest in using the UN, it is nevertheless fairly clear that the UN became particularly attractive because it provided opportunities for Washington and Moscow to move beyond unilateral or bilateral approaches to regional security. Yet in the period since the war over Kuwait and the peace settlement in Cambodia, there have been further tectonic shifts in the international political and strategic landscape. Most important, the disintegration of the USSR raises major questions about the future of co-operation between Moscow and Washington. There are several dimensions to this issue. One concerns the future of regional conflict and instability and the extent to which it will be seen as a problem for the USA. The second concerns the incentives for the USA to engage in co-operation with the successor to the USSR, the Russian state.

IV. Regional conflicts after the cold war

There are two broad views about the effect of the end of the cold war on the prospects for peace and stability in the developing world. One view is that superpower disengagement from regional conflicts in the developing world has already facilitated the termination of some long-standing conflicts. The corollary is that the absence of the overlay provided by superpower competition will make regional conflicts less likely and less dangerous. The other assessment is that the end of the cold war has created a less structured and more permissive environment for conflict in the developing world.

These contrasting views rest upon very different assumptions about the role of the two superpowers during the cold war. The view that disengagement will reduce the likelihood and intensity of regional conflicts rests upon the belief that the superpowers exacerbated, perpetuated and sometimes even created such conflicts to advance their own interests—they meddled, with negative impact. The assessment that the end of the cold war will encourage regional conflict rests upon a more positive and paternalist concept of the superpower role in restraining local clients and allies. The argument here is that superpower involvement on opposite sides of regional conflicts set limits to these conflicts. In the Middle East, in particular, superpower involvement circumscribed what could be achieved through the use of force. Soviet concern over the fate of the Egyptian Third Army at the end of the 1973 Middle East War, for example, and its abrasive signals and warnings to the USA about the depth of this concern, compelled the USA to exert pressure on Israel to relieve the position of the Third Army. In other words, the argument goes, the superpowers imposed stability during much of the cold war. The corollary is that without their

---

[16] See Wallander, C. A., 'Soviet policy toward the Third World in the 1990s', eds Weiss and Kessler (note 8), p. 45.

restraining influence, regions which were kept firmly under control may now boil over into conflict.

These different interpretations are presented as mutually exclusive alternatives. In fact they are not: the role of the superpowers in relation to regional conflicts was both restraining and exacerbating. There were times when client states saw superpower support and superpower arms supplies as a prerequisite for the use of force. Moreover, the superpowers themselves often encouraged regional powers to act as their proxies, thereby giving indigenous conflicts a superpower dimension. At the same time, when the superpowers were aligned on opposite sides of regional conflicts, their concern that they should not be dragged into a direct confrontation generally set limits to the permissible behaviour of their client states. In the final analysis, the superpower role in relation to regional conflicts in the developing world was essentially ambivalent. The concomitant of this is that the removal of the superpower overlay on regional conflicts in the developing world is likely to have mixed results. It presents new dangers and offers new opportunities for preventing and managing regional conflicts.

Part of the reason for this is that many regional conflicts had—and continue to have—indigenous roots. They were not a function of US–Soviet relations, and although they became subsumed in the cold war they were independent of it. In some cases, they have also outlasted the cold war. This is particularly dangerous in those situations where superpower disengagement has left 'regional power vacuums' which may offer temptation to some of the local actors.[17] Indeed, without the constraining influence of potential superpower involvement, the use of military force could become more widespread as a means of dealing with local and regional security problems.

Superpower disengagement will also have an effect where Moscow and Washington have propped up regimes with dubious internal legitimacy. Indeed, some analysts of developing world security believe that the major source of regional tension and conflict in the 1990s and beyond will be a lack of legitimacy leading to what is sometimes referred to as the Balkanization or 'Lebanonization' of new states, whether in the developing world or Central and Eastern Europe.[18]

'The central problem for developing and developed countries in the 1990s will be the growing inability of governments to meet the psychopolitical, cultural and economic needs of their constituents. The legacy of the 1980s is a crisis of legitimacy and political coalescence . . . In this sense the model for the era we have just entered is less Iraq than Kashmir, less Iran than Yugoslavia, less Argentina than Peru'.[19] Put very simply, the problem for the future is less one of strategy between states than one of politics within states.

---

[17] This possibility is discussed at several points in Weiss and Kessler (note 8).
[18] Norton, A. R., 'The security legacy of the 1980s in the Third World', eds Weiss and Kessler (note 8), p. 30.
[19] Norton (note 18), p. 23.

What is perhaps most striking is that these problems are not unique to developing world states. While each regional conflict is unique and distinctive, they also share certain characteristics. The disintegration of the Soviet external and internal empires has left in its wake the same kind of issues that have long existed in the developing world: security problems that are about ethnic and nationalist tensions, demands for autonomy and justice, and the lack of legitimacy of existing political structures. The particulars differ considerably but the parallels between the disintegration of Lebanon and the civil strife in Yugoslavia should not be overlooked. When Eastern Europe and the former Soviet republics threw off the Soviet yoke and left the Second World, in effect they became part of the Third World.

This is not to claim that future regional security problems will be confined to internal instabilities. Indeed, one of the problems of internal unrest is that it can encourage external intervention not only by the great powers but also by other local powers. Nor is the argument about political legitimacy intended to deflect attention from the strategic considerations that are likely both to exacerbate and to provoke regional conflicts in the future. Indeed, one of the most obvious of the trends which suggest that regional conflicts may be more prevalent, more disruptive and more dangerous than ever before is the proliferation of ballistic missiles, together with chemical and nuclear capabilities.

The presence of 'doomsday weapons in the hands of many' will pose unprecedented problems for regional security.[20] Moreover, there seems to be little that can be done to halt the diffusion of new weapon systems. With around 15 states in the developing world already in possession of ballistic missiles and with another 10 having active development programmes, it is clear that the Missile Technology Control Regime (MTCR) has done little to stem the spread of weapon systems that introduce new pre-emptive instabilities into already tense situations. In addition, over 20 countries are working on the development of chemical weapons, while the proliferation of nuclear weapons is unlikely to be stopped simply because Washington and Moscow are in the process of reducing their arsenals.

Moreover, the sources of potential conflict between and within states seem likely to increase. The late 1990s and the early years of the 21st century may well be a period in which conflicts over resources and the environment are much more prevalent than ever before. Cross-border environmental degradation could prove to be, at the very least, a source of irritation in relations between particular states, and on occasion may have much more serious consequences. Another source of concern for the future will be mass movements of peoples, a development that could both spark and be sparked by regional tensions and conflicts.

The implication of all this is that the new world order conceived by President Bush will be vulnerable to considerable disruption. Yet one of the elements in

---

[20] See Bailey, K. C., *Doomsday Weapons in the Hands of Many* (University of Illinois Press: Urbana and Chicago, 1991), for a fuller discussion.

this new order as envisaged by Bush was the prospect of superpower co-operation to deal with regional conflicts and instability. Closely linked to this, and emphasized by President Bill Clinton in his first months in office, was greater reliance on multilateral institutions such as the United Nations to deal with regional conflicts. In the conditions that have developed in 1994–95, however, it is uncertain whether co-operation between Moscow and Washington will be as compelling or as attractive as it appeared during 1990 and the first half of 1991. Indeed, it is to this question that attention must now be given.

V. Co-operation after the cold war

The elements of co-operation in what was always a complicated relationship between Moscow and Washington became increasingly obvious in the second half of the 1980s. Yet the disintegration of the USSR and its replacement by a loose confederation, the Commonwealth of Independent States (CIS), not only put the final seal on the end of the cold war, but also called into question the patterns of co-operation which had accompanied it. There are several reasons for this. The disappearance of the USSR and the end of the cold war changed the incentives for co-operation in preventing and managing regional conflicts, altered the opportunities to engage in such behaviour and, finally, may even influence the very capacity for co-operation.

In terms of incentives, the arguments were evident even prior to the failed August 1991 coup and the final disintegration of the USSR. The US need for co-operation was dismissed on the grounds that the USSR was no longer an effective player and it was therefore unnecessary to extend it the privilege of being involved in major regional crises. This argument became even stronger after the disintegration of the USSR and its replacement by the CIS finally removed traditional assessments of threat. The argument is that there is no longer a basis for continued collaboration between Washington and Moscow, whether Moscow is acting as the representative of the Russian state or as the main representative of the CIS. Chechnya may further strengthen this view.

The disappearance of one of the two superpowers has left what is effectively, if temporarily, a unipolar international system.[21] The traditional imperatives for superpower co-operation came from the dangers of competition in conditions of bipolarity and rough nuclear equality. With the disappearance of these conditions, the incentives for co-operation have also disappeared. A dominant USA is no longer compelled to take into account the views of its allies, let alone the views of Moscow, in responding to regional conflict and instability. Thinking about co-operation with Moscow is anachronistic, a result of attitudes and patterns of behaviour which became fixed in an era when the Soviet capacity to meddle in regional issues, its ability to project military power, its willingness to support regional clients opposed to those of the USA, and its capability of

---

[21] This is the term popularized by Charles Krauthammer. See in particular his 'The unipolar moment', *America and the World 1990/91, Foreign Affairs* , vol. 70, no. 1 (1991), pp. 23–33.

escalating conflicts to a nuclear level gave it a unique position as both rival and partner of the USA. Soviet power and status compelled attention. Indifference to Soviet preferences or behaviour was not possible for the USA when Moscow helped to determine the terms of engagement for superpower involvement in regional conflicts. Whether the successor to the USSR is regarded as Russia or the CIS, the transformation in Moscow's position has been astounding. The former superpower has become a supplicant. The adversary which formerly demanded respect because of its power now demands attention only because of fears of its complete disintegration. When US or other Western policy makers visit Moscow it is no longer to discuss military assistance by the USSR to areas of regional conflict; it is to discuss economic and humanitarian assistance to the CIS by the West. Moreover, from being a party to regional conflict, the USSR has itself become an arena in which such conflict may well be played out. Since Moscow is no longer an adversary, and no longer an equal player, it is no longer an appropriate partner for the USA in dealing with regional conflict. The experience of the cold war is not a prologue to new forms of co-operation but a self-contained short story which has clearly come to an end.

The contrasting view is that while the disintegration of the USSR has obviously had a major impact, some of the old patterns of co-operation remain relevant. There are several reasons for this. The first is that Russia is still a major actor with a powerful strategic nuclear force and a capacity for large-scale military intervention if it is deemed that circumstances warrant it. Moreover, it will retain such a status for the foreseeable future in spite of the reduction in nuclear arsenals that is taking place. Acknowledging that the USSR has disappeared as the second superpower is one thing; claiming that Russia can be ignored is quite another. Even with its weaknesses it retains at least some of the attributes of a great power. Consequently, acquiescent co-operation by Moscow may be a necessary if not sufficient condition for a more active and intrusive role by the USA in at least some regional conflicts.

Second, the very disintegration of a major nuclear power has already brought with it a set of potential developments relating to the possible spread of nuclear technology which could have very serious consequences for future regional stability. Even if there is no successor state which is able to play a role in its own right, the disintegration of the USSR has placed on the agenda a number of new issues relating to the possibility of regional conflict. The USA has to take this into account. US co-operation with Belarus, Kazakhstan, Russia and Ukraine under the Nunn–Lugar legislation is a recognition of the nuclear dangers associated with the disintegration of the USSR. Moreover, the willingness of Boris Yeltsin and other leaders of the CIS to discuss such issues with the USA suggests that the pattern of co-operation which developed between Moscow and Washington during the cold war may have continued relevance.

The third reason why Washington–Moscow co-operation may still be worthwhile is that, although economic weakness and the social and political dislocation caused by the transition to market economies mean that, in the short term, Moscow will be preoccupied with domestic matters, these domestic preoccupations may be the prelude to the re-emergence of Russia as a major player in regional conflicts and crises. Although the ideological antipathies which dominated international politics and exacerbated competition between regional powers are a thing of the past, it is unlikely that Russia will be indifferent to regional security problems not only in Central and Eastern Europe, but also in the Middle East, which has traditionally been regarded as the soft underbelly of the Central and Eastern European heartland. Moreover, Islamic fundamentalism is something that may be of even greater concern to Moscow now than it was before the disintegration of the internal Soviet empire. Moscow, of course, already has claimed special responsibilities in all the area of the former Soviet Union.

Closely related to this is the fact that Eastern Europe could well be one of the most crucial arenas of regional turmoil and instability through the 1990s and beyond. Not only does Moscow still have interests in this region, but there may well be limits to the kind of solutions to conflict and instability that it is willing to accept. Indeed, Eastern Europe now has an ambivalent status that under certain circumstances could precipitate problems not only between Moscow and Washington but also between Moscow and Bonn.

An additional reason for continued interest in co-operation with Moscow is the possibility that the war against Iraq, in one sense at least, provided a model for future regional crises. One of the most important characteristics of the crisis over Kuwait was the creation of an international coalition to deal with the problem. This is something that may be required again, especially as the USA proves unwilling to act alone as the guarantor of a new world order. It would be well to ensure that Moscow becomes a key element in this process. Treating Moscow seriously rather than as a negligible factor could be crucial in encouraging constructive rather than obstructive policies. Conversely, if it feels excluded from participation in efforts to manage or defuse regional crises, Moscow could prove to be a potential spoiler. Preoccupation with domestic issues does not imply a total or permanent indifference to international security matters or to what are seen as slights by the USA. Moreover, Russian involvement could prove to be a key element in efforts to obtain a broader consensus. The old pattern of purely bilateral co-operation between Washington and Moscow which characterized the cold war is unlikely to be repeated, yet co-operation between Moscow and Washington is likely to be an important and, on occasion, perhaps even the key element in broader multilateral efforts to deal with regional problems.

Another question concerns not the connection between Moscow and Washington but sentiment in the USA. It is possible to discern, with the end of the cold war, a new introspection developing in the USA. Although the Pentagon has contingency plans to deal with a variety of possible adversaries, there are strong sentiments for an 'America first' approach in which the USA acts militarily and diplomatically only when there are self-evident threats to US security. In this connection, one possible and attractive response to regional conflicts, whether in the developing world or in Eastern Europe, is to remain aloof. The USA initially took this position in response to the civil war in the former Yugoslavia, arguing that the conflict was primarily the responsibility of the European Community. To the extent that it believes itself to be insulated from the consequences of regional conflict—whether it occurs in the developing world or in Eastern Europe—the USA will have little interest in developing co-operative approaches. The difficulty with indifference, however, is that the USA will continue to have an interest in the overall direction of the international system. Moreover, although the Yugoslav case is an example, for now, of self-contained conflict, regional instability elsewhere may have more extensive and far-reaching consequences, particularly in circumstances in which it involves weapons of mass destruction. Moreover, there is significant potential for conflict among the former republics of the Soviet Union and within Russia itself. A conflict like Chechnya could happen again, and on a larger scale. In these circumstances, there is a real danger that the conflict would have major spill-over consequences. To avoid these the USA and its West European allies would have a very strong interest in providing assistance in crisis management.

This points to what is likely to be one of the most important features of crises in the post-cold war era—the participants themselves are not likely to have the same capacity for managing the confrontations and containing the possibility of large-scale violence that the USA and the USSR demonstrated during the cold war. In these circumstances, external involvement and perhaps even management begin to become far more necessary to prevent hostilities. There are many ways in which this can be done. One possibility is that Moscow and Washington can offer lessons from their own experience and suggest ways in which similar arrangements or procedures could alleviate regional tensions. Some of the lessons that have been learned about the need for communication and the establishment of direct communication links, of particular importance in times of crisis, could be passed on to other governments. The implicit assumption underlying such efforts, of course, is that the cold war was an important learning experience about crisis management and that at least some of the lessons which were learned could constructively be absorbed by less powerful states.

Yet it would be unwise to rely exclusively on management to keep potential conflict situations under control. It is also necessary to establish longer-term crisis prevention arrangements. In this connection, the USA acting alone, in conjunction with Russia, or as part of a wider international effort involving other great powers, could also emphasize the relevance of confidence-building measures as a way of easing the tensions caused by a security dilemma. There could also be co-operative efforts to manage proliferation in ways that would contribute to more stable structures of regional deterrence.

None of this is likely to be easy. The familiar problem of reverse influence in which client states manipulate their patrons may diminish but will not disappear simply because of the end of the cold war, nor will the resistance of developing countries to attempts by external powers to impose solutions on regional conflict. 'Third World conflicts often have their own indigenous roots, making them resistant to solutions imposed from outside the region'.[22] They will be even more resistant to outside involvement if it is perceived as an attempt to establish some kind of great power directorate, whether this is informal or channelled through the UN Security Council.[23] It is clear therefore that the 'exogenous limitations on great-power conflict management' cannot be ignored as was evident in US involvement in Somalia.[24] If this underlines the need for caution in efforts to devise crisis prevention and crisis management mechanisms for regional conflict after the cold war, it does not mean that these efforts should be abandoned. It does mean, though, that these efforts should be directed primarily at the development of regional security arrangements which, once established, are essentially self-regulating. This is perhaps nowhere more important than in relation to nuclear proliferation.

VI. Nuclear proliferation: from prevention to management

Nuclear proliferation was an issue on which the USA and the USSR very clearly had common interests. This was evident in the 1968 Non-Proliferation Treaty (NPT), which was one of the earliest arms control agreements and was signed in a period when superpower *détente* was still not fully developed. Moreover, as Joseph Nye has pointed out, during the 1970s the superpowers developed both 'an impressive degree of cooperation' and 'institutions for maintaining that cooperation' in their efforts to thwart further proliferation.[25] This was also an area in which co-operation continued, albeit with a relatively low profile, during the first half of the 1980s when the superpower relationship reverted once more to cold war. Paradoxically, it has taken on greater salience with the problems of nuclear smuggling precipitated by the disintegration of the USSR. Indeed, the USA has worked closely with the Russian Government under Boris Yeltsin in an effort to minimize the nuclear dangers inherent in the large number of nuclear weapons deployed in Belarus, Kazakhstan, Russia and Ukraine. In some respects, however, the emphasis on a single centre of control for nuclear weapons reflected a nostalgia for the old USSR, a knee-jerk reaction against the idea that the possession of nuclear weapons by states other than Russia might not be a bad thing for stability in the region—or for the non-Russian states which may have to contend with efforts at some kind of restoration of Russian hegemony in the region. In these circumstances it was not surprising that there were voices in Ukraine in particular—given a desire for independence from Russia—arguing that Kiev at least consider the option of being a nuclear power. The argument for this was that it might help to inhibit or avert a potential conflict with Russia. The argument against this option, of course,

[22] Kessler, M. A. and Weiss, T. G., 'The United Nations and Third World security in the 1990s', eds Kessler and Weiss (note 8), p. 109.

[23] Kessler and Weiss (note 22), p. 111.

[24] Kessler and Weiss (note 22), p. 109.

[25] Nye, J. S., 'US–Soviet cooperation in a nonproliferation regime', eds A. George, P. Farley and A. Dallin, *US–Soviet Security Cooperation: Achievements, Failures, Lessons* (Oxford University Press: New York, 1988), p. 337.

was the familiar one that if a clash between these two neighbours did occur then it will be all the more dangerous if they both possess nuclear arsenals.

Even so, the emphasis in the USA on the reversion to a single power centre in Moscow, with exclusive control over the nuclear armoury of the former USSR, reflected not so much a rational calculation of the dangers as a reflexive desire to retain the comfort of familiarity in a world that has changed dramatically. There was also a significant strand of continuity with a past in which the USA and the USSR had established an impressive record of sustained co-operation. The dominant approach to nuclear proliferation on the part of both Moscow and Washington focused—and continues to focus—on prevention rather than management. The desire to prevent or inhibit the spread of nuclear weapons has dominated thinking about the problem in both capitals. While these efforts will remain crucial and need to be strengthened and intensified, they also need to be supplemented by a more managerial approach. Such an approach is fatalistic about the inevitability of proliferation but acknowledges the need for ensuring that the regionalization of deterrence results in relatively stable security arrangements. This is a considerable challenge, especially in regions such as South Asia where the enmity between India and Pakistan has increasingly been given a nuclear dimension.

Although accepting the inevitability of such developments does not come easy to those who are committed to non-proliferation, it is arguable that a more comprehensive strategy is required in which efforts to stop the spread of nuclear weapons are increasingly accompanied by efforts to stabilize regional deterrence relationships. The main reason for this is that while regional powers may develop and deploy nuclear weapons, they are unlikely to have the resources or the technology to create the kinds of stabilizing mechanisms that were systematically and successfully incorporated into the US–Soviet nuclear relationship during the cold war. The result is that regional nuclear deterrence relationships are likely to exhibit the kinds of pre-emptive incentives and instabilities that helped precipitate the outbreak of the Arab–Israeli War of 1967. The incentives for going first would, of course, be strengthened by major disparities between the nuclear forces of the regional adversaries. Closely related is the danger of preventive strikes in the event that a nuclear state wanted to prevent an enemy from also acquiring nuclear weapons.

Enhancing regional stability in the developing world is something on which the interests of both Moscow and Washington will frequently converge, and there are several strategies that they could adopt to deal with the kinds of problem that could arise from the inexorable spread of nuclear weapons. The minimum form of co-operation is tacit agreement to exercise increased restraint on regional nuclear powers, especially those locked into an adversary relationship. In one sense this would be simply an extension of what was done during the cold war. In another, it would be a novel approach: Moscow and Washington would be explicit about what they are doing—even though they no longer had their own underlying competition to keep under control. The problem with this is that it could all too easily be seen as an attempt by Moscow and Washington to impose some kind of condominium—a development which would be unacceptable to many developing world states.

A more explicit and ambitious form of co-operation is to move from unilateral guarantees to clients to joint guarantees designed to enhance regional stability through mitigating some of the consequences of the security dilemmas that accompany the early stages of nuclear arms races. The difficulty with this, once again, is that it might not be acceptable to the regional powers themselves. Emergent or new nuclear powers are likely to be particularly sensitive about their prerogatives and reluctant to accept security arrangements that are seen as inhibiting or infringing on these prerogatives.

The same problem arises with perhaps the most ambitious form of co-operation in relation to proliferation management, that which involves the provision of technological stability. Perhaps the key to regional deterrence stability is the provision of capabilities that provide emerging or new nuclear powers with more secure and effective retaliatory capabilities. This is in some ways a potentially more fruitful approach as it would minimize long-term US and Russian involvement in the adversarial relationship between the regional powers, while making it easier for the regional deterrence relationship to become stable and self-regulating. The idea is that Moscow and Washington help not with the development and deployment of nuclear weapons, but with ensuring that these nuclear weapons are deployed in ways that minimize vulnerability, that they are subject to stringent and effective command and control arrangements, and that there are adequate and effective safeguards against unauthorized use. In other words, regional nuclear powers should be encouraged and assisted to take steps which would replicate some of the more desirable features of the old US–Soviet nuclear relationship as it evolved during the cold war. The crucial thing is to ensure that the regional balance of terror is not delicate, that there is no need for rapid launch decisions, and that temptations for pre-emptive action are eliminated.

There are several ways in which the USA, either acting alone or on a co-operative basis with Russia and perhaps other leading nuclear powers, could attempt to accomplish this. Probably the most ambitious would be to establish advisory teams which would be sent to both sides to provide technical advice and assistance on ways in which nuclear forces could be made less vulnerable. Although this would be in some respects the most logical way to proceed, it would also be the most difficult politically if it involved an attempt at co-operation between two or more nuclear powers. It would require not only a more formalized approach than has been evident in the past, but also a willingness to share information and pool expertise. While it is not certain that Moscow and Washington—let alone Paris and London—would be prepared to do this, it is an option worth considering. The co-operation should be formalized and specific, and would leave little opportunity for misunderstanding; it should highlight the fact that great power divisions of the past have come to an end, with the result that the opportunities for playing off one great power against another have declined very considerably. In a similar vein, it should avoid the kind of client–patron relationship that arises where assistance is provided as part of a purely bilateral relationship.

Such an approach would not necessarily be welcomed by the potential recipients. On the contrary, new nuclear powers might face serious problems in accepting nuclear-related aid from the great powers—especially if this involves a great power with which they traditionally have had poor relations.

An alternative approach therefore would be for the USA and Russia to act in parallel rather than in concert. Each one would send a team to its erstwhile client to provide similar kinds of advice, information and expertise. While this would have the advantage of being less sensitive, the danger is that it could have a further polarizing effect at the regional level and could encourage rather than dissipate regional tensions and complicate the Russian–US relationship. This need not happen, however, if some mechanism were devised at the Moscow–Washington level for information exchange and mutual reporting of activities. So long as there is a reasonable degree of trust between the two governments and transparency in their activities, there is no reason that the regional problems should spill over into their relationship.

None of this is meant to imply that managing the proliferation process is a viable alternative to non-proliferation, but if it is accepted that the spread of nuclear weapons is inevitable, then the key issues concern the pace, scope and consequences. The argument here is that a greater concern with mitigating consequences is something that could lead to a very fruitful co-operative approach by Washington and Moscow. Moreover, if some kind of joint or even co-ordinated approach would make clear that becoming a nuclear power involves far more than just acquiring a simple capability to explode nuclear weapons, in a sense it would not only raise the price of entry to the nuclear club but reaffirm that this club has certain rules and procedures which have to be observed. Ironically, if proliferation becomes associated with the creation of stable deterrence relationships in which the utility of nuclear weapons is very limited, this could act as an extra inhibition to further proliferation.[26]

This is not to agree with Kenneth Waltz that, so far as nuclear weapons are concerned, more may be better.[27] Nor is it to agree with John Mearsheimer, who has argued something very similar, although more specifically in relation to Central and Eastern Europe.[28] The assumption here is simply that proliferation is something to be discouraged, but that when it is clear that nothing can be done to stop it in particular cases, then the focus of attention should shift to mitigating its consequences. An analogy is with the provision of free needles for drug addicts as a way of minimizing the spread of acquired immune deficiency syngdrome (AIDS). Intravenous drug abuse is likely to occur anyway, and the provision of disposable needles (like assistance with the provision of

[26] The author would like to express his appreciation to Dr Joshua Epstein of the Brookings Institution for this point.

[27] See Waltz, K., *The Spread of Nuclear Weapons: More May Be Better,* Adelphi Paper, no. 171 (International Institute for Strategic Studies: London, 1981).

[28] See Mearsheimer, J. J., 'Back to the future: instability in Europe after the Cold War', *International Security*, vol. 15, no. 1 (summer 1990), pp. 5–56.

permissive action links to prevent unauthorized release, early-warning systems or technologies which reduce the vulnerability of retaliatory capabilities) is simply a way of mitigating consequences. This approach is, in effect, one of 'harm reduction'.

VII. Concluding observations

Recent events provide a warning against predictive confidence, let alone predictive certainty. There are many uncertainties relating to the future roles the USA and Russia will want to play in the developing world in the post-cold war era. Nevertheless it does seem fairly clear that developing world turbulence is likely to increase rather than decline in the future—and likely to be accompanied by some significant developments in relation to the spread of weapons of mass destruction. In these circumstances, the USA will either stay out of developing world conflicts altogether or adopt policies and strategies which are explicitly designed to have a stabilizing effect. If the USA decides that it is in its self-interest to pursue the former approach, this will not depend on co-operation with Russia or other great powers.

Enlightened self-interest would dictate that the USA help to provide a more stable and orderly environment even if this goal is not pursued with equal vigour by other great powers. At the same time, there will be incentives to develop co-operative partnerships both to prevent and to respond to regional conflicts in the developing world. This chapter, while far from exhaustive, has explored the kinds of co-operative action that the USA and Russia might find attractive. These range from tacit action through acquiescent co-operation to more explicit and formal measures. In the final analysis, the extent of co-operation in particular instances will depend on the balance between incentives and impediments and the constellation of domestic political forces in both Washington and Moscow.

3. The elements of a North–South security system

Sergey Rogov

I. Possible consequences of the end of the cold war for the developing world

The end of the cold war may mean that the East–West conflict will be replaced by North–South and South–South conflicts. Reliable security mechanisms in which the great powers and regional countries co-operate on both the regional and global level must be developed if the world is not to enter a period of greater instability. This chapter provides a conceptual outline of how such mechanisms could be achieved and describes the essential elements of a new North–South security system.

The end of superpower competition does not mean that the situation in the developing countries will stabilize, far from it. Regional disputes pose significant challenges to Russian–US co-operation in particular.

Political disputes in the developing world can escalate to dangerous levels, especially if the introduction of sophisticated conventional arms is accompanied by proliferation of nuclear, biological and chemical (NBC) capabilities. Unless controlled or managed, in a few years this arms race could bring about a series of military conflicts with unpredictable consequences. Russian–US co-operation can help to prevent this.

There may be 'a window of opportunity' for political and military stabilization of the developing countries through the introduction of arms control methods first tried in European and Soviet–US relations. Russia should take the lead in creating a North–South security system and proposing the establishment in the developing countries of a system of arms control and confidence-building. It should be kept in mind that in the near future no better means will exist to influence the situation in the developing countries. Such an initiative would help to counter deteriorating relations between Russia and the Western countries, especially the USA, caused by differences over regional disputes. In addition, it could become the most important element in facilitating the achievement of a comprehensive international security system. Much has been written about a 'Euroatlantic' security system. A North–South security system also is important to global peace and security. In the developing countries Russia may face a choice between developing co-operation with the USA in the field of security under the UN umbrella or large-scale US unilateral actions. This approach should also prevent a new division of the developing countries and the creation of new military blocs.

Key roles should be played by regional states. Previous experience, however, demonstrates that it will be extremely difficult to achieve such a solution through the efforts of the developing countries alone. Regional security can best be enhanced through co-operation of great powers, like France, Russia, the UK, the USA and so on, with regional powers.

The great powers may, of course, have either a stabilizing or a destabilizing influence on specific regions. On the positive side, Europe, Russia and the USA possess substantial experience in arms control and confidence- and security-building measures (CSBMs), which the developing countries lack. Some of these experiences are not applicable to all regions, but others have a more universal character and may be successfully applied after necessary adaptation to the conditions of the developing countries. On the negative side, there is abundant evidence that irresponsible behaviour on the part of states outside a region can fuel arms races and aggravate tensions in the region. The basic point is that the great powers have a significant capacity to influence the situation in various regions of the world and that co-ordinated efforts (e.g., the supplying or denying of weapons and other special military–political activities) with the countries of a region could lead to positive results. Unco-ordinated efforts may have the opposite effect.

It is also necessary to assess the role of the United Nations in such a process. The new prestige gained by the Security Council in recent years has proved that it is possible to realize the potential of the UN Charter when the great powers find it possible to co-operate. The end of the cold war has presented an opportunity for the UN to overcome its paralysis and gain the authority to oversee international peace and security as envisaged in its Charter.

II. The aims of a North–South security regime

The problems of militarization of the developing countries can be solved by the establishment of a framework (or several interconnected frameworks) for regional security with a system of common guarantees. Such a system would include France, Russia, the UK and the USA on the one hand, and the regional powers on the other. It should concentrate not on an immediate political solution of conflicts in the developing countries, but on prevention of potential escalation of tensions and crises, establishment of CSBMs, reduction of armed confrontation and arms races, and fostering political conditions which could lead to the peaceful settlement of conflicts. It should not be seen as a substitute for political solutions. Security building should ease the way to those political compromises which are necessary for peaceful settlements.

A lack of crisis prevention and crisis de-escalation mechanisms, as well as the absence of security guarantees for regional states, allow crisis situations to escalate. Some limited methods of arms control, for example CSBMs, could help to prevent or contain crises. If successful, these initial CSBMs would reduce tensions and provide the participants with their first experience of arms control. Recognition of not only the political but also the technical meaning of this type of interaction between 'enemies' can drastically change attitudes towards generations-old national, territorial and religious conflicts. The process could thereby begin to take root, becoming more self-sustaining and less dependent on external assistance, and perhaps ultimately leading to a true resolution of regional conflicts.

Arms control and CSBMs in developing world areas may differ substantially from the European model. There are major differences in the military–political situation in the developing countries in the arms control context:

1. Before the process of significant arms reductions and military disengagement began in Europe, Europeans had experienced more than four decades of peace. Many developing countries, however, have been (or still are) involved in domestic and international conflicts. The initial task in the developing countries will therefore be to terminate both 'hot' and 'warm' wars.

2. In the developing world national borders are not always universally recognized, and many countries have territorial disputes. It should be realized that unless the political and territorial dimensions of these conflicts are settled, it will be impossible to abolish the threat of war and establish security systems.

3. The situation in Europe excluded military 'victory' as a possibility, which meant that military solutions had to be discarded in favour of political solutions. In developing countries, military force is still an effective means to achieve certain political or territorial goals.

4. Many regional countries are involved in conflicts which have both a 'central' and a 'marginal' component, and a large regional war can result from the escalation of such secondary clashes. In any case, conflicts similar to that in Lebanon (in the Western Sahara or Yemen, for example) may have a negative impact on the more significant issues in the developing countries.

5. It must be remembered that there is no bilateral military balance in the developing world. Simultaneous management of the relations of several military forces in different regions presents a serious challenge which defies simple solution. The geopolitical situation places significant limitations upon the means that can be used to create a security system. In the Middle East, for example, the military confrontation between Israel and its Arab neighbours is a factor but so is the military balance between Arab powers such as Egypt, Iraq, Libya, Saudi Arabia and Syria.

The difficulties discussed above make it impossible to contemplate a uniform approach to the negotiations process. The framework for confidence- and security-building in other regions cannot be a carbon copy of the European model. The main tasks of a security and arms control system in the developing countries might be: (a) prevention of proliferation and use of NBC weapons and their delivery systems; (b) adoption of CSBMs and the creation of transparency[1] in the military sphere to prevent surprise attack; (c) improving the security environment in the region to reduce military tensions; (d) containment of the quantitative and qualitative arms race to limit the possibility of a large-scale military conflict; (e) prevention of the escalation of regional conflicts and border clashes; (f) diminishing the impact of internal political conflicts on inter-state relations; and (g) creation of conditions for political settlements.

In practical terms, regional security regimes can be constructed with two types of participation: by regional states, and by great powers which play the role of facilitators and guarantors of the process.

The functions of the great powers may be to: (a) provide security guarantees to all regional states on the basis of UN Security Council decisions; (b) provide monitoring functions to supervise the military situation in the region; (c) regulate arms transfers and military technology sales to the developing countries; (d) mediate political disputes between participants in a conflict (important because of the low levels of confidence); (e) provide diplomatic and technical assistance for the regional process of confidence- and security-building; (f) supervise the implementation of those arrangements which go beyond the boundaries of the developing world; and (g) support the stationing of multi-national forces under UN control if their presence in the developing world is considered necessary by regional states.

Permanent stationing of military forces from the great powers (or the establishment of facilities for them) should be avoided. A long-term, large-scale military presence in strategic regions on the part of any one of the great powers could develop into a major problem with the others, and the international community should commit itself to finding ways to avoid this.

In the Middle East, for example, multinational forces should preferably be provided by Arab countries (for the Persian Gulf area) or neutral states (in the Arab–Israeli area). Effective UN involvement in the region will probably demand a revitalization of the UN Military Staff Committee (MSC) and the creation of a structure for it, including formal assignment of certain national units to its control if deemed necessary by the Security Council. Russian and US participation should be limited to logistic and staff support. On the political level, however, it should be clear that multinational forces can rely on the full power of the permanent members of the Security Council if an aggressor tries to engage UN forces. Such a trip-wire role would not require the stationing of large forces in a region. Forces which are deployed should not be withdrawn unless there is agreement among all regional participants in the security system. It is also possible to consider the creation of a small multinational naval force under the UN flag to guarantee freedom of navigation in a region. In such a case, US and Russian involvement could be more substantial.

To initiate the peace process in the developing world, the great powers must stimulate interaction among regional states. Here Russia and the USA can be

---

[1] Transparency in the international security context refers to a reduction in the secrecy that often conceals military plans, capabilities and operations. Methods to achieve this include declarations by governments and invitations to observe military activities.

especially important in preventing unlimited arms transfers and military technology sales. West European countries and Japan can contribute financially to the costs of security systems in the Middle East and elsewhere.

III. Measures to reduce military tensions and build confidence and security

Types of measures

While an early and comprehensive solution is desirable, in practical terms the process of building a security system must go through several stages which would allow the step-by-step implementation of different types of measures leading to greater security for all participants. It is too early to provide a detailed blueprint of future security systems in the developing countries, but in order to facilitate discussion the following possible measures are suggested, which can be classified in three main groups:

1. Measures of a political and psychological nature, which do not demand drastic changes in existing military structures and foreign policy approaches, would comprise the first step since it is difficult to envisage more than this in the initial stage. Such measures could decrease current tensions and facilitate direct communication between nations, and this might bring about changes in declared postures. These measures could include ending war and, better still, reaching agreement on the main principles of future peace treaties. The successful implementation of such steps would decrease the threat of military activity and provide the basis for conflict resolution efforts, including direct negotiations.

2. Measures which partially change military structures, freezing them or controlling their buildup, would comprise the second step. They could lead to the institutionalization of elements of common security between regional participants.

3. Measures which fundamentally alter military postures and foreign policy systems could transform a system for regulation and control of competition in the security sphere to a system of co-operation. The implementation of such measures would most likely be connected with political solutions of regional issues and the development of diversified economic and cultural relations among regional participants.

While all these categories of measures are logically connected, they can hardly be implemented immediately as a package. They should be seen rather as a process which will take time to complete. It is important to begin the process, however, with what is attainable under existing conditions rather than wait for those conditions to change.

Stages of implementation

The creation of arms control and regional security systems should be done in two stages. The first stage would be a prerequisite for the second and would also include the step-by-step de-escalation of tensions in a region.

The first stage would aim to pave the way for future negotiations on the details and methods of arms control and CSBMs, and to create incentives for the participation of regional states in the peacemaking process. Major initiatives would be unlikely to be made by the regional parties themselves at this stage. This initial approach would probably be based on persuasion by the great powers, which in some cases might develop conceptual approaches for the regional parties, helping them to learn the essence of arms control. During this first stage it seems necessary and possible to prevent the resumption of Russian–US competition in the developing countries, to restrict the flow of arms, to reduce the threat of surprise attack and to prepare the basis for a future system of international guarantees in the developing countries.

The components of this stage might include:

(*a*) broad discussions of non-confrontational methods among the developing countries under UN auspices, with participation of the permanent members of the Security Council, and other countries such as Germany, India and Japan. These should not address the details of political settlements, but instead concentrate on possible CSBMs and security guarantees;

(*b*) the use of various political and economic incentives to gain acceptance of arms control and security regimes in the developing countries;

(*c*) the regulation of arms transfers by major arms producers to developing world areas with special attention to ballistic and cruise missile technologies and non-conventional military technology;

(*d*) the establishment of a system to monitor the military situation in the developing world as a basis for encouraging regional transparency;

(*e*) authorization by the UN Security Council of a multinational peacekeeping force for the developing countries; and

(*f*) convocation of regional conferences on security and arms control.

During this stage several basic tasks would be accomplished: (*a*) the USA and Russia would be disengaged from confrontational competition in the developing countries; (*b*) the great powers would co-ordinate their respective roles in a future security system; and (*c*) the danger of surprise attacks would be significantly decreased.

The goal of the second stage is to bring the regional states actively into the search for greater security and arms control by implementing practical steps towards reduction of military tensions, by disengagement from armed confrontation and by the formation of regional CSBM structures. At this stage regional countries should agree on measures that would amount to their response to the initiatives of the great powers. These might include: (*a*) regional agreements banning NBC weapons; (b) an agreement on import limitations for certain types of weapon systems; (c) the creation of disengagement zones and zones of limited military presence; (d) the organization of regional structures for monitoring and verification; and (e) the development of agreed approaches to the possible reduction of armed forces, in particular offensive weapons, to agreed ceilings.

These measures should be accompanied by progress in settling political issues and territorial disputes. It can be expected, however, that solutions to these problems will be reached only later. Military threats are not likely to be removed from the developing countries until the next stage of the arms control and security-building process is reached. The reduction of the military threat and the growth of confidence and mutual trust, however, will facilitate compromises on political issues, while greater political co-operation will ease the way for further arms control and co-operative security measures.

IV. Elements of a North–South security system

The future North–South security and arms control system has to include at least five major components: (a) control over arms transfers; (b) non-proliferation of NBC weapons and the means of their delivery; (c) measures to lower military tensions and limit regional arms races; (d) creation of a comprehensive transparency and information exchange system; and (e) prevention of increased international terrorism.

Limitation of arms transfers to the developing world

The arms race in the developing countries is fuelled mostly by weapons imported from developed countries. While there is a growing military industry in the developing countries, even Israel cannot become fully independent in crucial types of weaponry. For this reason, the prevention of an unrestricted arms race in the developing countries is a twofold task including both the establishment of a global regime for arms export, and limitations by developing countries on arms imports. It is inadvisable to urge a complete ban on all arms transfers since this could lead to unpredictable destabilization, but some measures can be taken.

Such an agreement must rely on verification procedures which would require a certain level of institutionalization. A centre for the control of arms transfers could perform this function utilizing some of the methods employed by the former Coordinating Committee on Multilateral Export Controls (COCOM). Consultations among permanent members of the UN Security Council, bringing China into the process, would also be important.

Exporters of arms such as Argentina, Brazil, China and North Korea cannot completely replace Russia, the USA and the European countries in markets in the developing world. These other exporters cannot produce the desired numbers, variety and quality of sophisticated 'smart' weapons used during the Persian Gulf War, or their next generation, which are becoming available in the mid-1990s. Nevertheless, these other exporters should be included in the process of arms transfer restrictions. Since the countries of the developing world have reached a significant degree of diversification of arms sources, curbing arms transfers demands a global agreement under UN auspices. The first step in this direction may be the UN register of all arms transfers,[2] which can perhaps serve as the basis for future more restrictive arrangements.

An agreement among exporters should lead to one among importers. The countries of a region should first declare support for restrictions imposed by exporters and later institutionalize specific arrangements. These might include establishing: (a) a regional agency for arms transfer control which will be provided initially with official information on weapon purchases and later be given the right to verify such information; (b) a procedure for early notification of planned arms transfers, including their timing, quantity, origin and so on; (c) restraints on the purchase of some types of offensive weapons; (d) a ban on the re-export of certain types of weapons; and (e) agreement on quotas for some types of weapons.

Such a regime will not be easy to achieve. Even more difficult may be future arrangements to control domestic production facilities in the developing countries. Currently, indigenous production of weapons is increasing, including that of aircraft, armoured fighting vehicles (AFVs) and artillery pieces. Without domestic production control, arms sales limitations will have limited impact. Domestic controls might include a ban on the production of certain types of weapons and production limits on others. The great powers and major weapon producers should also reach an agreement banning the licensed production of weapons in the developing countries. However, halting the production of weapons which has already begun seems highly unlikely.

Strengthening the non-proliferation regime for NBC weapons

The introduction of non-conventional weapons into the developing world will have especially serious consequences. Limiting the impact of the use of such weapons may be difficult to achieve: the use of chemical or nuclear weapons in one part of the region would inevitably affect the rest. In addition, most countries have a very limited potential to develop 'second-strike options'. The proliferation of non-conventional weapons would create incentives for pre-emptive disarming strikes. With limited early-warning capabilities and unreliable control and communication systems, such a development could lead to accidental or unauthorized use of these weapons even in peacetime.

It must also be recognized that a number of developing countries have made the production of nuclear weapons a priority; India, Israel, Pakistan and some

[2] See Laurance, E. J., Wezeman, S. T. and Wulf, H., SIPRI, *Arms Watch: SIPRI Report on the First Year of the UN Register of Conventional Arms*, SIPRI Research Report no. 6 (Oxford University Press: Oxford, 1993).

other countries have possessed a nuclear capability for some time. Nevertheless the situation is not yet completely out of control. The agreement between North Korea and the USA of October 1994 shows that a variety of incentives can be brought to bear on the problem. One incentive is partial nuclear disarmament by Russia and the USA. To prevent further nuclear proliferation, speedy implementation of the 1993 Strategic Arms Reduction Talks (START) Treaty is essential.[3] This would lead to more effective implementation of the 1968 Non-Proliferation Treaty (NPT) regime in the developing countries. Sanctions (economic, political, and the like) might be required against those parties which persist in their intention of creating an operational nuclear policy.

The problem of chemical weapons (CW), often defined as 'the poor man's nuclear weapon', is more difficult. Iraqi President Saddam Hussein made the CW option thinkable by Iraq's use of chemical weapons against Iran and Kurds living in Iraq. The danger of CW proliferation is enhanced by the proliferation of ballistic missiles, which can be used for their delivery.

The 1987 Missile Technology Control Regime (MTCR) agreement by seven developed countries to control missiles and missile technology transfers seems insufficient. One reason for its poor performance is that Russia has not been a party to it. Another is the existence of new exporters of missile technology, especially Argentina, Brazil, China and North Korea. It seems clear that Russia and the USA by themselves cannot completely block missile proliferation. On the one hand, the great powers have to strengthen restrictions and demand that others follow suit. On the other hand, developing countries must accept fully the provisions of the NPT and international inspections, and this could lead to a regional agreement on missile proliferation. In the Middle East, to cite one case, the possible 'package' might include: (a) acceptance by all Middle Eastern states of the NPT and international control by the International Atomic Energy Agency (IAEA); (b) acceptance by all regional parties of the 1993 Chemical Weapons Convention; (c) an agreement to refrain from purchase of new missiles with ranges greater than 50–100 km, except multiple launcher rocket systems (MLRS)-type systems and air defence systems; and (d) creation of a regional co-ordinating body to supervise the control and verification of these arrangements.

Constraints on military deployments and operations

After the end of the cold war in Europe the developing world may become an area where military tensions abound and where large armed forces are always ready for immediate large-scale action. The probability of large-scale conventional conflict is relatively high. The creation of a security and arms control regime in some regions of the developing world may be impossible without substantial reductions in accumulated conventional armouries. This creates a

---

[3] The US–Russian Treaty on Further Reduction and Limitation of Strategic Offensive Arms (known as the START II Treaty) was signed on 3 Jan. 1993.

frustrating impasse: political *détente* demands a reduction in military confrontation, but such a reduction can only follow relaxation of political tensions.

At the first stage of the process the best that can be hoped for is a political understanding or a declaration of intentions from the relevant parties. They could commit themselves to a rejection of aggressive actions and use of force against their neighbours. The next step might be an agreement on the disengagement of forces. Particular areas in the region could be designated as buffer zones, fully or partially demilitarized. In the fully demilitarized areas no troops (except a limited number of border guards without tanks, heavy artillery or missiles) should be deployed; in the partially demilitarized zones only units of multinational forces should be stationed. Such zones could be established along internationally recognized borders and demarcation lines.

The creation of buffer zones cannot substitute for other steps. In principle, buffer zones can fulfil two major tasks: they can remove the danger of surprise attack and lower the possibility of dangerous border incidents. This would lead to a significant reduction in the level of military confrontation and uncertainty. There could also be areas where offensive weapons are either restricted or completely prohibited. In addition, some areas inside the territories of the parties should be designated as zones in which troop movements are prohibited or restricted. Such zones could be asymmetrical but should be mutual. Centres for monitoring the military situation could supervise activities in those zones.

Besides restrictions on ground military activities it would be necessary to establish centres for the control of air space and air traffic. All recent military conflicts have begun with air offensive operations aimed at gaining air superiority. The key role of air power was once more demonstrated during the Persian Gulf War. These centres should initially be manned by personnel from the great powers, and only later by personnel from regional states. Restrictions on the flight of combat aircraft could include the creation of special corridors which aircraft would be prohibited from entering. Large-scale exercises would need to be prohibited, and there might be a ceiling on the number of aircraft which can be in the air simultaneously.

The first stage would probably also demand permanent stationing of new multinational peacekeeping forces.

At the second stage, front-line countries directly participating in regional conflicts could try to agree on substantial reductions of their forces (especially offensive armaments), and could shift to more defensive military postures and doctrines. The numerical ceilings in many cases cannot be based on 'parity'. Parity demands a more sophisticated country-by-country approach which would be extremely difficult to adopt. The reductions in conventional armaments should be synchronized with reductions of chemical and other non-conventional weapons. More promising are possibilities to agree on such CSBMs as restrictions on the number and scope of military exercises and a ban on large call-ups of reservists.

Success in these areas could help further to institutionalize an arms control and security regime, including the creation of a United Nations Arms Control

Agency to work together with other bodies (Security Council, MSC, centres for monitoring the military situation, centres for arms transfers, centres for control of air space) to create a more comprehensive regional security framework. At the next stage this agency could pick up some of the functions earlier performed by the great powers. Later it might be possible to further lower the armament ceilings and establish greater regional co-operation in various security matters. This might encourage a transition towards more defence-oriented military postures at some later stage.

During the reduction process it would be vital to take into consideration regular armies, paramilitary forces (which can significantly influence the military balance) and the reserve components of the military potentials of the countries. Anti-tank missiles and air defence weapons could be left unlimited in order to enhance the defensive orientations and defensive stability of the countries.

Transparency and confidence building

Confidence building is an integral part of the arms control process. As experience in Europe has demonstrated, without CSBMs no breakthrough in arms control is possible. The importance of such measures will be even greater in the developing world where mutual mistrust is extremely pervasive. CSBMs cannot, however, be simply transferred from Europe to developing countries.

In order to create the initial basis for co-operation between the participants it is vital to take the following bilateral or unilateral steps: (a) publication of data on military budgets by category; (b) provision of information on the size and structure of armed forces; and (c) preliminary release of information about planned military activities and exercises. Step b would not have a significant impact on the situation since the information is already widely known. Nevertheless, the release of information at the state level would have a positive psychological influence.

Countries in some regions of the developing world might be able to agree on direct exchange of information on troop movements and exercises, on principles of mutual control and verification of military activities and other CSBMs. More intrusive transparency measures could be provided with the assistance of outsiders, acting as 'honest brokers' to make relevant information available to all regional parties. Such a system might rely on satellites and ground stations under some form of UN control. It would appear useful to supplement the exchange of data with the following: (a) elimination of exercises near borders or disengagement lines; (b) limitations on the timing and size of exercises, prohibiting large-scale tank exercises in particular; and (c) observation of all exercises, including command exercises, first by UN representatives and then by the representatives of the regional participants.

A key role might be played by the centres for monitoring military activities, which could act as intermediaries to prepare and induce greater co-operation. The centres could also: (a) serve as banks for relevant information; (b) operate monitoring satellites and ground stations; (*c*) conduct ground inspections of suspicious activities; (*d*) provide 'hot lines' for direct communication between parties; and (*e*) take political actions as 'preventive diplomacy'.

The activities of the centres could prepare the stage for the creation of a UN Arms Control Agency, and lead the way towards the creation of a more comprehensive system of regional security.

Opposing international terrorism

Terrorism has become not only one of the scourges of the developing world, but also a global threat. Terrorism in the developing world is often state supported. Experience shows that the search for peace in these regions can provoke new waves of terrorism, sometimes of the most vicious form. In the early stages of the arms control process it will likely be impractical to expect participants to co-ordinate their anti-terrorist activities. Later, however, this could become an important aspect of the regional security effort.

Practically all developing countries, including those which co-operate with terrorists, are victimized by terrorist groups that threaten their internal security. This might allow the developing countries to co-ordinate their fight against terrorism when CSBMs become more sophisticated. Co-operation on the following could significantly strengthen regional security in the developing world: (*a*) agreeing on the definition of terrorist groups; (*b*) ceasing to support terrorist activities (including the provision of training facilities and safe refuge); (*c*) agreeing to extradite terrorists according to legal procedures; and (*d*) preparing a regional convention on the prevention of terrorism, especially hijacking.

V. Conclusion

For almost four decades regional conflict was seen as a part of the global Soviet–US struggle. The end of the cold war removes superpower competition as a restraining factor, complicating the regional situation. Today Russia and the USA can co-operate with each other and with other countries in developing a North–South security system that would promote peace and security in the developing world. Of course, they cannot and should not 'impose' peace on these countries, but they can facilitate political negotiation and be even more instrumental in helping to create a positive regional security environment—a North–South security system—as described above. Developing countries will find it more difficult to exploit great power antagonisms in such an environment. This will have a serious impact on their approach to security policy. Without trying to suggest a blueprint for 'comprehensive settlement' of the problems of weapon and military technology transfers, it is possible to conclude that successful regional negotiations between parties should be facilitated by the international environment. Co-operation between Russia and the USA will help to launch a step-by-step process and promote the goal of lasting peace in the developing world. This approach seems reasonable, but its implementation can be difficult. What is important, however, is that it recognizes that a North–South security regime should be developed in parallel to the effort to find political solutions and should not be delayed. Arms control and CSBMs can open the way to political solutions of political questions. The introduction of arms control and CSBMs to the developing world will help to realize political dialogue between the relevant parties.

4. Containing the introduction of destabilizing military technologies: the confidence-building approach

James Macintosh*

I. Introduction

The European security environment entered a period of fundamental transformation in 1986 with the negotiation of the Conference on Security and Co-operation in Europe (CSCE) Stockholm Document.[1] The adoption of this comprehensive collection of confidence- and security-building measures (CSBMs) formally marked a new level of co-operative openness in European security affairs and signalled the beginning of a profound change in security perceptions. By 1991 the process of transformation had assumed astonishing proportions with the structure of European security relations for ever changed. However, this transformation also helped unleash processes and create conditions that may eventually undermine the apparent progress of recent years. Time will tell whether or not the end result will be enhanced political and military stability.

One important consequence of the transformation of the security environment has been the multilateralization of both security problems *and* their solutions. This may make the management of military instability[2] within Europe and on

---

[1] It may seem arbitrary to single out specific dates and events as marking what has been in fact a complex process stretching out over at least a decade. Nevertheless, a good argument can be made that the final stages of the 1984–86 Stockholm Conference on Confidence- and Security-Building Measures and Disarmament in Europe and the coming to power of Mikhail Gorbachev in the Soviet Union clearly and unmistakably defined the start of a period of significant transformation in East–West security relations. The conclusion of the Stockholm Document in 1986 and the Gorbachev proposal for sweeping new conventional armed force reduction talks to replace the unproductive Mutual (and Balanced) Force Reduction Talks in Vienna (April and June 1986) signalled the threshold of a new era and a period of major change. The text of the Stockholm Document is reproduced in SIPRI, *SIPRI Yearbook 1987: World Armaments and Disarmament* (Oxford University Press: Oxford, 1987), pp. 355–69.

[2] Stability is a complex concept that embraces a variety of distinct phenomena. The origins of most international security-oriented considerations of stability lie in the analysis of Soviet–US strategic force relationships. The translation to multilateral conventional force relationships is not perfect but the basic characteristics appear to apply reasonably well. The two aspects of stability that are particularly relevant here are *arms race stability* and *crisis stability*. Each may be influenced by the introduction of new military technologies into complex military relationships.

Arms race stability refers to 'the degree of incentive to develop a matching or offsetting weapon system or capability in response to a new development or deployment' in a neighbouring state. *Crisis stability* is the degree of incentive to employ potentially vulnerable systems before they can be destroyed or neutralized in a surprise attack. A related characteristic of military relationships, sometimes referred to as *deterrence robustness,* is also relevant but somewhat more difficult to apply to conventional force deterrence. Deterrence robustness refers to the willingness (or lack thereof) of partners in an adversarial military rela-

---

* This chapter is based, in part, on research conducted under a NATO Research Fellowship.

REGIONAL CONFLICTS

its periphery much more difficult. Relatively straightforward quantitative arms control approaches such as symmetrical force reductions, particularly of key systems such as main battle tanks, may no longer be sufficient to address increasingly complex and primarily *psychological*[3] stability concerns.[4] The fragmentation of the previous, predominantly bipolar security structure makes that all but inevitable, even if the size and character of conventional military forces remain approximately the same as today.

Making matters more complicated, the introduction of 'militarily relevant technologies'[5] may have one of four basic types of impact on existing (but evolving and transforming) conventional military relationships. These technologies, at least in principle, may increase or decrease stability because of their specific character. However, the introduction of some militarily relevant technologies may also have a neutral impact where the stability of a military relationship is perceived to be unaltered. The most difficult case, of course, is that which sees both stabilizing *and* destabilizing results flow from the introduction of a specific military technology. It is necessary to identify which of these four potential outcome types is likely in each case before seeking arms control solutions to the impact of various technologies.[6] It should not be assumed that all

tionship to consider the use of force given the prospect of retaliation and escalation. It can also be thought of as the strength of a complex deterrence relationship. Although deterrence robustness is obviously a function of assessments of relevant military balances, these assessments are probably influenced by judgements about whether or not the use of force is appropriate. Thus, it combines judgements about whether force can be used and whether it should be used. All three of these concepts have a significant psychological character in as much as they entail personal and collective judgements about the meaning and nature of military force relationships. See Macintosh, J., 'Soviet–American strategic relations', eds D. Leyton-Brown and M. Slack, *The Canadian Strategic Review 1984* (Canadian Institute of Strategic Studies: Toronto, 1985).

[3] A central claim of this chapter is that stability problems in the military relationships among groups of states have a psychological as well as material character. 'Stability concerns' are very much in the eye of the beholder, a point that is easily overlooked. The same deployment of military forces may produce a very different reaction depending upon how decision makers in the relevant states think about those forces and the general intentions of their neighbours.

[4] Of course, it might be an exaggeration to suggest that straightforward quantitative reductions actually represented an effective arms control solution to NATO–WTO conventional force balance problems. It might be argued that the 1990 Conventional Armed Forces in Europe (CFE) Treaty constituted an effective arms control solution, but it should be remembered that the structure and process of East–West security relations was already under fundamental revision during the time the Treaty was being negotiated. As a consequence, there is not a clear-cut example of conventional force quantitative reductions to prove the effectiveness of this arms control approach.

[5] The term 'militarily relevant technology' is used in order to cover the widest range of technologies and technological origins, including those in the civilian sector. It is used in preference to 'military technology' because that term might be taken to include only those technologies specifically developed for military use, and perhaps only by government-funded military R&D facilities—restrictions that may be too narrow. This is particularly the case as distinctions between 'civilian' and 'military' R&D become more fuzzy and as shrewd military planners increasingly draw on civilian sources for use in military systems. This idea is explored later in the chapter.

[6] In this analysis, confidence building is considered to be a form of arms control, a view that is increasingly common within the analytic community. The understanding of arms control employed in this chapter is based on the work of Patrick Morgan. His definition states that 'arms control consists of measures, directly related to military forces, adopted by governments to contain the costs and harmful consequences of the continued existence of arms (their own and others), within the overall objective of sustaining or enhancing their security in international politics'. See Morgan, P., 'Elements of a general theory of arms control', ed. P. R. Viotti, *Conflict and Arms Control: An Uncertain Agenda* (Westview Press: Boulder, Colo., 1986), p. 285.

militarily relevant technologies can only have a destabilizing or negative impact on a military relationship. Neither should it be assumed that a given technology and the changes wrought in military capability as a result of adopting or developing it will have the same destabilizing (or stabilizing) impact in all security relationships. Instability is very much in the eye of the beholder—it is a phenomenon with a significant psychological component. In addition, analysis should not ignore the wide range of mitigating conditions that shape—or potentially even alter—that stability impact.[7]

Of particular interest are those militarily relevant technologies that can have a destabilizing impact. Some new military technologies may upset existing, relatively stable security relationships emerging in the new, much more multilateral world. Alternatively, these technologies may further destabilize relationships already troubled by quantitatively or qualitatively based instabilities. In either case, qualitative arms control solutions will be increasingly important, particularly once efforts have been expended to address basic quantitative asymmetries. Once approximately equivalent ceilings for major weapon systems have been established, the major source of capability change (and instability) will be either doctrine and training on the personnel side or qualitative changes in weapon systems. However, qualitative arms control approaches will not necessarily be very easy to develop or implement. They may also have limited amounts of leverage on the predominantly psychological dimensions of stability.

Indeed, it may be the case that only arms control approaches which are oriented towards confidence building and which work on a largely co-operative level will prove able to deal effectively with technologically induced conventional military instability. This will certainly be so if outright bans on key weapon systems and technologies prove to be unpalatable or unworkable solutions—a distinct possibility given the realities of the contemporary world. Industrial strategies, national security priorities, trade considerations and the extreme difficulty of developing 'leak-proof' non-proliferation arrangements across a wide range of 'conventional technologies' all caution against false optimism on this front.

This chapter explores the confidence-building approach to constraining the impact of militarily relevant technology on the stability of conventional military relationships among a number of states of varying power potentials and geostrategic realities within a region. The surprising conclusion to this exploration is that a modest-seeming regime of 'technology constraints'—CSBMs and CSBM-like measures which are to some extent foreshadowed or initiated in the

---

[7] The provisional analysis undertaken here focuses on the impact on stability of militarily relevant technologies (in principle, almost any technology) rather than attempting to assess the 'offensiveness' or 'defensiveness' of improved or modified weapon systems or new military technologies. The latter focus has not been very satisfactory, in large part because it tends to produce a 'dialogue of the deaf'. Contrasting analytic perspectives have acquired paradigm-like dimensions that conceptualize weapon systems and their impact in very specific, rather inflexible (and sharply contrasting) ways. Debates about non-offensive defence and the role of main battle tanks in modern militaries illustrate this tendency only too well.

CSCE's Vienna Document 1992[8]—may help provide a non-controversial yet constructive and useful degree of stability in asymmetrical conventional military relationships. However, a wide variety of considerations limits what can be achieved with multilateral, co-operative arms control efforts. This chapter examines both the opportunities for and the limits to qualitative confidence building with particular focus on the CSCE case. Although arms control lessons derived from the CSCE experience are not necessarily exportable to other regions, at least without suitable adjustments for changed contexts, it cannot be denied that the CSCE has been a productive 'hothouse' for developing new ideas about improving regional security relations.[9]

II. Background

Although a process of profound change in European security affairs began with the negotiation and implementation of the Stockholm Document in 1986, it has been during succeeding years that the most significant changes have occurred. The 1990 Conventional Armed Forces in Europe (CFE) Treaty and the parallel Vienna CSBM agreements of 1990[10] and 1992,[11] combined with various unilateral (primarily Soviet) conventional force reductions and withdrawals,[12] the dissolution of the Warsaw Treaty Organization (WTO) in March 1991, and of the Soviet Union have altered the European security environment fundamentally. The global security environment has also been changed profoundly by the melting away of cold war structures, perhaps to an extent that is not yet well understood by analysts or the general public. These unanticipated changes have transformed the East–West, North Atlantic Treaty Organization (NATO)–WTO conventional military relationship in Europe well beyond what any analyst could have predicted a few years ago. The changes are truly startling.[13]

---

[8] The text is reproduced in SIPRI, *SIPRI Yearbook 1993: World Armaments and Disarmament* (Oxford University Press: Oxford, 1993), pp. 635–53.

[9] For potential application of CSBMs in other regions, see Goodby, J. E., 'Transparency in the Middle East', *Arms Control Today*, vol. 21, no. 4 (May 1991), pp. 8–9; and Goodby, J. E., The context of Korean unification: the case for a multilateral security structure', eds P. Williams, D. M. Goldstein and H. Andrews, Jr, *Security in Korea* (Westview Press: Boulder, Colo., 1994).

[10] The text of the Vienna Document 1990 is reproduced in SIPRI, *SIPRI Yearbook 1991: World Armaments and Disarmament* (Oxford University Press: Oxford, 1991), pp. 475–88.

[11] For background, see the author's 'Confidence-building measures in Europe', ed. R. D. Burns, *Encyclopedia of Arms Control and Disarmament* (Charles Scribner's Sons: New York, 1993); and his 'Confidence building processes—CSCE and MBFR: a review and assessment' and 'European arms control developments', eds H. Rattinger and D. Dewitt, *Canadian and German Perspectives on East–West Arms Control* (Routledge: London, 1992). See also Dean, J., *Meeting Gorbachev's Challenge: How to Build Down the NATO–Warsaw Pact Confrontation* (St Martin's Press: New York, 1989).

[12] For example, the 7 Dec. 1988 unilateral reductions amounting to six divisions announced by General Secretary Gorbachev at the United Nations. These are discussed in Dean (note 11), pp. 54–56, 132–34. These reductions and other related actions are also discussed in the immensely useful *Arms Control Reporter*, an annual with monthly updates published by the Institute for Defense and Disarmament Studies, Brookline, Mass.

[13] Although it is clear that there have been startling changes in Europe (and globally) in recent years, there is some debate about how changed international security relations truly are. For some provocative views, see: Snyder, J., 'Averting anarchy in the new Europe', *International Security*, vol. 14, no. 4 (spring 1990); Mearsheimer, J. J., 'Back to the future: instability in Europe after the cold war', *International*

A unified and increasingly powerful—but potentially insular—Federal Republic of Germany now stands where two great military alliances once faced each other. It is almost impossible to exaggerate the consequences of this change. Concerns about significant conventional force asymmetries and the capacity of the WTO states to launch a no- or low-warning attack against the West no longer have substance or meaning.[14] The WTO—never a natural creation in any event—disappeared virtually overnight with unsettling effects, and NATO continues to struggle to redefine its *raison d'être*. Completing the picture of radical transformation, nuclear weapons ranging from intermediate to tactical and extending into the strategic nuclear realm are increasingly absent from the continent.[15] Although not a direct concern here, the changes in thinking about strategic nuclear issues have also been significant, with a clear tendency towards minimum deterrence thinking emerging in the policy-shaping and analytic world.[16] These changes may well increase the relevance of concern about conventional military instabilities as strategic nuclear forces decline further in relevance. To the uncertain extent that the existence of overwhelming nuclear forces influenced decisions to use conventional force in the past (either by or against a nuclear power), significantly reduced nuclear forces will be even less influential.

Security, vol. 15, no. 1 (summer 1990); Van Evera, S., 'Primed for peace: Europe after the cold war', *International Security,* vol. 15, no. 3 (winter 1990/91); Kupchan, C. A. and Kupchan, C. A., 'Concerts, collective security, and the future of Europe', *International Security,* vol. 16, no. 1 (summer 1991); Jervis, R., 'The future of world politics', *International Security,* vol. 16, no. 3 (winter 1991/92).

[14] Although there were developing suspicions among increasing numbers of Western analysts that the WTO really did not pose the sort of threat commonly assumed in the mid- to late 1980s, the forces of the two alliances nevertheless remained physically present in the centre of Europe. Regardless of opinions about the nature (and credibility) of the threats posed by those forces, it took their physical removal to actually change the nature of the military relationship in Europe. Views sceptical of the WTO threat emerged throughout the 1980s but remained controversial. See Mearsheimer, J. J., 'Why the Soviets can't win quickly in Central Europe', *International Security,* vol. 7, no. 1 (summer 1982). By 1985, more analysts were engaged in critical assessments. See, for instance, Posen, B. R., 'Measuring the European conventional balance: coping with complexity in threat assessment', *International Security,* vol. 9, no. 3 (winter 1984/85). For analyses at the zenith of doubt and uncertainty, see Chalmers, M. and Unterseher, L., 'Is there a tank gap? Comparing NATO and Warsaw Pact tank fleets', and Cohen, E. A., 'Toward better net assessment: rethinking the European conventional balance', both in *International Security,* vol. 13, no. 1 (summer 1988). The spring of 1989 saw what amounted to the last shots fired in these debates with Mearsheimer, J. J., 'Assessing the conventional balance: the 3:1 rule and its critics', and Epstein, J., 'The 3:1 rule: the adaptive dynamic model, and the future of security studies', both in *International Security,* vol. 13, no. 4 (spring 1989), together with related correspondence.

[15] A manifestation of this was the 16 June 1992 announcement by Presidents George Bush and Boris Yeltsin that the strategic forces of the United States and the Russian Federation would be reduced to 3000–3500 warheads by the turn of the century. This, of course, was negotiated even before the previous agreement (START) could be implemented. Reported in *New York Times,* 17 June 1992.

[16] See, for instance, Kaysen, C., McNamara, R. S. and Rathjens, G. W., 'Nuclear weapons after the cold war', *Foreign Affairs,* vol. 70, no. 4 (fall 1991).

III. Arms control

Despite these generally positive changes, the arms control agenda for the greater CSCE region—both its Eurasian and North American components[17]—is far from exhausted.[18] While some old concerns have been reduced or even eliminated, new ones have emerged to take their place. More will almost certainly develop to further complicate this dynamic CSCE-wide security environment. With few exceptions, these new problems are more complex and seemingly more intractable than the old ones. *This is largely a function of the emergence of genuine multilateral linkages and complex subregional relationships where once there was a significantly more structured, bilateral security order.*

The capacity of existing arms control approaches to deal with these new security concerns and realities is uncertain. Further CFE-style force reductions—both equipment and personnel-oriented—can help in some cases. However, the European security environment is far more complex than it was several years ago, which makes the calculation and attainment of meaningfully 'symmetrical' ceilings extraordinarily complicated, if not impossible.[19]

The whole notion of conventional force symmetry has become elusive in the new Europe. There are simply too many 'sides' with too great a range of fundamental power disparities for CFE-style approaches to work either easily or well. The essence of the CFE process, after all, was to bring two diverse alliances into greater symmetry at lower force levels. Now, some large and powerful European states have no hostile neighbours while smaller states may be surrounded by potentially unfriendly states. Former friends and neighbours may now be potential enemies. The sorts of security concerns that European states face may be quite different, too. Some may be preoccupied with maritime-oriented threats while others may focus on land-force threats of various types. Security concerns have become much more singularized and diverse. Much the same appears to be true of potential regional security groupings in other areas of the world where the former East–West cold war structure never really existed. Although this does not mean that CFE-style quantitative arms control

[17] Recall that some aspects of the CSCE apply to the land masses of all participating states, while the security dimension, as defined in the 1983 Madrid Mandate, only applies to the Atlantic-to-the-Urals sub-region.

[18] This chapter's assessment runs counter to the current perception within some parts of the CSCE security community that arms control *per se* within Europe is largely completed business, only requiring the resolution of details. From the perspective of this chapter's analysis, this view is wildly optimistic. Note that the CSCE Budapest document 1994 defined 'Further Tasks of the CSCE Forum for Security and Co-operation' to include 'new measures of arms control, including in particular confidence- and security-building' and the promotion of 'complementarity between regional and CSCE-wide approaches'.

[19] The successful attempt to divide the former Soviet Union's treaty-limited equipment (TLE) entitlements under the CFE Treaty among its successor states suggests that the development of new quantitative limits in multilateral settings is not impossible. However, the somewhat arbitrary nature of the reapportionment, the unique circumstances surrounding the adjustments and the possibility of further difficulties flowing from these limits should not be overlooked. The adjustments to the CFE Treaty involved 8 of 15 of the former Soviet republics (extending the CFE's area of coverage well into Central Asia) as well as 5 East European states from the former WTO. The new agreement was signed on 5 June 1992 with the NATO states. *New York Times,* 6 June 1992. Editor's note: Some of its provisions are being contested by Russia, and some were ignored in the Chechnya operation.

agreements cannot be developed for other regions or further developed within Europe, the problems will be severe.

Confidence-building agreements, for example, the CSCE's Vienna Document 1990 and Vienna Document 1992, may provide some measure of control and stability beyond what quantitative approaches can promise. However, there are limits here, too. Analysts and policy makers have yet to explore the qualitative constraint dimensions of confidence building to any great extent.[20] Therefore, it may be necessary to develop new—or at least significantly revised—arms control approaches to manage some dimensions of these 'stability' problems and developments.

IV. The arms control scene in more detail

In contrast to the last 45 years, many new security concerns within the CSCE region—and especially within its European domain—will increasingly revolve around perceptions of military instability in complex security relationships *among multilateral groupings*. This is in contrast to the more traditional security relationship defined by two major blocs during the cold war era. This assessment can hardly be seen to be controversial and represents a central element of the analysis here.[21] At least some of these security concerns already exist between former members of the WTO. More will doubtless emerge, in some cases among successor states of the USSR.

The potential for unstable security relations among European states should not be underestimated. Some of these states have little democratic experience and no real democratic tradition; in some cases their defence forces and militias are poorly controlled and lack professionalism; states are plagued by ethnic and religious friction that cuts across many borders; and they face dismaying economic problems as they attempt to manage the conversion to market-oriented economies. It is a volatile mixture of weaknesses and problems. Compounding matters, some regional and subregional animosities have histories that extend over many centuries and appear deeply rooted in the psyches of all currently living generations. These seemingly indelible animosities will inevitably also colour contemporary security relations.

This is fertile territory for miscalculation and misperception as well as outright, premeditated hostility. Inexperienced governments with little practice in dealing with volatile public sentiment may be poorly equipped to contain domestic demands for the use of force, making a dangerous situation even

---

[20] This is discussed in the author's *From Stockholm to Vienna and Beyond: The Confidence Building Process Revisited* (Department of Foreign Affairs and International Trade: Ottawa, forthcoming).

[21] This multilateralization process is important because it tends to make European or CSCE-related security issues more like those in other parts of the world where multilateral and multiple, independent bilateral security relations are the norm. This will likely make new security lessons and insights developed in or for Europe and the broader CSCE region more 'exportable' to other regions. The CSCE Budapest Document 1994 determined that 'specific arms control measures, including disarmament and confidence- and security-building, may vary in order to address the particular security needs of individual States or regions'.

worse. They may also be tempted to turn to externally directed violence in order to distract domestic critics. This situation can only be compounded by the occasionally fragmented control of armed forces, particularly when security agendas are set by emotional rather than rational considerations. The experience of extremely bitter internecine wars in the former Yugoslavia, major fighting between Armenia and Azerbaijan and other territorial disputes involving Georgia, Moldova, Russia and Ukraine underline these concerns. The potential for further explosive failures of the current European peace is real if still under containment. While few analysts expect to encounter many more Yugoslavia-style calamities in the near term, serious disagreements in several subregions are likely. Quantitative and qualitative force instabilities—or at least the perception of their emergence—can only add to the menu of problem-causing or crisis-exaggerating developments.

The CFE Treaty successfully addressed a number of very important bloc-to-bloc problems associated with the 'old' Europe, particularly problems identified with disparities in the armoured forces of the two alliances. However, the CFE Treaty has inadvertently helped to preserve a legacy of complex asymmetries among the various former WTO states as well as between them and various NATO and neutral states. The preponderance of the old Soviet Union—and now the new Russia—in comparison to the military strength of the remaining former WTO states can only be a cause of instability and concern. These asymmetries are complicated further by the emerging national forces of the former Soviet Union's successor republics (particularly Belarus, Moldova, Russia and Ukraine). Where once two alliances dominated power calculations, a host of subregional groupings has emerged to form a dynamic patchwork of new, more complex relationships.

While numbers and types of deployed weapon systems within each of these states matter in both relative and absolute terms, a major component in these emerging stability concerns will be the impact that *changes* in deployed weapon systems may have on perceptions of existing force relationships (especially when combined with doctrinal shifts towards more aggressive and mobile schemes).[22] Thus, for example, moderate quantitative asymmetries in approximately equivalent types of armoured vehicles may not contribute to a sense of instability in a military relationship among several neighbouring states. However, a change in that relationship—perhaps the introduction of a new generation of significantly more capable tanks or the acquisition of surface-to-surface rockets or missiles armed with 'smart' anti-armour submunitions—can

---

[22] This consideration is often overlooked. Changes in the way that existing or newly introduced weapon systems and other military equipment are to be utilized can produce a significant psychological impact, creating or exaggerating perceptions of instability. Doctrinal shifts that emphasize the development of rapid-reaction, highly mobile ground forces and the effective use of autonomous counter-offensives (including the use of long-range missiles and ground-attack aircraft) can easily trigger concerns about surprise attack that previously may not have been pronounced. Indeed, it could be the case that doctrinal shifts (if seen to be implemented successfully) can have as destabilizing an impact on a security relationship among neighbours as can the introduction of significantly more capable weapon systems.

generate a sense of instability where one was previously absent.[23] Moreover, a security relationship that already exhibits instability will almost certainly be aggravated by these sorts of qualitative changes. Both sorts of impact are important and are likely to be very difficult to assess or measure accurately.

This type of problem is fundamentally qualitative rather than quantitative, and as such it is much more difficult to deal with using arms control. 'Qualitative arms control' even when it was attempted by the two former superpowers or two well-disciplined blocs proved difficult enough to put into practice. How much more complicated will it be when as many as 10 subregional groupings, many with overlapping memberships and contradictory concerns, composed of from 2 to 16 or more states, replace the previous two blocs?

These difficulties will be complicated further by the different obligations, pretensions and geostrategic realities of the various CSCE states and the groupings in which they operate. Some states can contemplate relatively simple and, if they wish, severe military force constraint and reduction solutions, perhaps on their own or jointly with several neighbours. However, others are—or may feel themselves to be—obliged by more complicated circumstances to retain greater military flexibility and to pursue qualitative improvements within static or declining defence budgets. The need to maintain a viable defence industrial base, for example, can affect perspectives tremendously. CSCE states flanked by non-CSCE states of uncertain motivation can also influence perceptions of military need. The geostrategic circumstances of Hungary, Spain, Sweden, Turkey and the USA, for instance, are dramatically dissimilar. This has an inevitable impact on the tolerance that different states will—and can—have to qualitative or technologically oriented arms control. Nevertheless, there are likely to be modest yet useful standards and approaches that most will find acceptable, particularly if they are focused intelligently on key aspects of force modernization that threaten the greatest destabilizing impact.

V. A closer look at stability

Changes in military capabilities resulting from technological developments can produce instability in a variety of ways, some of which may be more worrisome than others.[24] The instability may be profound or trivial; it may be part of a larger process of stability-related changes or an isolated event in an otherwise stable relationship; and it might have an amorphous impact on long-term weapon system development programmes in other states or a specific and more upsetting impact on crisis behaviour in the very near term. However, militarily

[23] It is possible that the perception of change, a complex amalgam of emotional and rational assessments, is even more important than the actual 'objective' nature of the change. The perception that security relations have been altered for the worse is the critical aspect of change and can be wildly disproportionate to the actual material change in capability introduced, for instance, by the adoption of a new tank.

[24] The role of changes in personnel training and fundamental doctrine in producing destabilizing impacts on a security relationship should not be overlooked. They may be almost as important as the changes wrought by technologically induced modernization. A more comprehensive treatment of this subject would also include this dimension of capability change.

relevant technologies can also have a positive or stabilizing impact—at least in principle—on a military relationship under some circumstances. Any capability change that reduces the concerns of the deploying state about external threats while posing no offsetting threat to neighbours offers this contribution to positive stability.[25]

Everyday usage tends to obscure the complex nature of stability. To understand the sort of leverage that arms control (including confidence building) can have in moderating or damping instability in conventional military relationships (without impairing the enhancement of stability), it is necessary to understand in more detail the nature of stability and the ways in which the introduction of militarily relevant technologies can alter it. This section and the next deal with these two important components of qualitative arms control.

As indicated above, the introduction of increasingly sophisticated and advanced militarily relevant technologies can have varied impact on the operation of any existing conventional military relationship. The impact can be: (a) 'positive', (b) 'negative', (c) simultaneously positive and negative, or (d) neutral. These are the four dimensions of change that an existing security relationship can undergo as a result of qualitative weapon changes. It should be remembered, of course, that a conventional military relationship (the relations enjoyed on a bilateral as well as multilateral basis among a specific group of states) can range from extremely stable to very unstable *before* any effect is introduced by the adoption or development of new technologies. Thus, any assessments of this new impact must be sensitive to the existing context because that context gives important meaning to the degree of relative change. The consequences of a qualitative change in the capabilities of one state will almost certainly differ depending upon the overall state of stability enjoyed by a group of states. The changes may be considered almost irrelevant or deeply disturbing. The degree to which each state sees its fellow participants as either threats or partners will colour assessments of how the military relationship has changed as a result of technological changes. It is important to appreciate that these considerations are all *independent* of the particular characteristics of the militarily relevant technology or the weapon system capability changes that result from exploitation of the technology. This has substantial ramifications for the development of qualitative arms control, which must be at least equally sensitive to the defining context as it is to the technical characteristics of technologies and capability changes.

'Positive' stability impact in the context of the analysis here refers to relative increased stability, while 'negative' refers to relative decreased stability (viewed in terms of an existing stability baseline). At present, no specific qualitative (especially absolute) measures of stability or stability change recommend themselves for use in this type of analysis. Expressions such as 'increased' and 'decreased' or 'positive' and 'negative' stability create images of more formal,

---

[25] Movable, but not mobile, surface-to-air missile defence for military airbases and armoured vehicle facilities, for instance, could be seen as having a predominantly positive impact on stability.

quantifiable systems, processes and 'states of stability'. However, the work presented here does not yet support any such meaningful operational measurements of stability and stability change. Given the distinctly psychological nature of the basic analytic perspective and the context-dependent understanding of stability employed here, it is *not* clear what sorts of quantitative indicators or measurements—if any—would be appropriate beyond the implied intuitive 'more' and 'less' estimate.

On the basis of preliminary examination, it appears that the changes in conventional military capability brought about by the introduction or development of one or more militarily relevant technologies can have one of six distinct ideal-type categories of impact. Each category includes two distinctive variants. In one variant 'subjective' and 'objective' evaluations of the impact of a technology on stability generally correspond, at least in terms of their conclusions. In the second variant of each category the objectively derived assessment of impact (positive, negative or neutral) does not match up with the subjective estimate, again viewed primarily in terms of conclusions. This is an important but potentially contentious claim.

It is essential to the analysis here that some form of objective assessment is possible, at least in principle. Such assessment would permit independent observers to conclude whether a given technology and the changes in military capabilities that it facilitates would have, on balance, a neutral, positive (stability enhancing) or negative (stability degrading) impact in a given case. This constitutes the *objective* estimate of the impact that the technology would have on the state of existing stability in a conventional force security relationship, whether the technology or systems in question pertain to the state or its neighbour.[26] The important assessment, however, may be the more clearly subjective one performed by various civilian and military decision makers in the interacting countries as they think about their own development and deployment choices or respond to similar decisions made by neighbours. Different decision makers (with different backgrounds, principal concerns, bureaucratic–organizational allegiances, predispositions, etc.) will evaluate changes in military capabilities (and the technologies that facilitate them) in potentially diverse

[26] At the risk of complicating an already complex perspective, it is important to observe that a more comprehensive analysis of stability relations would distinguish between what are termed here 'objective' estimates of stability impacts and actual outcomes (i.e., observed impacts after the fact). There is a natural tendency to treat these two as functionally the same; a completely thorough assessment would almost by definition predict the eventual stability impact of a development or deployment choice. However, this assumption is improbably heroic. It almost certainly overstates the extent to which any analytic assessment could properly evaluate the complex environment (present and future) in which these decisions are actually played out. Thus, it will likely make sense in more comprehensive iterations of this analysis to treat 'objective assessments' and eventual outcomes as separate phenomena. It will also likely be necessary to distinguish between *ideal* objective assessments (hypothetically perfect) and *practically* objective ones that could be conducted by real world analysts observing from an intellectual and emotional distance from the policy world. The latter would aspire to perfection but not achieve it. Thus, it is possible to imagine not 2 but 3 conceptually distinct types of 'objective assessment' of stability impact: (*a*) observed outcome—after the fact, (*b*) an ideal type assessment and prediction, and (*c*) a deliberately but still imperfectly objective assessment performed by non-participants. As is the case with many other aspects of this preliminary look at qualitative arms control, much more work needs to be done to fully explore these important distinctions and the issues their identification raises.

ways. This will feed judgements about stability and the impact of qualitative change in important ways. It ensures that the stability assessments of policy makers will be heavily influenced by subjective considerations and will be context-dependent.

It seems plausible to speculate that the more relevant stability assessment is the one that policy makers *believe* in—the subjective assessments of stability impact (potentially independent of 'objective' facts and 'relational' analysis). This is the assessment, after all, that informs judgements about impacts on the stability of an existing military relationship. The thoughts of independent analysts might count for little in this process. Note, however, that objective and subjective assessments can also be identical or close to it. In principle, they can even employ similar processes of analysis. There is another consideration that links the two forms of assessment. A good argument can be made that genuinely objective assessments (i.e., those performed by genuinely independent and well-informed analysts) of the impact of a given technology (or, more directly, of a change in military capability facilitated by the technology) are very difficult to perform outside the reach of at least some extra-analytic influences. Many of the potential criteria that objective assessments might employ may have their own secondary subjective influences.

For instance, the value to attach to a given type of performance improvement in a particular weapon system flowing from the adoption of a new technological process can be influenced by ultimately quite subjective appreciations of how important it is compared with related performance criteria. Methods of comparison may also reflect idiosyncratic or institutional biases that have assumed the status of conventional wisdom. Consider a comparison of technologies that could improve the following aspects of main battle tank performance: standing-start acceleration, structural resistance to opposing tank fire (or crew survival) and fire control performance (acquisition speed and accuracy) while in motion. Which is most destabilizing? Which is most important for improved performance? How is a trade-off to be performed? While specific values can be attached to a given level of performance or performance improvement in each case, what they really mean may not be so obvious objectively. Analysts may argue endlessly over the relative value of, among other things, increased acceleration versus reduced signature (size and emitting characteristics) versus increased fuel efficiency (unrefuelled range) versus rate of fire and ammunition load, producing different estimates of how much and what type of 'change' and impact on existing levels of stability each actually entails. The implication is that objective assessments of capability change may also be prone to a variety of subjective components and/or influences.

Recognizing the possibility of objective and subjective assessments of stability impact is important to any reasonable analysis of military technology and qualitative arms control, as is recognizing the relative importance of subjective estimates even in apparently objective evaluation. It underlines in dramatic terms the context-dependent nature of thinking about technology and changes in military capabilities. Although there is little research to call on, it is probably the case that most analytic efforts to deal with qualitative developments tend to minimize or ignore subjective factors and contextual considerations (i.e., those things that help define the specific circumstances of a unique military relationship) and instead concentrate on abstract or technical assessments of how the introduction of certain technologies or capabilities will alter a given balance.

It is important conceptually to recognize that the perceptions of policy makers of both the state of stability in a security relationship and the likely impact of a given change in capability are influenced crucially by psychological—and perhaps analytically inaccessible—factors.[27] This conceptual point of view means that judgements about the impact of new technologies may be difficult to anticipate and have characteristics that make them particularly amenable to psychologically oriented arms control approaches. If judgements about the stability impact of capability changes (especially those facilitated by new technologies) prove to be relatively idiosyncratic and context-dependent, objective criteria for stability-oriented arms control may prove ephemeral at best.

This is why confidence building, because of its psychological focus and significant interaction with subjective assessments through its concentration on information, offers so useful an approach for dealing with the constraint of at least some potentially destabilizing technologies and the capability changes caused by them. Confidence building is very much concerned with the development of accurate information about military capabilities and activities. This is an absolutely central function in confidence-building agreements. It is also concerned with facilitating the positive transformation of security relationships, transformations that make *stability concerns less important*. Indeed, as is demonstrated below, confidence building is intimately connected with processes of transformation. Managing, constraining or even eliminating the introduction of destabilizing capabilities into relatively stable military relationships is a clear and obvious role for confidence building.

Forms of stability

In principle, the systemic impact on existing levels of stability caused by capability brought about by the introduction or development of a militarily relevant technology appear to fall into one of six basic categories as outlined in table 4.1.

In this simplified collection of categories several terms are used that warrant elaboration. For instance, in cases of negative impact, 'meaningful military

---

[27] Some analysts find this prospect either unappealing or unacceptable. The inner workings of the thought process of the various decision makers, however, may be critical to the causal processes that shape policy outcomes and interstate interactions. The fact that it is difficult to gain analytic leverage on these inner processes does not mean that they are unimportant or peripheral. It is a central analytic stand in this chapter that the perceptions (and other thought processes) of policy makers, regardless of how accessible they may be, are critical to understanding security issues.

Table 4.1. The systemic impact on existing levels of stability caused by changes in conventional military capability resulting from the introduction or development of a militarily relevant technology[a]

Category	Subjective assessment	Objective assessment
1A. Neutral impact	No relevant change in perceptions of stability	Objective assessment of impact corresponds to subjective assessment
1B. Neutral impact	No relevant change in perceptions of stability	Objective assessment of impact contradicts subjective assessment—actual destabilizing impact may follow
2A. Negative impact	States are perceived by each other to derive meaningful destabilizing military advantage by employing militarily relevant technology	Objective assessment of impact corresponds to subjective assessment
2B. Negative impact	States are perceived by each other to derive meaningful destabilizing military advantage by employing militarily relevant technology	Objective assessment of impact contradicts subjective assessment—the impact may not be destabilizing, but the expectation that it will be destabilizing may become a self-fulfilling prophecy
3A. Positive impact	States are perceived by each other to derive constructive (i.e., stabilizing) military capability by employing militarily relevant technology	Objective assessment of impact corresponds to subjective assessment
3B. Positive impact	States are perceived by each other to derive constructive (i.e., stabilizing) military capability by employing militarily relevant technology	Objective assessment of impact contradicts subjective assessment—the impact may not be stabilizing, but the expectation that it will be may become a self-fulfilling prophecy
4A. Complex and off-setting impact	No relevant change in perceptions of stability because the combined impact of employing several militarily relevant technologies is perceived to be offsetting	Objective assessment of impact corresponds to subjective assessment
4B. Complex and off-setting impact	No relevant change in perceptions of stability because the combined impact of employing several militarily relevant technologies is perceived to be offsetting	Objective assessment of impact contradicts subjective assessment—the impact may not be offsetting, but the expectation that it will be may become a self-fulfilling prophecy

Category	Subjective assessment	Objective assessment
5A. Complex and negative impact	Net negative change in perceptions of stability because combined impact of employing several militarily relevant technologies is perceived to be destabilizing	Objective assessment of impact corresponds to subjective assessment
5B. Complex and negative impact	Net negative change in perceptions of stability because combined impact of employing several militarily relevant technologies is perceived to be destabilizing	Objective assessment of impact contradicts subjective assessment—the impact may not be destabilizing, but the expectation that it will be may become a self-fulfilling prophecy
6A. Complex and positive impact	Net positive change in perceptions of stability because combined impact of employing several militarily relevant technologies is perceived to be stabilizing	Objective assessment of impact corresponds to subjective assessment
6B. Complex and positive impact	Net positive change in perceptions of stability because combined impact of employing several militarily relevant technologies is perceived to be stabilizing	Objective assessment of impact contradicts subjective assessment—the impact may not be stabilizing, but the expectation that it will be may become a self-fulfilling prophecy

^a It might prove necessary to add a fourth type of complex category although it would appear that its outcomes devolve into multiple, independent instances of categories 1, 2 or 3. In this fourth form—'parallel and independent'—each technology and the military capabilities that its adoption might alter would have an essentially independent impact on stability assessments yielding confusing and incommensurate perceptions and assessments. The somewhat incoherent result would reflect the incapacity of decision makers—either individually or (especially) collectively—to integrate separate assessments in order to make an overall assessment of collective impact. Vaguely resembling the style of decision making termed 'bounded rationality' discussed decades ago by Herbert Simon and James March, no clear, final or overall judgement is possible. Perceptions of stability impact would depend upon which technology, system and capability is salient at the time of selection as well as the institutional and basic ideological or paradigmatic perspective of each decision maker. Some would argue that this untidy and confusing situation closely approximates policy reality.

Source: See Macintosh, J., 'Cognitive rationality and the Sentinel ABM', unpublished MA thesis, York University, 1980.

advantage' is the perceived (or real) result of acquiring a new military capability, while in cases of positive impact, a 'constructive military capability' is seen to be the result. They are similar but not identical. Of the two, 'constructive military capability' clearly corresponds to the basic intent of confidence building and co-operative multilateral efforts to minimize the destabilizing effects of new weapon system development.

As is true for several other notions explored in this chapter, it is difficult to attach a precise definition to or develop a set of criteria for 'meaningful military advantage'. In principle, it might be possible to develop an objective standard for each major type of military system that would delineate the point beyond which military capability was improved 'significantly'. For instance, criteria could include the following measures compared against an existing performance baseline: (*a*) percentage increase (e.g., 10 per cent) in tank cross-country speed and/or acceleration, (*b*) tank unrefuelled cross-country range, (*c*) percentage increase in the velocity of tank ammunition at a given range (perhaps 2000 m), (*d*) percentage or absolute increase in the rate of fire of self-propelled howitzers, (*e*) percentage improvement in howitzer or mortar ammunition range, (*f*) percentage improvement in resisting shaped-charge explosives or armour-piercing cores, (*g*) percentage increase in armoured infantry combat vehicle (AICV) interior dimension or load capacity, or (*h*) percentage increase in unrefuelled range or weapon load of an attack aircraft. The potential range of candidate criteria is quite extensive.

At least as important, however, is a point made earlier: subjective estimates are what central decision makers act on, and they may be influenced by a variety of considerations not tapped by explicitly 'objective' approaches to assessment. Thus, meaningful military advantages are defined *subjectively*, at least in part, by relevant decision makers. *Advantages are meaningful when decision makers believe that they are*, and the basis for their conclusions might not be especially objective or rational. These decisions are likely to combine very subjective criteria (nuggets of conventional 'wisdom' and time-honoured—but perhaps inaccurate—aphorisms, unconscious biases generated by long-standing prejudice or institutional affiliation, ideological filters, broad myths, etc.) with generally objective ones to produce a complex, interactive mixture of reasons for concluding that a military capability is significantly improved, or not. Of course, defence budget politics further complicate the picture by encouraging threat inflation and the over-selling of new technologies. This can further distort an already quite subjective process.

It is important to recall that decision makers can perceive the exploitation of a militarily relevant technology by a neighbour to be destabilizing for reasons that can be very different compared with those identified in an 'objective' assessment. Equally, they can fail to appreciate that a development of their own might be seen as destabilizing when a more objective assessment would at least identify that possibility. The perception and the objective assessment of stability impact are kept analytically distinct in this examination whether or not they reach the same conclusion *because the grounds for reaching the conclusion (as well as its process) may be very different*. That may mean that judgements may shift suddenly on the perceptual or the objective side but not necessarily on both at the same time. These are two distinct dimensions that appear more similar than they are, regardless of the conclusions that emerge from the decision process.

The term 'constructive military capability' is used in the positive impact cases in preference to 'meaningful military advantage'. The latter term seems appropriate only for the negative impact cases. Many of the problems noted earlier in establishing criteria for what constitutes a meaningful military advantage also apply in the case of constructive military capability. Indeed, as is noted below, it may be even more difficult to develop objective standards for this concept. Viewed in the simplest of terms, a constructive military capability is one that is seen to be stabilizing by the principal decision makers in all of the states recognizing themselves to be involved in a military relationship. This can be as large a grouping as the expanded CSCE or as small a grouping as Hungary and Romania, and typically includes a main regional grouping (such as the CSCE) and subsets of subregional groupings.

The first three relatively simple categories of impact—neutral, negative and positive—are expanded in this analysis by considering the more realistic instance of some or all of a group of states exploring changes in *more than one* military capability through the use of various militarily relevant technologies at approximately the same time. Thus, the overall stability impact is a mixed or *complex* combination of more than one set of perceived and objective impacts.

Collectively, this represents a sizeable array of possible stability outcomes, some good, some bad, and some ambiguous or too complex to judge easily. It must be borne in mind, however, that there are at least two separate dimensions or forms of stability—arms race stability and crisis stability. Every distinct case noted above therefore must be considered in terms of these two separate dimensions of stability. This makes the design of arms control agreements intended to enhance conventional military stability and/or to moderate destabilizing developments a very complicated business *if* it is to be done explicitly and seriously.

The six categories in table 4.1 represent a checklist that can be used to help evaluate the impact of qualitative changes in conventional force capabilities. The stability focus is useful for identifying which qualitative weapon system developments warrant arms control attention in order to moderate their destabilizing impact or encourage their stabilizing impact. To be truly useful, however, the stability focus must be properly attentive to the dominant role of subjective assessments and case-specific context.

When the abbreviated set of categories is expanded to reflect the two fundamental types of stability—*arms race* and *crisis stability*—the number of distinct types is doubled and the complexity of the arms control enterprise is increased appreciably. Thus, for instance, a technologically induced change in conventional military capability, perhaps manifested in a new type of more precise guidance and targeting system for surface-to-surface missiles or a new type of 'stealthy' surface treatment for armoured vehicles, can have a negative impact on both crisis stability and arms race stability, but for different reasons and in different ways. It is also possible, at least in principle, for these sorts of changes in military capability to have a greater impact on one form of stability than on the other or even a positive impact on crisis stability but a negative impact on arms race stability. This obviously complicates judgements about capability changes and their impact on stability.

In many instances, particularly those that do not involve major changes, it will not be clear beforehand what the perceived (i.e., subjective) crisis and arms race stability impacts will be. That will depend very much upon the subjective reaction of various decision makers in different states and with different concerns. Indeed, the more closely one examines this subject, the more difficult it becomes to develop any general guidelines about which examples of change will produce perceptions of instability and which will not. Each case appears to be very context dependent. More disturbing for analysts, the *objective* assessment of the two stability impacts may also not be self-evident. As different technologies and the resulting weapon system changes are carefully scrutinized, it may be discovered that many of them are difficult to categorize in purely objective terms. They, too, may need a context to give meaning to the specific type of change that has occurred. Before it is possible to assess the potential role of confidence building in dealing with qualitative changes in military capability, therefore, these two forms of technologically induced instability ought to be explored further. The way in which they interact may influence decisions about preferred arms control approaches.

As suggested above, arms race stability refers to the degree of perceived need to develop a matching or offsetting weapon system or capability in response to a new development or deployment in a neighbouring state. Crisis stability, on the other hand, is the degree of perceived need to employ potentially vulnerable systems before they can be destroyed or their effectiveness neutralized in a surprise attack. The former assumes 'business as usual' in a generally suspicious and dangerous world, while crisis stability assumes an extraordinary event and concentrates on a 'use them or lose them' mentality.

The arms race stability concept assumes a continuous process punctuated by 'decision points' where qualitative and/or quantitative improvements in weapon systems are initiated and then developed. In its richer forms it includes a sensitivity to decisions made about the development of technologies and weapon systems as well as reactions to observed or anticipated developments in neighbouring states. It assumes a form of interaction in the defence planning processes of different states (the so-called 'action–reaction' interaction or some more elaborate form of it) that some analysts find suspect.[28] Crisis stability, on

---

[28] Indeed, a substantial literature developed in the 1970s and early 1980s that explored the nature of 'arms racing', generally in the context of US–Soviet strategic weapon systems. There was also a related literature that explored individual weapon system decision cases. It is too complex a subject to discuss here, but a more comprehensive discussion of arms race stability would necessarily have to re-examine that literature in some detail. The general conclusion of the arms race debates was that some doubt existed as to the degree of true interactiveness exhibited by arms acquisition patterns. Although no firm conclusion emerged, the case for intranational influences playing a predominant if not decisive role in explaining many system acquisition decisions appeared quite strong. This has a clear bearing on any effort to develop arms control approaches that can moderate what is, in effect, qualitative arms race behaviour conducted at a relatively slow pace. In principle, it would seem that at least several types of standard confidence-building approaches (especially those dealing with information) could be effective in moderating qualitative arms racing, whether the main causal pattern was interactive or intranational.

the other hand, is clearly event-oriented and has little process character.[29] However, it is influenced in part by the nature of perceptions of military capabilities developed in both those states that might attack and those that might be attacked. The capabilities, of course, are a function of arms acquisition processes. Thus, there is a clear conceptual connection between the two types of stability. Particular weapon systems or components therefore have (or at least can have) both an arms race and a crisis stability impact.[30] This is also true of the technologies that facilitate or permit the changes in military capability.

Despite the possibility that it may prove feasible to identify a single common stability criterion that can stand in the place of both the arms race and the crisis stability concepts, at present it is probably wisest to treat them as separate concerns, each warranting an independent arms control strategy. It might also prove analytically useful to isolate the two types of stability concern in order to underline what could be an important constraint on crisis stability-oriented arms control efforts: it may not be easy to distinguish systems (or technologies) that have special crisis destabilizing characteristics. Crisis instability can flow as much from the way a standard collection of conventional military forces is trained and deployed (and from the doctrine that informs their training and deployment) as it does from the characteristics of particular systems. Thus, there may not be an obvious list of systems or technologies that ought to be constrained in order to moderate or reduce the inherent crisis instability of a security relationship. Enhanced transparency and improved political relations may be the only practical methods of addressing force developments that can be seen to create or aggravate crisis stability problems.

It is difficult to say much more about different categories of stability, qualitative changes in military capability and the role of confidence building in constraining or otherwise managing those changes in order to minimize their stability impacts in the absence of more information about qualitative change and confidence building.

VI. A closer look at qualitative change

The already-classic example of technologically induced change is the introduction of so-called 'smart munitions' as dramatic force multipliers, but many other examples exist. They fall into relatively well-defined categories such as: (a) viewing devices, primarily thermal imaging and low-light image intensifier

[29] Both forms of stability bear a more-than-passing resemblance to the deterrence ideas of Patrick Morgan. His immediate and general deterrence concepts are quite similar in character to crisis and arms race stability, respectively. See Morgan, P., *Deterrence: A Conceptual Analysis* (SAGE Publications: Beverly Hills, Calif., 1977). This is a seriously underappreciated analytic work. A more comprehensive version of the exploratory qualitative arms control research undertaken here would explore this relationship in some detail.

[30] Indeed, it seems likely that those systems or capabilities that appear to be most suited to pre-emptive use might trigger, when developed, the strongest 'arms race' response in the development programmes of other states. Thus, systems that have a strong and negative crisis stability impact could be expected also to have a strong and negative arms race stability impact. This assumes, however, that all actors perceive these developments in the same way.

devices, that permit effective night combat; (b) developments that permit close to real-time battlefield data collection and analysis as well as the effective, real-time command and control of diverse forces—the net product of many technologies including remotely piloted reconnaissance vehicles, reconnaissance aircraft, multi-spectrum reconnaissance satellites, communications satellites and ground links, database software, distributed computing capabilities, communication management software, and so on; (c) precision location equipment; (d) stealth designs that permit combat aircraft, and missiles, to operate in high-threat areas with little chance of precise detection, particularly in precursor strikes; and (e) significant improvements in armoured vehicle protection, including threat detection sensors and advanced types of armour.

All of these, and many more, can upset a regional or local military balance if they are asymmetrically introduced. Indeed, their impact can be destabilizing even if they are introduced at the same time in several adjoining states. The impact can be difficult to measure or assess objectively because of the complex interaction among a host of factors, including doctrine, training and leadership. Some military forces may be better able to accommodate some new technologies because of other advantages such as doctrinal flexibility, leadership skills and the qualities of individual soldiers. At least as important as 'objective' considerations is the psychological component of technological change. The appearance of a new weapon system or broader technology can create the perception of a significant destabilizing shift even when little change in combat effectiveness has or will actually occur. Whether the change is 'real' or perceived, however, the effect of instability results. Thus, arms control solutions that can moderate or constrain these effects are definitely worth pursuing.

The arms control methods available to moderate or eliminate potential instabilities resulting from the introduction of new military technologies, particularly in the conventional military sphere, are poorly developed. Conventional, quantitatively oriented approaches (the dominant type) appear to offer little promise as they do not address qualitative issues. Conventional force-oriented non-proliferation arrangements do not offer much promise either. Outright bans on the deployment of key systems, analogues of the 1972 Anti-Ballistic Missile (ABM) Treaty, could be useful in some cases, but it is difficult to identify systems that have the same potentially destabilizing impact within the conventional force sphere.[31] Most weapon systems and most capabilities in the conventional sphere are genuinely useful in a variety of circumstances. This makes the identification of especially destabilizing systems, capabilities or changes quite difficult. The fact that there are competing analytic assessments, for instance, of 'offensiveness' and 'defensiveness' that see the same systems (especially tanks) in starkly different terms only underlines this problem. There is little difficulty in identifying systems that can be seen as destabilizing and needlessly provoc-

---

[31] Editor's note: For a discussion of the new class of US military systems used in Desert Storm, the Persian Gulf campaign, see Perry, W. J., 'Desert Storm and deterrence', *Foreign Affairs*, vol. 70, no. 4 (fall 1991), pp. 66–82. Perry argued that control over sale of *systems* like intelligence sensors, Stealth aircraft and precision-guided weapons will slow the spread of these capabilities.

ative or dangerous. Generating consensus is next to impossible. Confidence building probably offers the most varied range of options for avoiding these problems while still producing effective, positive results. What were once regarded as its limits now confer extra flexibility.

VII. The essential nature of confidence building

In order to appreciate what confidence building can—and cannot—do to moderate the effects of technologically induced change in the stability of security relationships, it is necessary to fully understand confidence building. This also helps to underline why the psychological focus of confidence building makes it such a promising approach to use in addressing the qualitative arms control problems so intimately tied to perceptions of stability change. It should be stressed, however, that the fundamental nature of confidence building assumes a level of interstate relations that is relatively constructive and co-operative. This means that any attempt to use the confidence-building approach to solve stability problems in a group of states that does *not* already enjoy improving relations is likely to be disappointing at best.

It appears that qualitative or stability-oriented CSBMs are best employed in a relatively mature arms control relationship where some security problems still remain. They appear natural follow-ons to quantitative reduction agreements and more modest information and activity constraint CSBM agreements. To put this observation in a practical context, it would not have made sense—nor would it have been possible—to attempt specific qualitative arms control in the CSCE before the successful completion of the Vienna Document 1992. It may still be too early to turn to explicitly qualitative CSBMs.

Confidence building is an arms control approach employing co-operative measures intended to help clarify the military intentions of participating states, to reduce uncertainties about their potentially threatening military activities and to constrain their opportunities for surprise attack or the coercive use of military forces. Confidence-building agreements are *not* intended to prevent deliberate, premeditated attacks. However, this type of agreement can be an effective method for minimizing accidental conflicts and, perhaps most important, for improving security relations among suspicious *but not belligerent* neighbours. It is in the latter role that confidence building is most effective and promising. This role also directly addresses those developments that can produce solvable arms race as well as crisis stability problems.

There are three distinct analytic perspectives that, when used together, can help to clarify confidence building more thoroughly.[32] These amount to differ-

---

[32] Variations on these analytic perspectives were first presented in the author's *Confidence (and Security) Building Measures and the Arms Control Process: A Canadian Perspective*, Arms Control and Disarmament Studies, no. 1 (Department of External Affairs and International Trade: Ottawa, 1985). They are revised and explored in greater depth in the author's *From Stockholm to Vienna and Beyond: The Confidence Building Process Revisited* (note 20). See also the author's 'Confidence- and security-building measures: Asia–Pacific application', Paper prepared for two associated conferences co-sponsored by The

ent ways of looking at the complex confidence-building phenomenon and include a general definition, a typology of categories and a practical example of a CSBM agreement.

The first analytic perspective involves the development and use of a general and abstract definition of confidence building. Based on over 10 years of exploration and refinement, the following has emerged as a comprehensive and abstract definition: Confidence building is a discrete security management activity entailing the *process* of exploring, negotiating and then implementing a package of confidence-building measures (CBMs). When successful, the process initiates and/or facilitates a significant positive transformation in the security relations of participating states. The transformation is the product of personal interaction, information and knowledge exchange, and the development of co-operative constraint. It is a psychological process that involves the transformation of specialist, government decision maker and public beliefs about the nature of threat posed by other states, primarily entailing a fundamental shift from a basic assumption of hostile intentions to one of non-hostile (although not necessarily friendly) intentions.[33]

The most important element in this process approach is the identification of transformation—the transformation of ideas and beliefs relating to the threat posed by neighbouring states, particularly when those neighbours in the past have been enemies.

An enhanced appreciation of what confidence building entails can be derived from an examination of the specific CSBMs that have been proposed in the past. They can be organized in two fundamental categories: information and communication CSBMs and constraint CSBMs (see table 4.2).

To the conceptually oriented perspectives can be added an illuminating example of confidence building in action. The Vienna Document 1992 on CSBMs is a concrete illustration of what a confidence-building *agreement* entails and demonstrates the way in which a collection of specific measures can reinforce each other to create a very constructive form of synergy. It included:

1. 'Annual exchange of military information', requiring the submission of information detailing land force organization, unit location, manpower and major weapon and equipment systems organic to formations. It includes non-active and low-strength formations and combat units. Additional requirements include information on military budgets and new weapon system deployments;

2. 'Risk reduction', employing the Conflict Prevention Centre (CPC)—a CSCE forum in Vienna with a small technical staff—entailing consultation regarding unusual military activities, co-operation as regards hazardous incidents and voluntary hosting of visits to dispel concern about military activities;

Peace Research Centre at the Australian National University, Canberra, 5–26 June 1992, and the Indian Ocean Centre for Peace Studies at the University of Western Australia, Perth, 29–30 June 1992.
[33] See note 20.

Table 4.2. Confidence- and security-building measures (CSBMs) which have been proposed in the past

Type of CSBM	Examples
Information and communication CSBMs	
Information measures Information about military forces, facilities, structures and activities	Publication of defence information, weapon system and force-structure information exchange, creation of consultative commissions, publication of defence budget figures and weapon system development information, doctrine and strategy seminars
Communication measures Provision of means of communication	'Hot lines' for exchange of crisis information, joint crisis control centres, 'cool lines' for regular distribution of required and requested information
Notification measures Advance notification of specific military activities	Advance notification of exercises, force movements and mobilizations, including information about forces involved
Observation-of-movement conduct measures Opportunity to observe specified military activities	Mandatory and optional invitations to observe specific activities (with information about the activity), rules of conduct for observers and hosts
Constraint CSBMs	
Inspection measures Opportunity to inspect and/or monitor constrained or limited military forces, facilities, structures and activities	Special sensing devices, special observers for sensitive movements, on-site inspections
Non-interference (with verification) measures	
Activity constraint measures Avoiding or limiting provocative military activities	Avoiding harassing activities (e.g., 'playing chicken' at sea), conducting non-threatening manœuvres or equipment tests
Deployment constraint measures Avoiding or limiting provocative stationing or positioning of military forces	Avoiding threatening deployments near sensitive areas (e.g., tanks on a border), constraints on equipment such as attack aircraft within range of a neighbour's rear area territory, manpower limits, nuclear-free zones
Technology constraint measures Avoiding or limiting development and/or deployment of specified military technologies, including systems and subsystems, having a destabilizing character or impact	Limiting improvement of armoured vehicle armour type, limiting improvement of tank main-gun technology, limiting improvement of fighter/attack aircraft radar systems

Source: *From Stockholm to Vienna and Beyond: The Confidence Building Process Revisited* (Department of Foreign Affairs and International Trade: Ottawa, forthcoming).

3. 'Contacts', enhancing openness and transparency through invitations to visit air bases, expanded military exchanges and the demonstration of new types of major weapon and equipment systems;

4. 'Prior notification of certain military activities', requiring notice 42 days in advance of exercises, concentrations and movements of at least 9000 troops or 250 battle tanks (or 3000 troops if the activity is an amphibious or parachute assault exercise);

5. 'Observation of certain military activities', where observers must be invited for land force exercise activities within and transfers from outside the region of at least 13 000 troops, 300 tanks or 3500 amphibious or parachute assault troops;

6. 'Annual calendar', requiring extensive information about notifiable military activities scheduled for the following year;

7. 'Constraining provisions', limiting notifiable major activities of more than 40 000 troops or 900 tanks to one per two years and smaller exercises (13 000–40 000 troops or 300–900 tanks) to six per year. Of these six activities per year, only three may be over 25 000 troops or 400 tanks;

8. 'Compliance and verification', providing for short-warning inspections of troubling sites and activities (limit of three received inspections per year for each state) as well as evaluation visits to confirm the data of the information measure (minimum of 15 received visits per year for each state);

9. 'Communications', establishing an efficient and direct communication network for CSCE use in distributing notifications, clarifications and requests; and

10. 'Annual implementation assessment', mandating an annual assessment of compliance.

Collectively, these different perspectives provide a rich and comprehensive understanding of what confidence building means, an understanding that goes far beyond the more usual appreciation that grows from an over-concentration on the nature of CSBMs. Several key conceptual issues develop some visibility when this multifaceted approach to understanding confidence building is employed. Most important among them is whether confidence building is an agent or artifact of change: *Is confidence building a process that helps to make change in broader security relations possible, or does change make confidence building possible?*

This is important as far as both timing and ambition are concerned. If advanced CSBMs are used to contain stability problems triggered by the impact of new technology on military capability, then at least two things must be understood. First, attempts to solve qualitative arms control problems will almost always follow efforts directed at quantitative problems (for instance, armoured force asymmetries). Therefore, qualitatively oriented or stability enhancing CSBMs will probably be second-, third- or even fourth-generation efforts. They will thus build on an existing record of arms control achievement. The second consideration is timing. At what stage in the evolution of relations within a region (or security regime) can attempts be made to develop, negotiate and then implement qualitative CSBMs?

The issue of timing is a difficult one. An answer is partly dependent on the first point made above: qualitative CSBMs are likely to be third-generation or later and therefore cannot be undertaken early in an arms control process. The nature of the evolving security relationship will also influence timing. It would appear that relations must be good enough to have supported the evolution of an existing regime (to approximately the level seen in the CSCE as of Vienna Document 1992) but not so good as to remove concerns about continuously evolving military capabilities within various participating states. There must still be the potential for conflict and worsening relations.

Current understanding of confidence building is derived largely from the CSCE experience. It assumes that there is a positive if still unclear connection between: (a) negotiating and then implementing CSBMs, and (b) basic changes in perceptions of threat. According to this emerging conception, doing the former both facilitates and is facilitated by the latter with the exact causal relationship still unclear. Contemporary analyses of confidence building are an attempt to characterize that imperfectly grasped real-world process that helps to transform the perceptions of key decision makers about the nature of military activities in hostile or potentially hostile neighbouring states. The transformation describes a shift in thinking and perception that sees national decision makers (and other élites as well as publics) increasingly confident that formerly hostile neighbours no longer represent a serious threat.

The notion of a perceptual shift is important. It suggests that CSBMs and confidence building may work best when some variety of positive shift in thinking is already taking place. It seems likely that a package of CSBMs will accelerate or facilitate that process of improvement, perhaps in a critically important way. Thus, the timing of negotiations to develop CSBMs and their eventual adoption may be critical to their success. If they are pursued too soon, they will produce a disappointingly marginal result—or none at all. However, if too much time is allowed to elapse the pursuit of a CSBM package will miss the 'window of opportunity' during which it can have a positive, constructive impact on security relations. Relations will either progress on their own (but perhaps with intrinsic, unresolved security weaknesses that will later cripple relations) or deteriorate. It is the lack of clarity about the precise causal role played by the negotiation and implementation of confidence-building agreements that causes uncertainty about their status as agents (causes) or artifacts (parallel phenomena) of changes. At present it appears that confidence building is more agent than artifact, but it also seems incapable (at least during the early stages of the development of a security regime) of initiating or sustaining a process of change independent of other change-inducing events and processes.

VIII. Tailoring confidence building to the technology constraint task

The goal of qualitative arms control arrangements is to put into place co-operative measures that will constrain and manage the destabilizing impact of changes in military capability, particularly those caused by the exploitation of militarily relevant technologies. The principal problem identified in the analysis thus far is the extraordinarily difficult task of generalizing across time or distinct regimes any observations or criteria about what should be considered as 'destabilizing'. Assessments appear to be potentially too variable and idiosyncratic. The lengthy discussion of stability above develops an argument that casts stability in highly context-sensitive terms and stresses the dominant role of subjectively informed perceptions of stability over objective and technical assessments. Given that understanding, general guidelines and all-purpose constraint regimes are next to impossible to develop. They would also be presumptuous. What appears to matter more are the perceptions of specific policy makers in a specific and perhaps unique military–political context. It is their understanding of what is and is not destabilizing that matters most.

This understanding of stability encourages a dual-track strategy for managing negative stability changes in an evolving security regime. One track should concentrate on the general improvement of security relations across the board to ensure that technical stability changes lose as much as possible of their meaning. The better the relations enjoyed by a group of states, the less consequential relative changes in military capability are likely to be perceived to be. The second track is the one more narrowly focused on specific capability developments. It generally does not concern itself with technological developments *per se* recognizing those to be beyond the grasp of any plausible regime in the complex, modern world. Indeed, it could be argued that for the time being technology ought not to be limited in case of unexpected developments. What needs to be constrained is the introduction into regular forces of weapons and related capabilities that can upset existing balances and perceptions of existing balances. This means that the exploration of technology and the preliminary development of capabilities is less a concern than the actual deployment of new systems.

Understanding the complex nature of conventional force stability and the ways in which technologically induced changes in capability can upset perceptions of stability in unpredictable ways helps to identify CSBMs that might moderate negative changes. The obvious place to start is with the typology of CSBMs presented in table 4.2. Of those fundamental categories, several look particularly relevant (e.g., information measures, inspection measures, activity constraints, technology constraints and, perhaps, deployment constraints).

Several of the specific CSBMs in the Vienna Document 1992 appear promising, either in their present form or as precursors to more advanced measures. A capability constraining, stability enhancing regime might highlight the following Vienna CSBMs as a starting point: (*a*) annual exchange of military information; (*b*) contacts; and (*c*) compliance and verification. The details of these measure are given above.

These measures provide the basis for an information-oriented programme that would focus on ensuring that participating states had a comprehensive and unbiased understanding of each other's military capabilities, both those which exist and, in particular, those under development. Accurate information is a powerful counter to various types of misperception. The requirement for demonstrations of new systems is a constructive step in this direction, but participants might want to consider limiting new or dramatically improved systems as a follow-on step. The existing information measure, with its expanded requirement for listing major system performance characteristics, is an obvious starting point for devising a method to limit capability 'improvements'.

It is possible to conceive of new measures that would add appreciably to the scope of a stability enhancing, capability constraining confidence-building regime. They include:

(*a*) expanded annual exchange of detailed defence budget information including forecasts of major weapon system developments (reporting perhaps triggered by the onset of prototype or pre-production testing);

(*b*) creation of annual 'co-operative force planning seminars', where the defence planning principles, objectives and concerns (including worst-case fears) of participating states could be discussed;

(*c*) a commitment not to replace deployed equipment of certain types—typically, tanks, heavy armoured combat vehicles (HACVs), self-propelled artillery, combat aircraft, combat helicopters—with new, more advanced types. This would require the specification of categories and lists of systems to clarify what would constitute an improved example and what a true replacement. This measure would not prohibit research and development (R&D) work nor would it preclude the testing of new systems—only deployment, including training. It would not prohibit the modernization of existing chassis and airframes, nor the replacement of key subsystems; and

(*d*) a commitment not to *modernize* deployed equipment of certain types (typically, tanks, HACVs, self-propelled artillery, combat aircraft, combat helicopters) in certain key, well-defined respects. One example would be a prohibition on replacing tank or HACV cannons with any 'new' type ('new' either in the sense of using new principles, such as liquid-propelled cannons or directed-energy devices, or in the sense of employing new fabrication techniques, materials or higher performance components).[34]

These examples provide a sense of how a confidence-building approach to constrain destabilizing military capabilities and developments might be structured and the specific measures it might employ. The above list constitutes a

---

[34] These potential CBMs are drawn from *Future CSBM Options: Post-Helsinki CSBM Talks*, a study conducted by the author for the Canadian Government in Mar. 1991.

relatively rich but reasonable menu of confidence-building options for adoption in specific contexts. Although they were developed with the CSCE regime in mind, they could also contribute to a confidence-building arrangement in other areas aiming to constrain the effects of new militarily relevant technologies and military capabilities. As with the CSCE, however, they would almost certainly be third- or fourth-generation measures building on quantitative reduction agreements and less ambitious CSBMs.

IX. Conclusion

This chapter provides a preliminary sense of how confidence building may provide a useful approach to the management of qualitatively oriented stability problems. Much of the discussion concentrates on exploring the actual nature of stability problems, highlighting the importance of policy makers' perceptions of stability and stability changes. This is central to understanding what qualitative arms control can accomplish—and what it cannot.

The discussion here is rooted in the example of the CSCE, where a significant series of arms control agreements has already been concluded. As a result of that progress, the future of arms control seems primarily located in the realm of qualitative change and its constructive management. Particularly in a regime where numbers of main weapon systems are frozen, it will be increased concern about existing qualitative disparities among specific types of systems or changes in the capabilities of deployed systems that will most trouble neighbours who remain nervous and suspicious despite the general improvement of security relations within their regions.

Probably the most important conclusion to emerge—if only tentatively—from this analysis is the seeming impossibility of establishing objective standards for gauging the destabilizing character of particular weapon systems, changes in weapon system capabilities and militarily relevant technologies. The stability of conventional military relationships appears to be very much in the eye of the beholder, the function of a wide range of organizational, ideological and psychological considerations. Arms control approaches must recognize this and build constructively on it. This is why confidence building, with its focus on increasing accurate information about military force capabilities and its underlying concern with transforming perceptions of threat, is well suited to the task of constraining and managing the potentially destabilizing impact of new technological developments and a seemingly constant urge to improve military capabilities.

5. Controlling the high-technology militarization of the developing world[*]

M. Granger Morgan and Mitchel B. Wallerstein[1]

I. Introduction

Developing states acquire military capability for most of the same reasons as developed states: in response to concerns about external threats to their security, in order to maintain internal security, as a 'legitimate' vehicle for subsidizing domestic industrial development, as a tangible symbol of national sovereignty and pride, and in some cases to advance the imperialistic interests of powerful rulers. As long as these underlying motivations remain, it is unrealistic to believe that the demand by developing states for military capability—and the technology that supports it—will significantly decline.

However, various external factors can modulate that demand and control the mix of weapons and capabilities that developing states acquire. This chapter argues that it is in the interests of the developed states, and especially the great powers, to work collectively to limit the spread of high-technology weapons and weapons of mass destruction in the developing world, and that the only effective means of achieving this objective is through collective action. The chapter outlines the basic strategies that appear appropriate, but largely leaves to others the tasks of conceptualizing and developing the foreign policy and diplomatic frameworks within which they can best be implemented.[2] Indeed, successful international implementation is likely to require a significantly less explicit and forthright discussion of many issues than is provided here.

This chapter focuses on weapons and systems that have the potential to act as important force multipliers. This implies more than the traditional concern about 'weapons of mass destruction' because it includes a variety of advanced weapons as well as selected dual-use technologies—many of them widely and

[1] The authors bear sole responsibility for the views expressed in this chapter, which have neither the expressed nor implied endorsement of their current or past employers. They acknowledge with thanks advice from William F. Burns and John D. Steinbruner. Partial financial support was provided by academic funds from the Program on International Peace and Security, Carnegie Mellon University.

[2] The problem of working out new political and diplomatic arrangements to control regional militarization is, of course, part of the broader task of evolving a new set of international security arrangements. Some of these issues have been addressed in Carter, A. B., Perry, W. J. and Steinbruner, J., *A New Concept of Cooperative Security* (Brookings Institution: Washington, DC, 1992).

[*] This chapter, written in 1992, first appeared in slightly different form in Wander, W. T. and Arnett, E. H. (eds), *The Proliferation of Advanced Weaponry: Technology, Motivations and Responses* (American Association for the Advancement of Science: Washington, DC, 1992), pp. 285–99. It is reproduced here with permission.

legally available on a commercial basis—that can be adapted for or integrated into military systems.[3] In addition to chemical weapons (CW) and biological weapons (BW), missile technology and nuclear weapons this chapter therefore also addresses such technologies as regional surveillance, advanced communications, stealth, precision navigation, smart targeting and high-performance platforms.[4]

II. Implications of shrinking defence budgets and rising unit costs

The cost of new generations of weapon systems is rising rapidly. Indeed, in a series of simple but elegant extrapolations, Norman Augustine, the chief executive officer of the Martin Marietta Corporation, has argued that unless fundamental technological changes occur, the cost of developing and acquiring new high-performance systems such as jet fighters will exceed the defence budgets of even the largest powers sometime early in the next century.[5] Some technological innovations, such as the development of improved interoperability standards and the adoption of 'open system architectures' in weapon systems hardware and software, may ease this cost escalation, but it is far from certain that the problem can or will be solved.

Hence it seems safe to assume that, for at least the next decade, it will be far more costly and difficult to develop new more advanced military systems than it has been in the past. This development is occurring in the face of shrinking defence budgets in most of the major developed states. At the same time, however, both national governments and defence contractors are attempting to sustain their defence production infrastructures. There are, as a result, growing pressures on the USA, on its NATO allies, on the former Soviet Union, and on certain countries of Eastern Europe, to maintain weapon production facilities by seeking markets abroad. The pressures on the People's Republic of China are somewhat different but it, too, faces strong incentives to export.

Pressures to export militarily sensitive technologies have historically been greatest in smaller advanced states, such as France, that have tried despite their size to maintain an independent arms industry. Today similar pressures are being felt increasingly even by the largest advanced states. These pressures are both domestic (e.g., primary and secondary economic effects and political and social impacts) and international (e.g., balance of payment considerations). The incentives for China, Russia and East European countries such as the Czech Republic are particularly strong, because advanced weapon systems appear to

---

[3] This definition corresponds to that used in a report on export controls by the National Research Council, *Finding Common Ground* (National Academy Press: Washington, DC, 1991), in which the authors were centrally involved. A number of the ideas discussed in this chapter had their origins in that study, but have been substantially extended.

[4] See, for example, the arguments on attack aircraft advanced by Harvey, J. *et al.* in 'Assessing ballistic missile proliferation and its control', working paper of the Stanford Center for International Security and Arms Control, Stanford, Calif., Oct. 1991.

[5] Augustine, N. R., *Augustine's Laws* (Viking: New York, 1986).

be one of the few areas in which they have products for which there is a significant, hard currency export market.[6]

One solution for the technically advanced states would be for groups of them, or even all of them, to rationalize their weapon systems acquisition and buy from each other, emphasizing their respective comparative advantages. Historically, even among the NATO allies, which have reasonably compatible values and foreign policy objectives, such an approach has not been particularly successful. The idea nevertheless continues to be discussed in various forms. US Ambassador to NATO William H. Taft, IV suggested the idea of a 'defence GATT [General Agreement on Tariffs and Trade]', which would involve a more rationalized system of defence trade and would at the same time create the possibility of greater multilateral control of weapon exports outside the trade group.[7]

There are some new signs of co-operation within the European Union (EU). For example, France, Italy and Spain agreed jointly to develop the 'future surface-to-air family' (FSAF) of ground- and ship-launched missiles, and Italy and the UK are co-operating on joint development and production of the Augusta/Westland EH101 helicopter. Co-operation between the USA and European states also occurs, but on a much smaller scale than is optimal. A decade of continually shrinking defence budgets could, of course, dramatically change this situation. At the moment, however, the prospect of wider co-operation is uncertain. Much will depend on the course of future developments in the former USSR (i.e., the extent to which it remains a threat), on the pace and intensity of domestic political pressure in the NATO countries for major reductions in military spending, and on the ways in which Western states choose to address problems of employment, regional development and industrial policy.

Clearly, there is a basic conflict. On the one hand, militarily advanced states face considerable short-term domestic, economic and political pressures to expand foreign sales of weapons and other military systems. On the other hand, the more the militarily advanced states are willing to proliferate their advanced weapon systems and technology, the more difficult it may be to sustain a major technical performance lead in future regional conflicts. Given recent cost trends, it is uncertain that even *with* a long-term commitment to public investments in military research and development (R&D) it will continue to be possible for the advanced states to maintain an acceptable edge over their potential adversaries if transfers of weapons and technologies are allowed to continue.

In short, with only minor modifications, the arguments about the importance of maintaining an edge through force multipliers can now be applied to the relationship between the developed world and militarizing, or potentially milit-

---

[6] The impact of the Persian Gulf War on demand for Chinese or Russian (as opposed to NATO) weapon systems will not be known for some time yet. In all likelihood, the determining factor will be the extent to which potential buyers believe that the poor performance of these systems was owing to the inadequate training of the Iraqi military versus fundamentally ineffective design.

[7] This proposal became the focus of a NATO staff study.

arizing, developing states. Just as in the earlier East–West context, in thinking about these issues a differentiation must be made between arms transfers (including licensing and co-production) and the export of dual-use civilian technology. Clearly, the direct transfers of arms and other military systems can have immediate and serious impact.

In the longer term, the transfer of dual-use technology may have more profound and far-reaching implications, since it creates the possibility of establishing a domestic capability. However, the situation is also more complicated than the historical East–West context. Under the old paradigm, collateral economic damage caused by technology denial had the not-unhelpful effect of keeping a potential adversary weak.[8] In the new situation, there should be no desire on the part of the technically advanced states to prevent developing states from attaining legitimate economic development objectives. Indeed, quite the contrary, they should be helping the development process. The problem, then, is how to draw and act upon legitimate distinctions, especially in the dual-use context, between technology necessary for economic advancement and the (often quite similar) technology used in military systems.

Some may argue that such concerns are misplaced, or at least overstated. They would point out that the USA and most other advanced states generally keep tight control on their highest-performance military systems. However, while the USA rarely, if ever, transfers its very best equipment, it has in the past regularly transferred very good equipment to its 'friends'. For example, M1 tanks and airborne warning and control system (AWACS) aircraft have been sold to Saudi Arabia. Shoulder-fired Stinger anti-aircraft weapons were made available to the Afghan rebels; and, of course, F-14 fighter planes were sold to Iran until the downfall of the Shah.

Unfortunately, as the last example demonstrates only too well, in a number of regional theatres, today's friend can often be tomorrow's adversary. Critics of this line of argument point out that it takes more than hardware to succeed. Training, maintenance and access to spare parts are all critical to success. Owing to their absence, revolutionary Iran made relatively ineffective use of the advanced weapons that the USA had transferred to the Shah.

The developed world would be foolish to assume, however, that the lack of these factors can always be relied on to degrade advanced systems that fall into unfriendly hands. Militarizing states in the developing world can and do look at the lessons of the past and learn. Owing to the fact that the necessary knowledge is now widespread, and many states can now manufacture sophisticated parts and components, it may be possible over time for a militarizing state to develop alternative solutions, especially if the supplier states do not closely coordinate their actions. Graphic proof of this assertion is given by recent revela-

---

[8] 'Economic warfare' against the Soviet Union was not an explicit policy objective under the Coordinating Committee on Multilateral Export Controls (COCOM) export control regime, but it is hard to argue that COCOM controls did not have significant negative impacts on the civilian economy of the former USSR.

tions concerning the Iraqi nuclear programme.[9] In addition, the advent of computer-based 'dumb interfaces for smart weapons' (i.e., user-friendly operational arrangements for military systems that do not require large amounts of sophisticated training) and more complete microelectronic control may make training and maintenance significantly less critical in the future.

III. Strategies for limiting militarization

If their fundamental foreign policy interests are sufficiently congruent, and if they are prepared to work together in ways that may require short-term economic, political and diplomatic sacrifice in the interest of longer-term international security, there are a number of parallel strategies that the developed states can adopt to reduce or respond to regional militarization and its associated risks:

1. They can reduce the demand for military capabilities by resolving the legitimate security concerns of developing states through the development of new regional security arrangements and regional arms control agreements, and by removing economic and other obstacles blocking the attainment of legitimate development needs.

2. Supplier cartels can be developed that limit the transfer of weapons and other military systems, as well as the associated production technologies and know-how, from developed to developing states.

3. Existing export control regimes can be co-ordinated and rationalized—or, particularly in the case of conventional arms, new ones can be developed—that limit the transfer to developing states of civilian technologies that have important military utility.

4. The actions of universities, professional societies and other organizations can stress the moral obligations that technical experts have to use their knowledge and skills in responsible ways. Specific steps can be taken to control the flow of technical experts into the militarization efforts of 'problem states'.

5. Military superiority can be maintained so that regional security can be imposed, should that become necessary. The resolute intention of the great powers to undertake *in extremis* joint military or other action to remove proliferation-related facilities that pose immediate and substantial threats can be made clear.

---

[9] The Iraqi case provides a compelling illustration of four aspects of the dual-use problem: (*a*) the possibility of using relatively unsophisticated technology, which is often no longer used in military contexts in advanced industrialized countries, in new and ingenious ways (e.g., use of calutrons to enrich uranium); (*b*) the ability of a militarizing state to assemble a powerful combination of dual-use technologies for military application while successfully obscuring the acquisition process and the origins of the products; (*c*) the inadequacy (and in some cases total absence) of loose and informal multilateral co-ordination of proliferation controls; and (*d*) the failure of limited and non-intrusive multilateral non-proliferation inspection regimes (i.e., the IAEA) to detect wilful violation.

Reducing demand

While policies that focus on the 'supply side' of the problem may slow the spread of high-technology military capabilities, in the long term the only way to avoid militarization is through policies that limit demand.

Resolving regional security concerns is an essential international security goal that should receive continuing and serious attention, yet, as experience in the Middle East, in South-East Asia and on the Korean Peninsula has demonstrated, progress is typically slow and difficult. If the developed states want to limit the military capability of developing states, they clearly will have to devote far more concerted political effort and economic resources to their respective spheres of influence.

Confidence-building strategies, originally developed in the cold war, may hold promise in some regional contexts.[10]

Regional arms control may sometimes also hold promise. Bruce Berkowitz[11] and others have argued persuasively, however, that arms control may do little to retard militarization if the basic factors that lead to demand for particular weapon capabilities go unaddressed. As noted above, there are many different motivations and/or national political pressures that may drive a developing state to seek to acquire weapons of mass destruction and advanced conventional weapons. Some of these pressures, particularly those arising from traditional interstate rivalries and conflicting territorial claims, may be responsive to aggressive diplomatic efforts and multilaterally applied political and economic pressure from the developed states. Indeed, on some occasions a change in political regime may create the opportunity for significant diplomatic progress. This has been demonstrated by the significant actions taken by the governments of Argentina and Brazil to suspend efforts to develop their own nuclear weapons.

Other motivations, particularly those emanating from the personal ambitions of autocratic rulers such as Iraqi President Saddam Hussein, are far more difficult to address or contain diplomatically. There is, of course, ample historical and contemporary evidence that weapon development programmes often proceed in these cases on a highly secretive basis and are frequently accompanied by professions of innocence and peaceful intent until after the fact. In the Iraqi case it is clear that existing International Atomic Energy Agency (IAEA) safeguards were inadequate to detect and prevent the covert nuclear weapon development programme that was under way. While regional arms control may slow proliferation in such a situation, it is unlikely to prevent it. Moreover, pressure for arms control under such circumstances may simply encourage the affected

---

[10] See, for example, Goodby, J. E., 'Confidence and security-building in the Korean Peninsula: the negotiating agenda', ed. E. Arnett, *Science and International Security: Responding to a Changing World* (American Association for the Advancement of Science (AAAS): Washington, DC, 1990), pp. 171–94; and Goodby, J. E., 'Transparency in the Middle East', *Arms Control Today*, vol. 21, no. 4 (May 1991), pp. 8–11.

[11] Berkowitz, B., *Calculated Risks: A Century of Arms Control, Why It Has Failed, and How It Can Be Made to Work* (Simon & Schuster: New York, 1987).

parties to innovate or engineer around the restrictions, often with the net result that overall military capability and political instability are increased.

A serious problem with arms control in the context of proliferation of nuclear weapons has been the double standard that the great powers have historically applied. With the end of the cold war, drastic cuts in the stocks of nuclear weapons and in the nuclear weapons programmes of the great powers should now be possible. Progress in this area should place the great powers in a much better position to exercise leadership with respect to proliferation in the developing world. Finally, developed states may be able to contribute to regional security through direct co-operative security guarantees of various sorts.

In addition to reducing the security threats faced by developing states, the great powers must also work to ensure that such states do not face insurmountable external obstacles in addressing their legitimate development needs. Better access to lucrative markets in the developed world is especially important. As a consequence, international trade negotiations, which have previously been viewed in strictly economic terms, will increasingly have important implications for regional security. Such negotiations have also become more important in the formulation and pursuit of US foreign policy. Conflicts between trade and security objectives lay at the heart of the quarrel between the White House and Congress over renewal of Most Favored Nation status for the People's Republic of China, in which Chinese missile sales in the Middle East and elsewhere became a central issue.

Supplier cartels

Supplier cartels are an obvious strategy by which the flow of weapons and other military systems to developing countries can be limited. However, such arrangements face a number of potential obstacles. Developed states have in the past been unwilling to forego the right to make arms transfers to meet the 'legitimate needs' of their 'friends'. Since situations of near unanimity among supplier states, such as the one that led to the UN embargo against Iraq, are rare, developing states have mostly been able either to find at least a few developed states that have been willing to make transfers for commercial or geopolitical reasons, or to meet their needs by means of the extensive international black market in weapons and related technology.

While they have not yet fully articulated it, nor evolved a suitable diplomatic framework within which to take action, the authors of this chapter believe that the great powers now share a long-term common interest in encouraging regional security and stability. Fostering conditions for economic prosperity plays a greater role in the broad national security objectives of all the developed states. Moreover, many of the developing states, including some that have come only lately to a market-oriented development philosophy, appear now to seek greater security and stability as a means of attracting foreign investment. Despite many problems, including the obstacles that have impeded the recent round of the GATT negotiations, a global system of trade has emerged in which all the great powers want to participate. The smooth operation of this system requires stability. Perhaps even more important in the long run, the sustained use of force, particularly if it results in significant casualties, is increasingly seen as politically unacceptable, especially in Europe, Japan and the USA.

If the great powers share a common interest in encouraging regional security and stability, then in principle these states should be willing to forego some of the short-term economic and geopolitical benefits they might receive from arms transfers. Getting states to give up short-term benefits from unilateral action in favour of possible long-term benefits from collective action has never been easy. This is the classic game-theoretic problem of the 'prisoner's dilemma'. Its solution will require careful diplomatic negotiation and a continuing process of confidence building.

One serious difficulty is that in assessing the trade-off between short- and long-term benefits not all states face the same 'effective discount rate'. The states of the former USSR, Eastern Europe and to a lesser extent China face a desperate need for hard currency. If they are to forego arms sales in the developing world, the other developed states must either help these countries find or develop other markets in which they can be competitive, or 'compensate' them in other ways, such as through easier access to international credit and long-term loans that will permit them to develop new industrial infrastructure and/or to retool and convert some portion of their military–industrial apparatus for modern commercial production. There may also be ways in which the short-term costs can be offset through co-operative approaches to developed world arms acquisition. While this seems most feasible among the members of NATO and in Japan, there appears to be no reason why, in certain restricted lower-technology domains (e.g., small arms, airframes for cargo aircraft or hulls for transport ships) it might not be possible now on a much wider basis.

The basic problem is that an effective suppliers' cartel will limit the individual freedom of action of its members. While the recent experience in the Persian Gulf offers only a partial model, it does demonstrate the possibility of developing forceful and effective collective action. However, to succeed in a number of such ventures over time, the USA is likely to have to adopt a stance that is more responsive to the interests and needs of other major suppliers. For collective action to be sustained, it will have to be collectively evolved. In the current global technological and economic environment, it is no longer possible (if it ever was) for such a cartel to be imposed from Washington because too many other states have comparable capabilities and resources and are capable of exercising independent action.

A successful developed world suppliers' cartel, which limits exports of weapons and other military systems and certain highly sensitive dual-use technology to developing states intent on militarization, is likely to prompt several responses. One will certainly be a widened search for alternative suppliers other than the great powers. A second likely response will be an increased effort to develop second-tier consortia for weapon system development. The complex international arrangements put together in support of the Condor 2 project appear to have failed.[12] However, success in limiting arms supply will almost certainly prompt similar and more sophisticated arrangements in the future, and it is by no means certain that these too will fail or that they can be stopped through external pressure. Finally, as with successful arms control, a successful cartel is likely to prompt militarizing states to seek alternative means to the same ends. For example, if access to the precision internal-guidance technology used in cruise missiles is successfully denied to developing states, alternative guidance systems based on civilian global-positioning technology may well be developed.[13] Such 'technological end runs' are in many respects more dangerous than second-tier consortia. They will require careful monitoring and prompt multilateral action.

Several international regimes now exist to impede the spread of weapons of mass destruction. The oldest and most formal is the 1968 Non-Proliferation Treaty (NPT) and the so-called London Nuclear Suppliers Group arrangement to control the spread of nuclear weapons, which requires the signatories to accept full-scope safeguards and inspection of nuclear facilities by the IAEA. Somewhat less formal in nature is the Missile Technology Control Regime (MTCR), which is based on a 1987 agreement among seven Western supplier countries to restrict the export of goods and technology that could be used to produce a missile capable of carrying a nuclear payload. The least formal proliferation regime is the so-called Australia Group, 26 nations that have met periodically under the auspices of the Australian Government to identify and agree upon control of precursor chemicals which can be used for the manufacture of chemical weapons. The Australia Group was an interim arrangement in anticipation of the 1993 Chemical Weapons Convention (CWC).[14]

It is significant that currently there are no fully functioning international arrangements to deal with the export of either conventional or advanced conventional weapons. In the latter case, in particular, the results of the war in the Persian Gulf suggest an urgent need to broaden the focus to include various new technologies that can have major force-multiplier effects, including high-precision location, battlefield surveillance and smart targeting systems.

The existing international regimes are, in many respects, an unco-ordinated patchwork, with different sets of targets, different sets of co-operating states, and different kinds of sanctions. Links are few or non-existent between the MTCR, the Australia Group, and the Nuclear Suppliers Group. Member countries of the MTCR have not been able to agree on targets of control or conditions of sale. As regards chemical weapons, until the CWC enters into force the

---

[12] Nolan, J. E., *Trappings of Power: Ballistic Missiles in the Third World* (Brookings Institution: Washington, DC, 1991).

[13] See, for example, Lachow, I., 'The global positioning system: managing the tensions between defense needs and civilian applications', Ph.D. thesis, Department of Engineering and Public Policy, Carnegie Mellon University, Pittsburgh, Pa., May 1994.

[14] For the text of the Convention on the Prohibition of the Development, Production, Stockpiling and Use of Chemical Weapons and on their Destruction (the CWC), see SIPRI, *SIPRI Yearbook 1993: World Armaments and Disarmament* (Oxford University Press: Oxford, 1993), pp. 735–56.

international community will not have agreed on any formal sanctions for violations of multilateral accords. Nevertheless, the synergy between these weapons—for example, Scud missiles equipped with CW warheads—poses potentially grave threats to international security. There is thus an especially urgent need not only for better cross-regime co-ordination, owing to the frequent overlap between projects of concern and developing state efforts to acquire the necessary technology, but also for wider and more rapid sharing of relevant intelligence.

Yet another dilemma is that a number of important states, including some republics of the former USSR and the People's Republic of China, are not formally parties to all of the existing proliferation control regimes. Indeed, some of the potential suppliers of weapons of mass destruction remain outside traditional proliferation controls. To be effective and politically realistic, future regimes are likely to require closer, informal co-ordination among all of the great powers, combined with a broad-based international political arrangement to which *all* relevant states can be parties.

Co-ordination among the great powers could be achieved on an informal basis through one or more existing international mechanisms or through some new organization. Moreover, the United Nations—particularly the revitalized Security Council—may also be a viable forum for achieving broad political consensus on these issues. In principle, it would be desirable to integrate the existing multilateral control regimes to manage nuclear proliferation, the proliferation of missile technologies and the proliferation of chemical and biological weapons. In practice, because of the differences in the basis and operation of these proliferation regimes and their varied country membership, and because of the obstacles to negotiating the necessary arrangements among large numbers of technically advanced states, it seems unlikely that complete integration of the existing regimes will occur in the near future. However, given the remarkable political developments that have occurred since the breakup of the Soviet Union, it remains a worthy, and potentially attainable, goal towards which to work.

Beyond the need for greater informal co-ordination and the eventual complete integration of proliferation control regimes, there are other problems that remain to be addressed. It is clear, for example, that regional arms control agreements and other agreements designed to prevent proliferation will encounter difficulty if the developed states apply a double standard with regard to the proliferation of CW, nuclear and missile technologies. The USA and the other great powers cannot afford to continue turning a blind eye to the behaviour of states friendly to their interests and expect to retain—or, in some cases, establish—credibility with other states whom they are in the process of confronting on proliferation matters. The implication is that developed states must take a greater leadership role both in reforming their own weapon and technology export policies and in promoting regional arms control arrangements.

The need for and limits of dual-use export control

More complicated than the exports of arms and related military systems to developing states are the exports of civilian technologies that also have significant utility in the development of military capabilities. There are many examples of these, including advanced computers, machine tools, measurement systems, and certain process chemical technology. Many of these technologies are important to developing a modern industrial economy. It is generally agreed that, for moral, humanitarian and practical economic reasons, the developed world should not attempt to hold the developing world in a permanent state of underdevelopment by blocking transfers of knowledge and technology. On the contrary, it is in the interest of the developed world to promote and facilitate economic development.

As with more traditional East–West controls, the USA and other developed states face basic conflicting national interests in applying export controls to the developing world such as: (a) military interests in slowing the spread of militarily critical technology and advanced weapons; (b) economic interests in promoting strength in international markets; and (c) foreign policy interests both in promoting the development of stable democratic states built on modern prosperous economies, and in using access to advanced technology and products to build enduring political and economic international relationships.[15] Clearly, too little thought has been given to the potential utility and limitations of export control as a policy tool in the developing world.

Before the developed world goes too far in implementing new dual-use export controls to limit the proliferation of high-technology weapons and weapons of mass destruction, some careful technology assessment and empirical research will be required to identify the contexts in which controls are likely to work and those in which they probably will not.[16] Such a determination is too important to be left to opinion, speculation or ideological preference. It is essential to identify systematically the contexts in which benefits exceed costs when the conflicting national interests in military security, economic competitiveness and foreign policy objectives of controlling states are balanced. Identifying the region in which the net benefits are positive will require careful, empirical research and analysis by the intelligence and policy communities. Experience in the East–West context has shown that, in a bilateral world, export controls can be effective *only* if used very selectively. Selectivity is likely to be an even greater prerequisite for the success of controls in a multilateral world. Even given significant selectivity, the domain of the effectiveness of export controls remains uncertain and is likely to be critically dependent on the broader policy context in which they are employed.

---

[15] For a detailed discussion of the problem of balancing these interests, and procedures that might be used to do this, see National Research Council (note 3).

[16] The process of expanding the application of export controls to address proliferation problems, without first performing thorough analysis, has already begun in Germany, the UK and the USA as a result of political pressures arising from the Persian Gulf War and the claims that a CW production facility had been established at Rabta, Libya.

Based on current knowledge, the authors of this chapter suggest the following guidelines for a dual-use export control regime for the developing world:

1. Because the volume of world trade is enormous, and the fraction of trade that is of serious concern for regional militarization is quite small, an effective strategy must be narrowly focused on selected technologies and destinations rather than directed across the board. This guideline is proposed for three reasons. First, there is the 'needle in the haystack' problem. If licences were required for *all* international trade to the developing world, even with advanced automation the volume of the paperwork would be so great that it would be impossible to maintain sufficient bureaucratic vigilance to catch the occasional problematic shipment. Second, because trade with the developing world is becoming increasingly important, any strategy that imposes across-the-board trade restrictions will present participating developed states with major incentives to cheat or relax surveillance activities. Third, many developing states are dependent on imports of high-technology goods which cannot be produced domestically for critically important development activities. Any action that impedes such trade is morally objectionable.

2. Owing to the fact that most high-technology products (or their rough equivalents) can be obtained from multiple sources in the developed world, any approach to selective export control must be widely multilateral in nature. This means that, in most instances, unilateral control will fail to achieve the desired control objective and will have adverse economic impact on the controlled suppliers. The argument that such impact is small because the volume of trade foregone is small can be seriously in error for two reasons. First, many builders of integrated systems will shy away from incorporating components that carry unilateral controls which may impede future marketing activities. For example, representatives of a number of major European firms have told the authors of this chapter that they have designed out or are in the process of designing out US parts and components because of fears that unilateral imposition of controls by the USA could constrain their future marketing flexibility. Second, there are often powerful 'first entry' effects in high-technology markets. Thus, restrictions that impede the rapid and early entry of new advanced technologies and products may have profound downstream implications for market share. Markets once lost can be very difficult to recapture.

The present authors hold the view that the best way to produce a system that is narrowly targeted is to insist on transparency and full disclosure in importing countries. Developed states need to be able to see easily that the goods and services they are exporting are going to support the peaceful economic development of importing countries. When a developing state is prepared to engage in such full disclosure, and is using imported technologies in peaceful ways, there should be few if any restrictions on the import of technology.[17] Using formal

---

[17] These ideas have been best articulated by John D. Steinbruner, Director of Foreign Policy Studies at the Brookings Institution, and are explored further in Carter, Perry and Steinbruner (note 2).

and informal international arrangements of the sorts outlined above in the discussion of proliferation control regimes, the developed world can track activities in transparent states and selectively impose restrictions for specific projects which it identifies as problematic. Developing states that wish to maintain their 'co-operating' standing should agree to prevent the internal diversion of imports to those projects that cause concern. Evidence that diversion had occurred would be grounds for losing 'co-operating' status and becoming subject to export licensing restrictions.

Openness and full disclosure can be encouraged with both incentives and penalties. Developing states that are prepared to operate with transparency should be guaranteed reasonable access to international markets. Developing states which are unwilling to operate with transparency should face restricted access to markets and be subjected to broad control on sensitive high-technology imports. The level of restriction and control should be adjusted in response to the level of disclosure. For example, states might be classified as: (a) co-operating states, to which export of virtually all dual-use high technology would be allowed, except for restrictions to identified 'projects of concern'; (b) nonco-operating states, to which export of more sensitive dual-use high technology would be licensed, and to which licences for most leading-edge technology would typically be denied; and (c) outlaw states, to which export of all high-technology items with potential military utility would be forbidden.

Recent US policy—in particular the Bush Administration's Enhanced Proliferation Control Initiative (EPCI)—has not conformed to the guidelines outlined above. Indeed, while the EPCI is couched in appropriate rhetoric about the importance of fully multilateral efforts to deny potential proliferating countries access to controlled technology, it is inherently a unilateral US approach in keeping with the historic tendency of the USA to react to events of the day (in this case, the Persian Gulf War) in a unilateral fashion.[18] Moreover, the list of controlled items covered under the EPCI encompasses a broad swath of technology, potentially far broader than is necessary or realistic given the nature of the threat. It is hardly surprising, therefore, that affected US industry sectors, such as the chemical industry, have expressed substantial concern about the regulations.

The flow of technical experts

Perhaps the most impressive and vexing aspect of the Iraqi proliferation effort is the considerable technical expertise of the team of scientists and engineers assembled by Iraq and the very considerable achievements they made with limited resources.[19] Technically trained people are clearly the single most

[18] Representatives of German firms have recently made similar complaints to the authors of this chapter about the unilateral nature of newly expanded German laws and administrative procedures.

[19] Cleminson, R., address to the AAAS Colloquium on 'Science, Technology and Security in the New International Order', Washington, DC, 22 Nov. 1991.

important ingredient to any programme of high-technology military development. Most of the basic knowledge for such programmes is now available in the textbooks and journals of the open scientific literature. Much of this knowledge and the technical skills to use it are routinely imparted to students in major universities throughout the world, particularly in institutions in advanced industrialized countries.

There is no way that this flow can be halted, and there is likely to be significant pressure on technically trained individuals who are citizens of a country that is mounting a sustained clandestine proliferation effort. On the other hand, major universities have done almost nothing to impress on their students the social responsibilities that go with advanced education. While such emphasis may be questionable, universities nevertheless have a moral obligation to address these issues in a continuous and explicit way.

Developed countries should also take steps to make it illegal for their nationals to provide technical assistance to proliferation efforts. In the aftermath of a series of serious infractions, Germany has now developed the most stringent rules of this kind. Some states, such as the UK, continue to argue that they do not at present have jurisdiction over technical assistance that their nationals provide abroad.[20] In this context, the development of a more coherent body of international law, perhaps under UN auspices, could be useful.

One pool of technical manpower that is of particular concern today is the staffs of the many weapon laboratories and design bureaux of the former USSR.[21] Most of these facilities are facing dramatically reduced budgets, and many employees will find it difficult to earn a living. There are reports that some have already received lucrative offers from militarizing states anxious to secure their services. Other offers, perhaps irresistible, will certainly follow. The developed states need to work aggressively with the CIS and the former republics to ensure that alternative, more constructive, forms of employment can be found for these people.

Another pool of technical manpower that is of concern, based on the recent experience in Iraq, is what might be called 'scientific and technological mercenaries' (i.e., technically trained individuals prepared to work on contract for nations seeking to develop weapons of mass destruction). Given the acceleration that such knowledgeable individuals can bring to a proliferation effort, governments (both individually and collectively) should pay greater attention to this problem.

It would appear that on at least some occasions in the past intelligence agencies have sought to limit the contributions of certain important technical experts

---

[20] The question of how to deal with this problem is currently under discussion in the British Government.

[21] For a discussion of this problem see Campbell, K. M. *et al.*, *Soviet Nuclear Fission: Control of the Nuclear Arsenal in a Disintegrating Soviet Union*, CSIA Studies in International Security (John F. Kennedy School of Government, Harvard University: Cambridge, Mass., Nov. 1991).

by killing them.[22] Abhorrent as such activities may be, it seems likely that some states will from time to time encounter circumstances in which they consider this solution to be the lesser of two evils. It should be emphasized, however, that this approach does not represent a viable element of a comprehensive multilateral political strategy for the containment of proliferation.

The continuing need for developed world military superiority and the direct removal of proliferation threats

Diplomacy, arms control and confidence-building activities may all contribute to regional security. Such strategies are not foolproof, however, and regional high-technology militarization may place nuclear and other advanced weapons in the hands of rulers prepared to use them both regionally and against the developed world. It is likely that both US national interests and the collective interests of other developed states will continue to be best served by also maintaining a capacity to project decisive military force in regional theatres if political means fail.[23] It thus remains important for the USA and its partners to maintain weapon systems and other military capabilities that are superior to those that can be manufactured domestically in developing regional states, and to those that it may be possible to acquire from abroad. In the past the USA derived such superiority almost as an automatic corollary of the same 'force multiplier' strategy that has been the basis of NATO doctrine for more than 40 years. With the end of the cold war, superiority in regional theatres has become less automatic. Despite the politically awkward and morally difficult issues that come with it, a strategy that has remained comfortably implicit in the past must now be considered explicitly if coherent policy is to be developed. Just as in the NATO–WTO confrontation, any strategy that depends on maintaining a technological lead inevitably has two requirements: to prevent the potential adversary from gaining access to the same technology, since this would neutralize military advantage, and to continue producing new technological advances to stay ahead.

If it is assumed that this is the desired objective, it is not self-evident that maintaining collective superior military capability will always serve both the interests of the technically advanced states and the more general interests of world peace. The maintenance of military superiority might increase the odds of military intervention; it is not clear how it will affect the willingness of great powers to work collectively, or how that willingness will affect the likelihood that interventions will occur. Collective action by the great powers would probably increase regional stability, if consistently and impartially applied; whether

---

[22] It is widely assumed that Gerald V. Bull, who was apparently assisting Iraq in the development of its 'supergun', was killed by Israeli intelligence. For a reasonably detailed account of the Bull case, see Toolis, K., 'The man behind Iraq's supergun', *New York Times Magazine*, 26 Aug. 1990, pp. 46–77.

[23] This chapter does not address the important and difficult task of specifying the circumstances under which such interventions are appropriate. Such circumstances can arise, and the problem of being prepared to deal with them should be addressed if this occurs.

an increased threat of external intervention would also have a positive effect on regional stability is a good deal less clear.

From the overall perspective of global security, the desirability of maintaining a developed world military advantage over developing states is theoretically arguable, and probably depends to a considerable extent on the political agenda of the great powers—most notably the issues over which they are willing to adopt the use of force—and on their ability and willingness to work collectively. On the other hand, from a starkly realistic perspective, the great powers are likely to do whatever is necessary to maintain their ability to project force when they perceive their vital interests to be threatened (as in the Persian Gulf). It would be unreasonable, in this view, for the great powers to do anything *other* than arm themselves with superior weapon systems and be prepared to use this capability if the situation requires. It can thus be assumed that the continued maintenance of military superiority is and will remain an objective of the great powers.

There is an additional option available to the developed states if they are confronted with compelling evidence that a militarizing state is attempting to acquire or develop domestically the capacity to produce weapons of mass destruction and advanced conventional weapons. This option is to remove the threatening facility by means of pre-emptive military action in those cases where it can be positively identified through human and other intelligence means. With the exception of the carefully targeted—but less than fully effective—bombing during the Persian Gulf War, which was intended in part to achieve this objective, pre-emptive military action for purposes of nonproliferation apparently has been attempted on only one previous occasion: the successful 1981 Israeli raid that destroyed the Osirak nuclear reactor in Iraq. Given the gross violation of national sovereignty inherent in this approach, sufficient multilateral consensus, even tacit consensus among the great powers, is likely to exist only on those rare occasions when the nature of the threat is large, immediate and undeniable.

Clearly, this policy course is an absolute *in extremis* action. To be justifiable in the court of world opinion—if not under international law—such action would have to be preceded by clear, unambiguous and deliberately escalated warnings. Preferably, it would be undertaken after debate within and approval by the UN Security Council, based on previously agreed-upon criteria for determining the nature, extent and duration of misconduct potentially justifying a military response. Even in the absence of a UN resolution, the great powers must be prepared to demonstrate by deeds as well as words their determination not to tolerate the construction or operation of threatening weapon design and/or manufacturing facilities that pose large and imminent risks to regional or global security. Unfortunately, it may only be through the 'demonstration value' of military force that additional proliferation schemes can be deterred or stopped.[24]

IV. Moral dilemmas

The above arguments undoubtedly raise a fundamental moral question: Given the bellicose history of the great powers, and indeed of all developed states, what right do they have, either individually or collectively, to constrain the militarization of developing states? There are two quite different answers to this question. To some extent, the issue of rights is not relevant. If a secure and peaceful world is in the interest of the developed states, and if they have the power and will to constrain the level of militarization in developing states, they may simply impose their will. Moral or immoral, it will happen.

As Graham Allison noted over two decades ago, states are not unitary actors.[25] Their actions result from a complex interplay of many forces. In the long run questions of morality are never irrelevant to the actions of democracies. The present authors suggest three responses to the 'moral' question.

1. Unconstrained militarization in regional theatres can substantially affect the security and well-being of people in the developed world. For this reason, constraining such developments is morally defensible as part of a programme of preventive self-defence.

2. Both because of the existence of nuclear weapons and because of the continuous evolution of social thinking, the great powers are in the process of trying to outgrow the use of force as a vehicle for settling international disputes. It can be argued that, by limiting the rate of militarization in developing states, the developed states may be able to accelerate this process in their own societies and thereby stimulate a similar process of social change in regional settings. Such a development would serve the collective security interests of the world.

3. In most cases, regional stability also serves the interests of most of the residents of developing regions. What most of these people need is improved economic conditions that can give them a better life; such conditions are unlikely to come about in the absence of stability or in circumstances where an inordinately large share of the national budget is dedicated to the procurement of armaments.

Dramatic social change, even revolutionary change, can sometimes be a necessary prerequisite to development, and none of the above precludes such

---

[24] Editor's note: On 24 Jan. 1995, US Secretary of Defense William J. Perry told the Senate Foreign Relations Committee that the USA had considered destroying North Korea's nuclear reactor: 'I can tell you flatly that we know how to do that, but on consideration I did not recommend that course of action to the President', Greenhouse, S., 'Administration defends North Korea pact', *New York Times*, 25 Jan. 1995, p. A6.

[25] Allison, G. T., *Essence of Decision: Explaining the Cuban Missile Crisis* (Little, Brown: Boston, 1971).

change. The authors of this chapter have neither called for preservation of the existing socio-political order in the developing world nor for a developed world police force that would routinely suppress military action in the developing world. It is indeed possible for developing states to undertake a limited military development programme for the purpose of maintaining a credible national defence *without* seeking to acquire the most technologically advanced weapon systems or weapons of mass destruction. The above discussion does not even call for significant levels of military intervention in the developing world by the great powers. Only in rare circumstances would the kind of action proposed above be justified; in general, the world would be a better place if there were significantly less intervention of this kind.

What is called for is a set of programmes intended to slow the rate of technological advancement of developing world militarization while allowing and supporting continued economic growth. Also needed is the maintenance to the greatest extent possible of developed world military superiority within an appropriate diplomatic framework that would allow intervention, preferably collective intervention, as a strategy of last resort in the face of dangerous proliferation. If it is prudently developed and wisely and equitably employed, the maintenance of such a capacity would serve the best interests of world peace and stability.

How the set of strategies proposed above is received, particularly in the developing world, will be critically dependent upon the diplomatic context in which they are developed and implemented. If the great powers are not sensitive to the legitimate needs of developing states, if they are not acting collectively, if they are not taking steps to limit their own arms (particularly their nuclear weapons), and if they appear to be motivated only by narrow national interests, then the developing world can be expected to object strenuously with charges of exploitation, arrogance, élitism and paternalism. If, on the other hand, a diplomatic context can be developed in which collective action, motivated by a genuine concern for collective security, emerges as the dominant motivation, then wide (though certainly not universal) acceptance, even in the developing world, should be possible. The opportunity is there; it is time for creative diplomats to go to work.

Part III

Where interests diverge: dilemmas of US–Russian security co-operation

6. Global co-operation and regional conflict: problems in co-ordinating the US and Russian security agendas

*Russell Leigh Moses**

I. Introduction

As Russia attempts to emerge from the rubble of what was once the Soviet Union, its participation in co-operative security endeavours will be especially crucial to the stable evolution and formation of a post-cold war international order. This chapter is an assessment of what both the Russian and the US governments can and should do to bring about Russian–US security co-operation, focusing on the issues of proliferation of advanced weapons technology and multilateral peacekeeping.

To understand the potential for Russian co-operation in such political–military areas, it is necessary first to examine the domestic context of Russian national security decision making. This chapter addresses the question of Russian decision making for political–military intervention by examining the Soviet decisions to intervene in both Afghanistan (1979) and the Persian Gulf War (1990–91). Examination of the emerging Russian policy in proliferation and multilateral peacekeeping is followed by evaluation of the potential strategies the USA might adopt to foster US–Russian security co-operation.

The major conclusion of this chapter is that because domestic concerns dominate, US–Russian co-operation in multilateral peacekeeping is likely to be more central to the US–Russian relationship than co-ordination to stem proliferation. The political situation in Russia, and in the former USSR generally, is almost overwhelmingly complex, and the capability of the USA to meet its security objectives regarding Russia is quite limited. Rebuilding the economic and social order along democratic lines while making sure that a more assertive Russian foreign policy does not exacerbate ethnic and regional tensions is a laudable goal, but the means are probably lacking as is a current plan for addressing these issues. The USA should adopt not a long-term strategy but one based on making sure that there will be a 'long term': a political strategy, in short, for the middle distance, for the latter years of the 1990s. This strategy

* My thanks to Sara Kearns, Bates Gill, Alexey Arbatov, James Goodby and Benoit Morel for their assistance, and to the Soviet Studies Research Centre, the Royal Military Academy at Sandhurst, England, especially Director Chris Donnelly and his assistant, Anne Hill, for their help at an early stage of this project. Bates Gill deserves special thanks for his careful reading of an earlier draft.

should aim to create a context for security co-operation, focusing on peacekeeping in the former Soviet Union.

II. Foreign policy uncertainties

Domestic political clashes and the battle over the direction and pace of economic reform still dominate political discourse in Moscow. The Government of Russia is still in the throes of selecting a set of political strategies to deal with its vastly changed domestic and international context. The Russian action in Chechnya and the political repercussions of this disaster no doubt will affect the course of events very significantly. Despite the ostensibly more democratic character of the Russian Government, indications are that there still exists a personalized, patronage-driven system of internal access, compelled more by crisis than by flexible policy process. The Chechnya decision appears to be an example of this.[1]

There is no clear way of predicting the politics or policies of a still-emerging Russia. It is impossible to know with any sort of precision who will be in charge of Russian foreign policy even in the short term or what their priorities and abilities to implement their policy preferences will be. In 1992 President Boris Yeltsin criticized Foreign Minister Andrey Kozyrev for managing a Russian foreign policy that was too passive.[2] Russian policies seem to be drifting towards the perspective held by former Russian Ambassador to the USA Vladimir Lukin, who acknowledged that Moscow and Washington had common interests in such areas as nuclear proliferation, democratic and market reform in Russia, and the conflict in the former Yugoslavia, but insisted that the centrality of US–Russian relations had been 'diminishing' for some time, to the point where it had lost its centrality.[3] The dramatic events of late 1993, including Vladimir Zhirinovsky's electoral success also must have had a profound impact on influencing Yeltsin's now more nationalistic foreign policy.

Institutional competition is nothing new in Russian foreign policy, and it should be possible to identify its main features and attempt to adjust co-operative policies accordingly. However, political chaos produced in large part by personal infighting does not make for predictable foreign policy. This persistent feature of the Russian political landscape, however, is depriving Russian and US decision makers of that element of reliable certainty that is generally at the foundation of co-operative efforts. Since Russian foreign policy is still in the early stages of its development, there is much to be learned (and perhaps

[1] See Dobbs, M. and Coll, S., 'In new Russia, old boys hold the best cards', *International Herald Tribune*, 27 Jan. 1993, pp. 1, 4; Checkel, J., 'Russian foreign policy: back to the future?', Radio Free Europe/Radio Liberty (hereafter RFE/RL), *RFE/RL Research Report*, vol. 1, no. 41 (16 Oct. 1992), pp. 15–29; Checkel, J., 'Ideas, institutions, and the Gorbachev revolution', *World Politics*, vol. 45, no. 2 (Jan. 1993), pp. 271–300; and 'The Chechen trap', *The Economist*, vol. 334, no. 7896 (7 Jan. 1995), pp. 25–27.

[2] See Yeltsin's speech to the Russian Foreign Ministry on 27 Oct. 1992, as discussed in Lepingwell, J. W. R., 'Yeltsin calls for tougher foreign policy', *RFE/RL Research Report*, vol. 1, no. 44 (6 Nov. 1992).

[3] See Lukin, V. P., 'Our security predicament', *Foreign Policy*, no. 88 (fall 1992), p. 66.

much continuity) from past Soviet foreign policy decisions. Analysis of Soviet decisions concerning Afghanistan (1979) and the Persian Gulf War (1990–91) can shed light on the methods and attitudes that Russian decision makers will bring to bear on questions of intervention or co-operation.

III. Afghanistan and the Persian Gulf War: Was Soviet intervention really different from Soviet co-operation?

At first glance Soviet military intervention in Afghanistan in December 1979 and the co-operation of the Gorbachev Government in the US-led effort to oust Saddam Hussein from Kuwait could not look more different. The former featured the introduction of Soviet military forces into an adjoining state to prop up an allied government; the latter displayed a willingness on the part of Moscow to stand by while a former adversary engineered an armed assault on a regional ally. In the first case, the Soviet leadership was roundly condemned by the international community; in the second, the Soviet Government became one of the leading political participants in efforts by many nations to expel Iraq from a Gulf state. In Afghanistan, the Brezhnev Government put much less effort into finding a diplomatic settlement than into conducting military operations,[4] while the period immediately preceding the inauguration of Coalition military operations against Iraq displayed a Soviet General Secretary willing to 'go to the brink' for a political end to the military confrontation.

However, studying cases that may appear very different can have considerable analytic and prescriptive value.[5] More importantly from the standpoint of this analysis, a comparison of the decisions to use force in Afghanistan and to forsake and seek to prevent the use of force in the Persian Gulf can reveal much about the thoughts of Soviet (and even post-Soviet) decision makers on: the utility of military force and diplomacy, the patterns of both the perspectives and process of decision making in Moscow, the factors that work to impel or restrain the use of force, and the willingness to co-operate in security matters to achieve a diplomatic resolution to conflict. In fact a comparison of the Soviet invasion of Afghanistan and Moscow's co-operation with the US-led UN Coalition's struggle with Iraq reveals a number of important similarities:

1. In both cases decisions were restricted to a very small group of individuals in the Soviet Government. These individuals did not seem to have participated as representatives of specific agencies or bureaucratic interests so much as officials with personal ties to the prevailing leadership. None the less, major elements of the Soviet military found themselves in opposition not only to the decisions made but to the way in which they were made.

---

[4] This is not to say that Moscow did nothing diplomatically. See Khan, R., *Untying the Afghan Knot: Negotiating Soviet Withdrawal* (Duke University Press: Durham, N.C., 1991), pp. 25–54.

[5] See, for example, Kaplan, A., *The Conduct of Inquiry* (Chandler Publishing: San Francisco, Calif., 1964).

2. The role of Islam appears to have figured in the deliberations behind Soviet policy choices. Concern about the impact of religious fundamentalism ranged from its role in regional circumstances in the Middle East to its place in the Soviet domestic realm.

3. In both Afghanistan and Iraq, the motives and course of US behaviour were viewed sceptically by Moscow. Washington's decisions were frequently seen as unpredictable, rash and potentially threatening.

The background of the Afghanistan and Iraq crises

The Soviet decision to use military force in Afghanistan came during a widening and deepening conflict that had raged in that country for over a year. Historically, Moscow's relations with regimes in Kabul had been troubled, and its ties to the Government of Nur Mohammed Tarakki, which came to power in April 1978 through a coup that may have had the support of the Brezhnev Government, were never warm or enduring.[6] However, far from spearheading a drive to stabilize a country on the Soviet southern border, Tarakki and his Prime Minister Hafizullah Amin antagonized Muslim and tribal leaders throughout Afghanistan and exacerbated the existing split between the Khalq faction they headed and the Parcham faction, led by Barbak Karmal. The reform strategy of the Khalq faction was meant to incorporate the Afghan countryside in a national drive for development and modernization but in fact succeeded in alienating major portions of it. The Tarakki regime also antagonized Pakistan, where many Afghan and Muslim intellectuals were in exile, and propelled Islamabad even further in its effort to support opposition groups based there in cross-border attacks.[7]

The Brezhnev Government, which must have been anxious about these developments (as well as the increasing Sino-US *rapprochement* and efforts by Washington to explore the possibility that a military coup would stabilize Iran), signed a Treaty of Friendship and Co-operation with the Tarakki Government in early December 1978. Apart from giving Moscow a more formal stake in Afghan affairs, the initialing of the document indicated that the stability of the Tarakki Government would be of direct and immediate concern to Soviet decision makers. Military support, in the form of aid and advisers, was accelerated and expanded.

However, the main problems in Afghanistan were political and social. The more the regime in Kabul attempted to transform traditional structures outside the capital, the greater was the level of local resistance. Between the signing of the Treaty with Moscow and the autumn of 1979, over one-half of the country fell out of government control. In Herat in February 1979, scores of Soviet military technicians and economic advisers were killed in anti-regime riots, and

---

[6] For background, see Dupree, L., *Afghanistan* (Princeton University Press: Princeton, 1978); and Ganovsky, Y. (ed.), *A History of Afghanistan*, rev. edn (Progress Publishers: Moscow, 1985).

[7] See Roy, O., *Islam and Resistance in Afghanistan*, 2nd edn (Cambridge University Press: Cambridge, 1990), chapters 5 and 6.

direct air support from the USSR had to be used to quell the eruption. These incidents against Soviet personnel and their families continued throughout the autumn of 1979. Tarakki and Amin began to press for even more direct Soviet military assistance.[8]

In September 1979, Amin overthrew Tarakki in a bloody palace coup and seized control of the Afghan Government.[9] The Brezhnev Government was evidently taken by surprise. Amin's rule only heightened the level of armed resistance, and Soviet military and civilian personnel continued to be attacked in many areas of the country. Amin, who had urged a more overt Soviet military presence for months, now renewed his requests for direct Soviet military assistance in the form of troops that would engage in offensive operations.[10] Sometime around the middle of December, elements of the Brezhnev Government made the decision to support an internal coup against Amin and to intervene militarily to stabilize the new Government in the short term. On 27–28 December 1979, Amin was overthrown (and apparently killed) during the operation, and replaced by Barbak Karmal. Soviet armed forces poured across the border.[11]

Iraq's invasion of Kuwait on 2 August 1990, and both Moscow's response to that action and the efforts of the US-led Coalition to retaliate against Saddam Hussein, evolved in a quite different environment—one marked by increasing Soviet–US co-operation. The invasion caught US Secretary of State James Baker and Soviet Foreign Minister Shevardnadze in a meeting on arms control and regional conflicts, and they issued a joint statement condemning Iraq's 'flagrant aggression' and called on support from the international community. President Gorbachev and the Soviet Government called for 'the urgent and unconditional withdrawal of Iraqi troops from Kuwait's territory' and insisted on the complete restoration of 'the sovereignty, national independence, and territorial integrity of Kuwait'. Moscow was quick to support the drafting of United Nations Security Council Resolution 660, which insisted on the complete and immediate withdrawal of Iraqi forces.[12]

Within weeks of these early efforts at co-operation, however, consensus both within the Gorbachev Government and between Moscow and Washington began to show signs of fracture. As it became clearer that the Bush Administration saw the use of military force as a first, rather than last, resort to oust

---

[8] See Bradsher, H., *Afghanistan and the Soviet Union*, rev. edn (Duke University Press: Durham, N.C., 1985), chapter 5.

[9] For the most complete account, see Bradsher (note 8), chapter 6.

[10] See Muratov, D., 'Secret documents on entry into Afghanistan', *Komsomol'skaya Pravda*, 27 Dec. 1990, p. 3, in Joint Publications Research Service–Soviet Military Affairs (hereafter cited as JPRS-UMA) JPRS-UMA-91-006, 4 Mar. 1991.

[11] For further elaboration, see Bradsher (note 8), chapter 9.

[12] *TASS*, 2 Aug. and 3 Aug., 1990. For two surveys of Moscow's actions in this crisis, see Freedman, R. O., 'Moscow and the Gulf War', *Problems of Communism*, vol. 40 (July/Aug. 1991), pp. 1–17; and Ekedahl, C. M., 'The Soviet Union and Iraq's invasion of Kuwait', ed. D. D. Newsom, *The Diplomatic Record, 1990–1991* (Westview Press: Boulder, Colo., 1992), pp. 83–108. For an impressive general interpretation of the war, see Newsom, D. D., 'Diplomacy and the Gulf crisis', in the same volume, pp. 5–20.

Saddam Hussein from Kuwait (and possibly from Baghdad itself),[13] Gorbachev began to press for an exhaustive search for diplomatic solutions to the crisis. When the UN Security Council passed Resolution 678,[14] which authorized 'all necessary means' to accomplish the implementation of Resolution 660 by early January 1991, Gorbachev argued for and eventually achieved a clause allowing a 'pause of goodwill' until 15 January 1991 as a window of diplomatic opportunity.

The Soviet President, handicapped by the presence of Soviet civilian and military advisers in Iraq and the historical ties between Moscow and Baghdad, also found himself under siege by independence movements in the Baltic states and growing opposition to this and other policies, both from reformers and conservative communists. Hampered from within and seen as a junior partner from without, Gorbachev continued doggedly to pursue the diplomatic path while the Bush Administration raced along the track of military coercion. On 12 January 1991 the US Congress authorized President George Bush to use force against Iraq. Four days later, in the absence of an adequate response and during continued diplomatic efforts by Gorbachev to convince Saddam Hussein to withdraw from Kuwait, the Coalition air war began. Gorbachev's attempts to construct a peace plan culminated in a comprehensive proposal that emerged on 18 February 1991, but Washington rejected the plan, and less than a week later the Coalition ground assault began. Four days later the Iraqi military was shattered and the Persian Gulf War was over.[15]

The character of the Soviet decision-making process and the role of the military

There is now abundant evidence to indicate that the Soviet decision to use force in Afghanistan was, as one Soviet source puts it, 'made as a result of "secret meditations" by a small group of politicians'.[16] Available indications are that the decision to intervene was made reluctantly (though suddenly) and with the advice of academics and outside experts dismissed or the opportunity for hearing their counsel perhaps bypassed altogether.[17] A Brezhnev-chaired subgroup

[13] See Woodward, B., *The Commanders* (Simon & Schuster: New York, 1991).

[14] The text of the resolution is reproduced in SIPRI, *SIPRI Yearbook 1992: World Armaments and Disarmament* (Oxford University Press: Oxford, 1992), pp. 525–30.

[15] See Freedman (note 12) and Ekedahl (note 12) for Soviet perspectives on the war and Woodward (note 13) for US decision making. For an interesting look at Gorbachev's role in the crisis, see King, C. A., 'Necessary but insufficient: the role of language in the Persian Gulf crisis' (Senior Honors thesis, Carnegie Mellon University, May 1992).

[16] 'Afghanistan—"As it was"—a historian's commentary', *Voyenno-Istoricheskiy Zhurnal*, no. 5 (May 1990), in JPRS-UMA-91-005, 13 Feb. 1991, p. 131. See also Bradsher (note 8), pp. 163–68.

[17] See 'Unsolicited memorandum sent to the appropriate levels, from the USSR Academy of Sciences Institute of the Economics of the World Socialist System', in *Literaturnaya Gazeta*, 16 Mar. 1980, in *Current Digest of the Soviet Press* (hereafter cited as *CDSP*), vol. 40, no. 8 (1988). According to Raymond Garthoff, a number of leading Soviet academic specialists who were in a position to provide policy guidance to the Brezhnev Government were stricken with heart attacks during the period immediately following the Soviet intervention. See his *Détente and Confrontation: Soviet–American Relations from Nixon to Reagan* (Brookings Institution: Washington, 1985), p. 933. The author is grateful

of the Soviet Politburo responsible for foreign policy and national security affairs, the Defence Council, probably made the final decision.[18] The original indecision and reluctance of the Brezhnev Government to intervene directly with Soviet military forces on a large-scale were evidently overridden by increasing pressure from Soviet Ambassador to Afghanistan Alexander M. Puzanov, KGB reports from the embassy in Kabul, various Soviet military liaison officers stationed in and around Kabul, and what a number of Soviet commentators referred to as 'the deteriorating international situation'.[19] Brezhnev himself said that the choice to use force in Afghanistan 'was not a simple decision'.[20]

What is especially interesting about the decision to intervene in Afghanistan was the part played by the Soviet military. According to reports in the Soviet press (the central press of the USSR was one of the best indicators of thinking in and behaviour by Moscow), the majority of the Soviet General Staff (and perhaps the entire General Staff) was opposed to the introduction of Soviet troops into Afghanistan on such a massive scale and with such short warning.[21] According to these accounts (which cannot be said to be completely unbiased), it was Soviet Defence Minister Dmitri Ustinov who overrode the objections of the General Staff and directed the implementation of the decision by the Defence Council to use force in Afghanistan. While the manner of this effort may have had a negative impact on the early ground operations of Soviet forces (if only because planning time was short), the relevant point is that Ustinov had close personal ties to Brezhnev and personality, rather than political expediency and bureaucratic logic, may have played the most prominent role in the decision to use military force.[22] Clearly, the choice to use force in Afghanistan was beset by difficulty and internal struggle, with much of the relevant policy-making machinery bypassed or shut out. The parallels with the Chechnya decision are obvious.

Soviet decision making concerning the use of force against Iraq and Saddam Hussein over a decade later also tended to be compelled by personality, rather than driven by process. Indeed, as in so many other foreign policy matters in the post-1985 period, Gorbachev aimed to supplant the established process with

to Alexey Arbatov for discussions relating to the decision-making process concerning the use of force in Afghanistan.
[18] See Muratov (note 10); and Rahr, A., 'Gorbachev discloses details of Defence Council', *Radio Liberty Research Bulletin*, no. 425/89 (30 Aug. 1989).
[19] See Muratov (note 10); and Moses, R. L., *Freeing the Hostages: Reexamining US–Iranian Negotiations and the Soviet Union, 1979–1981* (University of Pittsburgh Press: Pittsburgh, Pa., 1995), chapter 5.
[20] '*Pravda* interviews L. I. Brezhnev', *Pravda*, 13 Jan. 1980.
[21] See Yermshina, O. and Zubkov, A., 'We were not preaching evil', *Sovetskiy Patriot*, 27 Dec. 1989, in JPRS-UMA-90-007, 23 Mar. 1990, pp. 123–25; Belitsky, S., 'Authors of USSR's Afghan war policy', *Report on the USSR*, 28 Apr. 1989; and Herspring, D. R., *The Soviet High Command, 1967–1989: Personalities and Politics* (Princeton University Press: Princeton, N.J., 1990), pp. 283, 293. On the validity of the Soviet media, see Axelrod, R. and Zimmerman, W., 'The Soviet press on Soviet foreign policy: a usually reliable source', *British Journal of Political Science*, vol. 11 (1981), pp. 183–200.
[22] See Gelman, H., *The Brezhnev Politburo and the Decline of Détente* (Cornell University Press: Ithaca, N.Y., 1983), p. 95.

his own persona. While careful to issue many pronouncements in the name of the Soviet Government, Gorbachev adopted a high profile from the outset of the crisis. He also established himself as the main spokesman for the USSR on the crisis at the expense of Foreign Minister Shevardnadze. Shevardnadze was having his own difficulties with fierce opposition both within and outside the Soviet Foreign Ministry and was gradually driven out of many of the deliberations over whether or not the USSR should support the US call for the use of force against Iraq. Instead, Gorbachev relied on a close circle of advisers, including Yevgeniy Primakov (who would later become his special envoy to Iraq and the Middle East during the crisis), and he himself took on much of the workload associated with the aftermath of the invasion of Baghdad.[23] Even the newly revitalized Soviet legislative bodies, elevated to policy-making status by Gorbachev, found themselves dispatched to the diplomatic sidelines. After promising to confer with the Supreme Soviet, for example, Shevardnadze was forced to pull back on that promise when Gorbachev declined to give him public support for that position.[24]

Coverage in the Soviet press makes it clear that while Gorbachev restricted the circle of decision making during the Persian Gulf crisis, he did not act overtly to restrain debate about the use of force. The substance of Moscow's response to the Iraqi invasion was seen by many in the USSR as a direct test of its policy of 'new thinking', and Gorbachev's efforts began to be both exalted and criticized in that connection.[25] Not surprisingly, chief among the topics involved was the Soviet attitude towards the use of force as proposed in the UN Security Council. Here, the criticism ranged the loudest, widest and deepest, covering the fear among some of 'another Afghanistan', anxiety that the USSR was ceding its superpower status to Washington and growing concern that diplomacy was being eschewed for the sake of efficiency.[26]

Although throughout the debates and discussions it was Gorbachev who dominated the decision making, as Leonid Brezhnev did in the immediate prelude to Afghanistan, there were elements in the Soviet military which resented and attempted to resist this development. The Soviet High Command was not always unified in this respect, nor were its concerns directed specifically at Gorbachev; concern was expressed in some quarters of the armed forces about

[23] See Shevardnadze, E., *The Future Belongs to Freedom* (Free Press: New York, 1991), pp. 101 ff. See also Crow, S., 'Primakov and the Soviet peace initiative', *Report on the USSR*, 1 Mar. 1991, pp. 14–17; and 'Interview with Primakov', *Time*, 4 Mar. 1991. Shevardnadze does not mention Primakov at all in his memoirs.

[24] See Keller, B., 'Shevardnadze to consult Parliament on Gulf involvement', *New York Times*, 16 Oct. 1990; and Crow, S., 'Legislative considerations and the Gulf crisis', *Report on the USSR*, 14 Dec. 1990, for a general overview. Crow's analysis throughout the crisis was especially perceptive.

[25] See, for example, the survey in Crow, S., 'The Gulf conflict and debate on Soviet "national" interests', *Report on the USSR*, 8 Feb. 1991.

[26] See the surveys in Freedman (note 12), pp. 10–12; and Crow, S., 'Moscow struggles with decision on UN force', *Report on the USSR*, 30 Nov. 1990.

the assertiveness of the Bush Administration and the potential escalation of hostilities, as well as the presence of Soviet advisers in Iraq.[27]

To a Soviet military already caught between its own efforts at internal modernization and the transformation urged and directed by Gorbachev, a Soviet President who might bypass military counsel concerning the use of force yet again was an immediate problem. With the unrest in the Baltic states seen as another potential threat to their role and interest in maintaining order in Soviet society and their access increasingly curtailed, some in the Soviet armed forces evidently believed that they had little choice but to protest—and loudly. As Iraqi intransigence grew and Gorbachev's own personal involvement increased, many in the Soviet military saw themselves pressed between the fear of a wider war that had to be prevented and the Soviet President's continued efforts to consolidate decision making. It does not seem unreasonable to speculate that the bloody crackdown in Lithuania in early January 1991, arriving when it did, was a warning shot across the diplomatic bow of the leading civilian decision maker in Moscow.[28] The prevailing view in the Soviet military had to be one of not wanting to get pushed into 'another Afghanistan'. However, as was the case with Afghanistan, the military did not find itself pulled into the circle of decision making concerned with the use of force.

The role of Islam

Soviet decision makers, like their Western counterparts, have generally paid little attention to Islam as a political force in international and regional affairs, but the cases of Afghanistan in 1979 and Iraq in 1990–91 were important exceptions to this tendency. This suggests that Russian foreign policy towards proliferation and multilateral peacekeeping in the Middle East and perhaps in the 'near abroad' will be deeply influenced in the future by the religious dynamic in politics. Chechnya may accentuate this tendency.

In the case of Soviet military intervention in December 1979, Islam was not seen in Moscow as a problem indigenous to Afghanistan so much as a cross-national factor that could be exploited by the new revolutionary regime in Iran. In the eyes of many Soviet analysts and commentators, the issue was not a national problem in Afghanistan or Iran but a regional concern. The Brezhnev Government appears to have accepted the view espoused by the Iranian Communist Party (Tudeh) leader Nurredin Kianuri that Ayatollah Khomeini and Islam could be strong allies of the Iranian left and the USSR, but Tehran's proclaimed support for the Islamic opposition in Afghanistan in the months pre-

---

[27] See Lee, G. and Atkinson, R., 'Soviet general warns of world war', *Washington Post*, 20 Sep. 1990, p. A14; and Fuller, G. E., 'Moscow and the Gulf War', *Foreign Affairs*, vol. 70, no. 3 (summer 1991), pp. 55–76.

[28] On the events in Lithuania, see Kaiser, R. G., *Why Gorbachev Happened: His Triumph and His Failure* (Simon & Schuster: New York, 1991), pp. 390–400; and Foye, S., 'Gorbachev denies responsibility for crackdown', *Report on the USSR*, 25 Jan. 1991.

ceding the intervention must have played a role in the Soviet decision.[29]
Throughout the summer of 1979, Soviet statements expressed Moscow's
growing dismay at Iran's overt assistance to anti-regime forces in Afghanistan.
As one commentary put it, 'the anti-Afghan and anti-Soviet position of some of
Iran's mass media cannot possibly be reconciled with official Iranian assur-
ances concerning non-interference in the affairs of neighbouring states and a
desire to strengthen traditional Soviet–Iranian friendship'.[30] A month before the
intervention, one prominent Soviet commentator saw clear similarities between
the Islamic-led revolution in Iran and the crumbling political situation in
Afghanistan.[31] That the Soviet military intervention ran into unexpected and
well-organized opposition that tended to be Islamic in character only indicates
that the Brezhnev Government underestimated the strength of Islam. It does not
mean that the policy makers in Moscow who decided to use force were
unaware of the part it might play in the region as a whole and in the USSR
itself. The available record indicates otherwise.

The Persian Gulf crisis some 10 years later is a more complex affair as far as
the role of Islam is concerned. Gorbachev and his spokesmen were not reluctant
to condemn efforts by Saddam Hussein that they saw as attempting to play on
Islamic symbols and sentiment. Instead, Gorbachev spoke regularly of 'activating the Arab factor', appealing to the interests of the Arab, as opposed to the
Muslim, political community in the Middle East.[32]

At the same time, however, Soviet policy makers were clearly concerned
about the response of Muslims in the USSR to Moscow's stance on the Persian
Gulf War.[33] Some of the republics in the southern tier of the USSR, which had
large Muslim populations, were critical of the international pressure being
placed on Iraq, and there were some small-scale demonstrations in these areas
condemning the US-led coalition against Iraq and offering support for Saddam
Hussein.[34] While the Muslim community was split on whom to support in the
conflict (apparently along generational lines, with many younger members vol-
unteering to fight for Baghdad), decision makers in Moscow, already alarmed
by the independence movements in the Baltic states and separatist sentiment in
the south, were surely concerned about the effect support from some Muslim
quarters might have on Soviet leverage and Gorbachev's mediation efforts.
Given his own extraordinary self-confidence, it is not clear how anxious
Gorbachev was about the Muslim factor. However, by focusing on the 'Arab
world', especially at critical stages in the crisis, like his predecessors in the

[29] See Moses (note 19), chapter 3. See also Cottam, R. W., 'US and Soviet responses to Islamic political militancy', in Keddie, N. R. and Gasiorowski, M. J., *Neither East Nor West: Iran, the Soviet Union,
and the United States* (Yale University Press: New Haven, Conn., 1990).

[30] See *Pravda*, 22 Aug. 1979.

[31] See Kondrashov, V., 'Whose interference?', *Izvestia*, 23 Nov. 1979.

[32] See, for example, Gorbachev's message to President Hosni Mubarak of Egypt in *Pravda*, 11 Aug.
1990; and Drozdiak, W., 'Gorbachev urges Arab initiative', *Washington Post*, 30 Oct. 1990, p. A15.

[33] See, for example, the coverage in *Novosti* during this period.

[34] See the discussion in Stein, G., 'Soviet Muslims divided on Gulf War', *Report on the USSR*, 22 Feb.
1991; and Fuller (note 27).

Kremlin 11 years earlier, he appears to have tried to minimize it without in any way attempting to ignore it.

The role of Washington

The final, and probably most important, similarity between the Afghanistan and Persian Gulf crises is the perceived role of the United States. In both instances, US administrations were seen by major elements in Moscow to be the central factor influencing the development of the crisis.

From the perspective of the Brezhnev Government in 1979, Washington's efforts were designed to recoup the loss of a strategic ally, Iran. As early as the spring of 1979, as anti-government activity against the Moscow-supported regime in Afghanistan increased so did Soviet protests concerning 'outside interference' by the United States, China and Pakistan, as well as Iran.[35] The majority of the blame was laid on Washington and Beijing, citing their 'incessant attempts to push Iran towards a more active anti-Afghan position'.[36] By the autumn, with the seizure of the US embassy in Tehran, attention shifted almost entirely to efforts by the United States, and Soviet commentary provided increasing detail about US military manœuvres in the Persian Gulf and Indian Ocean.[37] Up to late November 1979, Soviet press coverage of the possibility of US military intervention tended to focus on the hostage situation specifically. By early December, as the situation in Afghanistan began to unravel completely for the regime in Kabul, the potential for US military action was referred to as having a strategic character, and the implications of an increased arms buildup in the region were highlighted.[38]

At the least, Soviet decision makers must have been anxious about US military intervention in a state with which it shared a 1900-km border. It should be recalled that while Soviet commentary was stating that 'American naval, air and landing forces are massing in the Middle East directly adjacent to Iran and represent the largest concentration of US naval forces there since the Second World War', the leadership in Moscow was almost certainly examining the contingencies associated with its own military intervention in Afghanistan to aid the besieged government there.[39] The potential implications of US forces in

---

[35] See, for example, *TASS*, 18 Mar. 1979; *Pravda,* 19 Mar. 1979; and *Izvestia*, 20 Mar. 1979. A complete version of the *Pravda* commentary can be found in *CDSP*, vol. 31, no. 11. The analysis in *Pravda* was written by 'I. Aleksandrov', also widely assumed by a number of Western scholars to be representing the views of high-level Soviet officials. See Ploss, S., *Moscow and the Polish Crisis* (Westview Press: Boulder, Colo., 1986), p. 81.

[36] *Pravda*, 10 Apr. 1979. Moreover, this analysis was advanced by A. Petrov, another pseudonym for high-level officials.

[37] For example, TASS, 1 Dec. 1979.

[38] For one clear case, see *Pravda*, 9 Dec. 1979.

[39] See Petrov's commentary in *Pravda*, 5 Dec. 1979. Jiri Valenta, citing Soviet sources, has argued that 'the Soviets feared that the fall of a pro-Soviet regime in Afghanistan might have been manipulated by the United States and China and maintained that the United States was attempting to "drive" Afghanistan into the "notorious strategic arc" which the United States "has been holding for decades close to the USSR's southern borders"'. Valenta asserts that '[i]n addition to any defensive measures was the Soviet desire to be in a better position to exploit future opportunities in unstable Iran'. See his 'Soviet decisionmaking on

Iran might have given pause to those in the Brezhnev Government supporting more direct military assistance to the Afghan regime. Alternatively, the possibility might have also helped the arguments of those Soviet decision makers who favoured intervention in Afghanistan. If the final decision to invade Afghanistan was made sometime in early to mid-December 1979 (and available evidence now suggests it was), then a US military move against the revolutionary government in Iran before the actual implementation of Moscow's decision to invade might well have produced a superpower confrontation, at least in the minds of some Soviet officials.

The Brezhnev Government could not have been unaware of the wide range of difficulties a US military intervention in Iran might have posed for the pro-Soviet regime in Kabul and any efforts by Moscow to support it. One leading Soviet analyst, insisting on the similarity between the political situation in Iran and that in Afghanistan, argued that 'talk of alleged "Soviet interference" as a rule, has been used as a cover, or to prepare the way, for real—imperialist—interference'.[40] It seems probable that some in the Brezhnev Government might have speculated on the possibility of a successful US move into Iran as emboldening the Carter Administration to confront, in a more direct fashion, any Soviet movement into Afghanistan. Perceptions of US behaviour may not have directly and unilaterally caused Moscow to use force to support the Kabul regime, but Washington, in its effort to coerce Iran and in its attempts to warn the Brezhnev Government about intervening in Afghanistan,[41] might well have created the very situation it was trying to avoid.

Co-operation, rather than confrontation, was the general hallmark of the Persian Gulf crisis of 1990–91 as far as the Soviet–US relationship was concerned. However, as the possibility of the use of force grew, so did anxiety among Gorbachev and others, particularly conservative members of the Soviet hierarchy. The USSR was quick to jettison its long-standing (if frequently abrasive) relationship with Iraq,[42] yet the emphasis throughout the crisis, by Gorbachev especially, was on finding a peaceful formula through negotiation. This meant that military operations (first ground and then air) had to be postponed. Moscow's support for US-led efforts to deploy military force was largely tactical, stressing the defensive nature of the preliminary deployment to protect Saudi Arabia. Soviet Foreign Minister Shevardnadze's continued efforts to draw US and Soviet diplomacy closer privately acknowledged the probability that Washington would have to use force.[43] It was this approach that eventually undermined his relationship with Gorbachev and helped compel

---

Afghanistan, 1979', eds J. Valenta and W. Potter, *Soviet Decisionmaking for National Security* (Allen & Unwin: London: 1984), p. 223.

[40] See Kondrashov (note 31).

[41] Author's interviews with former senior officials in the Carter Administration, 1987–88. See also Bradsher (note 8), chapters 8 and 9.

[42] For the evolution of these ties, see Smolansky, O. M. and Smolansky, B. M., *The USSR and Iraq* (Duke University Press: Durham, N.C., 1991).

[43] See Woodward (note 13), pp. 333–35; and Kondrashov, S., 'And this time in Helsinki', *Izvestia*, 4 Sep. 1990.

Shevardnadze's resignation. As Ekedahl has pointed out, the USA and the USSR disagreed both privately and publicly on the importance attached to a political resolution of the conflict, and on the roles of mediation and multi-lateral enforcement of the UN Security Council resolutions.[44] Despite its four joint statements with Washington that preceded the inauguration of the air campaign on 15 January 1991, the Gorbachev Government clearly preferred working through the UN rather than exclusively through the USA.

Following the beginning of hostilities between the US-led Coalition and Iraq, Moscow's questions about US intentions and conduct were amplified. In a major address immediately following the start of the air assault, Gorbachev warned of the 'dangerous escalation' that might ensue and made clear reference to the fact that his last-minute suggestion to contact Saddam Hussein directly had been rebuffed by the Bush Administration. From that point on doubts about US objectives increased markedly, and Gorbachev pursued a more unilateralist course, enlisting Primakov as his special envoy and leaving Shevardnadze's replacement, Foreign Minister Alexander Bessmertnykh, to cope with US officials.[45]

In all, Gorbachev appears to have miscalculated his ability to manage events and stave off US-led efforts to wage war in the Middle East. Just as there were limits to confrontation during the cold war and what Soviet scholars under Gorbachev liked to call 'old thinking', there were clearly limits to co-operation between Moscow and Washington in the era of 'new thinking'.

Implications: lessons from Soviet interventions

The cases examined here have many dissimilarities and a number of important similarities. As such, they provide rich material from which to draw conclusions.[46] In spite of the collapse of the USSR, the implications of these conclusions also contain important lessons for policy makers concerned with the causes and consequences of the use of force and the potential for security co-operation.

While it cannot be asserted with certainty that there is a direct relationship between the size of the decision-making unit and the use of force, both cases point to the primary importance of individuals in situations where the use of force is being contemplated. In both Afghanistan and Iraq, Soviet decision makers (not unlike their counterparts in other political systems) ignored organizational boundaries and coalesced around a very small group. Policy makers currently interested in preventing the use of force might attempt to expand the arena of decision making, but Moscow's co-operation in 1990–91 evolved in an environment where one individual—Gorbachev—was predominant in the foreign policy process. In instances where force is contemplated, individuals matter. Private contacts, personal histories, friendships and other forms of

[44] See Ekedahl (note 12), pp. 94–99.
[45] For a further discussion see Crow, 'Primakov and the Soviet peace initiative' (note 23).
[46] See Popper, K., *The Logic of Scientific Discovery* (Basic Books: New York, 1959).

individual relationships are likely to be paramount in helping to get one's message across. Efforts in this direction that aim at security co-operation are unlikely to be sufficient, but they are probably necessary.

In both cases, the Soviet military was not an active player in the deliberations and was excluded from the process much of the time. Still, affecting the decisions of another government is crucial to influencing a state to co-operate; this means, at a minimum, knowing what concerns another government and creating a consensus there to move in that desired direction. It also means recognizing what occupies its attention. In the Afghanistan situation, concern about the stability of the regime in Kabul and developments in the country as a whole appear to have exacerbated what were seen by some in Moscow as US efforts to recoup its position in the region following the loss of Iran. The prevailing view in the Soviet military in the Persian Gulf crisis more than a decade later also exhibited this anxiety about actual US objectives and intentions. Actions by Washington cannot help but affect the calculations of any government in Moscow and may well alter the balance of forces there away from co-operation to confrontation and escalation.

If individuals matter more in decisions about the use of force, then involvement by the Soviet armed forces may have depended on the presence of a charismatic military leader. Neither the Soviet nor the Russian culture is known for this breed. In the absence of such an individual, militaries as organizations are likely to play a more limited role in decisions to use force.[47] Their role in co-operation is likely to be institutionally driven and to evolve over a long period of time.

Assessing the impact of a social and religious force—in this case, Islam—is much more difficult than evaluating the relative importance of individuals versus organizations. Islam was a factor in the two cases examined here, but the extent of its impact is still uncertain. Decision makers at high levels in Moscow were clearly concerned that Islam would limit Soviet flexibility to act, and this perception is critical in and of itself. The political role played by Islam is seen by many as growing in the 1990s, but its impact, as in 1979 and 1990–91, is bound to be diffuse. What these cases in fact illustrate in this regard is the gap between anxiety and reality. The impact of Islam appears to have been a consideration but not the primary one for policy makers in Moscow. (Whether it should have been is another question.) Its presence shows that crises involving decisions about the use of force are unlikely to be compartmentalized and restricted but instead cross-national and regional. If Islam continues to be taken into consideration in deciding whether or not to use force, it is likely to be seen as a disruptive and destabilizing factor. However, its popularity carries with it the potential for unification, order and stability. Throughout much of history the use of force to realize religious aims or to forestall them has rarely been successful. Washington will need to pay more attention to Moscow's worries about

[47] What is known about another crisis, the 1962 Cuban missile crisis, also supports this conclusion. See Garthoff, R., *Reflections on the Cuban Missile Crisis*, 2nd edn (Brookings Institution: Washington, DC, 1990).

Islam, and Gorbachev's successors will have to pay less attention to Islam as a disruptive movement compelling the employment of armed measures.

In the view of many decision makers in Moscow, the effort to expel Iraq from Kuwait shows that US unilateralism is Washington's definition of co-operation.[48] Distrust of Washington was rampant during the Afghanistan crisis, and it reappeared at certain points (particularly in the period immediately preceding the beginning of the ground campaign) in the US-led effort against Iraq. Gorbachev himself expressed doubts about Washington's motivations.[49]

To combat Soviet distrust of the USA, and to prevent it from creating obstacles to future joint efforts, a number of analysts have spoken of the need to institutionalize co-operation between Washington and Moscow. In terms of building predictability and trust into the post-cold war relationship, the approach has merit.[50] However, the case studies presented here demonstrate that the patterns of decision making associated with military intervention and military co-operation are not easily separated. Efforts at institutionalizing security co-operation might supplant flexibility for the sake of predictability, while retaining some latitude for action appears to be the most comforting element for decision makers in an international crisis.[51] If the period after the end of the cold war is to be seen as one of rapid and unique transformation, predictability will not only be difficult to attain but is likely to be completely absent. The lessons concerning interventions that emerge from these two cases do not augur well for the development of sustained trust between Moscow and Washington if security concerns are to transcend the theoretical and confront the practical.

The most important conclusion about the use of force that emerges from these two cases—and the first taste of the post-cold war environment—concerns not the superpowers (former or otherwise) but their allies. In the cases studied here, the use of military force was contemplated and employed when former allies began to drift apart or acted in unexpected ways. If recent events in the former Yugoslavia and elsewhere are harbingers of problems in the post-cold war world, the next few years will provide much information about the limits of trust between Moscow and Washington, the potential for joint efforts in the realm of non-proliferation and multilateral peacekeeping, and the location of the fine line that joins and divides intervention and co-operation.

[48] See, for example, Kondrashov, S., 'Political observer's notes: desert carnage', *Izvestia*, 15 Feb. 1991; and the survey in Foye, S., 'The Gulf War and the Soviet defense debate', *Report on the USSR*, 15 Mar. 1991.

[49] See 'Transcript of Bush–Gorbachev news conference', *Washington Post,* 10 Sep. 1990, for one example.

[50] See, for example, Brement, M., *Reaching Out to Moscow: From Confrontation to Cooperation* (Praeger Publishers: New York, 1991).

[51] See Lebow, R. N., *Between Peace and War: The Nature of International Crisis* (Cornell University Press: Ithaca, N.Y., 1981).

IV. Declining Russian interest in the developing world

Likely difficulties and opportunities in those areas of potential Russian–US co-operation that show signs of being both immediate and potentially enduring can and must be identified. One of those areas is the developing world. There are indications that some form of security co-operation could replace the antagonisms of the cold war. Even under the leadership of Soviet President Mikhail Gorbachev and Foreign Minister Eduard Shevardnadze, Soviet interest and influence in the developing world was beginning to recede, as advisers and analysts in Moscow questioned the benefits of involvement there generally.[52] Russian Foreign Minister Kozyrev has argued that Russia has direct interests only in those areas of the developing world that are 'economically viable'.[53] While it may be difficult to separate practice from pronouncement, clearly Russian policy has continued and strengthened the trend of cutting subsidies and ending support for regimes and movements historically identified as being pro-Russian if there is no evident commercial return. (Cuba is the most obvious example.) The Yeltsin Government is now interested in working to maintain and enhance good commercial relations regardless of ideological orientation; to secure and extend reliable markets and sources of new materials; and to assist in the general effort to ease the transition in some states from existing political and social structures to a more democratic political order, thereby supporting long-term stability in commercial relations.[54]

However, problems exist. First, Russia has traditionally had a 'Northern' perspective and now has Northern political partners, but its economy is still more 'Southern' than Northern.[55] Consequently, Moscow not only may have less to offer potential partners but also risks being associated with nations and governments seen by the South as intrusive, dominant and even dictatorial in trade and resource issues. Russian flexibility and leverage might thereby be further circumscribed, and its willingness to co-operate in security matters (especially those broadly conceived to incorporate economic concerns) is likely to be reduced.

Second, while Russian capability to produce outcomes beneficial to its sputtering economy (thereby enhancing its own political and military security) might be augmented by co-operation with the West, co-operation usually features some measure of quid pro quo. As early as the Persian Gulf War, some foreign policy planners and decision makers in Moscow were aware of the dangers associated with co-operating with the West and feared being pulled

---

[52] See, for example, Sestanovich, S., 'Gorbachev's foreign policy: a diplomacy of decline', *Problems of Communism*, vol. 37 (Jan./Feb. 1988), pp. 1–15.

[53] See Checkel, 'Russian foreign policy: back to the future?' (note 1).

[54] This latter feature receives substantial attention in Lukin (note 3).

[55] On the North–South dichotomy, see Hansen, R. D., *Beyond the North–South Stalemate* (McGraw-Hill: New York, 1979), pp. 3–12.

into situations in which they were unwilling and ill-prepared to participate.[56] The same sort of anxiety has long been apparent concerning the spectre of overt US intervention in the former Yugoslavia.[57] This difference in attitude also reflects the fact that elements in Moscow believe that Russia has a stake in the fortunes and future of Serbia.

If economic relations are central to the Yeltsin Government, then bilateral or multilateral co-operation should focus on ensuring non-encroachment on commercial spheres of influence, non-interference in the supply, extraction and transport of raw materials, and managing the political environment in such a way that stable exchange and price structures are guaranteed. Co-ordination between long-time allies in this area is difficult;[58] co-operating with Moscow in this context will surely be sluggish and troublesome. Given its plummeting involvement and interest in its former allies in the developing world, Russia's reduced capability places significant restraints on its willingness to press for co-operation or advantage, even if elements in Russia or the developing world might wish otherwise. It is likely that in the developing world, where those commitments are less clear-cut and where Russian capability is waning, Moscow's interest in directly and forcefully assisting to create and maintain a stable order will decrease.

A major prerequisite for US–Russian security co-operation is therefore the construction of incentives which transform commitment to co-operation. Creating the context for co-operation means reducing uncertainty and compelling engagement in a process which, by itself, might confer a degree of predictability on present and future political relations. Therein lies the dilemma. A convergence of US and Russian interests (as well as those of Western Europe and Japan) rests on the mutual recognition that the reduction of unpredictability is necessary. In the post-cold war era, unpredictability and uncertainty are prevalent, but two problems in particular are of such major consequence that they alone might compel convergence towards a general policy of security co-operation: the problem of extended proliferation and the possibilities of multilateral peacekeeping.

V. The perils of proliferation

Proliferation problems have received much attention recently, exacerbated as they have been not only by the spread of advanced technologies but also by the

---

[56] Author's conversation with Alexey Arbatov. See also Golan, G., 'The test of new thinking: the Soviet Union and the Gulf Crisis', eds G. Breslauer *et al.*, *Beyond the Cold War: Conflict and Co-operation in the Third World* (Institute of International Studies: Berkeley, Calif., 1991).

[57] For indications, see Checkel, 'Russian foreign policy: back to the future?' (note 1); and Dobbs, M., 'Russians might join UN police in Bosnia once peace is won', *International Herald Tribune*, 25 Feb. 1993, p. 1.

[58] Cooper, R. N. *et al.*, *Can Nations Agree? Issues in International Economic Cooperation* (Brookings Institution: Washington, DC, 1989).

collapse of the Soviet Union.[59] Both the former Soviet nuclear stockpile and the Soviet conventional arsenal have elicited concern in the West. The concern in Moscow over the former appears to have been driven primarily by the potential threat from other former republics and co-operation between Russia and the USA in nuclear arms control is generally good. However, in the conventional realm both the ability and willingness to export conventional arms from sub-machine guns to submarines has been marked. As Deputy Premier Georgiy Khizha put it in September 1992, 'I think that every export opportunity must be tapped. There is no need to portray us as saintly paupers. The whole world trades in arms'.[60]

Part of the motivation in the conventional realm is certainly economic, but it is probably not entirely that. (Whatever financial return exists is likely to be used to service debt rather than to meet short-term liquidity needs.) In any event, in a disorganized decision-making environment, centralized direction or uniform motives should not be ascribed to political actions. More complex forces—from former communists to private, local entrepreneurs with ties to the military—are bound to be at work in Moscow, and their presence and activity make the task of finding common ground for co-operation all the more diffi-cult.[61]

Internal threats to the Russian state will be the commanding imperative for security co-operation sponsored or shaped by Washington. What concerns Rus-sian decision makers in the realm of conventional proliferation is not only culti-vating useful commercial ties, such as with China,[62] but staving off the growing political interference in Russian affairs by other adjoining nations, such as Iran. With the short-term focus of Russian policy being on the near abroad, countries such as China matter in terms of their effect on the CIS domestic environment. Put differently, to foreign policy planners in Moscow what is strategic is that which is local. An Iranian leadership confronted by Russian intransigence and inadvertently emboldened by Washington to proliferate in both the nuclear and non-nuclear realms, and possibly advanced conventional, proliferation is likely to be more willing to try to influence Central Asian Muslims, endangering the lives and interests of Russian minorities residing there. Russian minority popu-

[59] For the former, see Simpson, J. and Howlett, D., 'Nuclear non-proliferation: the way forward', *Sur-vival*, vol. 33, no. 6 (Nov./Dec. 1991); Matthews, R., 'The neutrals as gunrunners', *Orbis*, vol. 35, no. 1 (winter 1991); and Rubin, U., 'Ballistic missile proliferation: how much does it matter?', *Orbis*, vol. 35, no. 1 (winter 1991). For the latter see Campbell, K. M. *et al.*, *Soviet Nuclear Fission: Control of the Nuclear Arsenal in a Disintegrating Soviet Union*, Center for Science and International Affairs Studies in International Security, no. 1 (Harvard University Center for Science and International Affairs: Cambridge, Mass., Nov. 1991); and Hopf, T., 'Managing Soviet disintegration: a demand for behavioral regimes', *International Security*, vol. 17, no. 1 (summer 1992), pp. 50–59.

[60] See Lilley, J., 'Russian handicap: Moscow looks East but the picture is bleak', *Far Eastern Eco-nomic Review*, vol. 155, no. 47 (26 Nov. 1993), pp. 24–26; and Vatikiotis, M. and Cheung, T. M., 'Bear-ing arms: Russia poised to sell weapons in ASEAN', *Far Eastern Economic Review*, vol. 155, nos 51–52 (24–31 Dec. 1992), p. 20.

[61] See Dobbs and Coll (note 1). Compare Bogert, C. and Selly, R., 'Arms makers, yes: arms merchants, no', *Newsweek*, vol. 123, no. 10 (1 Mar. 1993), pp. 32–33.

[62] See *China Daily*, 20 Dec. and 21 Dec. 1992; and Kaye, L., 'Common interests', *Far Eastern Eco-nomic Review*, vol. 155, nos 51–52 (24–31 Dec. 1992), for accounts of Yeltsin's visit to China.

lations are now threatening to play into domestic politics in Moscow even more directly than economic considerations.[63]

Moscow's interest in responding to these challenges and taking advantage of opportunities unilaterally should concern Washington. Yeltsin and his advisers are bound to be anxious about those areas where massive proliferation of conventional and small arms threatens to flood into adjacent regions within the borders of the former USSR and directly threaten Russian minorities. If Moscow directly approaches Tehran and attempts to convince it to halt its attempts to acquire a nuclear military capability or to forestall its efforts to play a leading role in south-west Asia, it will probably be less effective and less important to Russia than an indirect effort to compel Beijing to help dispel similar Iranian aspirations. The same approach should also be taken to Russian policy towards India and Pakistan, where direct passivity on the part of Moscow might be supplanted by indirect activity only if the prevailing view in Russia sees a threat to internal stability to Russia in the near-term future.

It is not the proliferation of weapons that compels Russian foreign policy decision makers as much as the proliferation of cultural identities and ethnic loyalties. In this respect an added difficulty for foreign policy planners in Moscow—and for decision makers in Washington (as well as in Western Europe and Japan)—is not where the near abroad begins but where it ends. Clearly, one of the main areas of political battle is the shape of Russian policy towards a disintegrating Yugoslavia. Continued anxiety about the shape of the CIS is not limited to the political conditions in the post-Soviet republics but also embraces regions such as the Balkans, which are seen as harbouring lessons for the leaders of post-socialist states faced with a variety of clashing ethnic groups. Even in the period preceding Gorbachev's departure, Russian advisers and officials, with the wounds of Afghanistan providing the backdrop, were as wary of the origins of conflicts as of the arms that made them so difficult to manage and quell.[64] Yeltsin has expressed concern over ethnic claims in Russia for some time, as have Russian military planners over the danger of spillover from Yugoslavia, Romania and elsewhere.[65] Among analysts and advisers in Moscow, the 'outside' and 'inside' are blurred realms.

VI. The problems of peacekeeping

As with proliferation, the prospects for peacekeeping from the Russian perspective (if indeed such a thing can be said to exist beyond the political moment)

[63] According to Hopf (note 59), the following are the percentages of Russians residing in the former republics of the USSR: Azerbaijan 6%, Belarus 13%, Estonia 30%, Georgia 6%, Kazakhstan 38%, Kyrgyzstan 22%, Latvia 35%, Lithuania 9%, Moldova 13%, Tajikistan 7%, Turkmenistan 9%, Ukraine 22% and Uzbekistan 8%. For the compelling argument that it is internal politics in these regions that make ethnic issues so explosive, see Saroyan, M., 'The "Karabakh syndrome" and Azerbaijani politics', *Problems of Communism*, vol. 32 (Sep./Oct. 1990), pp. 14–39.

[64] Author's discussion with Alexey Arbatov. See also Lukin (note 3), p. 66.

[65] See, for example, Lough, J. B. K., *The Russian Army Enters Politics* (Soviet Studies Research Centre, Royal Military Academy: Sandhurst, UK, July 1992).

tend to be seen in the light of domestic events, which are affected by international developments incrementally and indirectly. While short-term domestic and commercial considerations dominate the foreign policy discourse in Moscow, they do not always necessarily dictate. Even a relative hard-liner such as Lukin admits that Russian interests in the international realm are important in and of themselves.[66] Prevailing Russian attitudes on the role and importance of international peacekeeping are ambivalent. Russia is willing to contribute men (although not money) to such missions outside the former Soviet Union but is wary of setting precedents even (or especially) in the former Yugoslavia, and it seeks to maintain its latitude to intervene unilaterally within the CIS.[67]

Given the relative lack of central control of non-nuclear military material and the fact that this material has frequently been shipped abroad for commercial purposes (in part to maintain and enhance market share), Russian interest in international peacekeeping as an aspect of security co-operation with the United States must be greater than Russian concern about proliferation. When Lukin speaks of 'a new encirclement of Russia', he is less worried about the number and type of cartridges that real and potential adversaries carry than the conflicts in the surrounding areas of Russia. These conflicts have the potential to spread and, even if they do not, serve to diminish Russian flexibility to cope with a variety of other problems—internal and economic—on the post-Soviet political agenda.

Ethnic and national conflicts further from Moscow than its immediate periphery concern Yeltsin and his advisers primarily in so far as they can be used as domestic cudgels in the political struggles in Moscow. At the same time, Foreign Minister Kozyrev and others in the Russian Foreign Ministry are sensitive to charges that they are not doing enough to restrain the United States and Western Europe from overt intervention in areas where ethnic issues are concerned, such as the former Yugoslavia.[68] Even the issue of the recognition of Macedonia has divided and diverted decision makers in Moscow.

It is difficult to envisage a situation in which Russian participation in peacekeeping operations in Somalia, for example, would be evidence of Moscow's willingness to allow internationally sponsored peacekeeping operations to proceed, say, in South Ossetia or Moldova, where Russian minorities have been under direct siege for over a year.[69] Military protection of minorities, unilaterally implemented and enforced, has been the prevailing public pronouncement

---

[66] Lukin (note 3).

[67] This latter feature seems precisely what Lukin speaks of when he asks for US 'understanding and support in terms of [Russia's] complex geopolitical situation', Lukin (note 3), p. 73. For the evolution of the US and European responses to the Yugoslav crisis, see Weller, M., 'Current developments: the international response to the dissolution of the Socialist Federal Republic of Yugoslavia', *American Journal of International Law*, vol. 86, no. 3 (July 1992), pp. 569–607; Goodby, J. E., 'Peacekeeping in the new Europe', *Washington Quarterly*, vol. 15, no. 2 (spring 1992), pp. 153–71; and Newhouse, J., 'The diplomatic background: dodging the problem', *New Yorker*, 24 Aug. 1992, pp. 60–71.

[68] See Lepingwell (note 2); and Crow, S., 'Competing blueprints for Russian foreign policy', *RFE/RL Research Report*, vol. 1, no. 50 (18 Dec. 1992). Also see Hopf (note 59).

[69] For an early, well-informed account, see 'Moldova imposes emergency rule and orders disarming of militias', *New York Times*, 29 Mar. 1992, p. 11.

and rule, not the exception, in the post-USSR thus far.[70] If Goodby is correct in stating that 'a central lesson of Yugoslavia is [that] borders can be changed by force so long as the struggle is between successor states to a former union, and in such circumstances the international community will not react with force of any kind',[71] then many in Moscow are unlikely to be attracted to anything other than a unilateral military solution conceived and imposed by Moscow. If the US Administration is interested in Russian–US security co-operation, what should it do?

VII. A political strategy for Washington

Heretofore, the US approach (along with that of Western Europe and, to a lesser extent, Japan) has focused on economic assistance and ensuring the political stability of the Yeltsin Government.[72] If it is accepted that peacekeeping and proliferation are critical problems for the Clinton Administration in forging Russian–US security co-operation—and that peacekeeping is the most critical—then a policy for the middle distance must bring economic concerns in line with political objectives. A more general and effective political strategy should include the following components:

1. There should be a direct expression of the link between economic assistance and Russian peacekeeping procedures. Contributors to the Russian economic revival must have a direct advisory role in peacekeeping operations in the former USSR. This role will not extend down to the tactical level, but will none the less help shape decisions to deploy or not to deploy Russian peacekeeping forces and under what conditions. Failure to heed these advisory conclusions should result in a decreasing level of aid to Moscow and an increasing amount of assistance to the former republics.

2. Permanent members of the UN Security Council should provide it with the authority and the ability to mobilize a military force to serve under UN command for the purpose of enforcing Security Council resolutions.[73] A majority of these forces should replace current and future Russian troops in the former republics for a period of two to three years, thus bypassing existing difficulties

[70] For an overview, see Crow, S., 'The theory and practice of peacekeeping in the former USSR' and 'Russian peacekeeping: defense, diplomacy, or imperialism', *RFE/RL Research Report*, vol. 1, no. 37 (18 Sep. 1992). See also 'Russia: imperfect peace', *The Economist*, vol. 325, no. 7785 (14 Nov. 1992), pp. 57–58.

[71] Goodby (note 67), p. 165. Some leading military spokesmen in Moscow insist that the armed forces, not civil officials, are responsible for securing Russian minority rights and protection in the former republics, while Yeltsin and Kozyrev reportedly favour such action only under international sanction. See Checkel, 'Russian foreign policy: back to the future?' (note 1).

[72] For an interesting treatment, see Havrylyshyn, O. and Williamson, J., *From Soviet Disunion to Eastern Economic Community* , Policy Analyses in International Economics no. 35 (Institute for International Economics: Washington, DC , Oct. 1991).

[73] This is the main policy recommendation contained in Russett, B. and Sutterlin, J. S., 'The UN in a New World Order', *Foreign Affairs*, vol. 70, no. 2 (spring 1991).

in the Conference on Security and Co-operation in Europe (CSCE) structure.[74] Existing Security Council procedures for deployment would still apply.

3. Individuals and groups fight, but armaments enable them to fight wars. Conventional weaponry represents the most direct threat to peacekeeping missions in the former USSR as a whole. Impressive technical progress has been made in the destruction of nuclear and chemical weapon stockpiles; the demolition of conventional arms should be easier. Economic incentives should be established to reward ethnic groups and former republics for achieving set levels of conventional weapon disarmament, rather than waiting for the successful conclusion of negotiations before seeking such disarmament. Efforts to collect weapons on a local scale in the United States by offering direct payment have had some early success.

4. Before the collapse of the Soviet Union, working groups on Soviet–US co-operation in the developing world attempted to identify troublesome areas and to exploit potential opportunities for further collaboration. (A number of these groups were first established and directed by academics and private citizens.) These should be reinvigorated by regular Russian participation and staffed by Russian and US officials, and should meet on a regular basis with flexible agendas outside the CSCE or UN structures. For the first two years of their operation, these groups would be primarily concerned with peacekeeping; in the following two years, proliferation would be directly addressed by the majority of these groups. Judging from experience in the multilateral talks on the Middle East in 1993, working groups focused on various issues and topics appear to make more progress than one working group attempting to resolve many issues simultaneously.

The above are components of a political strategy for the middle distance; the strategy as a whole assumes that Russia is the centrepiece of security co-operation with the former USSR in the short and intermediate term. Long-term developments, such as the increasing military prominence of China and changes in the Pacific generally, may well compel a focus on the states of Central Asia.

Washington and Moscow should recognize that the security interests of both are embedded in the domestic political intercourse of the other. This is especially true of security co-operation related to peacekeeping in the former USSR. Russia cannot be detached from US security concerns simply because there is no longer a distinctly Soviet threat. In the recent past the attitudes of both the USA and Russia towards each other were frequently the pivot of political and electoral debate. In that respect, little has changed. If national and ethnic conflicts multiply and escalate in the former USSR and proliferation opportunities increase and expand, the US Administration will almost certainly be held responsible in the USA, rightly or wrongly. If the Yeltsin Government is unwilling to co-operate in a regular and systematic manner in coping with prob-

---

[74] See chapter 10 in this volume for a discussion of the respective roles of the UN and the CSCE in Eurasian peacekeeping operations.

lems arising in the near abroad, the US Administration will be beset by foreign crises.

John Herz noted nearly 20 years ago that progress in achieving stability in international relations would only be made 'when the danger of nuclear destruction and the interdependence of humans and their societies . . . will have made nations and their leaders aware that the destiny awaiting us is now common to all'.[75] Even with the collapse of the cold war structure that produced the fear of nuclear war, the threat of mutual catastrophe is still present. Amid the rubble of the former USSR, the common destiny of Russian–US security co-operation could very well be domestic political destruction. Both the US and Russian governments should view that which is abroad as all too near and all too possible.

VIII. Epilogue[76]

The recent period of US–Russian co-operation indicates that the next phase is likely to be as stormy. It does appear, at this point, that the containment of the Soviet Union has been replaced only by the containment of further erosion of co-operation with Russia in coping with regional conflict. While this view may be premature, three major conclusions emerge from the experience of 1994.

1. Political co-operation in the use of preventive diplomacy is exceptionally difficult when financial aid is untied and inadequate, impossible to attain without such assistance.

The main complaint by spokespersons for Russian foreign policy has been the lack of adequate economic aid to the government in Moscow. Russian analysts and officials have seen this situation as responsible for everything from surging inflation to the political rise of Zhirinovsky.[77] Agreeing on objectives and means, synchronizing political strategies for co-operation, and establishing institutional ties mean little without economic incentives. However, the best time for this use of financial leverage may have passed as the economic environment in Russia appears to be becoming more stable.[78] Grants, loans and a broad-based and wide-ranging programme of assistance can help keep it stable. Deteriorating economic conditions did not prevent the Russian leadership from assisting efforts by groups in the near abroad to reintegrate with Russia through violent action,[79] but a stable economy might. The ensured stability of the

---

[75] 'The territorial state revisited: reflections on the future of the nation-state', *The Nation-State and the Crisis of World Politics* (David McKay: New York, 1976), p. 252.

[76] Editor's note: The author contributed this epilogue towards the end of 1994. It is his assessment of the main problems for US–Russian security co-operation as these had appeared in the months following his last review of his manuscript. It does not, of course, take into account the developments in Chechnya in 1995.

[77] See *America and the Russian Future*, Occasional Paper no. 252 (Kennan Institute for Advanced Russian Studies: Washington, DC, Aug. 1993), for some early indications of these perceptions. See also Sciolino, E., 'Russia pledges to join NATO partnership', *New York Times*, 11 June 1994, p. 3.

[78] Bohlen, C., 'After economic and political chaos, Russians now face an eerie calm', *New York Times*, 22 Aug. 1994, pp. A1, A7.

[79] See Rashid, A., 'Proxy state: Russia calls the shots in Tajikistan', *Far Eastern Economic Review*, vol. 157, no. 37 (15 Sep. 1994), p. 17.

market in Russia may be one of the better means of ensuring the security of the newly independent states outside it trying to establish their own economies.

2. Co-operation in the 'far abroad' (dalnye zaruhezhe) is neither a substitute for nor an indication of co-operation in the near abroad.

Despite charges of US hegemony that seem to emanate daily from the Russian Foreign Ministry,[80] officials in Moscow have shown a disarming tendency to co-ordinate policies with Washington on issues such as arms control, non-proliferation, international crime and UN-sponsored intervention in Yugoslavia while insisting on a free hand in the states that abut Russia. Divorcing Russian behaviour in these two areas is not in the interest of the Clinton Administration for it is clearly read by Yeltsin and others as acquiescence in spheres of influence.[81] Spheres of influence may have worked in previous centuries and through much of the early part of the cold war as a way in which to keep peace between the superpowers, but they make no sense in a post-cold war world of permeable borders and a porous sovereignty. A resort to a strategy based on spheres of influence is read in Ankara,[82] Beijing, New Delhi and Tehran as appeasement of Moscow and Washington by the other.

3. Russian assertiveness in the near abroad threatens to undermine US efforts to co-operate and could very well undercut the Yeltsin Government if a direct military role in one of the adjoining states turns into a lengthy or more expansive operation.

Assisting Russia may mean helping to save Russian policy in the near abroad from itself. Policy makers in Moscow and Washington must recognize that the domestic agendas of both countries are inextricably linked to each other's foreign policy fortunes. Each separately and both combined are indications of the ability of both governments to direct and manage policy. Perhaps too much emphasis has been placed on economic recovery in Russia at the expense of countenancing Moscow's external policy in the near abroad, thinking that one is more important than the other. Continuing this approach and allowing Moscow to act assertively without penalty will bring disappointment and, in the event of a military quagmire, make future co-operation impossible. Rebuilding economies, as both the Yeltsin Government and the Clinton Administration are doing, is a necessary condition for political survival in a democracy where elections loom on the distant horizon, but it is not likely to be a sufficient one.

---

[80] This was the case even during the heyday of public co-ordination. See Erlanger, S., 'U.S. peacekeeping policy debate angers Russia', *New York Times*, 29 Aug. 1993, p. 5.

[81] See Smith, M., *Russia and the Far Abroad: Aspects of Foreign Policy* (Conflict Studies Research Centre, Royal Military Academy: Sandhurst, UK, May 1994). For the genesis of the term 'near abroad', see Safire, W., 'What's near Russia but outside it?', *International Herald Tribune*, 23 May 1994. See also Arbatov, A., 'Russia's foreign policy alternatives', *International Security*, vol. 18, no. 2 (fall 1993), pp. 5–43.

[82] Kamm, H., 'Turks fear Russian role in ex-states', *New York Times*, 19 June 1994, p. 4.

7. Post-independence decolonization: a framework for analysing Russia's relations with neighbouring states

John J. Maresca

I. The USSR as an imperial system

Nations and peoples are rarely prepared when they gain their independence, but they forge their way ahead anyway, despite the difficulties. And the difficulties in new nationhood are enormous, complex and long-lasting. As each colonial empire has broken up into independent nation-states, both the new nations and the mother country have been convulsed in political, economic and human problems, often accompanied by violence, terrorism or war. The breakup of the USSR, that vast empire which the Russian Bolsheviks inherited more or less intact from the tsars, has been accompanied by similar convulsions.

In thinking about these problems, it should be recognized that the USSR was, indeed, an empire. In fact, the USSR was studied as an imperial entity for many years before its breakup. In the early 1980s, for example, Helene Carrere d'Encausse's book *L'Empire Eclate*[1] foresaw the coming problems of maintaining so large and diverse an entity as a single state. By analysing the demography of the Soviet Union she concluded that it was leading inexorably towards a situation in which Russians would be a minority in a USSR dominated by ethnic Asians and Transcaucasians.

The Russian empire which was forged in the 18th and 19th centuries was as much an empire as any other such organization of the period. The imperial rule of the tsars was just as absolute, perhaps even more so, as the rule of the Habsburgs in Vienna or the British monarchs in London. The fact that a revolution intervened in Russia made little real difference after a brief period of nominal independence for some colonial areas. It may even be that the facade of socialism actually helped to prolong the existence of this particular empire by seemingly exempting it from Third World pressures to decolonize after World War II.

Certainly the USSR had several distinctive characteristics in comparison with other colonial empires. First, the fact that it was inherited by a revolutionary regime from a monarchical regime was distinctive, though not perhaps unique. This gave the new rulers in the Kremlin the possibility of creating new relationships with the colonies, a problem to which they gave considerable thought. As

---

[1] d'Encausse, H. C., *L'Empire Eclate* (Flammarion: Paris, 1979).

a result, at least the vocabulary used was different during the Soviet period. After the Bolsheviks had consolidated control over the whole of the imperial territory the colonial power became a hybrid of Russian nationality and Soviet/communist ideology. The ideology was always hollow—the words meant little—but it helped to cover Russia's otherwise rather traditional colonial rule.

Since the USSR was being run as a centrally planned and controlled economy, decisions made in Moscow often had a far-reaching and all but permanent effect on the economic life of the colonial areas. Their effects still dominate the life of these regions. If Moscow decided to develop an industry in one of these areas, it became central to the local economy; if not, the potential of that particular sector was simply never developed.

Perhaps the most significant and lasting effects arose from the fact that Russia's colonies were contiguous to the mother country. This tended to disguise the very existence of a colonial empire long after others had dissolved. More practically, it meant that many arrangements which normally would have been separated by geography ran together across the unmarked internal frontiers, without, of course, any thought being given to the problems this would cause if and when these colonial regions became independent. Everyone assumed that the USSR would last forever, and that these internal frontiers, which were not marked or in some cases even surveyed, therefore had no real significance.

This contiguity of the Soviet space also largely accounts for the ambiguous attitude of the United States towards this empire. Traditionally, the USA had been the champion of decolonization, from the Declaration of Independence, which was grounded in the notion that colonial peoples had the right to independence, to the Monroe Doctrine, to the Wilsonian precepts brought to bear in Europe after World War I. More recently, the United States favoured the emancipation of British, French, Portuguese and other colonial areas after World War II, but was hesitant about the USSR. This was due primarily to the fact that the contiguity of the area, coupled with the ideological cover of socialism, confused Americans and made them uncertain about the exact status of Russia's colonial areas. In turn this encouraged the belief that Soviet citizenship had legitimately superseded loyalty to national or ethnic origins.

However, the fact is that the Russian/Soviet Empire had much in common with the other great European empires. In all of these cases there was a migration of nationals of the mother country to the colonies. In the USSR this migration was strongly encouraged, in some cases forced, as a deliberate policy of Russification. In certain areas the local populations were deported, so that Russian emigration was facilitated. Joseph Stalin's brutal transferral of the indigenous Tatars from Crimea and the Chechens from Chechnya stand as just two of many examples.

As in the case of other empires, the political system of the mother country was extended to Russia's colonial areas. When the Bolsheviks took over their system was also imposed. Like English and French, Russian was established as the official language and the lingua franca of the élite. Similarly, local languages continued to be used, but with an inferior official and social status. There was lip service to local culture, and local personalities were developed as figure-heads, but the real power was always held by the Russian *nomenklatura*.

As happened elsewhere, there was an attempt to obscure local ethnicities and nationalities in a broader identity based on the identification of the mother country. 'Soviet citizen' meant much the same for the non-Russian peoples in the Russian/Soviet empire as being called French meant to a Black African. School-books used throughout the French system, even in Africa, referred to 'our ancestors from Gaul'. The African knew he was not really French, and the Uzbek or Azeri knew he could never be the same as a Russian in the USSR.

Of course, the mercantile nature of these empires demanded the subordination of the economies of the colonies to that of the mother country, and this was no different in the USSR. Most advanced industries were established in Russia itself, or in areas deemed to be Russified, while Central Asia and Azerbaijan were primarily sources of raw materials. Borderline peoples, like the Armenians or Georgians, sometimes benefited from this arrangement.

Finally, a strongly paternalistic attitude developed in each of the mother countries towards its colonies. Many Russians, like the British, French or Portuguese thought very simply that the colonial peoples under their control 'cannot exist without us'. In fact, most Russians believed and still believe that peoples under their tutelage were actually profiting from the benevolence of the metropole.

Despite all of these common characteristics, official Washington was rather silent about the Soviet empire, even while encouraging the emancipation of colonies belonging to America's closest friends. There was, and remains, much ignorance in the United States and the West in general about the real nature of the relationships between Russia and the areas it colonized.

Then, suddenly, the Russian/Soviet empire broke apart. This happened because of a political struggle for control in Moscow, rather than after a long period of hostility and revolt against the mother country, as was typical in the other colonial empires. The breakup was similar in some ways to the Bolshevik revolution, when control over many colonial areas was relinquished. While the circumstances were thus different from what had been the case with other empires, the West, in particular the United States, immediately recognized the new situation, established diplomatic relations, including embassies in each of the newly independent states, and set out to learn more about these areas, their histories and their politics, than was ever dreamed of before.

However, at the moment when these areas became 'independent', the period of anti-colonial struggle actually lay ahead. This was because, unlike previous examples of decolonization, in the case of the USSR the period of struggle and violence in search of independence *was going to happen after the nominal independence of the colonial areas, rather than before. In fact, it is going on now, and is likely to continue for many years.* Analyses and attitudes will have to take this into account, or there will be major errors of understanding and policy formation.

This unique reversal of the sequence of the key stages of decolonization is the key to understanding the current situation in the newly independent states formed from the former USSR. What is happening essentially is the kind of long period of struggle and adjustment which has occurred elsewhere *before* independence. If the evolution in the former USSR is understood in these terms, many phenomena are more easily comprehensible. It may also be easier for governments to anticipate what lies ahead, and to adjust policies accordingly.

II. The struggle to end colonial rule

What are the characteristics of the period of struggle to end colonial rule, whether that struggle takes place before or after nominal independence?

First, there is a difficult process of consolidation of the identity of the colonial people. The local language is elevated to official status; historians scramble to identify past local heroes; and the political system is altered. Everything connected with the mother country is rejected. This is a period of choosing and winnowing. Local leaders conflict with each other, form rivalries or alliances, and develop groups of followers which later become political parties. Often these local leaders are very unsavoury characters when they first appear.

Second, many of those who identify more closely with the mother country leave the colony and return to the metropole, as was the case in Algeria, Angola, Zimbabwe and elsewhere. In past experiences this happened before independence, but in the Russian case it is happening now, and will continue for years to come.

Third, there is sometimes irrational violence as this process unfolds. Extremists seek to hasten the withdrawal of the mother country through terrorism or guerrilla warfare. The nationals of the mother country are bitter about losing what, in their view, they have built. They may attempt a *putsch* to retain or regain power in the colony, as happened in Algeria, and as has happened in Trans-Dniester. The locals resist the prolongation or reimposition of the authority or even the symbols of authority of the mother country. They organize and gain political momentum. That happened, or is happening, in one way or another in Azerbaijan, India, Latvia and Pakistan.

Fourth, there is incredible, seemingly uncorrectable, economic chaos. The world saw this in West Africa, and is seeing it now in many of the newly independent states created from the former USSR. Gradually, the economies separate (more or less), but the mother country usually retains the principal economic interest in the colony. Subsequently, new relationships form, even if they are different only in name.

There are other characteristics which could be mentioned, but the point is clear: except for the fact that in the case of the USSR these phenomena are occurring *after* nominal independence, the phenomena themselves are common with those of other colonial breakups.

III. The outlook for the future

What does this suggest as to what is to be expected in the former USSR?

First, there is likely to be a long period of difficulty and convulsion, with all the characteristics of a struggle which takes place before independence, including the consolidation of local identities, development of political, groupings and local leaderships. There is likely to be fratricidal conflict in many areas, along with the continuing struggle against the old mother country.

Many of the ethnic Russians in these former colonies will eventually have to leave, and this will undoubtedly be disruptive, possibly violent in some cases. The example of Algeria is perhaps the closest in many ways to the case of these Russian minorities. Like the Russians, the Algerian *pieds-noirs* had no place to which to return. In their case the problem was that most of them were not from France originally, but had emigrated from Greece, Italy or Spain and had become French only in Algeria. In the case of the Russians many were simply uprooted by the command decisions of the Soviet system, and thus they, too, do not really have a place to which they can go back. The process of their gradual return will be deeply resented in Russia, as it was in France.

It will be tempting for Russia, and the Russians in these former colonial areas, to think of trying to stop or turn back the clock. There may be cases where this is attempted, as has happened in Trans-Dniester. Such efforts would be a mistake, for the tide is running in the other direction, and the results could be like those in Algeria. In addition, there are legal obligations among the states of the Commonwealth of Independent States (CIS), as well as in established international instruments such as the UN Charter and the 1975 Helsinki Final Act, which prohibit activities of this kind.

A new attempt at union between Russia and the states around its periphery will bring Russia back to the problems pointed out by Helene Carrere d'Encausse[2] (i.e., the inherent instability of a polity in which the power is held by an ethnic group which is increasingly in the minority). The choice for the Russians would then once again be whether to become a minority in a larger state or remain the majority in Russia itself.

Outsiders can have little effect on all this. Western countries are unlikely to be able to strengthen 'westernizing' tendencies by anything they can reasonably do. None the less, the West should certainly be trying to analyse, advise, caution and help where it can, if only to show its good intentions. The ability to analyse this type of situation in a detached way and to bring attention to such an analysis does not exist in Russia.

The actual situation in each of the newly independent states is different, and while overall generalizations have their utility, it is also essential to consider the individual characteristics in these new states.[3] The following brief examina-

[2] See note 1.
[3] See Fane, D., 'Moscow's nationalities problem: the collapse of empire and the challenge ahead', eds J. E. Goodby and B. Morel, SIPRI, *The Limited Partnership: Building a Russian–US Security Community* (Oxford University Press: Oxford, 1993).

tion of the situation in each newly independent state starts in the western part of the former USSR, with the countries which are geographically and culturally closest to the West, and works eastward towards states which are geographically, historically, ethnically and culturally much further away.

The Baltic states

The Baltic states Estonia, Latvia and Lithuania were never recognized by the United States, and a few other Western countries, as legitimately part of the Soviet Union, because of their established independence between the world wars, and their forced incorporation into the USSR as the result of a secret pact with Nazi Germany.[4] The Soviet Union carried out a deliberate policy of Russification in all three states, deporting many natives and installing many Russians, often with special privileges—as in the case of retired military personnel. This has left behind a residue of resentment towards the Russians who remain, which has been aggravated by Russia's use of the timing of withdrawal of its troops to gain concessions which favour the ethnic Russians left behind, especially the retired military officers.

The United States encouraged Russia to withdraw its forces as soon as possible, while at the same time urging the Baltic governments to adopt tolerant attitudes towards the Russians who remain, including easing citizenship requirements so that many Russians can qualify. These three states have been the most successful of the entire former Soviet Union in establishing separate economies, and it seems likely that they will continue to move away from Moscow and closer to the West. It also seems likely that many Russians will eventually opt to leave. None the less there are possibilities for rearguard actions by Russians in parts of Estonia or Latvia, which could draw in the Russian Army.

A word should be said about Kaliningrad, the area between Lithuania and Poland which surrounds the former German city of Königsberg. This is clearly a colonial area, having been acquired by conquest and simply annexed by the USSR after World War II. The only problem is that the area has been determinedly Russified, and is now essentially a basing area for the Russian Army, an enclave with no direct physical connection to Russia itself. Since there are very few native people left there, it is unlikely that a strong independence movement could ever emerge. None the less, the current situation is based on an historical foundation which is difficult to accept, and is potentially destabilizing for its region. For these reasons, consideration will eventually have to be given to the question of the future status of this area.

---

[4] The Molotov–Ribbentrop Pact accorded Nazi Germany's recognition to Moscow's incorporation of the three Baltic states and Moldavia into the Soviet Union.

Belarus

Belarus is ethnically, politically and culturally the closest of all the newly independent states to Russia. The Belorussians themselves have a hard time distinguishing between their own national identity and that of Russia, and many do not want to make such a distinction. Recent economic and political developments suggest that Belarus will become increasingly closely linked to Russia, and perhaps even join it in some fashion.

Ukraine

Ukraine was the heartland of the Slavs, and historically Russia grew out of this area, so that ethnically there is little difference between Ukrainians and Russians. However, several centuries of Polish and Lithuanian rule resulted in enough differences to give the Ukrainians a distinctive language and identity, stronger in the Roman Catholic western areas of the country, and weaker in the Orthodox eastern areas. Economically Ukraine, largely industrialized and with a population of more than 51 million, was so closely linked to Russia within the USSR that it is difficult for many Russians to imagine a separation. There are currently disputes between the two states over nuclear weapons, military forces, fuel supplies, debts and economic relations in general. The Ukrainians are also sharply divided between those who want closer relations with Moscow and those who reject any relationship. The election of President Leonid Kuchma by 52 per cent in July 1994, together with the dismal overall economic picture, suggests that the country will accommodate to closer economic relations with Russia.

Crimea is a special problem. Stalin deported the native Tatars, and the population is now largely Russian. Nikita Khrushchev irrationally gave the area to Ukraine as an anniversary gift from Russia. Since internal Soviet repression eased, some Tatars have begun to return. Meanwhile the ethnic Russians are demanding a relationship with Russia, and the Ukrainian Government is adamantly resisting. All of this creates a kind of colonial situation within a post-colonial situation, with a strong potential for conflict.

Moldova

Moldova's history is based on that of the ancient principality of Moldavia, which existed in the same area in the 14th century. This is another clearly colonial area, obtained first by the tsars in 1812 as a prize of war, lost and regained by the Soviet Union on the eve of World War II. The native people are ethnically Romanian, but there is a large Russian minority living on the left bank of the Dniester River, called the Trans-Dniester, and the 14th Russian Army remained stationed there under the free-wheeling General Alexander Lebed. He led in establishing, with tacit and at times open support from Moscow, a declared 'Trans-Dniester Republic', which favours reunification with Russia.

This was a classic rearguard military action of the type seen in several decolonization periods, similar in many ways to the action of French generals in Algeria.

Georgia

Georgia, colonized by Russia in the early 19th century, has a distinctive national identity and language, with its own alphabet, culture and ethnicity. None the less, since Georgian independence Russia has manipulated the factions and ethnic minorities in the country to make them all dependent on Russian intervention. This tactic, clearly directed from Moscow, succeeded in forcing (the word is not too strong) the Georgian Government under President Eduard Shevardnadze to accept membership in the CIS and the presence of Russian troops. There will be a long and confused struggle here as Georgia seeks to establish itself as a viable independent state.

Armenia

Armenia, the tiny remnant of the vast Armenian kingdoms of ancient times, was also seized by the tsars in the 19th century. Armenia's clear-cut ethnic, linguistic and cultural identity is very strong, but its support for the Armenian community in the Nagorno-Karabakh enclave in Azerbaijan has led it into a near-war situation, brought blockades by Azerbaijan and Turkey, and all but ruined the economy. The conflict, which began in 1988 and has continued for several years, is both an internal problem within Azerbaijan and an international issue. This has made Armenia heavily dependent on Russia for economic and military support, and the country's ability to separate from Russia is now in doubt. To what extent Moscow manipulated the war in order to gain this influence, and the level at which such a policy might have been approved in the Russian Government, is debatable, but the result was clear.

Azerbaijan

Azerbaijan was bought from the Persian Qajar Shahs as part of a peace settlement in the early 19th century. The Islamic Azeri people belong to a larger ethnic and religious group, the Azeri Turks, who also inhabit Iranian Azerbaijan and are very closely related to the Turks of Turkey. Azerbaijan, under the brief rule (1991–92) of popularly elected nationalist President Ebulfez Elcibey, succeeded in obtaining the withdrawal of all Russian forces (except for a radar station) and border troops. However, Elcibey was overthrown and replaced by former KGB General Gaidar Aliev, and since that time Russia has increased its pressure for the re-entry of its forces, using the Karabakh war as leverage.

Russia has been attempting to re-establish its control of the Azerbaijan–Iran frontier by bringing back its border guards. In addition, Russia clearly hopes to benefit from the vast oil reserves of Azerbaijan, and has forced the Azeris to grant it a share in the oil rights. Almost anything could happen here, from outright Russian military re-entry to a protracted and bloody struggle, ostensibly growing out of the war over Nagorno-Karabakh. Since it is clear that the Azeris do not want the Russians back, this is perhaps the most striking example of the kind of post-independence colonial struggle which is going on more subtly in virtually all of the newly independent countries.

Turkmenistan

The vast area of Central Asia to the east of the Caspian Sea was colonized by Russia in the 19th century, and was generally known by the single appellation Turkistan until the early part of this century. This was because, with the exception of the Tajiks, all the peoples of the area were essentially Turkic and nomadic, and more precise definition of their individual identities, particularly linked in some way to a specific territory, was difficult. It was only with the establishment of Soviet-imposed internal frontiers that many of the currently recognized ethnic identities became internationally known and accepted. These have now formed the basis for newly independent states, but in each of these areas the real sense of national identity linked to territory, which is normally the basis of statehood, is still in the process of formation.

Turkmenistan is a primarily desert area with a population of only 3.5 million people, among whom there are relatively few Russians. Turkmenistan holds considerable resources, especially natural gas, however, and it will certainly be under Russian pressure to draw closer to Moscow. The country is isolated and Islamic, with only Iran as an offsetting nearby influence. There seems little likelihood of conflict here, but a continuing dominant Russian role is probable.

Uzbekistan

Uzbekistan, with almost 20 million inhabitants, is the most populous state in central Asia, with potentially important mineral resources and agricultural production. Its fabled silk-route cities of Boukara, Khiva and Samarkand also suggest a potential for tourism. However, the state has problems: an environmental disaster caused by Soviet central planning's overproduction of cotton, a repressive Soviet-style regime, an explosive mix of different ethnic groups and an active political opposition. The likelihood here is of fratricidal struggle as rival groups compete for leadership, and as the national identity is consolidated.

Tajikistan

Tajikistan has been the scene of a full-scale civil war, partly an extension of the war in Afghanistan, just across the border. The same groups which are rivals in Afghanistan are also rivals in Tajikistan, which is the only new state formed from the former USSR that has ethnic ties to Iran, and whose language is based on Farsi. Ethnic Russians have largely fled from the fighting in an exodus which made a deep impression on Moscow's view of the plight of Russian minorities throughout the so-called 'near abroad'. Russian forces are present in a 'peacekeeping' role, but their real mission is to control the instability and to prevent it from spreading any further north. True independence seems impossible for Tajikistan in current circumstances.

Kyrgyzstan

Kyrgyzstan is the smallest and most remote of the Central Asian states. It has economic problems as well as smouldering rivalries among its ethnic groups. Yet it has come closer to real democracy than any other new country in the area, and achieved a certain stability and balance between Russian interests and independence.

Kazakhstan

Finally there is Kazakhstan, a gigantic country stretching from the edge of Europe west of the Ural Mountains, along the north coast of the Caspian Sea, across empty deserts to the mountainous frontier of China. The central demographic feature of Kazakhstan is that there are almost as many ethnic Russians living there as there are Kazakhs. The country has enormous potential wealth in the form of oil and gas reserves and minerals, but to be able to export these resources the Kazakhs must maintain good relations with Russia.

The government has been stable since independence because of the strong-willed leadership of President Nursultan Nazarbayev, but the unhappiness of the Russian minority is becoming more of an issue as the Kazakhs consolidate their sense of nationhood and confidence. At some point Russian sensitivities over the status of the ethnic Russian population, together with ambitions to control or share the exploitation of Kazakhstan's resources, are likely to clash with the growing sense of Kazakh nationhood.

IV. Russian intentions

In the current state of political turmoil in Moscow it is difficult for many people in the West to believe that there is a centrally orchestrated Russian plot to regain control of all these former Soviet Republics. Russia is like a force field which exercises influence in the surrounding areas in a variety of ways, whether or not this is a conscious objective of the Russian state, and many Westerners believe that what appears to be deliberate Russian assertiveness is really nothing more than the natural effect of this force field. However, since the beginning of 1994 the Russian Government in fact has been increasingly open about its intention—which Moscow sometimes calls its responsibility—to control these areas. This evolution has paralleled the political rise of figures like Vladimir Zhirinovsky who advocate a sharply more assertive foreign policy.

Many, perhaps most, Russians believe their country should and can regain its dominance, or indeed that it was never lost. This is a mistake. If Russia could not bring peace and prosperity to these areas in 200 years or more of well-organized, financed and determined activity, how can it be expected that Russia will be able to do so at a time when it needs to concentrate its attention on ensuring the economic survival of Russia itself, with its own internal ethnic problems.

Moreover, all the lessons of history seem to suggest the contrary. Every colonial power which has attempted to keep its colonies has been dragged into bloody, costly and politically destructive wars, and virtually all of them have failed, with the possible exception of the 1982 Falklands/Malvinas War. However, in that case there was no indigenous people with which to contend.

If this analogy is even partly correct, Russia now faces the same temptation which other mother countries have faced as their empires crumbled, but in Russia's case it is happening after the nominal independence of the former colonies. It would be better for Russia, the former colonies and the world if Russia chose another path: building constructive new relationships with these new states on the basis of an assumption of their independence, rather than attempts to cut back on that independence.

There are many people in Russia who understand this, do not want these colonial areas back again under Russian responsibility and believe Russia has enough problems of its own without them. However, these people do not appear to be in control of policy at the present time.

Russia has been: (*a*) focusing on the problems of the Russian minorities in ways which will guarantee that this is an emotional issue when and if a broad exodus begins; (*b*) trying to control the economies of all its former colonies by pressing them to accept such control through the CIS; (*c*) attempting to station its troops throughout the CIS; (*d*) seeking control over all the former external frontiers of the USSR with Russian border troops, rather than making an effort to demarcate new frontiers around Russia; and (*e*) trying to use a variety of levers to control energy resources throughout the CIS.

V. The response of the international community

Once again the attitude of the West, particularly that of the United States, has been ambiguous in response to these developments. While the West has interests in some of these former Soviet Republics—particularly the Baltic states, Ukraine, Moldova, the Transcaucasian countries and Kazakhstan—few Westerners would argue that these interests are 'vital'. The result is that there is a tendency to turn a blind eye towards these areas, to give Russia and the CIS the benefit of the doubt and to recognize that there is little the West can do to influence events, at least in the more remote regions.

It seems clear that the world has to expect a very long period of difficulty, during which Russia's efforts to deal with its problems will have to be viewed with patience. However, Russia should not be misled to think that attempts to recolonize the former USSR are acceptable to other countries. On the contrary, Western states, particularly the USA, should be pressing Russia to understand where its real interests lie.

Of course, Russia has major interests in the so-called 'near abroad'—Russian minorities, security and economic links. The rest of the world recognizes that, but there are limits to what will be viewed as acceptable ways to pursue and protect those interests. Those limits are the norms established for the rest of the world in relation to neighbouring states. There cannot be a separate set of standards for Russia. The international community has a responsibility to make this clear to Moscow. Indeed, The Tashkent Treaty on Collective Security of 15 May 1992,[5] which established a new mutual security relationship among most of the newly independent states, requires UN involvement in certain situations.

It will be better for Russia to involve the international community in taking responsibility for the problems in the newly independent areas, even if that means taking a lesser role. The peculiar sensitivities of the post-colonial relationship make this even more important. Russia is not just a powerful and influential neighbour; it is the former colonial master. This means it must behave towards these new states with exceptional restraint, if they and the rest of the world are not to accuse Moscow of aggressive neo-imperialism. In any case, Russia will be stronger if it is not carrying this responsibility by itself.

Of course, a prominent direct US role in these areas would also not be a good idea. Such a role would provoke a hostile response among many Russians, and could therefore be counter-productive. The United States also has neither the resources nor the motivation to carry out by itself the types of activities which will be needed to stabilize the newly independent states.

The most promising possibility for accommodating Russia's need to protect its interests in these areas, while avoiding the appearance of neo-imperialism, is through the involvement of international organizations. Russia can continue to play a significant and useful role in the development of international approaches, and in the activities of international organizations in the area. If these activities are under the control and responsibility of the international community, the inference that Russia is seeking to re-establish its colonial dominance will not be there, or at least will be muted. The United States can contribute by encouraging Russia in this direction, by energizing international organizations to become involved and by promoting agreed arrangements.

---

[5] The Tashkent Document is reproduced in the *SIPRI Yearbook 1993: World Armaments and Disarmament* (Oxford University Press: Oxford, 1993), pp. 671–77.

Thus far efforts to develop multilateral approaches involving subordinate Russian participation have not been particularly successful, either in the Conference on Security and Co-operation in Europe (CSCE) or the United Nations.[6] This has been owing partly to: (*a*) the reluctance of the international community to get involved in certain areas, such as Tajikistan, which are particularly remote and dangerous; (*b*) Russian inflexibility and unwillingness to cede the leadership in these areas to any entity other than the Russian-led CIS; and (*c*) the extraordinary difficulty of the problems themselves and the stubborn opposition of the factions involved in them to any compromise.

These multilateral efforts have focused on the development of peacekeeping forces which might be under international control but include large Russian contingents. The traditional UN rule against including forces from neighbouring countries in peacekeeping operations has made it difficult to conceive of UN-sponsored Russian or CIS operations in Azerbaijan or Georgia. The Russian military's understanding of peacekeeping is also so different from that in the West that it has been difficult to reach agreement on how a hybrid international/Russian operation might work, or what its objectives would be. The Russian approach concentrates on suppression of violence, while the established international approach is to avoid violence in order to lay the basis for mediation of a political solution.

However, more than just peacekeeping is needed; the former Soviet areas will need a variety of preventive diplomacy and reconciliation efforts for years to come to help to ensure stability. There are already a number of preventive diplomacy missions deployed in the former USSR, either by the CSCE or the UN. Perhaps the CSCE missions, with their tailored mandates, are the most creative in this field. In Estonia and Latvia, for example, CSCE missions are helping to ease the confrontations between members of the local ethnic group and the Russians living in these countries.

A concentrated effort should be made to bring Russia's activities under the control and responsibility of one or the other of these international organizations. This will require much greater attention, particularly by the United States, to the situations in these countries. Unless the international community shows that it is seriously interested in helping to head off or resolve their problems, Russia will be unwilling—even politically unable—to leave them alone. These areas are simply too important for Russia.

If there is a serious, sustained attempt to absorb Russian interest in a true international effort, there can be hope that these new countries will succeed in establishing their new nationhood on a firm basis. That will be better for them, for Russia and for the world.

---

[6] Editor's note: See chapter 10 in this volume for a discussion of the CSCE and the Budapest decisions of 6 Dec. 1994.

8. Intervention in the 'new world order': US use of force in Latin America and the Persian Gulf

William W. Newmann

I. Introduction[1]

The selections in this volume take their cue from a single premise—that the end of the cold war marks a new era in the international balance of power. The changes in the former Soviet Union have had far-reaching consequences throughout the world that will reverberate into the next century. This chapter examines the effect of these changes in the USSR and the end of the cold war on US decision making for military intervention. It focuses on the introduction of military forces for the specific intention of initiating combat or establishing a defensive posture in a combat area.[2] The interventions considered are those in Latin America and the Persian Gulf.

The USA has already undertaken two post-cold war military interventions—one in Panama during December 1989 and the second in the Persian Gulf during 1990–91. A comparison of the decision-making processes leading to these post-cold war interventions with those that led to cold war era interventions can reveal a great deal about how Washington views its role, and its relationship with Moscow, in the 'new world order'. The cold war interventions used for comparison are the invasion of Grenada in 1983 and the Persian Gulf reflagging of Kuwaiti tankers in 1987 and 1988. Using only cases from the Reagan/Bush years adds a control to the comparison. If one assumes that the approaches of Ronald Reagan and George Bush to foreign affairs were somewhat similar, the changes in intervention policy can be seen as responses to the end of the cold war and not simply the result of a change in administration.[3]

This chapter explores three main questions:

---

[1] Secondary journalistic sources were used in the collection of some data on recent events. Individual articles are cited only as necessary. These sources are: *New York Times, Washington Post, Los Angeles Times* and *Wall Street Journal.*

[2] Limiting the study in such a way excludes the Multinational Force in Lebanon. The deployment of peacekeeping forces entails a significantly different type of decision from one that dispatches troops into combat environments. One of the criticisms of the Reagan Administration's ill-fated deployment of troops in Lebanon was that peacekeeping forces were deployed into a situation not yet restrained by cease-fire rules of engagement. This limitation also precludes discussion of peacekeeping-type operations in Bosnia and Somalia. These situations were still developing as this chapter went to press.

[3] Given the limited space allowed, this is a useful assumption. The foreign policy record also exhibits a strong measure of consistency from the second term of the Reagan Administration through the Bush Administration.

1. Did the end of the cold war really change the way US decision makers (at least those in the upper levels of the Reagan and Bush administrations) perceived the strategic framework that guided their decisions on intervention?

2. If so, how did that framework change?

3. What might be the implications of that change for future US interventions?

An analysis of the strategic framework that guided US decision making in each case study illustrates the decision makers' perceptions of the threats to US national interests that prompted the intervention. These perceptions have been called the 'shared images' of the foreign policy élite or elements of an 'operational code' that define the way foreign policy decision makers view the world.[4] For the purposes of this study, the relevant 'images' are those perceptions of the USSR that shaped US policies towards security threats and possible reactions to those threats.

The invasion of Grenada was a classic battle of the cold war in the Western hemisphere. Although at first glance the intervention in Panama seems to be 'business as usual' for the USA in Central America, it was not the typical US intervention in Latin America (i.e., an action taken against a left-wing regime or rebel group). In the cases of the Kuwaiti tanker reflagging and the war against Iraq, the end of the cold war rearranged the entire strategic framework of US decision makers. A comparison of the strategic framework guiding decision making for the two regions suggests that, while the end of the cold war ushered in a new era of co-operation in US–Soviet/Russian relations in the Persian Gulf and the Middle East, in Central America the USA may still act unilaterally (although with a new set of justifications for that intervention).

The Clinton Administration's actions in the Haitian situation suggest that the USA will try to refrain from acting unilaterally, even in the Caribbean. The Clinton rhetoric and intervention timetable were clear attempts to cast the US action in the multilateral mould of the Persian Gulf War, as opposed to the more traditional unilateral model of US intervention in Latin America that was most recently illustrated by the Bush Administration's invasion of Panama.

The following analysis suggests a number of things about the future of US–Russian relations with respect to the potential for US military intervention. These are discussed in the concluding section of the chapter. However, it is important to point out that US–Russian relations will most likely be the post-cold war equivalent of US–Soviet relations. The USA recognized Russia as the successor state to the USSR—supporting its bid to take the USSR's United Nations Security Council seat, making the US Ambassador to the USSR the new Ambassador to Russia and working steadfastly to bring all nuclear

---

[4] The term 'shared images' is used in Halperin, M., *Bureaucratic Politics and Foreign Policy* (Brookings Institution: Washington, DC, 1974), pp. 11–16. The idea of an 'operational code' that frames the beliefs of decision makers about the nature of the world is best outlined in George, A., 'The operational code: a neglected approach to the study of political leaders and decision-making', *International Studies Quarterly*, vol. 13, no. 2 (June 1969), pp. 190–222. The concept was first explored in Leites, N., *A Study of Bolshevism* (Free Press: Glencoe, Ill., 1953).

weapons on the territory of the old USSR under Moscow's control.[5] The implications of changes in the US strategic framework will therefore shape US policy towards Russia, and it will be Russia that the USA looks to for partnership or feels compelled to reassure the next time a US President contemplates the use of US forces abroad.

While the cold war years were marked by decades of conflict and competition, in the years to come the USA and Russia may often find themselves on the same side of an issue, as the USA and USSR did during the 1990–91 conflict with Iraq. However, this 'alliance' may become more and more difficult to achieve diplomatically as independent Russia grows more confident and assertive in pursuing its own foreign policy goals. Even if this is indeed a new world order, some aspects of the old world order may last into the next century. US policy towards Latin America may hold to some of the old patterns of unilateral US actions (although the rationale for these actions will most likely be the war against the drug trade and not the battle against international communism). These actions in Latin America, however, are unlikely to damage growing US–Russian co-operation. In this sense, the post-cold war world seems one in which the USA views Russia as a partner in the fight against instability and aggression in many regions.

In fact, recent events concerning US intervention in Haiti and Russian intervention in Georgia suggest that Russia and the USA may need each other's co-operation to deal with regional threats close to their own borders. Both the Russian 'peacekeeping' operation in Georgia and the US intervention in Haiti have been followed with charges of 'imperialism' or 'unilateralism' from many quarters of the international community. Russia and the USA have co-operated to use the UN Security Council to legitimize their actual or potential foreign policy activities, to deflect criticism and to enable both nations to police their traditional spheres of influence. The conclusion of this chapter addresses these issues in the context of the events of the summer and autumn of 1994.

II. Strategic framework of decision making

For the purposes of this chapter, the term 'strategic framework' refers to the decision makers' general perceptions of the nature of international conflict and US interests in any given international situation. An analysis of the way in which decision makers perceive the necessity for military intervention will reveal their notions of the strategic framework. The most important question remains how the perceived strategic framework within which US decision makers operated changed following the sweeping changes in the USSR and Eastern Europe, and in what ways the new framework might shape the direction of US–Russian relations. In this chapter the decisions for intervention in Latin

---

[5] On US relations with Russia after the fall of the USSR and the birth of the CIS see Newmann, W. W., 'History accelerates: the diplomacy of co-operation and fragmentation', eds J. E. Goodby and B. Morel, SIPRI, *The Limited Partnership: Building a Russian–US Security Community* (Oxford University Press: Oxford, 1993).

America and the Persian Gulf during the 1980s provide a useful comparison. Two sets of decisions are illustrated and compared: (*a*) the Grenada intervention of 1983 (cold war) and the Panama intervention of 1989 (post-cold war); and (*b*) the reflagging of Kuwaiti tankers in 1987–88 (cold war) and the Persian Gulf War of 1990–91 (post-cold war).

III. Latin America

Grenada

The US invasion of Grenada occurred at the height of the renewed cold war of the early 1980s—six weeks after the USSR shot down the Korean Air Lines 007 passenger flight and only a month before the USSR walked out of arms control negotiations in Geneva. In the tradition of US actions in Chile, the Dominican Republic, Guatemala and Nicaragua, the intervention was a US move in its cold war chess game with the USSR in Latin America.

On 13 March 1979, Maurice Bishop led the leftist New Jewel Movement (NJM) to power on the island nation of Grenada.[6] Only five years after gaining independence from the UK on 7 February 1974, an authoritarian right-wing government had been overthrown by what would become an authoritarian Marxist regime under the leadership of new Prime Minister Bishop. Factional infighting between moderate elements of the NJM Government led by Bishop and a more extremist, Leninist group led by Deputy Prime Minister Bernard Coard erupted into the violent events of October 1983.

Since coming to power, the Reagan Administration had been instinctively suspicious of Soviet and Cuban ties to Grenada. In March 1983, President Reagan had spoken out against Cuban influence in Grenada and the construction of a large airstrip at Point Salines which was long enough to accommodate military aircraft.[7]

It has been reported that the Central Intelligence Agency (CIA) was plotting Bishop's overthrow but cancelled such planning when the information leaked to Congress.[8] Concern over the use of Grenada as a staging base for Soviet and Cuban expansion and regional destabilization deepened within the Reagan Administration as the Government in Grenada deteriorated during the autumn of 1983.

On 13 October 1983, Coard and Armed Forces Chief of Staff General Hudson Austin arrested Bishop in a coup attempt. The USA had already discussed the situation in Grenada at the regular morning meeting of the National

[6] For an analysis of the immediate pre-invasion history of Grenada see Glass, C., 'The setting', ed. P. M. Dunn and B. Watson, *American Intervention in Grenada* (Westview Press: Boulder, Colo., 1985).
[7] Cypher, D., 'Grenada: indications, warning and the US response', eds Dunn and Watson (note 6), p. 48.
[8] 'Britain's Grenada shut-out', *The Economist*, 10 Mar. 1984. For a sense of the Reagan Administration's assessment of the Bishop regime see the memoirs of Reagan NSC staffer Menges, C., *Inside the National Security Council* (Simon & Schuster: New York, 1988), pp. 43–76.

Security Council (NSC) staff.[9] The following day, as word of Bishop's arrest reached the USA, the State Department began to assess its plans for evacuating US citizens attending St Georges Medical School on Grenada, while the Joint Chiefs of Staff (JCS) were instructed to examine the Pentagon plans for a non-combatant evacuation of US citizens from the island.[10]

As the political situation deteriorated, fear for the safety of US citizens soon became an excuse for pursuing the larger cold war foreign policy goals of the Reagan Administration. The fate of potential hostages was overshadowed by the potential opportunity to rid the Caribbean of a Soviet–Cuban client.[11] Debate within the bureaucracy was overtaken by events on 19 October 1983. Prime Minister Bishop was released from jail during a mass rally by thousands of his supporters. Later that day he was recaptured by General Austin's forces and executed; Austin added to Washington's concern by announcing a 24-hour shoot-on-sight curfew.[12]

In Washington, on the morning of 22 October 1983, the Administration's Special Situations Group (SSG) met to discuss the intervention. At the meeting US objectives were outlined: (a) to save US citizens; (b) to restore democracy to Grenada; and (c) to remove Cuban influence.[13]

It is interesting to note that the first objective listed is saving the lives of the students at St Georges Medical school.[14] The most vivid images of the operation were of grateful students kissing the tarmac after stepping off the military aircraft that had returned them safely to the USA. The SSG included veterans of the Reagan presidential campaign; they were acutely aware that President Jimmy Carter's inability to free US hostages in Iran was a major factor in Reagan's victory. This fear of another hostage crisis greatly influenced the decision. There was much discussion about how similar General Austin and his

[9] Menges (note 8), p. 49.

[10] *Full Committee Hearing on the Lessons Learned as a Result of the US Military Operations in Grenada*, Hearing before the Committee on Armed Services, US House of Representatives, 98th Congress (US Government Printing Office: Washington, DC, 24 Jan. 1984), pp. 10, 46.

[11] Latin American specialists from both the State Department and the NSC staff favoured using the crisis as an opportunity to capture Grenada itself, overthrow the Marxist Government and rid the island of Soviet and Cuban influence. Senior Pentagon decision makers, including Secretary of Defense Caspar Weinberger and Chairman of the Joint Chiefs General John Vessey, urged a more cautious approach. See Gelb, L., 'Shultz with tough line, is now key voice in crisis', *New York Times*, 7 Nov. 1983, p. 1; Menges (note 8), pp. 51–52; and Brands, H. W., 'Decisions on American armed intervention: Lebanon, Dominican Republic and Grenada', *Political Science Quarterly*, vol. 102, no. 4 (winter 1987/88), p. 617.

[12] Schoenhals, K. and Melanson, R., *Revolution and Intervention in Grenada* (Westview Press: Boulder, Colo., 1985), p. 75–78; Cypher (note 7), p. 49.

[13] The SSG, chaired by Vice-President George Bush, was the NSC-level crisis management forum during the early years of the Reagan Administration. During the Grenada crisis it included Bush, Weinberger, Secretary of State George Shultz, General Vessey, Attorney General Edwin Meese, acting CIA Director John McMahon, Under Secretary of Defense Fred Iklé, US Ambassador to the Organization of American States William Middendorf, Under Secretary of State for Political Affairs Lawrence Eagleberger, Assistant Secretary of State for Inter-American Affairs Langhorne Motley, and NSC staffers Oliver North and Constantine Menges. President Reagan, Shultz and National Security Advisor Robert McFarlane participated in the meeting via loudspeaker phone from Augusta, Georgia. Details can be found in Menges (note 8), pp. 56, 59, 64; and Adkin, M., *Urgent Fury: The Battle for Grenada* (Lexington Books: Lexington, Mass., 1989), pp. 118–20.

[14] Approximately 1000 US students attended St Georges Medical School. See *Full Committee Hearing on the Lessons Learned as a Result of the US Military Operations in Grenada* (note 10), p. 1.

supporters were to those who took power in Iran in 1979; as the final decision was made to proceed with the intervention, President Reagan was reported to have commented that he was 'no better off than Jimmy Carter'.[15]

Although fear of a potential hostage situation is listed as the most important of the operation's objectives, such a rescue operation did not demand seizure of the entire island of Grenada.[16] Diplomats were in contact with the students before the operation began, and some analyses of the crisis suggest that the students were not in danger until after US forces landed on the island and combat resulted. Reportedly, General Austin's junta was eager to co-operate in getting the students out.[17]

It is impossible to assess whether the students were really in danger. However, in response to criticism that using the students as justification for the invasion was disingenuous, the Reagan Administration released a compendium of documents captured during the intervention that illustrated the Bishop Government's ties with the USSR, Cuba and other leftist regimes.[18] These documents were intended to prove that Grenada was being turned into a staging base for Soviet–Cuban expansion in the Caribbean. The use of these documents as justification for the intervention suggests that, within the minds of the relevant decision makers, stopping the spread of Soviet and Cuban influence was all the motive the USA needed to invade Grenada. At the height of the cold war, such arguments were the very core of the strategic framework of the decision makers.

Panama

No such cold war thinking was apparent in the US decision to invade Panama in 1989. The decision to intervene was specific to US–Panamanian relations and the controversial rule of General Manuel Noriega in Panama. There is little need here to detail the long relationship between the USA and Noriega.

[15] See Schoenhals and Melanson (note 12), p. 141; and 'Britain's Grenada shut-out' (note 8), p. 32.

[16] The hostage problem did have an impact on the decision to proceed with the operation so quickly. Fear that the students would be taken hostage caused the Administration to set the operation in motion almost immediately. US forces landed on Grenada only six days after Bishop was assassinated. This fear may also have been the real reason that the operation included forces from both the Army and Marines. Richard Gabriel cites William Lind's thesis that the use of Army Rangers and elements of the 82nd Airborne Division was simply a way of dousing the flames of inter-service rivalry that would have set Washington ablaze if the Army had been excluded. See Gabriel, R., *Military Incompetence* (Hill and Wang: New York, 1985), pp. 178–79. However, another source contends that Army units were deployed because it would have taken eight days to move an additional Marine Amphibious Task Force by sea from California, through the Panama Canal to Grenada which lies off the coast of Venezuela, north of Trinidad. Given the fear of a hostage crisis it seems logical that the Administration would choose to eschew a time-consuming and visible movement of Marines in favour of simply airlifting fully equipped Army forces directly to the area. See Bolger, D., 'Operation urgent fury and its critics', *Military Review*, vol. 66, no. 7 (July 1986), pp. 57–69.

[17] Initially, US diplomats could not secure release of the students because Pearls Airstrip, the only operational airport on the island, had been closed. See Schoenhals and Melanson (note 12), pp. 144–45; and Adkin (note 13), p. 108.

[18] A discussion of the documents and a sampling from the collection appears in Valenta, J. and Ellison, H. (eds), *Grenada and Soviet/Cuban Policy: Internal Crisis and US/OECS Intervention* (Westview Press: Boulder, Colo., 1986), pp. 241–485.

Noriega's dealings with the CIA can be traced as far back as 1970.[19] Panama had always been a stalwart ally in Washington's fight against communism in Latin America; Noriega proved to be particularly useful in the Reagan Administration's efforts to destabilize the Sandinista Government in Nicaragua. With the passage of the second Boland Amendment in 1984 it became illegal for any US Government intelligence agency to fund or assist the Nicaraguan Contras in their war with the Sandinistas.[20] Noriega agreed to fulfil this role by allowing the Contras to train in Panama on Panama Defense Forces (PDF) bases.[21]

Noriega's involvement in drug trafficking, known within the intelligence community and US Justice Department, was tolerated as Noriega's usefulness in the cold war continued.[22] For example, Senator Jesse Helms convened hearings of the Western Hemispheric Affairs Subcommittee of the Senate Foreign Relations Committee in the spring of 1986 for the purpose of providing a public forum for the Panamanian opposition to PDF rule and revealing Noriega's abuses of power. Assistant Secretary of State for Inter-American Affairs Elliott Abrams had contacted Senator Helms's office in an effort to convince the Senator to cancel the hearings. The hearings began as scheduled, however, and Abrams defended the US policy of support for the PDF and the Noriega regime itself by, among other reasons, citing the threat from Nicaragua.[23]

It could be argued that Noriega's usefulness as an ally in the fight against communism declined as US–Soviet relations warmed. US policy towards Panama during the Reagan and Bush administrations, however, illustrates that changes in policy were caused by actions in Panama City, not Moscow. It was the political fall-out from revelations about Noriega's role in the drug trade that eventually led to the US invasion. The Reagan Administration first came to the conclusion that Noriega must be removed from power, and the Bush Administration finally decided that this could only be accomplished through the use of US armed forces.

Reagan Administration policy

The real blows to Noriega's rule in Panama began with a series of newspaper articles in US papers that detailed Noriega's role in drug trafficking. Two front page articles in mid-June, one in *The New York Times* by Seymour Hersh and a second in *The Washington Post* by Charles Babcock and Bob Woodward,

---

[19] Analyses of the US relationship with Noriega can be found in Koster, R. M. and Sanchez, G., *In the Time of the Tyrants* (W. W. Norton: New York, 1990); Dinges, J., *Our Man in Panama* (Random House: New York, 1990); Buckley, K., *Panama: The Whole Story* (Simon & Schuster: New York, 1991); and Watson, B. W. and Tsouras, P. G., *Operation Just Cause* (Westview Press: Boulder, Colo., 1991), pp. 1–46. On Noriega's ties to the CIA, see Dinges, pp. 49–53.

[20] Arnson, C., *Crossroads: Congress, the Reagan Administration and Central America* (Pantheon Books: New York, 1989), pp. 166–69.

[21] Buckley (note 19), p. 44.

[22] Dinges (note 19), pp. 57–72.

[23] See Dinges (note 19), p. 237; and *Situation in Panama*, Hearings before the Subcommittee on Western Hemispheric Affairs of the Committee on Foreign Relations, US Senate, 99th Congress (US Government Printing Office: Washington, DC, Mar./Apr. 1986), p. 39.

detailed Noriega's role in the drug trade and questioned the Reagan Administration's support for Noriega.[24]

Although the Reagan Administration cancelled military sales to the PDF following publication of these articles, the Administration continued to support Noriega. NSC staffer Oliver North maintained a close relationship with Noriega in North's attempt to maintain the Contra effort, while CIA Director William Casey tried without success to convince Senator Helms to withdraw an amendment requiring the CIA to report to Congress on the possible role of the PDF in many illegal activities, including the drug and arms trade. This amendment passed as did another Senate resolution calling specifically for the end of Noriega's rule.[25]

It took the Reagan Administration another year to join Congress in its condemnation of Noriega. Following a public airing of Noriega's illegal activities in June of 1987 by Deputy Commander of the PDF Colonel Roberto Diaz Herrera, Administration policy became one of open opposition to Noriega's leadership of the PDF.[26] In February 1988, Noriega was indicted by two Florida grand juries on drug charges, including a strong relationship with the Medellín drug cartel of Colombia.

This reversal of policy had little to do with a lessening of cold war tensions. The Administration's new policy towards Panama was critical of Noriega, not the PDF, nor the role of the PDF in support of Administration policies in Central America. Although the Iran–Contra affair had discredited the Contra effort by revealing some of the NSC's potentially illegal backchannel gymnastics in support of the Contras, and the Administration's last request for military aid to the Contras was defeated in the House, the Administration continued to support the Contras.[27] In addition, the Administration had successfully convinced the Drug Enforcement Agency (DEA) to drop indictments of the PDF as a whole and to indict only Noriega.[28] Having decided that Noriega must go, the next policy decision was to find a way to remove him from power. From March to May 1988, the Reagan Administration attempted to negotiate with Noriega to bring about his resignation.[29] After the failure of these negotiations, the Administration would have turned to covert action if it had not been for the Senate Intelligence Committee's warning that US involvement in a coup resulting in Noriega's murder would violate US law prohibiting government-sponsored assassination.[30]

[24] Hersh, S., 'Panama strongman said to trade in drugs, arms and illicit money', *New York Times*, 12 June 1986, p. 1; Babcock, C. and Woodward, B., 'Report on Panama general poses predicament for US', *Washington Post*, 13 June 1986, p. 1.
[25] Dinges (note 19), pp. 252–53, 269.
[26] Horowitz, S., 'Indications and warning factors', eds. Watson and Tsouras (note 19), p. 50.
[27] One month following the House defeat of the Administration's request for Contra aid the Sandinistas and Contras signed a cease-fire accord. This, however, did not end the conflict within Nicaragua. See Arnson (note 20), pp. 205, 224–25.
[28] Buckley (note 19), pp. 117–18.
[29] Buckley (note 19), p. 360; Weymouth, L., 'Panama: the May 1988 option', *Washington Post*, 31 Dec. 1989, p. C1.
[30] Horowitz (note 26), p. 51.

Beginning in March 1988, US forces permanently stationed in Panama, the Southern Command (SOUTHCOM), and the PDF entered a period of confrontation that one analyst describes as 'low-intensity warfare'.[31] Essentially, this was a period of mutual harassment between PDF and US servicemen in Panama.

Bush Administration policy

The newly inaugurated Bush Administration still hoped that the PDF itself could remove Noriega even following the frequent clashes between US and PDF forces. However, following the obviously fraudulent elections of May 1989, even as President Bush called on the PDF to overthrow Noriega, the Administration seriously doubted the prospects of such a coup.[32] The failed coup of 1988 and a classified US study that questioned the PDF's ability to overthrow Noriega were leading to a consensus within the Administration by May 1989 that US forces might be needed to end Noriega's rule.[33] The changes within Eastern Europe and the USSR were irrelevant to the slow growth of support for an armed overthrow of Noriega.

To this end, the USA began to prepare for military action. Several days after the May 1989 election President Bush ordered the deployment of a battalion of the 7th Light Infantry Division to Panama, increasing the total of US troops in Panama to approximately 13 000.[34] The US military also began a series of training exercises specifically designed to prepare forces for an intervention in Panama.[35] The Administration replaced General Fred Woerner, Commander of the SOUTHCOM forces which would have undertaken any potential operations against Panama; Woerner had been a consistent critic of plans to use force within Panama. Woerner was succeeded by General Maxwell Thurman, considered by many to be a more aggressive general, whose retirement was postponed specifically for the mission of dealing with Panama. Outgoing Chairman of the Joint Chiefs Admiral William Crowe had informed Thurman that his mission at SOUTHCOM was to prepare for a US intervention in Panama. Crowe could not specify when the move might be made but made it clear that Thurman was to ready US forces for such an operation.

---

[31] Koster and Sanchez (note 19), p. 359.

[32] Buckley (note 19), pp. 183–84.

[33] Engelberg, S., 'US had inklings of a coup attempt', *New York Times*, 4 Oct. 1989, p. 4; Pichiarallo, J. and Tyler, P., 'Long road to the invasion of Panama', *Washington Post*, 14 Jan. 1990, p. A1.

[34] *1989 Events in Panama*, Joint Hearings before the Senate Armed Services Committee and Senate Select Committee on Intelligence, US Senate, 101st Congress (US Government Printing Office: Washington, DC, Oct./Dec. 1990), p. 121.

[35] Preparations for the intervention began as early as July. Both troops in the US and those stationed in Panama participated in 'joint contingency readiness exercises' beginning in July. A series of single-unit exercises, entitled Sand Fleas, and joint-service exercises, entitled Purple Storm, were held regularly. In September, elements of the 82nd Airborne Division rehearsed their planned tasks for the intervention. See Ropelewski, R., 'Planning, precision and surprise led to Panama successes', *Armed Forces Journal International* (Feb. 1990), p. 28; and *Department of Defense Appropriations for FY 1991*, Hearings before a Subcommittee of the Committee on Appropriations, House of Representatives, 101st Congress (US Government Printing Office: Washington, DC, 1990), part 2, p. 161.

The final turning point in the decision to use force to remove Noriega came in early October. Again, the decision had nothing to do with changes in East–West relations. A failed coup attempt by members of the PDF finally convinced the Bush Administration that US forces would indeed be necessary to overthrow Noriega.[36] The Bush Administration was heavily criticized by members of Congress for its crisis management during the coup situation and its failure to assist the rebels. Although the Administration felt it had made the right decision, criticisms of its handling of the coup had a strong influence on the direction US policy would take thereafter. The USA moved up its timetable for intervention and prepared to act sooner rather than later to erase the political damage caused by the October coup. All units eventually involved in the intervention received two months of practice for the operations they would undertake during 'Just Cause'.[37]

In addition, following the failed coup Noriega launched a major crack-down against dissident PDF officers and other critics of his regime.[38] President Bush seems to have taken Noriega's actions personally. Bush felt that Noriega was 'thumbing his nose at him', and friends of the President felt that Bush had 'become obsessed with' Noriega.[39] These feelings may have been major factors in the increased military activity undertaken by the USA after the coup. With the decision made that intervention was necessary and with preparations under way to ready US forces for action in the near future, the Administration was merely waiting for the right time. On Friday, 15 December 1989, and the weekend that followed, Noriega and the PDF gave the USA a justification for invasion. Noriega's self-appointed National Assembly made Noriega 'maximum leader of national liberation' on 15 December and also declared that the USA and Panama were in a state of war. The following day a US Marine was killed and another serviceman and his wife were threatened by the PDF. US forces were placed on alert in response to the increased tensions. On Sunday, 17 December, Bush and his top advisers met in Washington at the end of a White House Christmas party and decided to proceed with the intervention at 1 a.m. on 20 December.[40]

Essentially, the actual decision to intervene by the Bush Administration was the result of political embarrassment and an increasingly confrontational situation within Panama. This certainly was no cold war battle as in the case of the

[36] For details on the coup see the testimony of General Thurman in Joint Hearings before the Senate Committee on Armed Services and the Senate Select Committee on Intelligence (note 34), pp. 55–112; and Rosenthal, A., 'Panama crisis: disarray hindered White House', *New York Times*, 8 Oct. 1989, p. 1.

[37] For details of the numerous military exercises designed as practice runs for the invasion see Hughes, D., 'Night airdrop in Panama surprises Noriega's forces', *Aviation Week & Space Technology*, 1 Jan. 1990, p. 30; Crowell, L., 'The anatomy of Just Cause', eds Watson and Tsouras (note 19), p. 77; Horowitz (note 26), p. 55; Fulgham, D., 'Army tells Congress that aviators rehearsed US invasion of Panama', *Aviation Week & Space Technology*, 11 June 1990, p. 29; 'Inside the invasion', *Newsweek*, 25 June 1990, p. 29; Healy, M., 'Panama lessons: soldiers need police and urban war training', *Los Angeles Times*, 14 Feb. 1990, p. A6; and *Department of Defense Appropriations for FY 1991* (note 35), p. 216.

[38] Horowitz (note 26), p. 55.

[39] Dowd, M., 'Doing the inevitable', *New York Times*, 24 Dec. 1989, p. 5; Apple, R. W., 'Bush's obsession', *New York Times*, 26 Dec. 1989, p. 5.

[40] Ropelewski (note 35), p. 26.

Grenada intervention. The above analysis suggests that Noriega's overthrow was an indication that within the strategic framework of the Bush Administration there was still a perceived necessity to use military force even after the end of the cold war. Although the fight against communism had dominated US foreign policy for most of this century, it was not the only threat to US interests in Latin America. The implications of the above for future US–Russian–Latin American relations are discussed in the conclusion of this chapter.

IV. The Persian Gulf

Kuwaiti tanker reflagging

The reflagging of Kuwaiti tankers in 1987 and 1988, similar to the invasion of Grenada, is an example of a decision made within the strategic framework of the cold war. Concern over an expanded Soviet presence in the Persian Gulf had kept US decision makers awake at night since the Iranian Revolution and the Soviet invasion of Afghanistan. The proclamation of the Carter Doctrine committing the USA to securing the flow of oil out of the Persian Gulf, the establishment of the Rapid Deployment Joint Task Force (RDJTF) and its elevation to a Unified Command—Central Command (CENTCOM)—laid the groundwork for US Gulf policy in the 1980s.[41]

These fears of a Soviet foothold in the Persian Gulf were foremost in the minds of US decision makers in November 1986 when the Kuwaiti Government asked the USA for protection against the spreading violence of the six-year-old Iraq–Iran War. Iraq had escalated the war in the Persian Gulf in March 1984 in hope of depleting Iranian resources for the land battle that had turned in Iran's favour.[42] By 1986, Iran responded to Iraqi attacks on Iranian shipping using small, armed patrol boats as well as mines that began to take a heavy toll on shipping destined for Kuwait and Saudi Arabia.[43]

After consultation with other members of the Gulf Co-operation Council, the Kuwaiti Government asked both the USA and the USSR to secure safe passage of Kuwaiti tankers through the Gulf.[44] Initially, the US State Department

[41] A detailed look at US policy in the Persian Gulf as it evolved following the fall of the Shah and the Soviet invasion of Afghanistan can be found in McNaugher, T., *Arms and Oil* (Brookings Institution: Washington, DC, 1985); and Epstein, J., *Strategy and Force Planning* (Brookings Institution: Washington, DC, 1987).

[42] Rubin, B., 'Drowning in the Gulf', *Foreign Policy*, no. 69 (winter 1987/88), pp. 120–34; *Persian Gulf*, Report to the Majority Leader of the US Senate from Senator John Glenn and Senator John Warner on their Trip to the Persian Gulf May 27–June 4 1987 (US Government Printing Office: Washington, DC, 17 June 1987), p. 8.

[43] Stein, J. G., 'The wrong strategy in the right place: the United States in the Gulf', *International Security*, vol. 13, no. 3 (winter 1988/89), p. 147. From 1984 to May 1987, Iran had attacked 93 ships, while Iraq had attacked 168 ships: *Overview of the Situation in the Persian Gulf*, Hearings before the House Foreign Affairs Committee, Subcommittee on Arms Control, International Security and Science and Subcommittee on Europe and the Middle East, 100th Congress (US Government Printing Office: Washington, DC, May/June 1987), p. 52.

[44] Stein (note 43), p. 148. It is unclear whether Kuwait initially asked for assistance from both the USA and the USSR. Several sources indicate that the Kuwaiti Government turned to the USSR first for protection of its tanker fleet. Only after the Reagan Administration learned of the Kuwaiti overture to the

responded to the Kuwaiti request by explaining that reflagging would take six months under US law. Dissatisfied with this answer, the Kuwaiti Government seems to have prodded the USA by claiming it would put six of its tankers under US flag and the other five under the Soviet flag.[45]

Whether or not the Kuwaiti response was simply a ploy to speed up the time-table of a US reflagging or signified a real possibility of Kuwaiti tankers being placed under the Soviet flag is irrelevant for the purposes of the current analysis.[46] The Kuwaitis eventually received the response they desired. On 4 March 1987, in a meeting with National Security Advisor Frank Carlucci, Secretary of Defense Caspar Weinberger and Secretary of State George Shultz, President Reagan approved the reflagging of 11 Kuwaiti tankers.[47]

Although Kuwait was seeking protection from the ravages of the Iraq–Iran War, the USA was operating from the framework of the cold war. In a message to the Kuwaiti Government on 7 March 1987, the Reagan Administration offered to reflag the Kuwaiti tankers if, in return, Kuwait would agree not to give the USSR the right to use Kuwaiti ports.[48] When the Kuwaiti Government balked at the conditional acceptance, the USA agreed to proceed with reflagging.

It can be argued that in reflagging Kuwaiti tankers the USA was attempting to prevent Iran from becoming the pre-eminent power in the Gulf, or was simply defending the principle of freedom of navigation.[49] At the root of the policy, however, lay the cold war. If the threat from Iran and the freedom of navigation were the only concerns of the Reagan Administration, the USA would have been satisfied to join the USSR in a joint superpower operation. As Assistant Secretary of State for Near-Eastern Affairs Richard Murphy explained, the USA sought a 'Western shipping protection regime', but did not support 'an international shipping protection regime' simply because such a regime would 'legitimize a permanent Soviet Naval presence in the Gulf and ease its access to port and repair facilities in the Gulf'.[50]

USSR did it take interest in reflagging the Kuwaiti ships. If the Kuwaiti Government doubted the credibility of the USA after the revelations of Iran–Contra this seems like a logical step; see Ottaway, D., 'US sees success for its Gulf Policy in Iranian acceptance of cease fire', *Washington Post*, 20 July 1988, p. A12. Representative Lawrence Smith of Florida repeatedly charged at congressional hearings that the Administration turned down the initial Kuwaiti request for reflagging, leaving Kuwait no alternative but to turn to the USSR. No Administration witness addressed the charges. See, for example, *Overview of the Situation in the Persian Gulf* (note 43), p. 83.

[45] Weinberger, C., *Fighting for Peace* (Warner Books: New York, 1991), pp. 395–96.

[46] Kuwait did have relations with the USSR and had chartered three Soviet tankers which were provided with Soviet naval escorts. *Overview of the Situation in the Persian Gulf* (note 43), p. 286.

[47] Stein (note 43), p. 148. At the time Kuwait had 22 tankers. Eleven were candidates for reflagging; 2 were chartered from the UK and received protection from the Royal Navy, while the remaining 9 were smaller tankers that did not operate in the Persian Gulf. *Overview of the Situation in the Persian Gulf* (note 43), p. 52.

[48] Stein (note 43), p. 148.

[49] On the possibility of Iran eclipsing other powers in the Persian Gulf see Johnson, R. H., 'The Persian Gulf in US strategy: a skeptical view', *International Security*, vol. 14, no. 1 (summer 1989), pp. 148–50. In his memoirs, Weinberger cites 'freedom of the seas' as the major reason for the US reflagging. See Weinberger (note 45), pp. 387–429.

[50] *Overview of the Situation in the Persian Gulf* (note 43), p. 275.

ssibility of undertaking the operation under the flag of the United
as suggested in Congress by Chairman of the Senate Foreign Rela-
mittee Claiborne Pell and Chairman of the House Foreign Affairs
Dante Fascell. Former US Government officials Cyrus Vance and
ardson also proposed UN sponsorship of the operation. The Administration counselled against UN involvement, arguing again that this would
legitimize a Soviet role in the Gulf.[51] This is a critical difference between the
strategic calculus of 1987 and that of 1990. The intent of the policy is clear and
consistent with a strategic framework based upon the cold war. As will be illustrated below, it stands in sharp contrast to the willingness of the USA to involve
the USSR in the Persian Gulf War.

The Persian Gulf War

To illustrate the changes in the strategic framework within which US decision
makers operated during the Persian Gulf crisis of 1990–91, this section focuses
on the portrayal by the Bush Administration of this crisis as the first 'post-cold
war crisis' and an opportunity to create a new world order. The efforts of the
Bush Administration to make the defence of Kuwait and Saudi Arabia a
multinational operation that included both the USSR and a major role for the
United Nations illustrate a new approach to conflict in the Middle East. As an
example of this desire to present a unified international stand against Iraq, this
section also examines the Bush Administration's struggle to achieve passage of
a UN Security Council resolution allowing the use of force in support of the
UN embargo of Iraq.

Before Iraq's invasion of Kuwait both the USA and the USSR had a history
of friendly relations with the regime of Saddam Hussein. Iraq had been a Soviet
ally and a major consumer of Soviet arms.[52] During the Iraq–Iran War the USA
attempted to remain neutral yet began to tilt towards support of Iraq as early as
1984.[53] Reportedly, the US relationship with Iraq dated back to the sharing of
US intelligence with Baghdad in 1982.[54]

---

[51] Madison, C., 'A reflagged policy', *National Journal*, 28 Nov. 1987, p. 3029. During the congressional hearings on reflagging the Kuwaiti tankers Administration witnesses repeatedly cited the Soviet
threat. Both Secretary of Defense Weinberger and Under Secretary of State for Political Affairs Michael
Armacost flatly stated that if the USA had not agreed to reflag the Kuwaiti tankers, the USSR would have
accepted the role. Allowing the USSR to gain such a prominent role in the Persian Gulf would have
completely undermined the foundation of US policy in the Gulf since the end of World War II. Some
Administration officials even claimed that decision makers feared being accused of 'losing the Gulf' if the
USSR were allowed to gain access to ports in the Gulf. See *Overview of the Situation in the Persian Gulf*
(note 43), pp. 147, 177; and Trainor, B., 'Weinberger on the Persian Gulf: cap the chameleon?', *New York
Times*, 9 Oct. 1987, p. A20.

[52] See Smolansky, O. and Smolansky, B., *The USSR and Iraq* (Duke University Press: Durham, N.C.,
1991).

[53] Among other things the USA provided Iraq with agricultural credits and possibly intelligence data.
On the diplomatic front the USA condemned Iran at the UN and normalized relations with Iraq, see *War
in the Persian Gulf: The US Takes Sides*, Staff Report to the Committee on Foreign Relations, US Senate,
100th Congress (US Government Printing Office: Washington, DC, Nov. 1987), pp. 21–22.

[54] Hersh, S., 'US secretly gave aid to Iraq early in its war against Iran', *New York Times*, 26 Jan. 1992,
p. 1.

More recently, US policy had been to take an approach similar to the 'constructive engagement' policy towards South Africa and post-Tiananmen Square relations with China, in which the USA maintained relations with governments that have violated human rights in the hope of encouraging progressive trends.[55] Following Iraq's use of chemical weapons against its Kurdish minority, the Reagan Administration had lobbied against the Senate's passage of a sanctions bill, eventually preventing it from becoming law. The Bush Administration continued this policy despite a number of incidents including Iraqi threats to 'burn up half of Israel'.[56]

Up to the eve of Iraq's move into Kuwait, even as US intelligence estimated the number of Iraqi forces lined up on the Kuwaiti border to be nearly 100 000, the Bush Administration argued against bills pending in both the House and the Senate that would impose sanctions against Iraq.[57]

Although US attempts to better relations with Iraq can be seen as an effort to wean Baghdad from the USSR as Moscow's ability to act forcefully in the international arena began to decline, Iraq's 2 August 1990 invasion of Kuwait rearranged all the old alliances and conflicts. *Glasnost, perestroika* and the revolutions in Eastern Europe had changed the US view of the USSR to such an extent that on 1 August US Secretary of State James Baker and Soviet Foreign Minister Eduard Shevardnadze began an unprecedented effort to present a unified US–Soviet stand.

The dialogue between the USA and the USSR, a dialogue that could even be considered a partnership, actually began before Iraqi forces entered Kuwait. Although US intelligence was well aware of Iraqi forces on the Kuwaiti border on 30 July, analysts agreed that, lacking the communications infrastructure, artillery, munitions supplies and remaining logistical package, these forces were unready to move into Kuwait. The movement of forces was perceived as merely another tactic in Saddam Hussein's strategy to bully the Kuwaiti Government into resolving the dispute over Kuwaiti over-production of oil and the Rumaila oil field. However, by 1 August, Iraqi forces had completed their logistical buildup; in presentations to the White House and Pentagon officials, the CIA concluded that Iraq was about to invade Kuwait.

Already in Irkutsk at a scheduled meeting with his Soviet counterpart, Baker consulted Shevardnadze about the impending Iraqi invasion and asked whether

---

[55] An explanation of this policy can be found in *United States–Iraqi Relations*, Hearing before the Subcommittee on Europe and the Middle East of the Committee on Foreign Affairs, House of Representatives, 101st Congress (US Government Printing Office: Washington, DC, 26 Apr. 1990), p. 3.

[56] Gigot, P., 'A great American screw-up', *The National Interest*, no. 22 (winter 1990/91), pp. 5–6; *United States–Iraqi Relations* (note 55), pp. 9–11.

[57] US intelligence estimates of Iraqi troops can be found in Woodward, B. and Atkinson, A., 'Mideast decision: uncertainty over a daunting move', *Washington Post*, 26 Aug. 1990, p. 1. On the Administration's opposition to broad sanctions against Iraq, see *Developments in the Middle East, July 1990*, Hearing before the Subcommittee on Europe and the Middle East, Committee on Foreign Affairs, House of Representatives, 100th Congress (US Government Printing Office: Washington, DC, 31 July 1990), particularly pp. 23–24. The controversy over US policy towards Iraq, particularly the mixed signals sent to Iraq as its forces began to move to the border during July 1990, is legendary, yet still unsettled. For an overview of the immediate pre-invasion diplomacy see Oberdorfer, D., 'Mixed signals in the Middle East', *Washington Post Magazine*, 17 Mar. 1991, pp. 19–23, 36–41.

the USSR could prevent the invasion; Shevardnadze assured Baker on 1 August and again shortly before the invasion on 2 August that there would be no invasion.[58] After Iraq did invade, it was Baker who informed Shevardnadze of the attack. A two-day effort spearheaded by Baker aide Dennis Ross and Shevardnadze aide Sergey Taserenko to draft a joint US–Soviet statement condemning the invasion began immediately.

In Washington President Bush and his key advisers worked to build a multinational response to Iraq's invasion from the very beginning of the crisis. After flying to Aspen, Colorado, to deliver a scheduled speech on defence policy, Bush consulted with prime ministers Margaret Thatcher of the UK, Brian Mulroney of Canada and Toshiki Kaifu of Japan, Secretary-General of NATO Manfred Wörner and several Arab leaders.[59] The USA had undertaken multinational efforts in the past. The Persian Gulf reflagging of 1987–88 included assistance from Belgium, France, Italy, Japan, the Netherlands and the UK.[60] However, the Gulf crisis is unique in that for the first time since World War II the USA perceived the USSR as an ally in a conflict against a third party.

At Camp David, on 3 August 1990, the Bush Administration decided that US forces should be used to defend Saudi Arabia if the Saudis requested. It was not until 6 August that Saudi King Fahd was persuaded to accept US troops under the conditions that US forces would leave once the crisis had ended and US commanders would seek Saudi approval before undertaking any offensive military operations.

Once the decision to deploy troops to the Middle East had been made, the Bush Administration informed the USSR; fostering a common US–Soviet stand demanded that the USSR would not be surprised by the actions of the Bush Administration. In the most unprecedented move and the most startling indication of the shift in the strategic framework that guided its decisions, the Bush Administration asked the USSR if it desired to send its own naval and ground forces to the Gulf.[61] Such a request was in stark contrast to the US attitude towards a Soviet presence in the Gulf during the decision on Persian Gulf reflagging.

The USA had also argued against a role for the United Nations in the reflagging of Kuwaiti tankers. However, the Bush Administration from early in the Gulf crisis sought a major role for the UN. Since 1986 the USSR had been advocating a central role for the UN in international affairs and the settlement

---

[58] The details of the Baker–Shevardnadze meetings before and immediately after the invasion are described in Warner, M. G., 'The Moscow connection', *Newsweek*, 17 Sep. 1990, p. 24.

[59] It is ironic that the invasion which would lead to the largest US military effort since the Viet Nam War would occur on the eve of a Bush speech announcing the much-awaited Pentagon plan for reductions in the US military. For details of the Pentagon's plan see Gordon, M., 'Pentagon drafts new battle plan', *New York Times*, 2 Aug. 1990, p. 1; and Morocco, J., 'New Pentagon strategy shifts from Europe to regional conflicts', *Aviation Week & Space Technology*, 13 Aug. 1990, pp. 25–27. The President's speech, 'In defense of defense', given at the Aspen Institute Symposium, Aspen, Colo., is reprinted in US Department of Defense, *Report of the Secretary of Defense Dick Cheney to the President and Congress*, annual report (US Government Printing Office: Washington, DC, Jan. 1991), pp. 131–33.

[60] Weinberger (note 45), p. 421.

[61] Warner (note 58), p. 25.

of international conflict.[62] President Bush seems to have taken this idea to heart as he chose the Security Council—a body whose decision-making rules required US–Soviet agreement—as the forum that would legitimize US policy and spearhead the multilateral opposition to Iraq.[63] The night of the Iraqi invasion the UN Security Council passed the first of many resolutions condemning it.

Upon being informed that the USA was ready to deploy forces to the Persian Gulf, Shevardnadze suggested that military actions taken in defence of Saudi Arabia should be co-ordinated by the UN Security Council Military Staff Committee (MSC).[64] Use of the MSC to oversee multinational operations would truly make the coalition against Iraq an international one. The USA agreed to study the possibility. The MSC was originally designed to act as the military arm of the Security Council. Composed of the Chiefs of Staff of the five permanent members of the Security Council, the role of the MSC was to oversee the collective security functions of the Security Council. The MSC had been ignored since the inception of the UN, meeting regularly but with little, if any, input into Security Council decisions. The simple act of considering the use of the MSC was a concession to the USSR made by the Bush Administration to ensure Soviet support of the use of force. Ultimately, the MSC played no significant role in the military operations against Iraq.

The strategic framework guiding US policy had changed drastically, and the Bush Administration went to great lengths to publicize this notion. In a statement before the House Committee on Foreign Affairs Secretary Baker called the Iraqi invasion 'a political test of how the post-cold war world will work'. Baker acknowledged the Administration's belief that the changes in the USSR had made such a multinational alliance possible: 'we should remember what this conflict would have looked like if old-style zero sum thinking was still driving Soviet policy in the Persian Gulf'.[65] To some within the Bush Administration the creation of an international coalition against Iraq, including both the USA and the USSR, was the method to ensure the creation of a 'new international order'.[66] The Administration stressed this new world order by calling for a Bush–Gorbachev summit in early September that would stand as a symbol of co-operation.

It could be argued that the Bush Administration's new international order consisted of only one superpower, plus a second-rate power treated as an equal

[62] See Newmann (note 5).

[63] Many sources indicate that within the Bush Administration Secretary Baker was the strongest advocate of using the UN to support the US position on the Gulf crisis. Other senior officials, notably National Security Advisor Brent Scowcroft, were less sure about the need for the UN during this crisis.

[64] Warner (note 58), pp. 25–26.

[65] *Crisis in the Persian Gulf*, Hearings and Markup before the Committee on Foreign Affairs, House of Representatives, 100th Congress (US Government Printing Office: Washington, DC, Sep./Oct. 1990), pp. 7, 9.

[66] See President Bush's speech of 11 Sep. 1990, reprinted in *The Persian Gulf Crisis: Relevant Documents, Correspondence, Reports*, Report Prepared by the Subcommittee on Arms Control, International Security and Science, Committee on Foreign Affairs, House of Representatives, 102nd Congress (US Government Printing Office: Washington, DC, June 1991), pp. 24–27.

partner to legitimize the unilateral designs of the superpower. According to one Administration official, co-operation with the USSR was viewed by National Security Advisor Brent Scowcroft as a way to illustrate 'the United States and the USSR working together, with the USSR clearly the junior partner'.[67] This may have been true. Whatever the motivation, it seems clear that not only did the USA no longer see the USSR as a threat to US interests in the Middle East, but the USA felt that its interests could be furthered through co-operation with the USSR.

The desire of the Bush Administration to legitimize its efforts against Iraq through a multinational coalition and a partnership with the USSR was not merely rhetoric. A brief look at the events leading up to the Security Council resolution approving the use of force to enforce the embargo of Iraqi goods shows that the USA went to great lengths to ensure a Soviet role in the crisis.

On 6 August 1990, the day the USA was informed by King Fahd that US forces would be accepted on Saudi territory (but two days before the agreement was announced publicly), the UN Security Council passed Resolution 661 asking nations of the world to join in a trade and financial embargo of Iraqi and Kuwaiti assets seized during the invasion.[68] The USA also announced that it would use its navy to enforce the embargo if non-military means could not maintain Iraq's economic isolation. Other members of the international Coalition, including the other four permanent members of the Security Council (China, France, the UK and the USSR), were not as eager to use their navies to enforce the embargo. The dispute became a sticking point in the Coalition efforts on 12 August 1990 when the Bush Administration announced that it had given its naval commanders permission to use force—including disabling Iraqi ships and boarding them—to maintain a blockade of Iraqi shipping. The USA felt that the resolution gave each member of the Coalition the right to use its military to maintain the blockade, even if this required using force.

The other members of the Security Council felt that Resolution 661 establishing the embargo merely gave Coalition ships the right to monitor Iraqi trade in an effort to detect violations of the embargo; it was argued that the use of force in support of that embargo would require another Security Council resolution. In addition, diplomats at the UN warned the Bush Administration that the USA was beginning to become 'isolated'.[69]

Events began to overtake the debate over whether force could be used in the Gulf on the weekend of 17–18 August 1990. US naval forces stopped and then released two Iraqi cargo ships off the coast of Bahrain. In two additional incidents US ships fired warning shots at two Iraqi tankers that had failed to stop when US forces asked them to do so. The tankers continued on their way after

[67] Warner (note 58), p. 25.

[68] For the text of the resolution see *The Persian Gulf Crisis: Relevant Documents, Correspondence, Reports* (note 66), pp. 155–57; or *New York Times*, 7 Aug. 1990, p. A5.

[69] Sciolino, E. with Pace, E., 'How the US got UN backing for use of force', *New York Times*, 30 Aug. 1990, p. 1.

the warning shots, yet the USA refrained from disabling the two ships, choosing simply to follow them.

This restraint was a direct response to criticism of the US announcement that it had the authority to use force without a specific UN resolution approving such measures. The Bush Administration felt that the maintenance of the international Coalition was more important than stopping the two Iraqi tankers. On 20 August 1990, as US naval forces began to follow the Iraqi tankers, in an emergency session of the Security Council the USA began an intensive effort to convince the other Security Council members to pass a resolution allowing the USA to use force against Iraqi shipping. US Ambassador to the UN Thomas Pickering was instructed to keep the Security Council in session until a resolution was passed. The urgency stemmed from the fact that the two Iraqi tankers were scheduled to reach Yemen on the following day. The Bush Administration hoped to achieve passage of a resolution that would allow US ships to act before the two tankers reached their destination. The emergency passed, however, when Yemen announced that it would not allow the tankers to unload their cargo at Yemeni ports.

Throughout the following week a resolution on the use of force was debated in the Security Council. The major impediment to a resolution was the Soviet desire to allow force only if major violations of the embargo were detected. In addition, the USSR continued to argue for use of the MSC to co-ordinate Coalition naval forces. The deadlock was broken by direct negotiation between Secretary Baker and Foreign Minister Shevardnadze. On 22 August 1990, Shevardnadze asked Baker to give the USSR 48 hours to convince Iraq to withdraw from Kuwait. If these talks failed, the USSR would support a US resolution on the use of force. Iraq refused to yield and early on the morning of 25 August, the UN Security Council passed Resolution 665 authorizing the Coalition to use force in support of the embargo against Iraq.[70]

The resolution itself represented real co-operation between the USA and the USSR. Restraining the use of its military forces for the sake of maintaining a common stand with the USSR, the USA illustrated the lengths to which it would go to present a unified international alliance against Iraq. The resolution itself also represented a compromise between the USA and the USSR. The US draft resolution initially authorized a 'minimum use of force'. The USSR protested against the explicit reference to the use of force, and the two nations eventually agreed on ambiguous terminology that authorized 'measures commensurate to the specific circumstances as may be necessary . . . to halt all inward and outward maritime shipping'. The USA, in another concession to the USSR, agreed to give the MSC the role of co-ordinating any military action. The MSC actually met on 29 October 1990 to discuss the use of force, although

---

[70] For the text of the resolution see *New York Times*, 26 Aug. 1990, p. 9; or *The Persian Gulf Crisis: Relevant Documents, Correspondence, Reports* (note 66), pp. 160–61. By the time the resolution passed, US naval forces were trailing 12 Iraqi ships. Any real fighting at sea which might have resulted from passage of the resolution was avoided when Iraq ordered its ships to allow US inspection of their cargo.

the Western nations made it clear that they would not place their forces under UN command.

The USA used a similar strategy to gain passage of a resolution to allow the use of force against Iraq to push Iraqi troops out of Kuwait. Setting the 15 January 1991 deadline, the USA again attempted to legitimize its policy by internationalizing it.

A comparison of the decision making during 1987–88 Persian Gulf reflagging and the 1990–91 Persian Gulf War illustrates a US Government operating under a vastly different strategic framework. In 1987 US decision makers undertook an operation with the goal of preventing the USSR from expanding its role in the Persian Gulf. In only three years, the end of the cold war had led to such a major revision of the strategic framework that the USA courted Soviet involvement, delayed the use of force in the embargo of Iraq and even asked the USSR to contribute land and sea forces to the Coalition. This was such a break with the past that within the US State Department career officials in charge of Middle East policy were reportedly shocked and angered as the Administration completely reversed 45 years of policy towards the USSR in the Middle East.[71]

V. Implications[72]

The implications of the changes in the US strategic framework are revealing. The end of the cold war created a convergence of interests between the USA and the USSR that seemed as if it would only grow stronger as reform proceeded in independent Russia. However, events of 1994 hint that this 'cosy' relationship between Russia and the USA will become more complex as independent Russian foreign policy develops. The USA seems ready to accept a democratic Russia into the community of nations just as Moscow seeks entry into the Western world. Although Russia still wishes to remain a world power, it no longer has the resources to act unilaterally on a global scale as the USSR had. It still has foreign policy goals and national interests abroad that it will try to protect, but these interests seem ever more closely aligned with the interests of the USA. As recent events attest, post-cold war national security threats may be defined, by both nations, as aggression and instability.

A convergence of interests can mean many things. It is too early to tell what the eventual US–Russian relationship will become. If the Persian Gulf crisis can be viewed as a precedent, the USA and Russia may work together to forge a common stand and may each make concessions to the other's slightly different view of a given situation in order to solve international problems and preserve a growing friendship.

This is not an altogether new phenomenon. The *détente* of the 1970s sought to ensure that US–Soviet competition did not destroy a growing understanding

---

[71] Warner (note 58), p. 26.
[72] Much of what is contained in this conclusion is drawn from Newmann (note 5).

between the two nations that competition should not lead to direct conflict. In the Gorbachev era unilateral military withdrawals and negotiated agreements such as the 1990 Conventional Armed Forces in Europe Treaty (CFE), the 1991 Strategic Arms Reduction Treaty (START I) and the 1987 Intermediate-range Nuclear Forces (INF) Treaty illustrated Moscow's attempt to see that Soviet military deployments in Europe did not prevent the realization of the USSR's hope to enter the democratic world and gain economic aid from the West. The announced withdrawal of Soviet forces from Cuba, the end of massive Soviet aid to Cuba, discussions on the possible return of the Kurile Islands to Japan and independent Russia's policy continuity on these issues all suggested that Moscow was willing to subordinate some foreign policy goals to the urgent need of economic reform and better relations with the West. More recently, however, the Yeltsin Government has been willing to risk Western aid in pursuit of both domestic and foreign policy goals. Western ability to influence Russian politics is declining; ties with the West are even becoming liabilities for Russian politicians. Students of Russian politics should take care to remember that the late 1980s and early 1990s were witness to a revolution. It is unclear where that revolution is headed or even if that revolution is over.

While the future is uncertain, the recent past has been encouraging. Already the USA and USSR have co-operated in an attempt to settle conflicts in Afghanistan, Angola, Cambodia, El Salvador, Ethiopia, the Korean Peninsula, the Middle East and Namibia. The Persian Gulf crisis is only the most obvious example of US–Soviet security co-operation outside Europe. Mutual US–Russian interests are most pronounced in non-Russian areas of the former USSR, Eastern Europe, East Asia and the Middle East. The lack of critical interest in Africa on the part of both nations makes co-operation less complex, but also less compelling.

Latin America may be an exception to this pattern of co-ordinated US–Russian co-operation. During the cold war the idea of spheres of influence defined the parameters of US–Soviet competition. Although the USA could protest and condemn the Soviet interventions in Hungary and Czechoslovakia and the political intimidation of Poland during the early 1980s, there was little that it could do about these situations without initiating actions that could escalate to nuclear war. The USSR was similarly unable to influence US actions in Chile, Guatemala or Nicaragua. It is not a trivial point to remember that the USA and USSR came closest to nuclear confrontation when the USSR took the bold step of placing missiles within the US sphere of influence in Cuba.

In the post-cold war era Russia has lost the old Soviet sphere of influence, and following the failed coup of August 1991, the borders of the Western world moved to the east. Russia's sphere of influence may only lie in the areas that had been the territory of the former USSR, an area that has been called the 'near abroad'. Even those nations, however, may begin to look elsewhere for support in the early stages of nationhood. Ukraine is looking to the West in the hope of forestalling economic and political domination by Moscow, while the Central Asian nations may seek stronger ties to nations of similar socio-cultural and religious patterns, such as Iran or Turkey. However, Russia, as the dominant power in the region, will still see the near abroad as a primary concern of its foreign policy. Similarly, the USA has not lost its interest in its own near abroad—Latin America and the Caribbean. Both nations have remained active in their traditional spheres of influence. For the purposes of this chapter, the salient question is whether these concerns will be shaped by post-cold war US–Russian co-operation.

If the Panama intervention is used as a guide, the Monroe Doctrine has outlived the fears of European imperialism of the 19th century as well as the cold war era US–Soviet rivalry of the 20th century.[73] It seems that only the rationale for such interventions may change. The USA will continue to see Latin America as its foreign policy 'backyard', and may feel free to act unilaterally within the region, regardless of what Moscow or any other nation or international organization might have to say about the issue. The Clinton Administration has been reluctant to continue this pattern, however, seeking UN approval and participation in its actions towards Haiti.

While US–Russian mutual interests are apparent, several years after the collapse of communism Russian foreign policy may be entering a new phase. Recent events have suggested that post-cold war US–Russian co-operation is evolving towards a pattern reminiscent of classic great power politics. Russia and the USA have recently forged a diplomatic compromise to gain UN support for activities within their own traditional areas of concern. In areas such as the Middle East, however, where foreign policy interests may not be in harmony, US and Russian leaders seem more willing to air their differences of opinion in public. This is a departure from the level of co-operation that existed during the Gulf War, and implies that Boris Yeltsin is developing a foreign policy more in tune with Russia's historical interest as a great power. This may have little impact on US policies towards Latin America, but can become a serious complicating factor for US foreign policy in the rest of the world.

Both Russia and the USA face regional foreign policy challenges. Russia has intervened against separatists in newly independent Georgia. In support of Georgian President Eduard Shevardnadze's Government, Russian troops have begun CIS peacekeeping operations.[74] Many within the CIS region and around the world have accused Russia of attempting to recreate the Soviet empire.

The USA has been dealing with the repercussions of the overthrow of Jean-Bertrande Aristide, the constitutionally elected President of Haiti.[75] A continuing refugee crisis and growing domestic pressure had forced the Clinton Administration to consider military intervention to overthrow the military junta

---

[73] For a useful discussion of post-cold war US policy in Latin America, see *United States Interests in Post-Cold War Latin America and the Caribbean,* Hearing before the House Committee on Foreign Affairs, Subcommittee on Western Hemispheric Affairs, 102nd Congress (US Government Printing Office: Washington, DC, 19 Feb. 1991).

[74] A summary of the conflict can be found in Glenny, M., 'The bear in the Caucasus', *Harper's,* vol. 288, no. 1726 (Mar. 1994), pp. 45–53. Shevardnadze was Foreign Minister in Mikhail Gorbachev's Soviet Government.

[75] Martin, I., 'Haiti: mangled multilateralism', *Foreign Policy,* no. 95 (summer 1994), pp. 72–89.

and restore Aristide to power. Though a hostile military intervention was averted at the last minute through the diplomatic efforts of former President Carter, former Chairman of the Joint Chiefs of Staff General Colin Powell and Senator Sam Nunn, US military forces did deploy peacefully to Haiti as part of a transitional force that would clear the way for Aristide's return to power. While the intervention was similar to the insertion of peacekeeping forces and was certainly different in motivation from cold war interventions, the mere appearance of US troops descending upon a Caribbean island raises the spectre of US imperialism in the eyes of many Latin American nations. From the Latin American point of view, the Panama invasion should be the last intervention of the old world order and not a reflection of continued US unilateralism during the new world order. Within the USA, the issue of Haiti has become quite controversial. Republican opponents have chastised the Clinton Administration's intervention in Haiti, and have begun a general assault on Clinton foreign policy since taking control of the House and Senate in the 1994 mid-term elections. Both the USA and Russia have been criticized by domestic opponents and by international public opinion as they try to deal with these issues in their traditional 'backyards'.

At the UN Security Council it seems that Russia and the USA have found a way to help solve each other's problems. The USA had sought a Security Council resolution that would authorize the USA to lead a multinational invasion of Haiti to overthrow the military junta and place Aristide in power. Russia, a permanent member of the Security Council with a veto over any resolution, made it clear that it would not support any resolution on Haiti without exacting a diplomatic price. That price was stated clearly—Russia would support a US-led invasion of Haiti if the Security Council would pass a resolution legitimizing Russia's intervention in Georgia as a UN peacekeeping operation.

On 21 July 1994 UN Security Council Resolution 937 was passed essentially endorsing Russian intervention. The resolution stated that the Security Council 'commends the efforts of the Commonwealth of Independent States directed towards the maintenance of a cease fire', and 'welcomes the contribution made by the Russian federation' in Georgia.[76] The following week, on 31 July, the Security Council passed Resolution 940 which authorized a 'multinational force' to use 'all necessary means to facilitate the departure from Haiti of the military leadership'.[77] While the resolution did not mention the USA directly, it did specifically mention a role for states within the region. Given the diplomatic manœuvring at the UN, the intentions of the USA and the traditional role of the USA in the region, this was tantamount to UN approval of a planned US-led invasion of Haiti. The deal itself was explicit. The only constraints placed upon these operations were the inclusion of UN monitoring groups to watch both Russian and US forces in their respective activities.

[76] United Nations document S/RES/937, 21 July 1994.
[77] United Nations document S/RES/940, 31 July 1994.

Most nations of the former USSR and most Latin American nations were disappointed by these UN actions. From their perspective, Russia and the USA are going back to 'business as usual'—policing their spheres of interest. Even US Ambassador to the United Nations Madeleine Albright has referred to these two UN operations as 'sphere-of-influence peacekeeping'.[78]

In some ways Russia and the USA are acting in the traditional role of great powers—rewarding their regional friends and punishing their regional enemies. Importantly, however, Russia and the USA count each other as friends in the post-cold war world. During the cold war US intervention was officially justified by the threat of Soviet communism, while Soviet intervention was officially justified by the threat of US imperialism. In the cases of Georgia and Haiti intervention is not officially justified on the basis of Soviet or US threats. Instead, intervention is enabled and legitimized on the basis of Russian and US co-operation within the UN Security Council.

Some may argue that this perverts the UN missions of collective security and peacekeeping by allowing Security Council members to use the UN to hide unilateral regional domination under the facade of multinational peacekeeping. Others may say that, given the strains placed upon the UN system in the post-cold war world, as ethnic crises flare, humanitarian catastrophes take hundreds of thousands of lives and the ability of the UN to deal with each subsequent crisis declines, the UN has no choice but to turn to regional powers for help.

A trend in which the UN 'contracts out' its peacekeeping operations seems natural. The UN Security Council is dominated by the nations with the greatest military capability to undertake peacekeeping operations. These nations seem to shoulder a great deal of responsibility; it is only logical that they may begin to merge that sense of international responsibility with their own foreign policy goals—directing the attention of the Security Council towards international crises that are of most concern to their own national goals. Both Russia and the USA, though no longer antagonists, still have foreign policy goals that might require the use of force. In an era where Russian and US interests converge, there is much room for co-operation, co-operation that may be bargained within the Security Council.

The autumn 1994 crisis between Iraq and the USA revealed some cracks in this Security Council alliance. Iraqi troop movements towards the Iraq–Kuwait border were met with a sharp response by the Clinton Administration—the rapid deployment of US forces into the region. While Moscow denounced the Iraqi actions, Russian Foreign Minister Andrey Kozyrev came to the UN Security Council on 17 October to argue for a phased lifting of the economic embargoes against Iraq. Kozyrev's argument at the UN coming immediately after a trip to Baghdad suggests that Yeltsin foreign policy may seek to build bridges to old allies such as Iraq. The USA, however, maintained its hard line towards Iraq. The Clinton Administration made it clear that sanctions would

---

[78] Williams, D., 'Powers assert influence in peacekeeping roles', *Washington Post*, 30 July 1994, p. A12. This label also refers to French intervention in Rwanda.

not be lifted, and that Iraq was seriously mistaken if it thought that threatening gestures, such as the movement of troops towards Kuwait, would convince the USA that Iraq had changed its ways since the Gulf War. Russian diplomacy on behalf of Iraq may not have changed Washington's mind about sanctions, but it did reveal new Russian assertiveness, and did place strains on the US–Russian relationship. Russia may no longer be willing to be the 'junior member' in the Washington–Moscow partnership that had begun under Bush and Gorbachev. Russian and US interests that had been closely co-ordinated seem to be diverging. In the future, forming alliances behind US policy in the Middle East will not be the diplomatic juggernaut of 1990, but a more difficult and uncertain process. This may be true in other regions as well. Changes in the dynamics of Russian domestic policy, both in terms of the pace and shape of economic and political reform, and in terms of dealing with calls for limited autonomy, as in Chechnya, will continue to mould Russian foreign policy. The Russian actions in Chechnya may be a reminder to the overly optimistic that Russia was a great power before the USSR existed, and may stay a great power after the collapse of communism.

The recent UN Security Council resolutions may be the start of a new trend, not isolated incidents. Both Russia and the USA have supported a move towards multilateralism in the conduct of foreign affairs. Multilateralism was one of the keystones of Gorbachev's 'new thinking', and Boris Yeltsin has continued to move Russia towards more co-operative ventures with the West. The Bush and Clinton administrations have supported multilateralism in the Persian Gulf War, Somalia, the Balkans, North Korea and Haiti. If this pattern within both countries continues to hold, then US–Russian co-operation becomes a necessity. The possession of a UN Security Council veto by Russia and the USA requires co-operation when the UN is chosen as the venue for multilateral action. Co-operation may not be necessary if Russia acts through the CIS, or if the USA acts through the Organization of American States, as in the case of Haiti. However, both nations seem to see the UN as the preferred legitimizer of foreign policy activity and the most useful multilateral forum.

This will be the case when US and Russian interests converge. However, if US and Russian interests grow apart, veto power at the UN Security Council may become an impediment to action at the UN. Both nations could return to policies that are more unilateral in nature to avoid dealing with opposing interests of the members of the Security Council. As a result, the Security Council could again become a minor player in international affairs as it had been during the cold war. The model for the future role of the Security Council may be the often furious bargaining over the Bosnian situation. In this case, real differences over approaches to the conflict had to be ironed out diplomatically while the fighting continued, the death toll increased and the UN appeared increasingly irrelevant.

The issue is relatively simple. Even after the cold war nation-states have national interests. The USA has its political, economic and social traditions that affect its foreign policy interests, as does Russia. If there are mutual interests, multilateralism is possible. Where interests are at odds, unilateral action may be the norm. The balancing of those interests can be seen as a return to great power politics, some form of a 'global concert of powers' within which the UN may play a central role. The difference after the cold war could be that those interests may be shared interests more often than in the past.

9. Conflict in Europe: the case of Yugoslavia*

James E. Goodby

I. Introduction

The nation of Yugoslavia sat astride the fault line between Rome and Byzantium, between Catholic and Orthodox Christianity, between the Habsburg Empire and the Ottoman Empire, between the Christian and Muslim worlds. Other areas are split linguistically, ethnically and by religious faith, but no other country was so marked by history for so long and so profoundly as the dividing line between warring empires and conflicting ideas of how human beings should think, act and organize themselves.

Even today the former Yugoslavia occupies the sensitive borderland between areas influenced by the leading countries of Western Europe, most importantly Germany, and those areas that traditionally, at least, have ties to Moscow. As Russian influence receded from Eastern Europe, Western influence advanced, but Serbia is still a place where Russian opinion helped determine the limits of Western intervention. In fact, the onset of war in Yugoslavia raised several uncomfortable images in Europe. German support for Croatia and Slovenia coupled with Russian support for Serbia and the Yugoslav Federal Government in the early days of the war evoked the image of alliance and *entente* from World War I. The first post-cold war crisis in Europe tended to pit Russia against the West.

For Russia and the United States, Yugoslavia may offer lessons about acting in common or, failing that, about avoiding disputes among themselves. Russia and the USA began to co-operate in a serious way only in 1994, when NATO announced a readiness to use force against the Bosnian Serbs. The situation in Russia prior to that time did not encourage Moscow's intervention in Yugoslavia, nor did the situation in Yugoslavia itself. Both Russia and the USA were on the sidelines when a more vigorous role and a united stance might have helped prevent the catastrophe.

Many of the elements in the explosive mix of the former Yugoslavia can be found in other places, and an examination of these discrete problems therefore

* In writing this chapter the author drew, in part, on his 'Peacekeeping in the new Europe', *Washington Quarterly*, vol. 15, no. 2 (spring 1992), pp. 153–71. He also acknowledges with thanks the support provided by the US Institute of Peace, Washington, DC, and, especially, the invaluable help of Daniel O'Connor while he was analysing the conflict in Bosnia and Herzegovina.

may yield some insight into preventive diplomacy and crisis prevention.[1] For example, the question of how ethnic minorities can possess equal legal, economic and cultural rights in a state where another ethnic group is in the majority was a Yugoslav problem that has its counterpart in many parts of Eurasia. Whether the international community should intervene when an incipient conflict is still at the talking stage or wait until violence has broken out is an issue governments faced in Yugoslavia and will face in many other situations.[2] The question of what assets are available to those who would prevent a crisis or promote a political settlement is one that the Yugoslav experience may answer. Russia and the USA should put as much energy into the analysis of such problems as they did into managing the nuclear confrontation during the cold war. The conceptual problems are even more difficult.

II. Setting the stage for a tragedy

Earlier and firmer action by the international community could have headed off the conflict in the former Yugoslavia or at least limited its scale. This was the view of many commentators on the Yugoslav disaster. It was an opinion guardedly expressed by spokespersons for the Clinton Administration to explain why so few options were left to it following the passivity of the Bush Administration.[3] The basic dilemma is a familiar one: as events move from a minor dispute to a major crisis greater effort obviously will be required to deal with the situation. However, at its earliest stage the case for external intervention in a diplomatic dispute cannot be convincingly made, owing to the following obstacles:

1. There is no clearly definable point in a deepening crisis at which outside forces—great powers, neighbouring states, or international organizations—should begin to concert their policies to deal with the crisis.

2. It is difficult to identify a point in a crisis beyond which lies violence on a major scale.

3. Nations are unwilling to use coercive measures before a crisis reaches a level of violence that shocks the international community into action.

4. The international community is not well organized for crisis prevention activities that involve less than crystal-clear state-on-state aggression.

---

[1] In the author's usage, 'preventive diplomacy' refers mainly to the events leading up to the stage where armed conflict seems possible and 'crisis prevention' to the stage where armed conflict is recognized as a real possibility.

[2] This chapter uses the term 'international community' for any organized group of nations with an interest in European security affairs. In practice this means the Conference on Security and Co-operation in Europe (CSCE), the European Union (EU), formerly the European Community, the North Atlantic Treaty Organization (NATO) and the United Nations (UN).

[3] Williams, D., 'Clinton's policy in Balkans puts U.S. prestige, power on the line', *Washington Post*, 11 Feb. 1993, p. A35. Prior to the inauguration of President Bill Clinton the Clinton team also discussed the need to take a preventive approach to global crises before they boiled over and monopolized Clinton's time. See Sciolino, E., 'Clinton urges stronger U.S. stand on enforcing Bosnia flight plan', *New York Times*, 12 Dec. 1992, p. A1.

5. There is no method by which the international community can gauge the ultimate impact on international peace and security of a slowly developing crisis.

6. There are few criteria to determine whether the better course would be to contain and isolate a dispute or to intervene to settle it.

In the discussion that follows these obstacles provide a background for the analysis. The material for the analysis is derived from those events concerning the former Yugoslavia that preceded the outbreak of fighting in June 1991 and those that occurred in the second phase of the crisis leading to the outbreak of conflict in Bosnia and Herzegovina in April 1992. The events that precipitated co-operation, finally, between Russia and the West in 1994 and led to a decision to impose a settlement are discussed in connection with the series of efforts that were made to find a political exit from the war.

From preventive diplomacy to crisis prevention

Conventional wisdom had predicted practically since the end of World War II that after the death of President Josip Broz Tito Yugoslavia, lacking his unifying leadership, would fall apart. The crisis that became full-blown in 1991 was therefore one for which ample warning existed. Tito died in 1980, a success in having prevented ethnic conflict during his reign but a failure in preparing the way for a peaceful breakup of the country or, alternatively, in creating an enduring sense of Yugoslav nationhood. The result of this failure was a slow fragmentation of the country, marked by devolution of authority to the republics and a disavowal by the leadership of those republics of a real sense of responsibility for the future of Yugoslavia as a whole. The exception to this general trend was the Yugoslav National Army (JNA), 60 per cent of whose officers were Serbs, for whom Tito's vision of a unified Yugoslav state was both holy writ and a matter of self-interest. Fear of an outside threat, part of the glue that held Yugoslavia together, probably retained some unifying influence during most of the 1980s. With the revolutions of 1989 in all of East Central Europe and the decline of Soviet power in that region, even that influence faded and centrifugal forces gained momentum. This momentum was not the product of supposed ethnic self-expression alone. It was, in fact, generated by the leaders of the republics who found that nationalism was an effective device for justifying their staying in office after the collapse of communist ideology.

These leaders felt no responsibility to the outside world for settling their growing disputes over the nature of the Yugoslav federation and the sanctity of republican boundaries imposed by Tito. Although there were standards the international community had a right to ask these leaders to consider as they moved towards their bloody confrontation, hardly any pressure was actually exerted on them. The principles and practices of the 1975 Helsinki Final Act—of the Conference on Security and Co-operation in Europe (CSCE)—provided ample grounds for expecting the leaders of the disintegrating federation to settle their differences peacefully, if not amicably. Neither the Yugoslav politicians nor the leaders of other countries saw fit to insist that these norms be observed until it was too late. There were several times during the 1980s when the international community would have been justified in offering its good offices to help settle the disputes among the republics.

In May 1989, for example, Slovenia held an informal vote on its 'sovereign right of secession, free multiparty elections, and private property'.[4] In Bosnia and Herzegovina, inter-ethnic tensions increased sharply in 1989. There were reports of local Serb clashes with Bosnian Government militias in September 1989 and the formation of Bosnian Serb militias in October 1989. Dr Sabrina Ramet remarks that 'the obituary for Yugoslavia seemed to be at hand in October 1989, as it became clear that the republics were withdrawing into themselves and cutting off real ties with each other'.[5] In 1989 the rifts between the six republics were deepening. Slovenia and Croatia wanted a confederal system at a minimum. Serbia and Montenegro wanted to maintain a strong federal system. Bosnia and Herzegovina and Macedonia sought some sort of middle ground between the two positions.

By early 1990 the CIA was forecasting a breakup of Yugoslavia with probable armed conflict accompanying the collapse of the federation.[6] The leaders of the republics were publicly leaving themselves very little room to avoid a military clash. Serbia was arming Serbs living in Croatia, while the Croatian Government was also arming and attempting to disarm the Croatian Serbs. Elections held in Slovenia and Croatia in April and May of 1990 led to the ousting of communist parties in those republics. The winners of both elections, the Democratic United Opposition of Slovenia and the Croatian Democratic Union, made strong nationalistic appeals. The Croats called for a 'greater Croatia' that included parts of Bosnia and Herzegovina. Serbia's President Slobodan Milosevic declared that the Serbs too could go their own way with 'major changes in "administrative borders" of the existing republics such that all Serbs would live within one Serbian state'.[7] The Serbs living in Croatia set up a Serbian National Council on 25 July 1990 and elected Milan Babic president.[8] Ominously, in late 1990 and early 1991 Croatia and Slovenia began to shop abroad for more armaments. Croatia bought an estimated 10 000–20 000 AK-47 rifles from Hungary. The republics also purchased US and Soviet anti-tank and anti-aircraft equipment.[9]

At the latest therefore by 1990, and early in the year at that, the international community had every reason to consider collective policies to be adopted in the face of the inability of the Yugoslav republics to find some peaceful way out of

---

[4] Gagnon, Jr, V. P., 'Yugoslavia: prospects for stability', *Foreign Affairs*, vol. 70, no. 3 (summer 1991), p. 22.

[5] Ramet, S., 'The breakup of Yugoslavia', *Global Affairs*, spring 1991, p. 104.

[6] See Rusinow, D., 'Yugoslavia: Balkan breakup', *Foreign Policy*, vol. 83 (summer 1991), p. 143.

[7] Gagnon (note 4), pp. 23–24.

[8] Ramet (note 5), p. 99.

[9] Gow, J., 'Deconstructing Yugoslavia', *Survival*, vol. 33, no. 4 (July/Aug. 1991), pp. 299–300; and Gagnon (note 4), p. 28.

the impasse they were creating for themselves. In November 1990 the USA raised the matter in the North Atlantic Council (NAC), NATO's most senior standing committee, in Brussels. Several of the European allies objected, with France being the most vehement. Internationalizing the dispute, it was argued, would exacerbate rather than ease the quarrels. The European Community, however, added to its list of conditions that Yugoslavia had to fulfil for EC membership the demand that it continue as a single state.[10] All of this may have given comfort to Serbia in its dispute with the other republics. It is impossible to say whether the historic sympathies of France for Serbia, and Germany for Croatia, affected their judgements or in what way. No doubt there was an effect.[11]

The USA had decided to withdraw its cautious support for Milosevic when it concluded that he was aggravating the federal crisis. It suspended aid to Yugoslavia and withdrew its backing for Yugoslavia to borrow in financial markets in May 1991. Secretary of State James Baker's statement that assistance would be on a case-by-case basis gave the republics some hope of gaining *de facto* recognition from the USA.[12]

Granted that diplomatic intervention was clearly justified by 1990, could the scale of the violence have been anticipated in 1990 or before? Was it even possible to predict that armed conflict of any kind would occur in the early years of the process of disintegration? If not, the case for diplomatic intervention would be a weak one.

History and public statements emanating from Yugoslavia made it clear beyond a reasonable doubt that war would almost certainly accompany a break-up of the federation, and the CIA made that estimate based on its information. As the 1980s ended, alternatives to a breakup were being cast aside, leaving little room for doubt that war would ensue. Dr Sabrina Ramet, who closely followed events in Yugoslavia, predicted in early 1991 that a full-scale civil war could last one to five years and that it would disrupt the entire economy with the possible exception of Slovenia.[13] What is surprising is that these predictions were not followed by any public debate or analysis as to the consequences of war in the Balkans.

The West Europeans had turned their backs on the problem in the autumn of 1990 when the USA had raised the issue. The USA gratefully and quickly passed the buck to the Europeans in 1991.[14] In May 1991, an EC mission headed by Jacques Delors, President of the Commission, and Jacques Santer, Prime Minister of Luxembourg and President of the Council of Ministers,

[10] Gow (note 9), p. 305.

[11] See Josef Joffe's discussion in 'The new Europe: yesterday's ghosts', *Foreign Affairs*, vol. 72, no. 1 (winter 1993), p. 32.

[12] Joffe (note 11), p. 306.

[13] Ramet (note 5), pp. 108–9. Others were not as pessimistic at this time. V. P. Gagnon stated, 'The future of Yugoslavia is by no means certain. But it is also by no means doomed to violence and anarchy'. See Gagnon (note 4), p. 35.

[14] See Joffe, J., 'America's in the balcony as Europe takes center stage', *New York Times*, 22 Dec. 1991, sec. IV, p. 5.

travelled to Yugoslavia. Their aim was to promise economic help in return for a peaceful settlement, but by then it was too late.[15] In the late 1980s this kind of intervention might have helped, but as the crisis was building to proportions that made its prevention next to impossible there was no leader, no organizing agent, that could galvanize the international community, or that part of it most affected by the crisis in Yugoslavia.

Events began to accelerate from late 1990 through the first six months of 1991. What had been a relatively slow buildup of pressures became an avalanche of developments that made crisis prevention almost impossible. On 23 December 1990 Slovenia held a popular vote on independence and with 93 per cent of the electorate voting, some 88 per cent of the voters supported independence.[16] Following its plebiscite Slovenia gave the other republics six months to negotiate a new confederation or face Slovenia's unilateral withdrawal from the federation. Croatia and Slovenia had declared their sovereignty in 1990. Both Bosnia and Herzegovina and Macedonia declared that they would not stay in a Yugoslavia that did not include Croatia and Slovenia. In February 1991 Bosnia and Herzegovina declared its sovereignty.[17] Talks were held between Milosevic and the leaders of the other republics in April and May 1991. An agreement reached on 9 May 1991 between the leaders of the republics provided a temporary solution to the crisis. Under the terms of that agreement, the Serbs accepted the existing borders and recognized the Croatian authorities while Croatia agreed to negotiate with its Serb population on disputed issues and agreed to recognize the role of the JNA in preventing violence.[18]

From crisis prevention to dispute settlement

On 25 June 1991 the governments of Slovenia and Croatia declared their independence from the Yugoslav federation.[19] The JNA reacted and the crisis passed into war. Crisis-prevention efforts had failed to divert the disputants from confrontation and move them towards the conference table. The diplomatic activities during this phase principally concerned dispute settlement between Serbia and Croatia but they also amounted to crisis prevention as regards the rest of the former Yugoslavia and the Balkans. In the last six months of 1991 the world outside the Balkans reacted as it had not done in the decisive years and months before the war erupted.

In contrast to the inaction of the pre-war period there ensued a flurry of mediation attempts, threats to use force, and specialized missions to the war zones.

[15] Zametica, J., International Institute for Strategic Studies, *The Yugoslav Conflict*, Adelphi Paper, no. 270 (Brassey's: Oxford, 1992), p. 60.

[16] Rusinow (note 6), p. 144.

[17] Gagnon (note 4), p. 26.

[18] Gagnon (note 4), p. 30.

[19] Zametica (note 15), pp. 15, 18. On 15 May 1991 Serbia blocked Croatia's Stipe Mesic from becoming President of the Yugoslav Federation, paralysing the Yugoslav Federation and helping set the stage for Croatia and Slovenia's declarations the following month.

The effort was led by the EC with the encouragement of the Bush Administration, which had decided to distance itself from the diplomacy of conflict settlement in Yugoslavia. The last pre-war statement of the Bush Administration on the situation was made by Secretary of State Baker, speaking in Belgrade on 21 June 1991. The Secretary met at the Federation Palace in Belgrade with the Federal Prime Minister, the Foreign Minister and leaders of the republics. He said that what he had heard from them in his meeting did not allay his concern about the disintegration of the country which, he thought, would have very tragic consequences in Yugoslavia and in Europe. He stressed the importance of human and minority rights, of democratization and of a dialogue to create a new basis for unity. Asked about recognition of Slovenia, he said the USA would not do so because it opposed 'pre-emptive unilateral actions'.[20] Secretary Baker's statement was a clear declaration of a US preference for a united Yugoslavia. The crisis, however, had moved beyond that stage, as was soon to be shown by the Slovenian and Croatian statements of secession from the federation and the response of the JNA.

III. European and UN mediation in the Serbian–Croatian conflict

In the main it was the European Community that bore the burden through most of 1991 of working for cease-fires, monitoring these cease-fires and searching for formulas to get negotiations started between Croatia and Serbia. A review of the efforts of the EC is instructive. It shows the EC divided over the fundamental question of whether it was worth saving the Yugoslav federation and at odds over whether armed force should be used under any conditions. The record reveals that the EC negotiated with few instruments of coercion, and chose to deny itself those it had throughout most of the period from July to October 1991. The voice of the USA, the world's only superpower and self-proclaimed advocate of a 'new world order', was muted, no doubt because of *realpolitik* logic. Even the task of orchestrating the sounds of public opprobrium was neglected. The picture that emerges is one of selfless, even heroic manœuvring by brilliant West European and UN diplomats harnessed to national commitments that can only be described as half-hearted.

The mission was truly heroic—it nearly led to fatalities among the mediators and did result in the deaths of observer personnel. It was certainly creatively and energetically carried out. From early July 1991 onwards, it was one of the chief preoccupations of Dutch Foreign Minister Hans van den Broek in his capacity as President of the EC Council of Ministers for the latter part of 1991. EC mediation was successful almost immediately in the case of Slovenia. The Community negotiated an agreement that called for the JNA to return to barracks in both Slovenia and Croatia and for the two republics to suspend for

---

[20] Secretary James Baker, 'US concerns about the future of Yugoslavia, 21 June 1991', *US Department of State Dispatch*, 1 July 1991, p. 468.

three months the declarations of independence they had made on 25 June 1991.[21] The agreement was carried out in Slovenia, where EC observers were quickly introduced, but not in Croatia, where over 11 per cent of the population is Serbian. Clearly a major reason for the success in Slovenia was the decision of the Serbian military leaders to concentrate their assets on Croatia.

The EC resorted to a whole arsenal of mediation techniques. As its efforts to resolve the Yugoslav dispute expanded, it organized a peace conference in The Hague and later co-chaired, with the UN, the International Conference on the Former Yugoslavia in Geneva. It invented an arbitration mechanism for the settlement of disputes, offered ideas for the reconstitution of Yugoslavia and sent observer teams to monitor cease-fires that had been brokered by the EC mediators between Serbia and Croatia. Repeatedly, EC spokesmen talked about economic sanctions, but over four critical months the EC failed to impose sanctions on Yugoslav republics that refused to end the fighting and seek a diplomatic solution to the war.

The peace conference was chaired by Lord Carrington, former British Foreign Minister, former NATO Secretary-General, and one of the most successful mediators of the past 40 years. The conference met for the first time on 7 September 1991 in The Hague and held several meetings over the next months. Its full complement of participants included the leaders of Yugoslavia's six republics, the eight-member Yugoslav collective presidency and EC ministers. Those issues that could not be resolved by negotiation were to be handed to a five-member arbitration board whose decisions would be binding. The five members would be the heads of constitutional courts in France, Germany and Italy, plus one judge each from Croatia and Serbia. The board would be required to reach a decision within two months after Lord Carrington submitted a case to it.[22]

The EC put forward formal proposals designed to nudge the Yugoslav republics not just towards a cease-fire but also towards a long-term settlement. The proposals would have replaced the Yugoslav federal structure with a looser association. Guarantees for the rights of minorities would be provided, ethnic enclaves would be disarmed, and a customs union and programmes for economic co-operation would be established. There would be no unilateral changes in borders. Early in October 1991 an agreement along these lines had seemed possible, partly because it required Croatia to continue in some form of association with Serbia and required Serbia to renounce the use of force to change its borders. All the republics except for Montenegro, Serbia and Slovenia (which considered itself fully independent) had accepted the EC plan for restructuring Yugoslavia. On 7 October, however, the three-month delay in implementing their declarations of independence expired for both Croatia and Slovenia. They then proceeded to nullify their legal connections with the Yugoslav Federal

---

[21] Engelberg, S., 'Europeans try again to calm Yugoslavs', *New York Times,* 28 July 1991, p. A6.
[22] This is based on reports by Blaine Harden and William Drozdiak under the headline 'Yugoslav peace conference scheduled', *Washington Post,* 4 Sep. 1991, pp. A21–22.

Government. By the end of October, Serbian President Milosevic was dismissing the EC plan as a violation of Yugoslavia's federal constitution.

Soviet President Mikhail Gorbachev's efforts at friendly persuasion were equally fruitless. On 15 October 1991, the presidents of Croatia and Serbia met with Gorbachev in Moscow and issued a communiqué calling for an immediate cease-fire and the beginning of negotiations within a month under the sponsorship of the EC, the USA and the USSR. This promising opening failed to materialize.[23]

At a meeting in Belgrade on 23 October 1991, the leaders of Serbia began to unveil their plans for a Greater Serbia as the successor state to Yugoslavia.[24] On 8 November, the EC announced that it was imposing economic sanctions. These included suspension of a 1980 trade and co-operation agreement, limits on the imports of Yugoslav textiles, elimination of benefits under the General System of Preferences and exclusion of Yugoslavia from an EC-backed economic recovery programme. A more direct blow to the war-making capability of the JNA was the EC's intention to seek a UN-ordered oil embargo against Yugoslavia. Most of Yugoslavia's oil imports came from the USSR and Libya.[25] On 9 November 1991, President George Bush personally declared that the USA would support these sanctions.[26]

Most of the mediation effort of the EC had been directed towards the limited objective of a cease-fire. Getting agreement to cease-fires proved to be an easy thing to do, but none of the combatants took them seriously and none actually took hold. One problem was that irregular forces were not fully under the control of the Serbian or Croatian governments. Twelve cease-fires were brokered and broken before the EC decided to impose sanctions. A thirteenth was negotiated and ignored shortly afterwards. Observers were sent to Yugoslavia, however, and some precedents were set that should be relevant for future peacekeeping operations in Europe. At a meeting in Prague on 8 and 9 August 1991, the CSCE's Committee of Senior Officials—Yugoslavia concurring—agreed 'to include other CSCE participating states invited by Yugoslavia' in the observation teams.[27] Yugoslavia agreed to accept observers from Canada, the Czech and Slovak Federal Republics, Poland and Sweden. The observers were therefore CSCE-sponsored, not just EC-mandated. The costs were to be borne by the governments that furnished the monitors, a procedure which allowed

---

[23] For more details on this effort to reach a settlement see the following articles: Harden, B., 'Yugoslav sides accept peace pact', *Washington Post*, 5 Oct. 1991, p. A1; Montgomery, P., 'Serbian chief rejects peace plan at Yugoslav parley in The Hague', *New York Times*, 19 Oct. 1991, p. A2; Montgomery, P., 'Bid on Yugoslavia is again fruitless', *New York Times*, 26 Oct. 1991, p. A5; Sudetic, C., 'European countries warn Serbs to accept plan or face sanctions', *New York Times,* 29 Oct. 1991, p. A10; Zametica (note 15), pp. 61–62.

[24] Sudetic, C., 'Top Serb leaders back proposal to form separate Yugoslav state', *New York Times*, 24 Oct. 1991, p. A17.

[25] Riding, A., 'European nations declare sanctions against Belgrade', *New York Times*, 9 Nov. 1991, p. A1.

[26] Greenhouse, S., 'U.S. goes along with sanctions on Yugoslavia', *New York Times*, 10 Nov. 1991, p. A1.

[27] 'Yugoslavia agrees to more truce observers', Special to the *New York Times*, 9 Aug. 1991, p. A5.

groups within the CSCE to engage in peacekeeping operations at their own expense while the full membership legitimized the effort.

The EC did not want to send peacekeeping units to areas where a cease-fire had not yet taken hold. This was one of the main obstacles to inserting peace-keeping forces into the war zone, then and later, and various ideas were floated to deal with it. For example, the EC mission to Yugoslavia in early August 1991 suggested that monitors of a cease-fire should consist of 'units of the federal armed forces, representatives of the authorities in Croatia in co-ordination and cooperation with European Community monitors'.[28] That EC suggestion failed when Serbia boycotted a scheduled meeting with the EC ministers and Yugoslavia's collective presidency.

Yugoslavia also had its own cease-fire monitors, charged by the federal government with enforcing an 'absolute and unconditional cease-fire'[29] approved by the six Yugoslav republics. The observers consisted in part of plain-clothes federal police from Macedonia and Bosnia and Herzegovina. One of the members of the cease-fire commission reported on 23 August 1991 that the commission was unable to enforce a cease-fire because the JNA refused to defend both Serbs and Croats. Instead, he said, he saw Serbian guerrillas wearing army uniforms and driving vehicles with army licence plates.[30]

Recognizing that the European Community was placing self-imposed limits on the effectiveness of its mediation efforts, some EC members understood almost at once that escalation of the EC commitment might be necessary. As early as August 1991, Hans van den Broek said that he had 'no great objections in principle' to deployment of an armed European peacekeeping force in Croatia.[31] The *New York Times* reported on 1 August 1991 that officials from France, Luxembourg and the UK had privately acknowledged that military personnel might have to augment the EC observer teams.[32] Croatia would probably appeal to the CSCE and the UN for peacekeeping forces to be sent to the country, said President Franjo Tudjman of Croatia in early August, also according to the *New York Times*.[33] Nothing happened.

President of the EC Jacques Delors remarked that 'the Community is like an adolescent facing the crisis of an adult. It now only has the weapons of recogni-tion and economic aid. If it were 10 years older, it might be able to impose a military peacekeeping force'.[34] France had suggested in July 1991 that EC observers should carry sidearms for their own protection.[35] On 11 September 1991, French President François Mitterrand, referring to peacekeeping forces

[28] Sudetic, C., 'Serbs refuse to negotiate in Croatia', *New York Times*, 5 Aug. 1991, p. A6.

[29] Harden, B., 'Croatians seek high-tech arms on world's black market', *Washington Post*, 15 Aug. 1991, p. A38.

[30] Harden, B., 'Clashes in Croatia escalating: army pullout deadline looms', *Washington Post*, 24 Aug. 1991, p. A38.

[31] Harden, B., '80 Croatian police reported slain', *Washington Post*, 3 Aug. 1991, p. A15.

[32] Riding, A., 'Europeans try to ease Croatian crisis', *New York Times*, 1 Aug. 1991, p. A3.

[33] Sudetic (note 28).

[34] Drozdiak, W., 'Lack of an armed option limits EC's Yugoslav peace initiative', *Washington Post*, 5 Sep. 1991, p. A23.

[35] Riding (note 32).

for Yugoslavia, stated that 'if for legal reasons, the United Nations excuses itself, France expects the European Community to take the initiative'.[36] On 17 September, the *New York Times* reported that Dutch officials had proposed a 'lightly armed' force for Yugoslavia, not to impose a cease-fire but rather to use a European show of arms to discourage a resumption of warfare after a new cease-fire had gone into effect.[37]

John Tagliabue, the Balkans correspondent of the *New York Times*, perceptively summed up the situation as of 15 September 1991:

Efforts to establish a cease-fire, despite the presence of dozens of cease-fire monitors operating under the flag of the community, were failing miserably . . . the little war was increasingly becoming a test of the effectiveness of forging a common European foreign policy in a post-cold war world. With ethnic rivalries and nationalist conflicts like those in Yugoslavia abounding throughout newly democratic central Europe, the test was not going well at all.[38]

As if to underscore this judgement, the EC foreign ministers, meeting on 19 September 1991, failed to reach agreement on organizing an armed peace-keeping force. France, Germany and Italy had backed the Dutch proposal but the UK blocked agreement. British Foreign Secretary Douglas Hurd drew on British experience in Northern Ireland to make two points that certainly need emphasis in considering peacekeeping operations:

1. It is easier to put troops in than to take them out.
2. The scale of the effort at the start bears no resemblance to the scale of the effort later on.[39]

The Western European Union (WEU), despite British hesitations, was asked by EC ministers to draw up contingency plans for the use of armed forces. Options developed by the military staffs of the WEU included a 30 000-man force, a lightly armed corps and a force of 10 000 or fewer.[40] None of these plans was ever activated. The possibility of intervening with naval forces was endorsed on 18 November 1991, when the WEU foreign and defence ministers offered warships to protect Red Cross ships evacuating the wounded from Yugoslavia. France, Italy and the UK were prepared to make warships available. Hurd said, however, that the offer would have to be negotiated with Serbia and Croatia.[41] The idea of small-scale intervention was discouraged in

[36] Drozdiak, W., 'Mitterrand seeks talks on USSR', *Washington Post*, 12 Sep. 1991, p. A25.
[37] Riding, A., 'European force is proposed for Croatia', *New York Times*, 17 Sep. 1991, p. A3.
[38] Tagliabue, J., 'Croatia's dying dream', *New York Times*, 15 Sep. 1991, p. E2.
[39] Riding, A., 'Europeans not sending peace force to Croatia', *New York Times*, 20 Sep. 1991, p. A4.
[40] Riding, A., 'Community action', *New York Times,* 1 Oct. 1991, p. A8. According to conversations between the author and a well-informed source, Austria, Hungary and Poland had also engaged in contingency planning for peacekeeping operations in Yugoslavia.
[41] 'Warships offered for Yugoslav aid corridor', *New York Times*, 19 Nov. 1991, p. A7.

public statements by US officials suggesting that the scale of any military effort to halt the fighting in Yugoslavia would be prohibitively large.[42]

Chancellor Helmut Kohl of Germany and President Mitterrand had proposed as early as 19 September 1991 that the EC seek a UN mandate for a peace-keeping force to establish a 'buffer zone' between the warring forces in Yugoslavia.[43] The JNA had flatly opposed the introduction of peacekeeping forces, but this position was overruled in a letter to the UN from Yugoslavia's' collective presidency. In November 1991 the three EC members of the UN Security Council—Belgium, France and the UK—drafted a resolution to imple-ment the EC decision to seek an oil embargo and included in it a request to the UN Secretary-General to seek a cease-fire that would last long enough to permit the deployment of UN peacekeeping forces between the Serbian and Croatian forces. Included also was a proposal for a mechanism to tighten com-pliance with a UN-imposed embargo on arms shipments to Yugoslavia.[44] Activating the UN machinery created one immediate result. It shifted the burden of seeking a cease-fire from the EC mediators to a UN team headed by former US Secretary of State Cyrus Vance.

On 17 November 1991, the day that Vance arrived in Yugoslavia to assess the prospects for introducing UN peacekeeping forces, the defences of Vukovar, a city of key importance to Croatia, were overcome after three months of a siege conducted by the JNA and Serbian irregulars. The JNA at once began to move its tanks and artillery to the nearby Croatian cities of Osijek and Vinkovci, inhabited largely by ethnic Croatians. This movement was accompanied by new cease-fire negotiations among the Croats, Serbs and the UN mission, which led to the signing of a fourteenth cease-fire by Tudjman, Milosevic and Yugoslav Defence Minister General Veljko Kadijevic in Geneva on 23 November 1991. The cease-fire conditions were similar to those of earlier cease-fires. They included a requirement that Croatia should allow fed-eral forces trapped at bases inside Croatia to go to Serbia. Another condition was that all paramilitary or irregular forces on either side would also observe the cease-fire, a very difficult objective to achieve.

The fourteenth cease-fire lasted long enough for Vance to report to the UN Security Council that it seemed to be working. Thus encouraged, the Security Council unanimously adopted a resolution on 27 November 1991 that enabled Vance to return to Yugoslavia to work out the arrangements for the deployment of up to 10 000 UN peacekeeping troops. Two aspects of the Security Council's action require special note. The EC decided not to press for an oil embargo, thus once again dropping any real element of coercion. Second, the support of the Yugoslav delegation was indispensable to win the votes of India and other like-minded countries. Significantly, the role of the UN in resolving internal—

---

[42] This was the sense in which the Deputy Secretary of State and former US Ambassador to Yugo-slavia, Lawrence Eagleburger, spoke on the MacNeil-Lehrer Newshour in early November. See also Talbott, S., 'Fiddling while Dubrovnik burns', *Time*, 25 Nov. 1991, p. 56.

[43] Riding (note 39).

[44] Lewis, P., 'Three European nations propose a UN peace force for Yugoslavia', *New York Times*, 14 Nov. 1991, p. A1.

as opposed to external—disputes was seen by these countries as unwanted meddling in domestic matters.[45]

Thoroughly frustrated by their experiences in Yugoslavia, the EC's monitoring team in that country had drafted a highly critical report for the EC presidency. The report leaked as the fourteenth cease-fire began to collapse. The strategy of the JNA, it said, was to 'pour heavy artillery fire onto a target . . . send in undisciplined irregulars, then move into the villages and assume overall control'. Military intervention by outside forces could deal with the situation, the report suggested: 'There is good reason to believe that selective show and use of force—to intimidate and hit the J.N.A in places where it hurts can cow its bluster and bluff'. The monitors accused the JNA of fighting only 'for its own status and survival'.[46]

At the same time the German Government renewed its threats to recognize Slovenia and Croatia by the end of 1991, whether or not other members of the EC did so. Bonn also imposed a ban on air, land and sea links with Serbia. Partly to encourage recognition, the Croatian Parliament decided to grant Serbian enclaves in Croatia a degree of self-rule. In Bonn, Chancellor Kohl told the presidents of Croatia and Slovenia that Germany would grant them recognition before Christmas, a move opposed by France, the UK and the USA. Some of Yugoslavia's neighbours, however, warned that they might follow Germany's lead. The concern of those opposing recognition was that this should await an overall peace settlement and that Serbia's response would be to escalate the conflict rather than negotiate.[47] Stepping up its own pressure on all the republics, the USA announced on 6 December 1991 a series of economic sanctions to take effect on 21 December.

On 12 December 1991, UN Secretary-General Javier Pérez de Cuellar announced plans for a UN peacekeeping force of more than 10 000 troops. The force would consist of 10 infantry battalions and police units. It would be deployed in regions where Serbs and Croats lived in proximity to one another and would assist in humanitarian work, including resettlement of displaced people. The JNA would be withdrawn from Croatia. The Secretary-General stipulated, however, that 'an effective cease-fire' would have to be in place before the plan could be implemented. The report of the Secretary-General made clear that Serbian irregular forces continued to block an effective cease-fire.[48]

Efforts in the Security Council to organize a peacekeeping force coincided with efforts by Washington to block German diplomatic recognition of Croatia and Slovenia. On 12–13 December 1991, Deputy Secretary of State Lawrence Eagleburger gave 'stern warnings' to the 12 members of the EC that premature

[45] Lewis, P., 'UN promises to send force to Yugoslavia', *New York Times*, 28 Nov. 1991, p. A1.

[46] Quoted in Sudetic, C., 'Observers blame Serb-led army for escalating war in Croatia', *New York Times*, 3 Dec. 1991, p. A8; Silber, L., 'EC lifts Yugoslav sanctions, excepts Serbia and Montenegro', *Washington Post*, 5 Dec. 1991, p. A9.

[47] Kinzer, S., 'U.S. is at odds with German backing for Slovenia and Croatia', *New York Times*, 8 Dec. 1991, p. A18.

[48] Lewis, P., 'UN peacekeepers seen for Croatia', *New York Times*, 13 Dec. 1991, p. A6.

and selective recognition of Yugoslav republics would damage prospects for peace and lead to greater bloodshed. These warnings followed letters to the EC from Lord Carrington and Pérez de Cuellar also cautioning against early recognition. In the Security Council, France and the UK sought to head off the German action by sponsoring a resolution calling for military observers to be sent to Yugoslavia to begin arrangements for deployment of the UN peacekeeping force once a cease-fire had taken hold. The two delegations also proposed a clause that would warn against 'political actions' (i.e., recognition that would harm the reconciliation process).[49] All this was to no avail. German Foreign Minister Hans-Dietrich Genscher responded to the UN Secretary-General by asserting that denying recognition would only encourage the JNA in its 'policy of conquest'.[50] Germany and Austria pushed very strongly for EC recognition of Croatia and Slovenia, finally announcing that they would unilaterally recognize the two republics on 15 January 1992.[51] On 15 December 1991, the UN Security Council adopted a resolution that watered down the non-recognition appeal and authorized the dispatch of 18–20 military police and political observers to Yugoslavia. Reportedly, the USA had objected to a more ambitious French–British proposal to send as many as 100 military observers there.

President Bush added his voice to the debate on 15 December by saying 'we want to see a peaceful evolution'. Adding that the United States had been 'strongly supportive' of the UN and of the EC, Bush said 'their advice has been to go slow in recognition and I think they're right'.[52] The USA maintained that it would not recognize any republic until there was a general settlement of the crisis.[53] The position of the Bush Administration was that the parties to the Yugoslav conflict must first reach a peaceful settlement through negotiation and with firm protection for minorities.

Germany's advice carried the day, however, in the meeting of the EC foreign ministers in Brussels on 16 December 1991. The ministers agreed unanimously that they would extend recognition by 15 January 1992 to any Yugoslav republic that asked for it by 23 December 1991, provided certain criteria were met. The decision, however, permitted EC members to extend recognition even if standards had not been met.[54] Thus, as 1992 dawned, the conflict in Yugoslavia would cease to be a civil war and become an international European war. The media speculated that fighting would soon spread to Bosnia and Herzegovina. There was a brief respite: Vance succeeded in negotiating an end to the first

---

[49] Binder, D., 'Bonn's Yugoslav plan faces more flak', *New York Times*, 14 Dec. 1991, p. A3.

[50] Leopold, E., 'Informal accord reached on Yugoslav peace force', *Washington Post*, 15 Dec. 1991, p. A42.

[51] See Tagliabue, J., 'Kohl to compromise on Yugoslavia', *New York Times*, 18 Dec. 1991, p. A3.

[52] Lewis, P, 'UN yields to plans by Germany to recognize Yugoslav republics', *New York Times*, 16 Dec. 1991, p. A1.

[53] See Kinzer, S., 'U.S. is at odds with German backing for Slovenia and Croatia', *New York Times*, 8 Dec. 1991, p. A18; Tagliabue, J., 'Germany insists it will recognize Yugoslav republic's sovereignty', *New York Times*, 15 Dec. 1991, p. A1; Kinzer, S., 'U.S. not jumping on bandwagon', *New York Times*, 16 Jan. 1992.

[54] Drozdiak, W., 'EC envoys agree on recognition of Croatia, Slovenia next month', *Washington Post*, 17 Dec. 1991, p. A15.

phase of the Yugoslav war with a cease-fire between Serbia and Croatia on 3 January 1992. The agreement provided for stationing peacekeeping units in Croatia.

The failure of containment

Crisis prevention now turned to the problem of forestalling the spread of the conflict beyond Serbia and Croatia. For several months in 1991–92 it had seemed possible that the war in the former Yugoslavia could be contained. The fighting had been essentially limited to border areas between Serbia/ Montenegro and Croatia. Slovenia ceased to be a war zone after a few days of limited combat when the JNA pulled out to focus its attention on Croatia. The other republics, Macedonia and Bosnia and Herzegovina, maintained neutrality between the combatants and remained at peace. Kosovo and Vojvodina, which had been autonomous administrative units under Tito, lost their autonomy between the autumn of 1988 and spring 1990. Vojvodina fell first, with Milosevic taking control of the political apparatus in the region. Milosevic dissolved the Kosovo Assembly and Government on 5 July 1990. These areas remained quiescent during the fighting in 1991, the latter under harsh repressive control by Belgrade.

The period between July 1991 and April 1992 thus was a critical juncture for preventive diplomacy. Crisis prevention had failed to deal effectively with events in Yugoslavia prior to July 1991 but there was still a chance to prevent war in those parts of Yugoslavia not affected by the dispute between Croatia and Serbia.

What was the best that could have been expected of the three communities in Bosnia and Herzegovina in this period and how could the international community have encouraged it? Immense caution regarding the governance of the republic and a maximum commitment to intensive dialogue among the communities was what was required. It cannot be said that this was met by any of the parties or by the international community. John Zametica notes that 'the national question in Yugoslavia was . . . most strongly represented in Bosnia-Herzegovina'.[55] This is not surprising as Bosnia and Herzegovina was a microcosm of the Yugoslav federation. In the November 1990 elections in Bosnia and Herzegovina the following resulted: Muslims—86 seats, Serbs—72 seats, and Croats—44 seats, a near perfect representation of their relative percentages of population.

The Bosnian Muslims watched the conflict between Serbia and Croatia with considerable alarm. As 1991 wore on, the communities in Bosnia and Herzegovina began to split along ethnic lines. The Serbs opposed independence while Croatia armed the Croats in western Herzegovina.[56] The Muslims still entertained the idea of ethnic pluralism but expected to be the dominant group.

[55] Zametica (note 15), p. 36.
[56] Sudetic, C., 'Bosnia fears it's next in Yugoslavia's civil strife', *New York Times,* 28 Dec. 1991, p. A6.

The turning point came in December when the EC agreed to extend recognition to any Yugoslav republic that asked for it, subject to conditions designed to establish that the new states would be bona fide democracies: (*a*) respect for human rights, the rights of ethnic minorities and the democratic process; (*b*) acceptance of border changes only by peaceful means; and (*c*) agreement to submit territorial disputes to binding arbitration.[57]

The Germans hoped that this move would delegitimize any Serbian claim to be fighting for the integrity of the Yugoslav federation, but it exerted enormous pressure on the Muslims and Croats in Bosnia and Herzegovina to seek independence before working out the necessary inter-ethnic conditions for it.

In January 1992 a legal commission to the EC recommended that a referendum be held by those republics asking for independence and recognition in order to determine whether the citizens really wanted to opt for a status outside the Yugoslav federation.[58] The decision of the Bosnian Government to accept this condition and to conduct a referendum on independence predictably led to a refusal of the minority Serbs to take part in the voting. The question of whether minorities could safely live in republics dominated by another ethnic group had been at the heart of the question of whether alternatives to a federated Yugoslavia could be created without bloodshed. At the time the voting took place in Bosnia and Herzegovina the Serbian–Croatian conflict clearly foretold that disintegration of the federation would most likely not proceed without violent conflict. The Bosnian Serbs rejected the referendum, and fighting began in April 1992.

There could have been no question that violence would ensue under the conditions that developed in Bosnia and Herzegovina during the latter half of 1991 and especially the first quarter of 1992. A vague hope that Serbia had exhausted itself and was war-weary after the fierce struggles in Croatia probably led to some complacency, but the cease-fire between Croatia and Serbia came after Serbia had delivered about one-third of Croatia into the safekeeping of Serbs in Croatia with UN peacekeepers to watch over them. The precedents were far from encouraging. If there was ever a time for vigorous preventive diplomacy, this was it. The behaviour of the Western nations gave little sign that this was recognized. Once again, as during 1990 while the crisis of Yugoslavia was building and during the final months of deepening crisis in 1991, the main feature of Western diplomacy was a Micawber-like tendency to hope something would turn up. The predictions of disorder in Bosnia and Herzegovina may have been insufficiently cataclysmic but they were surely grim enough to warrant vigorous diplomatic activity before the Bosnian war began to prevent it. Western statesmen, however, still behaved as though they thought the war could be contained and that not much could be done to stop it. There was also an underlying doubt that Bosnia and Herzegovina was a viable state since it had no history of having been one.

---

[57] Drozdiak, W., 'Europeans' Balkan stance attests to rising German influence', *Washington Post*, 18 Dec. 1991, p. A25.
[58] Zametica (note 15), p. 39.

During the last six months of 1991 the EC mediators were preoccupied with stopping the fighting in Croatia. This meant that no one, essentially, was working on the problem of defusing the elements of the impending explosion in Bosnia.

Cyrus Vance and Lord Owen undertook five missions to the former Yugoslavia from mid-October 1991 to 8 January 1992. They went to Sarajevo on 2 January 1992, but it seems that they were then most concerned with concluding the Serbian–Croatian cease-fire agreement that took effect the next day.[59] They headquartered the United Nations Protection Force (UNPROFOR) in Sarajevo in the hopes that this might act as a moderating element.[60] Although the international community had been aroused to action by the war between Serbia and Croatia there was still no organizing agent to deal with the broader political problems of a disintegrating Yugoslavia and its ramifications for the Balkans, and, least of all, with internal power-sharing. As fighting increased in April 1992, Vance was sent to Bosnia to try to head off further fighting in Bosnia and Herzegovina. The UN planned to send 100 observers, destined for Croatia, to Mostar and the Bihac region.[61] There was also the problem that Vance and the UN simply did not have the resources to mount a second massive peacekeeping operation in Bosnia. Said Vance in April 1992, 'We are not going to put in any additional forces. We simply do not have any resources to do it'.[62]

The containment policy of the Bush Administration had to focus eventually on Kosovo since that came to be seen as the trigger that would involve the other Balkan states in a wider war. Bush therefore wrote to Milosevic in December 1992, saying that if Serbia used force in Kosovo the USA would retaliate against Serbia, including Serbia proper. He wrote, 'in the event of conflict in Kosovo caused by Serbian action, the United States will be prepared to employ military force against the Serbians in Kosovo and Serbia proper'.[63] President Bill Clinton reaffirmed this policy.[64] The negotiators in Geneva, Lord Owen for the EC and Cyrus Vance for the UN, also worked hard to contain the fighting, urging the Bosnian Government not to launch counter-attacks at critical negotiating junctures, and on one occasion urging the US State Department and the White House not to receive Bosnian President Alija Izetbegovic.[65] Ideas about safe havens and lifting the arms embargo on the Bosnian Government were floated in the media, but these notions were generally thought to be an escalation and not in keeping with a policy of attempted containment of the war.

---

[59] See Binder, D., 'Yugoslav's "war weary" envoy stays', *New York Times*, 8 Jan. 1992, p. A3.

[60] Burns, J. F., 'U.N. peacekeeping force moves into Yugoslavia', *New York Times,* 15 Mar. 1992, p. 6.

[61] Binder, D., 'U.N. to send 100 observers to Bosnia and Herzegovina', *New York Times*, 13 Apr. 1992, p. A6.

[62] Sudetic, C., 'Vance appeals to Serbs to halt Bosnia fighting', *New York Times*, 16 Apr. 1992, p. A1.

[63] Goshko, J. M., 'Bush threatens "military force" if Serbs attack Kosovo Province', *Washington Post,* 29 Dec. 1992, p. A10. Also quoted in Joffe (note 11), p. 36.

[64] Goshko, J. M., 'U.S. takes more active role in Balkans', *Washington Post*, 11 Feb. 1993, p. A1.

[65] Sciolino, E., 'Bosnian arrives, U.S. embarrassed', *New York Times*, 8 Jan. 1993, p. A6.

IV. Approaches to political settlement

The international community was brought to the point of active diplomatic intervention in the former Yugoslavia only by the outbreak of armed conflict in June 1991. Much of the time of the international negotiators therefore was taken up by brokering cease-fires and trying to sequester heavy weapons. Consistently, however, the negotiators declared that the conflict could end only when a political settlement had been achieved. The nature of the political settlement, naturally, evolved in response to events in the former Yugoslavia. The first of these proposals, Lord Carrington's Arrangements for a General Settlement of 18 October 1991, spoke of 'sovereign and independent republics with international personality for those who wish it'.[66] It steered clear of the issue of self-determination for ethnic minorities within sovereign states, and it insisted that frontiers could not be changed by force.

The spring of 1992 witnessed a second attempt at political settlement as the focus shifted to Bosnia and the issue of self-determination had to be confronted. The EC negotiator at that time, Ambassador Jose Cutileiro of Portugal, concluded that separate districts for each of the three ethnic groups would be the only way to settle the conflict. He made some progress towards establishing the goal of 'cantonization' as the basis for the negotiations with an understanding that power-sharing among the ethnic groups would be the basic constitutional principle. Ten rounds of talks took place under the chairmanship of Ambassador Cutileiro with senior representatives of the three main Bosnian parties. The high-water mark in progress was reached on 18 March 1992 when agreement was reached on a Statement of Principles for New Constitutional Arrangements for Bosnia and Herzegovina. Additional principles on human rights were agreed to on 31 March, but both agreements were repudiated soon after and fighting broke out almost immediately.[67]

This effort for a settlement collapsed in April 1992. The Bosnian Serbs had accepted the idea that Bosnia and Herzegovina would be divided into three ethnically defined regions but that the country would remain intact and not be divided between Serbia and Croatia.[68] The referendum of February 1992, however, had yielded a vote for independence, with the Serbs abstaining. This was followed by recognition of the Bosnian Government by the EC and the USA on 7 April 1992. By that time, the Bosnian Serbs had concluded that the republic would have to be forcibly divided. War on a large scale was guaranteed when, on 19 May 1992, the JNA pulled out of Bosnia and Herzegovina, leaving weapons and Bosnian members of the Army to augment the forces of the Bosnian Serb leader Radovan Karadzic.

[66] Zametica (note 15), p. 62.

[67] Report of the Co-Chairmen on Progress in Developing a Constitution for Bosnia and Herzegovina', a document of the International Conference on the Former Yugoslavia, 25 Oct. 1992, paragraphs 2 and 3, p. 1. See also Sudetic, C., 'Yugoslav groups reach an accord', New York Times, 19 Mar. 1992, p. A9; and Cutileiro, J., 'Horrors built on delusion', International Herald Tribune, 15–16 Aug. 1992, p. 4.

[68] See Sudetic (note 67), p. A9.

A third approach to political settlement was to bow to power realities and allow the strongest parties—Serbia and Croatia—to hammer out an agreement on the future of Bosnia. On 7 May 1992 the Serbs and the Croats met at Graz, Austria, to discuss the future of Bosnia. The map that resulted from that meeting granted large tracts of land in the north, east and south-east to the Bosnian Serbs, most of Herzegovina to the Bosnian Croats, and the central portion of Bosnia and the Bihac pocket to the Muslims.[69] Under this plan the central government of Bosnia would lose control over most of its territory. It was also assumed that the Serb and Croat areas would have a right to merge with their brethren across the border. The plan was rejected at the time because the international community did not want to condone the territorial conquests of the Serbs and because the Bosnian Government rejected anything like a solution which would deprive them of control of most of their territory. Later, during the summer of 1993, deprived of international support, the Bosnians would be encouraged to acquiesce in partition on terms acceptable to the Serbs and Croats. The Clinton Administration was threatening to bomb Serb-occupied heights around Sarajevo but only if the Bosnians actively participated in the Geneva talks, where Lord Owen was now advocating partition.

The fourth approach to a political settlement and the most elaborate came from the International Conference on the Former Yugoslavia, which replaced the EC Conference on Yugoslavia. Cyrus Vance and David Owen were named Co-chairmen of the Steering Committee, representing the UN and the EC, respectively. Martti Ahtisaari, a distinguished Finnish diplomat and later President of Finland, was named Chairman of the Bosnia and Herzegovina Working Group. The problem they faced as they began work in Geneva on 3 September 1992 was that the Bosnian Government and the Bosnian Serbs had diametrically opposite ideas about the future of Bosnia and Herzegovina.[70] The Bosnian Government advocated a centralized, unitary state arranged for administrative reasons into a number of regions. The Bosnian Serbs wanted Bosnia and Herzegovina divided into three independent states, one each for the Muslim, Serb and Croat populations. The Croats took an intermediate position.

The co-chairmen concluded that the intermingling of the population meant that three separate sovereign territories based on ethnicity could only be achieved through enforced population transfer. Furthermore, the new Serb and Croat states could be expected to form ties with Serbia and Croatia, rather than with the Muslim-dominated state. A centralized state, on the other hand, would not be accepted by the Bosnian Serbs and Croats who would fear that it would not protect their interests. From this reasoning, Vance and Owen came to the conclusion that the only solution left would be a decentralized state. This meant that the central government, in the words of the Vance–Owen report, 'would have only those minimal responsibilities that are necessary for a state to func-

[69] Harden, E., 'Serbs, Croats agree to carve up Bosnia', *Washington Post*, 8 May 1992, p. A17.

[70] The description of their positions is drawn from the 'Report of the Co-chairmen on Progress in Developing a Constitution for Bosnia and Herzegovina', 25 Oct. 1992, submitted to the UN Secretary-General by them on 26 Oct. 1992.

tion as such'.[71] The country would be divided into 7–10 autonomous provinces which would independently handle most of the affairs of the republic. The Vance–Owen analysis did not accept the idea that the boundaries of the provinces should be determined exclusively by ethnic considerations. Geographical, historical, economic and other factors also should be taken into account. Their report of 25 October 1992 stated, however, that 'a high percentage of each group would be living in a province in which it constitutes a numerical majority, although most of the provinces would also have significant numerical minorities'.[72]

As the Vance–Owen Plan evolved, the number of provinces became 10, but essentially the same thinking lay behind the proposals. By 30 January 1993 Vance and Owen had succeeded in securing the agreement of the three groups to nine principles that reflected the concept of a decentralized state with most governmental functions carried out by the provinces.[73]

Other features of the proposed political settlement were not accepted. The Croats accepted the constitutional principles and the map drawn up by the Vance–Owen team defining the boundaries of the 10 provinces. The Bosnian Government and the Bosnian Serbs, however, did not accept the provincial boundaries.[74] The Bosnians also would not sign the agreement on Military and Related Issues, believing that UN provisions for the internment and monitoring of Serb heavy weapons were inadequate.[75]

Another document was presented to the three Bosnian parties on 29 January 1993, entitled Interim Arrangements for Bosnia and Herzegovina. This was a proposal for establishing an interim central government through a procedure that envisaged each of the parties nominating three representatives who would be subject to the approval of Vance and Owen. The existing Presidency of Bosnia and Herzegovina would then transfer its powers and authority to the interim central government which would remain in power until elections could be held. There would also be interim governments in each of the provinces. A governor would be nominated by one of the three parties, depending on the ethnic composition of the particular province. The allocation to ethnic groups was designated in the document. Needless to say the Bosnian Government found it difficult to agree to its own liquidation and so this document, too, was rejected by representatives of the Bosnian Government.

Vance and Owen had decided that the Geneva negotiations should be suspended after the January effort to reach a political settlement, and the effort to reach agreement shifted to UN Headquarters in New York. There, the co-chairmen hoped, pressure could be brought to bear on the Bosnian Government by the Security Council to accept the proposals worked out by the Vance–Owen team. Owen stated at the time, 'I hope that by the time we get to the

---

[71] 'Report of the Co-chairmen' (note 70), p. 5.
[72] 'Report of the Co-chairmen' (note 70), p. 6.
[73] The text of the nine principles is in UN General Assembly Document A/47/869, 18 Jan. 1993.
[74] See 'Report of the Secretary-General on the activities of the International Conference on the Former Yugoslavia', UN Security Council document S/25221, 2 Feb. 1993, p. 3.
[75] See S/25221 (note 74).

Security Council we will have all the parties signed up. That is why we brought it deliberately to a crunch. We have the feeling it can be resolved in New York'.[76] According to aides to Vance and Owen the negotiators hoped to isolate the Bosnian Serbs and to get the rump Yugoslavia and Russia to press the Bosnian Serbs to settle the conflict.[77]

The hope entertained by Vance and Owen was dashed in fairly short order, in part by a 10 February 1993 announcement by Secretary of State Warren Christopher regarding the policy of the Clinton Administration towards the former Yugoslavia.[78] This statement made it clear that the Clinton Administration would not put pressure on the Bosnian Muslims to accept the Vance–Owen Plan. On 3 March 1993 President Izetbegovic signed the document on separation of forces and cessation of hostilities, leaving the map of the provinces and the interim governmental arrangements the only proposals not accepted by the three parties.[79] The negotiators were talking about adding some territory to the Muslim-dominated provinces, but the war, rather than the efforts to reach a political settlement, was the more decisive factor in the spring of 1993.

On 25 March 1993 the Bosnians signed the agreement on interim governmental arrangements and accepted a revised map of the provincial boundaries.[80] The Bosnian Serbs continued to reject the map and the interim arrangements stating that they had to be sent to their Assembly for its consideration and decision. The Bosnians stated that their signature would not be valid if the other parties did not sign within a reasonable time period, if the international community did not undertake to enforce the agreement and if the aggression continued.[81] The Bosnian Serbs signed the interim arrangements and agreed to the map on 2 May 1993 in a meeting in Athens, but Karadzic stated that his signature would be void if the Bosnian Serb Assembly did not support the decision in a vote on 5 May 1993.[82] The Assembly rejected the accord, as did a 'popular referendum' held on the accord two weeks later. The Vance–Owen Plan expired at that point for all practical purposes. Lord Owen declared the plan officially dead on 16 June 1993 and shifted his support to a partition solution.[83]

The Bosnian Serb rejection of the Vance–Owen Plan had no other repercussions, since the international community was unwilling to force the issue. President Clinton sent his Secretary of State to inquire whether the Europeans would support a 'lift and strike' strategy of lifting the arms embargo and using

[76] Binder, D., 'Talks in Geneva on Bosnia hit an impasse', *New York Times*, 31 Jan. 1993, p. A1.

[77] Lewis, P, 'Bosnian peace talks yield no progress', *New York Times*, 8 Feb. 1993, p. A10.

[78] Goshko, J. M., 'U.S. takes more active Balkans role', *Washington Post*, 11 Feb. 1993, p. A1.

[79] See 'Report of the Secretary-General on the activities of the International Conference on the Former Yugoslavia', UN Security Council document S/25403, 12 Mar. 1993.

[80] See 'Report of the Secretary-General on the activities of the International Conference on the Former Yugoslavia', UN Security Council document S/25479, 26 Mar. 1993.

[81] 'Report of the Secretary-General on the activities of the International Conference on the Former Yugoslavia' (note 80), annex V, Statement of Izetbegovic of 25 Mar. 1993.

[82] 'Report of the Secretary-General on the activities of the International Conference on the Former Yugoslavia', UN Security Council document S/25709, 3 May 1993, annex V. See also Drozdiak, W., 'U.S. seeks support for force in Bosnia as Serb leader signs U.N. peace plan', *Washington Post*, 3 May 1993, p. A1.

[83] Ottoway, D. B., 'Mediator backs partition for Bosnia', *Washington Post*, 18 June 1993, p. A1.

air power to strike at the Serbs. They did not and the strategy was shelved. A plan to protect six safe havens in Bosnia was later agreed among France, Russia, the UK and the USA, but continued Serb and Croat aggression revealed the hollowness of this approach as well. Finally, even Lord Owen urged the Bosnian Government to sit down with the Serbs and Croats and hammer out an end to the agony. Lacking the option of force, the international community could do little else.

Critics of the Vance–Owen Plan believed that the proposed political settlement awarded too much to the aggressors and that there was much that was unclear about enforcing it. The Cutileiro Plan had the same defect and, appearing at an early stage of the war, it seemed premature to abandon the idea of a multi-ethnic society. However, the fundamental question that these proposed political settlements raised demanded an answer: the question of how ethnic groups should be governed, protected and guaranteed their basic human rights within a single state.

In the Vance–Owen Plan, ethnic groups were given constitutional recognition, the central government was to be organized along ethnic lines, the constitution would regulate all matters of vital concern to any of the constituent parties and could only be amended in these respects by consensus among the three groups. The governments of the individual provinces would essentially be assigned to an ethnic group depending on the composition of the population. Critics of the plan argued that the dominant ethnic group in each province would probably indulge in ethnic cleansing. Some felt that the central government lacked sufficient authority under the Vance–Owen Plan and that the Serbian and Croatian provinces would develop stronger ties with Serbia and Croatia than with each other or with the central government. Most agreed, however, that the struggle had gone too far to base the constitution on anything other than ethnic power-sharing. As noted, some pointed out that Bosnia and Herzegovina had never been an independent, sovereign state and that Vance and Owen were essentially creating a state where none had existed before.[84]

What was clear was that the plan would not be self-enforcing and that tens of thousands of outside troops would be required, probably for years, to police the settlement. Close observers also thought that a civilian-run administrative structure would have to be put in place by the UN to parallel the tripartite central government structure created by the Vance–Owen Plan. Bosnia and Herzegovina would be virtually a UN trust territory for many years to come.

The fifth major effort to find a solution that would end the war stemmed from a series of developments that brought Russia, the USA and the European Union to assume joint responsibilities for the first time since the war began. Russia's bond with the Serbs served as one limit to Western action in the conflict from the beginning. On the other hand, Russia supported the oil embargo and the freezing of assets proposed by the United States in the United Nations in late May 1992. Russia, in fact, supported all of the numerous UN Security Council

[84] Rosenthal, A. M., 'Needed: U.S. goal in Bosnia', *New York Times*, 2 Feb. 1993, p. A19.

resolutions, including those concerning the use of force. Furthermore, the question of the use of force divided the West as frequently as it divided Russia and the West. Russia distanced itself from the Clinton Administration's first idea of lifting the arms embargo on Bosnia and mounting airstrikes against the Bosnian Serbs in early 1993, but so did the West Europeans.

The question of the use of force did not become a truly divisive issue between Russia and the West until the winter of 1993–94. In January 1994 the Europeans and the USA demanded the relief of Srebrenica and the opening of the airport at Tuzla, threatening to use force if necessary. Russia responded that fresh Security Council authorization on the matter would be necessary but France, Great Britain and the United States countered that new authorization was not needed for the Secretary-General to order strikes to protect UNPROFOR troops in Srebrenica, or to get humanitarian aid into Tuzla. The Russian Government came under increased pressure domestically as the Russian Parliament voted that the sanctions on Serbia should be eased.

A Bosnian Serb attack on a market-place in Sarajevo on 5 February 1994 left 68 dead and hundreds wounded and changed the complexion of the options being considered. The USA and the European Union quickly agreed to set a deadline for Bosnian Serbs to withdraw artillery and mortars or face NATO airstrikes. Russia opposed the move, saying first there should be an investigation into the attack. Russian Foreign Minister Andrey Kozyrev's early statements were ominous; he was quoted as saying that airstrikes would 'cast a very dark shadow over our relationship'[85] with the West. Russia seemed particularly incensed that the forum for discussing the issue was NATO and not the United Nations. Russia conceded that NATO had the authority under existing resolutions to carry out the airstrikes, but nevertheless insisted on a Security Council meeting. The Security Council met on 14 February 1994, but Russia was unable to get enough support to change the previous resolution. Faced with the unappealing prospect of the use of force by NATO in the Balkans, Russia became much more active in the negotiations. Special envoy Vitaliy Churkin played a major role in the compromise for a Bosnian Serb withdrawal of heavy weapons around Sarajevo with all that implied for future influence. This was managed by Churkin's proposal to place some 800 Russian peacekeepers in Sarajevo for unspecified duties and was worked out between Churkin as the Russian representative and Bosnian Serb leader Karadzic. In doing so Russia won the support of a somewhat nervous West, which wanted the shelling stopped but feared Russian influence in the Balkans, and the support of the Serbs, who saw Russia as a friendly protector.[86]

Communications between Russia and the United States as regards the use of force in Bosnia obviously did not work very well, which is inevitable when matters of military operations are concerned. From the Russian point of view, Moscow was not being treated as a great power that needed to be consulted

[85] Lewis, P., 'Russia a barrier to NATO air strike', *New York Times*, 9 Feb. 1994, p. A12.
[86] Lewis, P., 'Russia backing Serbs', *New York Times*, 11 Feb. 1994, p. A6.

before decisions were made. On the other hand, when Russia placed peacekeepers in Sarajevo to head off a NATO airstrike, the Clinton Administration found out about the initiative via television through the Cable News Network (CNN).

The search for a political settlement was a more fertile field for co-operation between Russia and the West. The West came to see Russia as a valuable partner and a link to the Serbs. As early as July 1992, Lord Carrington noted that the USA and Russia might do better than the West Europeans in getting the negotiations going. Russia took an active part in the International Conference on the Former Yugoslavia. When the Clinton Administration in its first decisions on Bosnia resolved to ask for better terms for the Bosnian Government, Ambassador Reginald Bartholomew went to Moscow first to consult with Russia. Russia, the United States and several European powers also agreed on a Joint Action Programme in which the warring parties would agree to a freeze on hostilities while the outside powers maintained the long-term pressure of sanctions to reverse the Bosnian Serb conquests.

Russia also became increasingly involved in the negotiations for a long-term settlement of the Croatian–Serbian dispute. In early 1994 UN strategy was developed by Churkin and Charles Redman, the US representative in the former Yugoslavia, and was based on the premise of normalization of relations between the Croats and the Serbs in Croatia and then negotiating a political settlement. As a sign of its influence with the Krajina Serbs, Russia persuaded them to go to Zagreb to negotiate with the Croatian Government using the Russian embassy there as a venue. Russia supported Croatian sovereignty over the Krajina areas. Russia noted that close co-operation with the USA was instrumental to the progress of the negotiations.

While the USA played the leading role in the negotiations between the Bosnian Croats and the Bosnian Government concerning a federation between the two, and between Croatia and Bosnia concerning an economic confederation, Russia was not absent from those negotiations. To cite one instance, the Bosnian Prime Minister and the Croatian Foreign Minister met in Moscow in mid-March 1994 to discuss the peace process. The primary mission of Russia, however, was mediating between the Bosnian Serbs and the other Bosnian communities.

In April 1994 a Contact Group was established, consisting of Russia, the European Union and the USA. The EU was represented by France, Germany and the UK. The Contact Group began work on 25 April 1994 and, on 5 July 1994, presented a map defining the areas that would be assigned to a Croat–Muslim federation and to the Bosnian Serbs. The map was offered by the five powers on a take-it-or-leave-it basis as the first step in a process that would lead to discussions of constitutional arrangements for Bosnia and Herzegovina within its existing frontiers. The Bosnian Muslims and Croats would be awarded 51 per cent of the territory of the country while the Bosnian Serbs would receive 49 per cent. It was envisaged that implementation of the plan would very likely require 50 000 troops, including US forces under NATO command. Sarajevo would come under UN control. The Serbs would be required to hand back to the Bosnian Muslims areas around Gorazde, Srebrenica and Zepa—the Muslim enclaves in eastern Bosnia—and to the Muslim–Croat federation lands in the north that would shrink the size of the corridor linking Serb-controlled lands to the west and east. The five powers agreed that economic sanctions would be the punishment of first resort if their take-it-or-leave-it plan was rejected. The map was accepted by the Bosnian Government and the Croats but was effectively rejected by the Bosnian Serbs.[87]

The five powers that worked out this plan differed on many issues but much of the time they preserved their unity in the face of temptations to go their separate ways. Russia exerted strong pressure on Milosevic and the Bosnian Serbs. The Clinton Administration, under pressure from the US Congress to lift the arms embargo on Bosnia and Herzegovina, agreed to defer this action and to rely on sanctions in the first instance. This method of working together is not yet a 20th-century Concert of Europe, but the experiment shows promise even though splits in the unity of the Contact Group have been apparent. The lifting of the arms embargo, if carried out unilaterally by the USA, would threaten the ability of the group to carry out its work.

V. The warnings of the Yugoslav experience

A lack of clarity about what the international community could do about the deepening crisis no doubt contributed to the paralysis. The time for economic sanctions or military measures had not come by 1990, if only because the international community was so divided as to whether any external interference was justified. On the other hand, recourse to the traditional diplomatic tools of mediation, conciliation and arbitration was certainly called for by 1990. Moreover, economic assistance offered early enough might have made a difference. None of this was offered, although EC membership and borrowing in the international markets were used as bargaining chips at the early stages of the crisis.[88] The case for diplomatic intervention in 1990 was not persuasive enough to carry the day; it is instructive to ask why that should have been the case.

One of the problems was that the dispute was seen as an internal matter. Observers were divided on the question of whether the independence of several of the republics was desirable or unavoidable, but the inclination to favour holding the country together was strong. There was, therefore, very little discussion about what a breakup of Yugoslavia might mean for Europe. By 1991, Washington had become worried about the example that the fragmentation of Yugoslavia might set for the republics that still composed the USSR. The impact on the Balkans or on Europe as a whole was hardly considered. It is particularly unfortunate that the consequences of war in Yugoslavia for Western Europe were ignored. There was no discussion of refugees streaming

---

[87] Drozdiak, W., 'Big powers give final endorsement to partition plans for Bosnia', *Washington Post*, 6 July 1994, p. A21; Riding, A., 'Bosnian Serbs said to reject mediator's partition plan', *New York Times*, 21 July 1994, p. A3.
[88] See Gow (note 9), pp. 303–8.

out of Yugoslavia into Germany or about the implications of the expansion of the war into Albania, and the revival of the barbaric practice of ethnic cleansing was not foreseen. No effort was made to reach collective judgement about what war in Yugoslavia might mean for international peace and security, and consequently, the basis was not laid for collective diplomatic intervention.

The case of Yugoslavia demonstrates that until an internal crisis reaches the stage where it presents a clear and present danger to states that are powerful enough to assume some responsibility for international peace and security, the international community is unlikely to intervene in a meaningful way. Even in 1992 it was possible to believe that the worst effects of the conflict could be contained. Identifying and coalescing around a direct threat to international peace and security is probably the most difficult issue nations face in crisis prevention or collective security generally, and particularly in cases that can be thought of as civil war. If their own interests are not clearly and directly damaged by a crisis and its more obvious consequences, there are always substantial grounds for governments to prefer the hands-off approach to an active, possibly military, intervention. If that is their basic predisposition then clearly there is little incentive to open a Pandora's box by beginning to consult about potential crises. What amounts to a 'head in the sand' attitude is derived from an absence of conviction that there is a common interest in preventing crises. This works against even the most modest of diplomatic interventions.

Who should have assumed responsibility for heading off the conflict in Yugoslavia? President Clinton and US pundits attacked the Europeans for not forcefully handling a problem on their doorstep; Europeans blamed Washington for its aloof attitude. NATO and the WEU and their supporters vied for the role of senior peacekeeper in Europe. The UN was ignored while the war raged on for six months. Turf battles had started to develop among the international organizations and their leading members. Some European nations, notably France, saw in the Yugoslav crisis a chance to strengthen the security side of the EC. This was encouraged by the USA which had no desire to become involved. NATO therefore was not at that stage a part of the struggle for the mantle of premier peacekeeper of Europe. The organization that was cut out, by the USA and by Europeans, was the United Nations. This was not an oversight. US spokespersons doubted publicly that there was a role for the UN.[89] It was obvious from the start that the UN's experience and authority could be useful in the crisis. Not until the soon-to-retire UN Secretary-General Pérez de Cuellar enlisted former US Secretary of State Cyrus Vance and Herbert Okun, former Deputy US Permanent Representative to the UN, to be his representatives in the former Yugoslavia did the UN begin to play the role it could have played all along. This did not happen until November 1991.

The images of Munich, Viet Nam and Lebanon were evoked in the Yugoslav crisis as reminders, respectively, of appeasement, quagmires and a failure to

[89] See the statement by an Administration official quoted in Goshko, J. M., 'Yugoslavia is puzzling problem for U.S. allies', *Washington Post*, 22 Sep. 1991, p. A31.

identify clear political objectives to be achieved by military force. Other recent analogies exist, however, in which great nations patiently and firmly led the world away from war. Such was the case in Berlin, Cuba, southern Africa and the Middle East. A resolution of the dispute concerned was not always or even frequently attained, but durable settlements or interim solutions were found. The striking thing about these particular achievements was that the USA took the lead. Of course, there are other cases and other nations that did the same thing in this era, often in the context of decolonization and the birth of new nations. There is little prospect of effective action, however, unless at least one of the major powers makes a determined effort to head off a growing crisis.

The Bosnian Government or the EC could have anticipated the reaction of the Bosnian Serbs to the referendum and pursued some course other than the one it did. Abstract principles were allowed to become the guide to action by the EC; the overly ambitious goals pursued by the dominant Muslims in the Bosnian Government compounded the problem. The situation as it actually existed called for a more cautious approach based on negotiations among the three groups. The EC call for a referendum for or against independence only made the situation worse in Bosnia and Herzegovina. The Bush Administration maintained a position of non-recognition with regard to Croatia and Slovenia until April 1992. With respect to this position, Secretary of State Baker stated: 'It is not sufficient in our view for countries to simply declare their independence and then forcefully seize border posts or customs posts in order to implement that declaration and thereby trigger a civil war. And that's what happened in Yugoslavia'.[90]

The Bosnian referendum was only a triggering mechanism, however, not the root cause of the conflict. Its main lesson for this analysis is that it demonstrates the need for responding to crises on their own terms. Once the EC, by its December 1991 decision on recognition, had invited the republics to secede from the Yugoslav federation it was next to impossible for the Bosnian Government to refuse the invitation. The EC action thus presented the Sarajevo Government with a no-win situation.[91] The Belgrade Government, of course, saw the EC actions as a blatant German design to break up the federation and extend German influence in the Balkans.[92] From Foreign Minister Genscher's point of view, it was necessary to present Serbia with Croatian independence as a *fait accompli* in order to stop the fighting.[93] It may have had that effect in the Serbian–Croatian conflict but the EC move failed badly to anticipate the situation in Bosnia and get ahead of events. Lord Carrington, the EC Special Representative, and Cyrus Vance, the UN Special Envoy, did warn that recognition would carry the danger of spreading the war to Bosnia and Herzegovina and

[90] Quoted in Binder, D., 'U.S. set to accept Yugoslav breakup', *New York Times*, 12 Mar. 1992, p. A7.
[91] President Izetbegovic realized the possible danger he faced. Minutes after he faxed his application to the EC for recognition he faxed a request to the UN Security Council for peacekeeping forces to be deployed along Bosnia and Herzegovina's borders and within the republic. See Sudetic (note 56).
[92] Harden, B., 'Balkans entangle big powers—again', *Washington Post*, 24 Dec. 1991, p. A9.
[93] Kinzer, S., 'Slovenia and Croatia get Bonn's nod', *New York Times,* 24 Dec. 1991, p. A3.

Macedonia.[94] For their part, the Serbs let the EC know that it would recognize the Serb areas of Croatia and Bosnia as part of a new Yugoslavia.[95]

Some of the effects of a war in Bosnia and Herzegovina were predicted, but many were not. It was suggested that the communities were so thoroughly mixed in Bosnia that neighbour would be pitted against neighbour. That happened, but most Serbs, Croats and Bosnian Muslims continued to live peaceably among themselves in Sarajevo during most of the siege. Not all Bosnian Serbs held the extreme nationalist views that Karadzic championed nor did all Serbs support the extreme positions of Milosevic. None the less, predictions of disaster were not far off the mark. What was not foreseen, at least in public commentary, was the Nazi-like ethnic cleansing strategy of the Serbs and later of the Croatians. Vukovar, a largely Croat city in Croatia, had been subjected to exactly this treatment by Serbia in the first phase of the Serbian–Croation War. It appears that the objectives of the Serbs caught most observers by surprise. This, in turn, meant that three profoundly important effects were minimized: the precedental importance of state-sponsored racism in post-cold war Europe, the destabilizing effect of refugees, and the propensity for the dynamics of the situation to involve other Balkan states.

The Bosnian experience is most revealing for what it tells us about the limits of the international community's vocation for preventive diplomacy and crisis prevention. The EC assumed the role of peacemaker in the former Yugoslavia in June 1991. The EC had its greatest opportunity to affect the course of the crisis in Bosnia and Herzegovina by promoting a political structure for Bosnia that would satisfy the three elements of the population. In October 1991 in the context of The Hague Peace Conference sponsored by the EC, Lord Carrington floated a proposal for a political settlement. It essentially offered EC recognition of the independence of each Yugoslav republic within a loose Yugoslav confederation. Holding Yugoslavia together even if only tenuously might have delayed the outbreak of hostilities in Bosnia. However, this solution would almost certainly have been insufficient since it did not address the internal governance of Bosnia. The idea did not find favour at the time with the Serbs since it did nothing to provide for self-determination for Serbs outside Serbia.[96]

There are other models for solving the problem of ethnic rights. The pre-war Bosnian model recognized that some power-sharing among the groups was necessary. Bosnia and Herzegovina was a republic of three nations. One analyst notes: 'the assumption . . . was that no far-reaching decisions could be taken without the consent of all three nations. This position of constitutional equality had been the cornerstone of existence in Tito's Yugoslavia'.[97] The mingling of the three communities, however, did not encourage the principle of territorial dominance for any one group. Rights were vested primarily in individual citizens rather than in ethnic communities. This could work while Yugoslavia

---

[94] Drozdiak (note 57), p. A25.
[95] 'Serbia strikes back', *New York Times,* 19 Dec. 1991, p. A8.
[96] Zametica (note 15), pp. 61–62.
[97] Zametica (note 15), p. 37.

existed but the appeals to ethnic nationalism by Milosevic, Karadzic and others found a receptive audience once Yugoslavia no longer existed.

The Czech and Slovak Federated Republic was another model. There was substantial mixing of Czech and Slovak populations throughout the country, but the country was divided territorially between the two dominant groups. The union fell apart under economic pressures which fostered a belief that it was not advantageous to either ethnic group. Political leaders in the two parts of the country, however, forced the pace of disunion beyond what the people themselves apparently thought necessary.

The German minority in Poland and the much smaller Polish minority in Germany were the subjects of attention in the 1991 German–Polish 10-year Treaty of Good Neighbourliness and Friendly Co-operation. Minorities were to be given encouragement to preserve their language and culture within the larger society but had no special role in the governance of the country. Similar situations were common in the treaties that defined the new states created in the aftermath of World War I.

Autonomy for ethnic groups that dominate a given region is another approach. This amounts to self-rule in domestic affairs while leaving international relations and the governance of the country as a whole in the hands of a central government. This is what Tito did for Albanian-dominated Kosovo and the Hungarian-dominated Vojvodina in 1974. Essentially the same situation would have prevailed in the case of the provinces in Bosnia under the Vance–Owen Plan. The Soviet model in theory provided autonomy for the ethnic-based republics of the USSR but in practice the republics were dominated by Moscow and conformed to policies centrally decided and administered. Table 9.1 illustrates the range of possibilities for dealing with ethnic groups.

The superiority of one system over another can be debated but is not the issue here. The two questions that are important in a discussion of crisis prevention are:

1. What can be done to resolve pressures for changing existing methods of dealing with ethnic groups before the crisis stage is reached?

2. To what extent should the international community give encouragement to the norm of self-determination for ethnic groups?

In response to these questions the CSCE has established means of acquiring early warning of minorities issues. In July 1992, a summit meeting of the CSCE created a High Commissioner for Minorities specifically to look into such matters. In addition, the CSCE has dispatched missions to crisis areas both to monitor and to encourage solutions to ethnic and other issues. This was a promising development of the CSCE institutional process, but of course governments must ultimately decide to act on early warning or the process becomes meaningless.

Table 9.1. Possible approaches to dealing with ethnic groups

Principle	Example
Rights invested in individuals, no special constitutional rights for ethnic groups	Most Western nations
Ethnic groups provided legal assistance to acquire full rights of citizens	Most Western nations
Ethnic groups given legal protection and special rights to preserve language and culture	Central and Eastern Europe
Ethnic groups guaranteed representation in government but no territorial division	Pre-war Bosnia
Ethnic-dominated territories given autonomous status within a country dominated by other ethnic group(s)	Russian Federation, Serbia under Tito
Country territorially divided along ethnic lines with strong central government and power-sharing at that level	Czechoslovakia pre-breakup
Ethnic groups dominate political units below national level, weak central government	Proposed solution for Bosnia and Herzegovina

Whether self-determination for ethnic groups should be seen as a worthy goal in all circumstances is debatable. As Max Kampelman notes, 'The right of self-determination of peoples does not include the right of secession. These are two separate rights, which must be viewed separately'.[98] The end of the cold war has led to a revival of nationalist sentiment, partly because politicians have used it as a rallying cry and partly because it is a natural reaction to the foreign domination that many identified with the bipolar order. Underlying these factors are more basic trends that have a more lasting impact on attitudes towards self-determination for ethnic groups.

The most salient of these considerations is that even for the most powerful nations sovereignty operates differently than it did in the earlier decades of the 20th century. There are more limitations on state sovereignty and, certainly in Europe, more recognition that most major internal actions have external effects. Moreover, the communications and information revolutions have also tended to make state frontiers more porous than before.

Local autonomy in these circumstances may be a more important value to people than the fortunes of the larger states of which they are a part. In an almost universal culture and economy in which central governments clearly have limitations in terms of protecting citizens and improving their well-being, local customs and ties offset the feelings of being alienated from a community too large to identify with in any tangible sense. From this perspective, stronger local management of human affairs is a natural concomitant of a perceived stronger influence exercised by a global economy on the lives of individuals. Fragmentation and integration have been occurring in parallel in recent years as

[98] Kampelman, M., 'Secession and self determination', *Washington Quarterly*, vol. 16, no. 3 (summer 1993).

scholars have observed.[99] This is likely to continue and is a factor that conflict and crisis prevention must work with, not against. In essence, the lessons should be: (*a*) that organizations representing the international community should be less hesitant about taking up issues that formerly were considered internal matters; and (*b*) that trends towards particularization at local levels should be accommodated and the shocks of change absorbed within the larger international community. Otherwise, effective countermeasures will almost certainly lag behind events. To wait until armed conflict breaks out is to wait too long.

[99] Gaddis, J. L., 'Toward a post-cold war world', *Foreign Affairs*, vol. 70, no. 2 (spring 1991), pp. 102–23.

Part IV

International security organizations as instruments for great power co-operation

10. The utility of international organizations for collective action in regional conflicts*

James E. Goodby and Daniel B. O'Connor

I. Introduction

Great powers are likely to have so much at stake in areas of strategic interest to them or where weapons of mass destruction might come into play that they will dominate the responses to regional conflicts in these cases. The regional conflict models discussed in parts II and III of this book therefore may not present occasions for international organizations to play leading roles except as legitimizers or facilitators. In many parts of the developing world, however, Russia and the United States may have shared interests in seeing an end to conflicts but may lack strong motivations to become directly involved themselves. In such cases, international organizations may have to carry the burden of collective intervention.

Misunderstandings between the United States and Russia could occur unless they operate on the basis of some common assumptions about what international security interests are at stake and what international organizations are expected to do. Common or shared assumptions also would make Russian and US responses more predictable.

Obviously, state-against-state acts of war or threats of war fit the category of events that are likely to be threats to international peace and security. Russia and the USA clearly should strive to concert their policies to deal with a problem that Hans Morgenthau saw as the main concern of diplomacy from the beginning of the modern state system to World War I: 'to localize an actual or threatening conflict between two nations, in order to prevent it from spreading to other nations'.[1]

Intervention becomes a more complex issue if the dispute is an internal matter as so many regional conflicts are in the post-cold war period. For this reason and because national self-interests have not been perceived to be at risk in many of these conflicts, the idea of international order has been very difficult to invoke as a guide to action. Responses instead have been limited to humanitarian assistance which does not necessarily contribute to a predictable international order.

---

[1] Morgenthau, H., *Politics Among Nations* (Alfred A. Knopf: New York, 1953), p. 335.

* This chapter draws, in part, on an essay written by the authors while in residence at the US Institute of Peace (USIP), Washington, DC. The essay was entitled 'Collective security, an essay on its limits and possibilities after the cold war' and was issued by USIP in April 1993.

The human tragedies that are represented by Haiti, Rwanda, Somalia and the former Yugoslavia, however, show that international security in the post-cold war period requires a collective response to violations of international norms *within* as well as between states. The long-understood need for the enforcement of international norms in relations between states, while still important, is being extended: the international community has begun to stake out a position that provides for intervention, even armed intervention, in the internal affairs of states on grounds that are derived only partly from humanitarian concerns. The other grounds for intervention stem from concerns about international peace and security. This is an important development, marking a conceptual departure from the thinking of earlier periods.

Of all the possible areas of US–Russian co-operation, however, joint actions directed at resolving or quelling internal conflicts are probably the least understood and the least accepted by the people of the USA and Russia. This chapter explores the implications of this rationale for collective action, focusing on the weaknesses of international organizations as a means of underscoring the fact that here is a critical and difficult problem area for future US–Russian co-operation. First, the chapter lays some necessary groundwork with a discussion of the collective use of force and a set of proposed guidelines for collective action.

II. The use of force in collective actions

Since the decision to intervene collectively even for mediation purposes is not easily made, it follows that the decision to intervene with members of the armed forces must be given the most profound consideration. However, not all uses of force are equally dangerous and consequential. The range of possibilities embraces the following: (*a*) crisis prevention, (*b*) peacekeeping, (*c*) protective security, (*d*) peace enforcing, and (*e*) peace-building.

Crisis prevention is generally regarded as involving mediation, conciliation, arbitration or simply diplomatic efforts to induce parties to a dispute to start talking to each other. It could also involve the use of military forces. In his report, *An Agenda for Peace*, United Nations Secretary-General Boutros Boutros-Ghali suggested the 'preventive deployment' of a UN presence.[2] This suggestion was put into effect as a deterrent in Macedonia, with the deployment including a small number of US troops.

In *peacekeeping*, the usual assumption in UN practice, and in the CSCE as well, is that a cease-fire is in place. No military action, in the sense of armed combat, should be required except in self-defence, but the peacekeepers are usually military contingents. This has been the classic type of operation man-

[2] United Nations Security Council, *An Agenda for Peace: Preventive Diplomacy, Peacemaking and Peace-keeping*, Report of the Secretary-General pursuant to the statement adopted by the Summit Meeting of the Security Council on 31 January 1992, UN document A/47/277 (S/24111), 17 June 1992. The text is reproduced in SIPRI, *SIPRI Yearbook 1993: World Armaments and Disarmament* (Oxford University Press: Oxford, 1994), pp. 66–80.

aged by the UN in Africa, the Middle East, South Asia and elsewhere for decades.

Protective security is a term that can be used to refer to operations that are essentially defensive but that may require taking sides in a conflict, for example, by providing safe havens or protecting humanitarian efforts. In UN circles, these operations are sometimes called 'Chapter VI1/2 operations'. They occupy a 'grey area' between Chapter VI of the UN Charter which is aimed at helping countries to maintain a cease-fire, for example, and Chapter VII, which gives the Security Council the right to impose peace in a conflict zone. This type of operation is important because it covers situations that are becoming the most likely contingencies, judging by experiences in Somalia and the former Yugoslavia. Enforcing a no-fly zone, as in Iraq, also falls into this category. Security zones or safe havens are likely to be fairly common requirements in the future, and not necessarily within the context of peace enforcement.

Peace enforcing implies a readiness to take sides and the possibility of combat, perhaps even heavy fighting, to bring an end to a conflict. The best known examples are the 1950–53 Korean War and the 1991 Persian Gulf War, both involving coalitions led by the USA but approved by the UN. However, not all peace-enforcing operations need involve conflict on this scale. Isolating a specific territory (i.e., cutting it off from access to trade and normal traffic) is a military problem to which solutions short of large-scale ground combat can be found. This type of intervention could be a 'peace-enforcement' response. Not all peace-enforcement operations will rise to the extreme end of the scale of violence, and yet decision makers must consider that possibility while avoiding a policy paralysis in the process.

Peace-building is a term used by Secretary-General Boutros-Ghali in *An Agenda for Peace* to signify operations necessary to create conditions conducive to peace in countries that lack the basic necessities for supporting a normal existence. Cambodia is a good example of a situation in which military forces have been used for this purpose. *Nation building* is an analogous term, but the idea has fallen into some disrepute in the USA because of the experience in Somalia.

When any government or international organization considers intervention in a dispute, the natural inclination is to look to non-military measures as the first remedy. While the correctness of this tendency cannot be disputed, it is important that two principles always be factored into the calculation:

1. Ruling out the use of force will almost certainly weaken the ability of the international community to influence events.

2. Intervening in a dispute without giving some consideration to whether force may be necessary at some stage means that decisions are being made on the basis of incomplete analysis.

III. Guidelines for collective intervention

Intervention in a dispute should be related, if at all possible, to the achievement of a resolution of differences and to the establishing of a predictable inter-national order and not just to humanitarian ends. Intervention for humanitarian purposes, as in Somalia and the former Yugoslavia, cannot contribute to a reso-lution or to the reinforcing of recognized norms of behaviour in and of itself. As was seen in Somalia, humanitarian reasons may suffice to justify peace-enforcement operations if the cost of intervention is sufficiently low. However, peace-building in Somalia, at least with sizeable US forces, was seen in Washington as a cost not justified by the benefit, to the obvious regret of Secretary-General Boutros-Ghali. A true resolution of the disputes in Somalia is not in sight at the time of writing. In Bosnia and Herzegovina humanitarian reasons have not been sufficient to justify anything more than peacekeeping operations because the costs of a more serious intervention, even to defend safe havens, were judged to be very high. It is clear that a humanitarian effort alone will not produce a resolution of the underlying problems in Bosnia and Herzegovina, but instead will postpone a resolution. Haiti may turn out to be a better example of the need for linkage between humanitarianism and conflict resolution goals but it is too early to say, in early 1995.

Collective action to enforce international norms will never be automatic, but instead will be highly dependent on specific circumstances. Decisions to inter-vene militarily, especially in the case of conflicts *within* states, must be based on self-interest, and in both Russia and the USA the publics must be convinced that the national self-interest is engaged. Whether to engage in dangerous col-lective operations that might require the use of force should be a question not lightly or randomly answered. The question should be judged by at least four criteria: (*a*) whether, in the absence of intervention, there is a serious potential for wider conflict; (*b*) whether there is likely to be a significantly adverse impact on international norms, particularly those related to the use of force to change established frontiers; (*c*) whether moral considerations such as war crimes, crimes against humanity or the survival of large populations come into play; and (*d*) whether the survival of a democratic government is at stake.

These criteria should be equally meaningful in Russia and in the USA as their governments and publics consider conflicts in the developing world. If all four of these criteria can be answered affirmatively, the case for collective interven-tion should be a powerful one, perhaps sufficient to overcome natural hesi-tations regarding the potential human costs of taking collective action.

It is evident that the application of these criteria requires a considerable exer-cise of judgement. There cannot be anything automatic about decisions regard-ing intervention even with the help of guidelines like those above. Their main use is not to allow the suspension of judgement but rather to ensure that the implications of a serious conflict are analysed in terms relevant to the national interests of Russia and the United States. They are meant to fill the void between automatic responses and inaction in framing issues of international peace and security. They should help provide consistency, rather than *ad hoc* answers to questions regarding collective intervention, and thus help to reinforce an international regime, or predictable international norms.

IV. International organizations and their uses

International organizations almost always play some role in regional conflicts even where Russia and the United States have decided they must intervene directly and perhaps even unilaterally, whether by preference or necessity. These organizations can help to define the public's understanding of a regional conflict and thus affect public attitudes towards intervention. This is particularly the case with the United Nations. US intervention in the Gulf War would have been exceedingly difficult to conduct on the scale US military planners thought necessary if the intervention had not been approved by the United Nations. Where the great powers elect to place the burden of intervention on the shoulders of an international organization, all the inherent problems of collective action sooner or later make their appearance.

Collective decision making frequently produces lowest-common-denominator results, thus leading to an outcome in which military means are inadequate and political objectives murky. Often collective decision making means no decision making. Despite these problems, there is no way around collective decision making. Preventing crises entails extensive international consultation in advance of hostilities. Collective military operations require constant exchanges of views among the governments trying to deal with the situation. In deciding to intervene collective decision making may depend more on national governments than on the international organizations they have established to support their collective actions. After international organizations have been entrusted with peacekeeping operations, responsibility for success or failure shifts to the leadership and management teams assembled by the international organizations.

The relative effectiveness of regional organizations in collective operations will be determined by four elements: (*a*) charter mandate—whether the charter of the regional organization has provisions for conflict mediation or even intervention in the internal affairs of member states; (*b*) political will—whether there are political cleavages in the organization that will prevent effective action or whether there is sufficient interest among members to mount a collective response; (*c*) available resources—whether the members of the organization have the military and financial assets for intervention, should it be decided to do so; and (*d*) perceived legitimacy—whether the proposed intervention is motivated by the criteria listed above, or is seen as a justification for the interference in the affairs of a weak state by one or more stronger states.

By these standards, hardly any organizations besides the United Nations and certain European regional organizations meet the test of effectiveness. The following discussion assesses the utility of several international organizations in managing collective action in regional conflicts.

The United Nations

The disaster of Yugoslavia may spell the end of the role of the United Nations in European security, but it is too soon to come to that conclusion. Its pre-eminence as the leading international organization for collective action in the rest of the world is unchallenged. Quite apart from its expertise and experience, and despite recent setbacks, the UN is a valuable legitimizing agent. A resolution adopted by the Security Council can be used to justify military action by individual nations joined in an *ad hoc* coalition or in a formal alliance. The former was the situation in the Persian Gulf War; the latter has been the case with NATO in the Yugoslav conflict. The approval of the UN carries a cachet that no other organization can bestow, and therefore collective actions endorsed by the UN can be carried out under circumstances in which the involvement of other organizations would be barred. The United Nations is also unique in that it brings together the world's great powers in one forum for collective decision making. It is a vital and perhaps underutilized tool for bringing Russia and the West more closely together in the post-cold war world.

Chapter VII of the UN Charter confers major responsibilities on the UN Security Council for peace enforcement. There is nothing comparable at present in the charters of other relevant international organizations. For this reason also the UN is likely to become the principal legitimizing authority for collective actions requiring military force. Unfortunately, but probably justifiably, the UN has been under fire for several years for *inter alia* alleged mismanagement of peacekeeping.[3] Secretary-General Boutros-Ghali's report, *An Agenda for Peace*, contained many good recommendations for strengthening UN preventive diplomacy and peacekeeping operations. For example, the Secretary-General proposed that the Security Council begin negotiations under Article 43 of the UN Charter to have member states assign armed forces, on a readily available basis, to the UN. The hard reality is that shortages of money and human resources as well as political differences are major obstacles that will not be easily or quickly overcome. The UN Military Staff Committee is a potentially useful collective security instrument which the Secretary-General hoped could support the negotiations under Article 43. Any attempt to reform or replace that moribund committee will require the assent of at least the permanent members of the Security Council, and obtaining this consent will take time.

In 1995, in his *Supplement to An Agenda for Peace*, Secretary-General Boutros-Ghali also emphasized that ending conflicts is not just a matter of mediation or of the proper application of enforcement mechanisms. He noted

---

[3] An example is the quote from Branigan, W., 'As U.N. expands, so do its problems', *Washington Post*, 20 Sep. 1992, p. A1: 'Peace-keeping operations, some of which drag on for decades, have become a source of soaring costs with minimal oversight'.

that 'implementation of the settlement in the time prescribed may not be enough to guarantee that the conflict will not revive. Coordinated programs are required over a number of years and in various fields to ensure that the original causes of war are eradicated'.[4]

The experiences of Somalia and other operations have shown how difficult it is for the United Nations to find people to serve as special envoys of the Secretary-General.[5] Boutros-Ghali noted that the UN representatives and special envoys would be greatly strengthened if they had a small support mission on a full-time basis. However, as he goes on to state, 'there is no clear view amongst Member States about whether legislative authority for such matters rests with the Security Council or the General Assembly, nor are existing budgetary procedures well geared to meet this need'.[6] He offers two possible solutions: a contingency budget of $25 million per biennium, or to enlarge the 'existing provision for unforeseen and extraordinary activities and to make it available for all preventive and peacemaking activities, not just those related to international peace and security strictly defined'.[7] Expanding the definition of threats to international peace and security has been one of the most important development of recent years and one of the most controversial.

The United Nations has come under harsh criticism from its chief patron, the United States. The Clinton Administration, responding to domestic criticism of the UN, has laid out stiff conditions for its participation in UN peacekeeping operations. Madeleine Albright, US Ambassador to the United Nations, stated on 24 September 1993 that several questions must be answered before the USA will decide to support a peacekeeping operation: 'Does the mission have clear, definable objectives? Is a cease-fire in place, and have the parties agreed to a U.N. presence? Are the necessary human and financial resources available? Can an "end point" to U.N. participation be identified?'[8] President Bill Clinton has stated that, 'The United Nations simply cannot become engaged in every one of the world's conflicts . . . If the American people are to say yes to UN peacekeeping, the United Nations must know when to say no'.[9] In May 1994 he signed Presidential Decision Directive 25 (PDD-25), formalizing the Administration's approach to peacekeeping and peace-enforcement actions. The Administration outlined several strict conditions for US participation in peace-

---

[4] United Nations Security Council, *Supplement to An Agenda for Peace: Position Paper of the Secretary General on the Occasion of the Fiftieth Anniversary of the United Nations*, Report of the Secretary-General on the work of the Organization, UN document A/50/60 (S/1995/1), 3 Jan. 1995, p. 6. See appendix 10A in this volume.

[5] Mohamed Sahnoun in his memoir of his experience in Somali not only notes this fact, but also his frustrations in working with the United Nations. See Sahnoun, M., *Somalia: The Missed Opportunities* (United States Institute of Peace: Washington, DC, 1994).

[6] *Supplement to An Agenda for Peace* (note 4), p. 8.

[7] See *Supplement to An Agenda for Peace* (note 4), p. 8.

[8] Goshko, J. M., 'U.S. sets stiff conditions for troop role in U.N. peace keeping', *Washington Post*, 24 Sep. 1993, p. 19. For the Clinton Administration conditions for sending forces to Bosnia, see Sciolino, E., 'Christopher explains conditions for use of U.S. forces in Bosnia', *New York Times*, 28 Apr. 1993, p. A1.

[9] Friedman, T. L., 'Clinton at U.N., lists stiff terms for sending U.S. force to Bosnia', *New York Times*, 28 Sep. 1993, p. A1.

keeping activities. These included 'the advancement of American interests, the availability of personnel and funds, the need for American participation for an operation's success, the support of Congress and the presence of clear objectives, a clear ending for American participation and acceptable command and control arrangements'.[10]

Under PDD-25 there would have to be a threat to international security coupled with a need for widespread relief aid, sudden interruption of democracy or gross violation of human rights, clear objectives, consent of the warring parties before entering the country, a realistic mandate and a clear exit strategy, as well as sufficient amounts of money and troops for the mission.[11] PDD-25 also states that the USA will not support a UN standing army, that the USA will not earmark any of its forces for UN peacekeeping in advance and that US troops will not serve under foreign commanders. Finally, PDD-25 states that the USA is bearing too much of the financial burden for peacekeeping and that the USA should seek to reduce its share of the peacekeeping budget to 25 per cent.[12]

In the wake of the November 1994 elections, the US Congress also called for much reduced funding for the United Nations. The proposal mandated that US payments for peacekeeping operations be reduced by the US costs for participation in peacekeeping operations for the preceding fiscal year.[13] This would include Haiti, where the United States sought and obtained a UN mandate to use US forces. If enacted the USA would get credit for the approximately $1.2 billion it spends annually on UN peacekeeping activities such as naval embargoes, no-fly zones, and humanitarian relief.[14] This would wipe out about one-third of the $3.6 billion annual UN budget for peacekeeping operations. Bills before the House and Senate of the US Congress in the spring of 1995 would bar US troops from serving under foreign command without specific congressional or presidential authorization, require reports to Congress on the costs and funding of all peacekeeping operations and call for the withholding of 20 per cent of the US payment to the UN until the new UN Inspector General 'obtains powers to investigate a wide range of UN documents and programs'.[15]

In terms of the four criteria cited above, the UN has the mandate, will and legitimacy for collective actions, but financial resources are a constant and worsening problem. Given its financial problems, the UN may be unable to carry the burden of collective interventions alone. Boutros-Ghali has identified

---

[10] Sciolino, E., 'New U.S. peacekeeping policy de-emphasizes role of the U.N.', *New York Times*, 6 May 1994, p. A1. For discussions of the PDD-25 draft, see Williams, D., 'Clinton peacekeeping policy to set limits on use of U.S. troops', *Washington Post*, 6 Feb. 1994, p. A24.

[11] Sciolino (note 10).

[12] Sciolino (note 10).

[13] US Congress, House of Representatives, National Security Revitalization Act, introduced 4 Jan. 1995, 104th Congress, 1st session, section 501. The bill, HR-7, was passed by the House of Representatives in Feb. 1995.

[14] Smith, R. J., 'Republicans seek to curb U.N. funding', *Washington Post*, 23 Jan. 1995, p. A1.

[15] See Smith (note 14); and National Security Revitalization Act of 1995, House Bill 7, and US Congress, Senate, Peace Powers Act of 1995, 104th Congress, 1st session, introduced 4 Jan. 1995.

several forms of co-operation between the United Nations and regional organizations, based in part on the experience of recent years:[16]

1. Consultations and exchanges of views.

2. Diplomatic support in which the regional organization participates in peacemaking activities with UN diplomatic support and/or technical support. He cited support for CSCE activities in Abkhazia and Nagorno-Karabakh.

3. Operational support of UN diplomatic initiatives by regional organizations, such as the provision of NATO air support to the United Nations Protection Force (UNPROFOR), or UN technical advice to regional organizations that undertake peacekeeping efforts of their own.

4. Co-deployment of forces in which the regional organization bears the military brunt and the UN deploys a small mission to ensure that the regional organization is behaving in ways consistent with Security Council resolutions. He notes missions deployed in support of the Economic Community of West African States (ECOWAS) forces in Liberia and CIS forces in Georgia.

5. Joint operations in which the UN and the regional organization share costs, staffing and direction of the operation. He gives the joint Organization of American States (OAS)–UN operation in Haiti as an example.

The problems regional organizations face become more apparent in the following discussion. It begins with a description of European regional organizations, each of which has been specifically assigned peacekeeping responsibilities by its members, and then examines regional organizations in the rest of the world.

Europe

The Conference on Security and Co-operation in Europe[17]

In 1990 the members of the CSCE (at that time all the governments of Europe, except Albania, plus Canada and the USA) decided at a summit meeting in Paris to create an organizational structure within the CSCE framework. The leaders at the Paris summit meeting envisaged a CSCE that would begin to deal with the instabilities that would be the obvious consequences of the end of the cold war. At the June 1991 meeting of the CSCE's new Council of Ministers, and especially at the Helsinki CSCE summit meeting of July 1992, the participants strengthened the collective security function of the CSCE.[18] Consensus was no longer required to call emergency meetings. The idea of early warning of conflict was built into the Helsinki Document, for example, by establishing a

---

[16] *Supplement to An Agenda for Peace* (note 4), p. 20.

[17] As noted in the introductory remarks (chapter 1), the editor has elected to use the word 'Conference' instead of 'Organization' since the former title will be more familiar to most readers.

[18] 'The Charter of Paris Declaration for a new Europe', 21 Nov. 1990, is reproduced in SIPRI, *SIPRI Yearbook 1991: World Armaments and Disarmament* (Oxford University Press: Oxford, 1991), pp. 603–10; see also 'Key CSCE documents in 1992', *SIPRI Yearbook 1993* (note 2), pp. 190–209.

High Commissioner for National Minorities. Several mechanisms have been established to encourage early consultations on emerging crises. Fact-finding and rapporteur missions have been created and used in, for example, Albania, Armenia, Azerbaijan, Belarus, Chechnya, Georgia, Kazakhstan, Kyrgyzstan, Moldova, Tajikistan, Turkmenistan, Ukraine, Uzbekistan and the former Yugoslavia.[19]

At the December 1994 Budapest summit meeting the heads of state or government of the participants in the CSCE took several decisions that seem to foreshadow a pre-eminent position for that organization in the preventive diplomacy of Eurasia. If the first steps taken at Budapest are pursued in a consistent way, the United Nations will not be the major force in future Eurasian conflicts that it became in the former Yugoslavia. The Budapest decisions show that Russia is inclined to back the CSCE with its weak peacekeeping mandate rather than the UN with its stronger Charter provisions, even though Russia has a veto in the UN Security Council. Although Russia has suggested a new CSCE structure like that of the United Nations in some respects there can be little doubt that Moscow's decision makers know that the prospects for changing the CSCE into an effective manager of peacekeeping operations are bleak.

What does this Russian preference for the CSCE suggest? Certainly Moscow would prefer the CSCE as an alternative to NATO's peacekeeping role in Europe. This is advantageous also because the CSCE Helsinki Decisions of 10 July 1992 specify that 'the peacekeeping mechanism of the Commonwealth of Independent States (CIS) may also be asked by the CSCE to support peacekeeping in the CSCE region'. This refers to the Tashkent Document of 15 May 1992 which endowed the CIS with a peacekeeping function.[20] Here, of course, the question of the impartiality of CIS peacekeeping forces is an issue because in recent experience these forces have been Russian.

Russia's tilt towards the CSCE rather than the United Nations may also be motivated by the CSCE's peacekeeping mandate. It was agreed at the Helsinki summit meeting that the CSCE would undertake peacekeeping operations of the type carried out traditionally under Chapter VI of the UN Charter, as a regional agency of the United Nations of the type envisaged in Chapter VIII. CSCE members ruled out anything like Chapter VII responsibilities, the provisions that give the UN Security Council peace-enforcing responsibilities. The CSCE has been positioned by its members as a useful service agency for those who might wish to call upon it for help, but it has effectively been removed from responsibility for any military intervention that might be necessary while armed conflict is taking place. For military intervention to occur, the UN or some improvised coalition would have to be used. This restricted scope of the

[19] For a review as of mid-1992, see 'CSCE missions', a summary prepared by the staff of the Commission on Security and Co-operation in Europe of the US Congress (US Government Printing Office: Washington, DC, Sep. 1992).

[20] See *SIPRI Yearbook 1993* (note 2), pp. 671–77; Hiatt, F., '6 ex-Soviet states sign collective security pact', *Washington Post*, 16 May 1992, p. A16; CSCE Helsinki Document 1992, *The Challenges of Change*, section III, paragraph 52; see also 'Key CSCE documents in 1992', *SIPRI Yearbook 1993* (note 2), pp. 190–209.

CSCE means that it will be unavailable for use in many conflicts throughout its area of membership; nations contemplating protective security or peace-enforcing operations will have to turn to the UN for a mandate. The rejection at Budapest of a proposal to include a reference to the UN and its Chapter VII responsibilities shows how difficult that would be.

The Budapest decisions were important in several ways. Two of the most important affected peacekeeping and the role of the military in the individual CSCE states. In their decisions on 'regional issues' the heads of states and government addressed the conflict in Nagorno-Karabakh and declared their political will to provide, with an appropriate resolution from the UN Security Council, a multinational CSCE peacekeeping force following an agreement among the parties for cessation of armed conflict.[21]

In addition to resolving, at least tentatively, the question of whether the CIS or the CSCE should manage peacekeeping in Nagorno-Karabakh, this decision set a precedent that may have to be repeated in other conflicts in the vicinity of the Russian Federation. The outcome was made possible by US–Russian co-operation, as well as the co-operation of the European participants, and it may turn out to be the most important achievement of the Budapest meeting. At this writing many significant details of the peacekeeping force remain to be resolved, but at least the permanent machinery and the political authorities of the CSCE have become engaged in a major peacekeeping enterprise.

The other decision that may have important consequences was the agreement on a Code of Conduct on Politico-Military Aspects of Security.[22] Although the Code of Conduct repeated the principles long familiar in CSCE affairs, it also includes a long section (VII) on the role of the military in democracies. As with other pronouncements of the CSCE, section VII cannot be enforced except through moral and political pressure. However, CSCE experience in the past has shown that pressure to observe norms does have an effect. Already criticism of Russia's military action in Chechnya has been based on paragraph 36, which states that:

Each participating State will ensure that any decision to assign its armed forces to internal security missions is arrived at in conformity with constitutional procedures. Such decisions will prescribe the armed forces' missions, ensuring that they will be performed under the effective control of constitutionally established authorities and subject to the rule of law. If recourse to force cannot be avoided in performing internal security missions, each participating State will ensure that its use must be commensurate with the needs for enforcement. The armed forces will take due care to avoid injury to civilians or their property.

---

[21] The *CSCE Budapest Document 1994: Towards a Genuine Partnership In a New Era*, Budapest, 6 Dec. 1994. *The Budapest Summit Declaration* is reproduced in SIPRI, *SIPRI Yearbook 1995: Armaments, Disarmament and International Security* (Oxford University Press: Oxford, 1995).
[22] See appendix 10B to this chapter.

The CSCE observer mission to Chechnya in January 1995 is a post-Budapest development of great value, not least because it shows that the Budapest decisions on the role of the military in democracies are to be taken seriously.

The Budapest decisions also resulted in a name change for the CSCE. Henceforth, it was decided, the CSCE will be known as the Organization for Security and Co-operation in Europe (OSCE). However, as the heads of state and government noted, the name change alters neither the character of the CSCE commitments nor the status of the CSCE and its institutions.

NATO, the North Atlantic Cooperation Council and the Partnership for Peace

NATO embarked on its peacekeeping vocation in accordance with a mandate of the UN Security Council.[23] The mandate authorized nations to enforce a naval blockade of Serbia and Montenegro to ensure that the sanctions on strategic goods earlier imposed by the UN were fully effective.[24] The blockade began late in the afternoon on 22 November 1992. By the end of the first day, 23 November, Western warships had stopped and inspected three merchant ships. NATO's mandate expanded in April 1993 when it began to enforce the no-fly zone over Bosnia with regular patrols by NATO aircraft.

In August 1993 the heads of state and government of the NATO nations pledged to carry out airstrikes to prevent the strangulation of Sarajevo. They reaffirmed this pledge on 11 January 1994. Following a Bosnian Serb attack on a Sarajevo market-place on 9 February 1994, the North Atlantic Council issued an ultimatum to the warring parties that any heavy weapons found in an exclusion zone of 20 km from the centre of Sarajevo (with an exception for a 2-km area around the centre of Pale) after 20 February would be subject to NATO airstrikes.[25]

On 28 February 1994 NATO engaged in its first military action ever as two US F-16s downed four aircraft attacking a factory in Bosnia. On 10 April 1994 US aircraft bombed Bosnian Serb positions outside the safe area of Gorazde at the request of the UN commander. This represented NATO's first mission against a ground target. NATO aircraft attacked Serb positions again the next day in order to protect UNPROFOR troops in the town.[26]

This was a significant threshold in the history of NATO. Forces assigned to NATO had been used in coalitions led by the USA, the Persian Gulf War being the main case in point. This was the first time, however, that NATO—as a collective defence alliance—had decided to use its forces in a UN-authorized military operation in Europe.

[23] See Schmitt, E., 'A naval blockade of Belgrade seen within a few days', *New York Times,* 18 Nov. 1992, p. A1; and Drozdiak, W., 'NATO agrees to impose blockade of Serbia', *Washington Post,* 19 Nov. 1992, p. A31.
[24] On the earlier sanctions, see Lewis, P., 'UN votes trade sanctions against Yugoslavia, 13 to 0; air travel and oil curbed', *New York Times,* 31 May 1992, p. A1.
[25] North Atlantic Treaty Organization, *Press Release* (94)15, 9 Feb. 1994.
[26] Sudetic, C., 'U.S. planes bomb Serbian positions for a second day', *New York Times,* 12 Apr. 1994, p. A1.

The North Atlantic Cooperation Council (NACC) was established at the end of 1991 to provide a link between the NATO countries and the members of the former Warsaw Treaty Organization (WTO). It was not therefore envisaged as an all-European organization with membership to include the neutral and non-aligned nations of Europe. NACC had a special role in helping to manage the allocation of conventional force reductions among the states of the former Soviet Union. It has become a forum for exchanging information among the NATO and former WTO countries on many types of security issues, including peacekeeping.

The Partnership for Peace (PFP) is not, strictly speaking, a multilateral organization. It was created at the NATO summit meeting of 9–10 January 1994 to provide a framework for bilateral co-operation between NATO and other European nations.[27] Over 20 countries had signed agreements by the end of 1994 to co-operate in military training and other activities, with a considerable emphasis on peacekeeping. Multinational training exercises were held during 1994 to develop those skills.

NATO and its related institutions, in principle, are well positioned to deal with collective military operations. Supreme Headquarters Allied Powers Europe (SHAPE), the Military Committee, the International Military Staff at NATO Headquarters and the several NATO military commands have many of the best planners, military leaders and logistic experts in the Western world. NACC, the national delegations to NACC and the NATO International Staff constitute a permanently operating consultative mechanism. The PFP provides an excellent mechanism for joint training in peacekeeping on an all-European basis. The integrated military command of NATO offers a unique advantage in that the command arrangements of the national forces committed to the alliance are already in place and functioning. The US military, always sensitive to serving under foreign command, operates smoothly and well in NATO's integrated command structure.

There is a limit on the extent to which military forces connected even tenuously to NATO could be used for peacekeeping. This is the geographic limit likely to be imposed by Russian sensitivities and Western reluctance to challenge those sensitivities. Moscow will not welcome the use of NATO-committed forces anywhere in the territories of the former Soviet Union. This attitude would apply as much to Moldova as it would to Tajikistan. NATO-committed forces therefore are most likely to be used in East-Central Europe and the Balkans *outside* the territory of the former Soviet Union, while many of the potential applications of collective military force in Eurasia are likely to be *within* the territory of the former Soviet Union. Russia was even uncomfortable with NATO's role in Bosnia. Possibly the NACC or the PFP mechanisms could provide a way around this problem but, so far, it would appear that the CSCE is the more likely candidate for operations in the border regions of Russia. In connec-

---

[27] For the text of the announcement, see 'Partnership for Peace: invitation and framework document', *US Department of State Dispatch*, vol. 5, no. 1 (Jan. 1994), pp. 5–7.

tion with proposals and studies regarding the possible extension of NATO membership to certain East-Central European countries, the question of Russia's relationships with the Atlantic Alliance was forced to the top of the US–Russian security agenda in late 1994. Section 604 of HR-7, which called for eventual membership in NATO for the Czech Republic, Hungary, Poland and Slovakia, helped keep the issue in the forefront of US–Russian discussions in early 1995. Russian leaders strongly and publicly opposed expansion of NATO-defended territory in an easterly direction. Owing to this and to pressure from the Republican majority in the US Congress it became necessary to define with some precision Russia's relationship to NATO.

An obvious option for the future would be to develop NACC as a forum for Russia's association with NATO. NACC was not utilized as fully as it might have been during 1993–94, probably because of the Clinton Administration's focus on the Partnership for Peace. NACC provides a politico-military forum for Russia's participation in security discussions, and it is collocated with other NATO organizations. It could be a kind of steering committee for the PFP, and thus develop a responsibility for peacekeeping and humanitarian activities in Eastern Europe and possibly beyond. The question arises of whether NACC or the PFP could do a better or a different job in the area of collective military actions than the CSCE. Unless the CSCE develops its military potential very significantly in the years ahead, NACC and the PFP would, by default, be better equipped to deal with military operations. As a bridge between the nations of Eastern Europe and NATO, NACC and the PFP might be better positioned than the CSCE to be the main consultation forum for collective actions that could require military forces. In this case the CSCE would be entrusted with establishing and monitoring norms for human rights and treatment of minorities and long-term conflict resolution assistance, while NATO and NACC, armed with UN mandates, would perform the time-urgent fire brigade role. Russia's current attitude suggests, however, that the more likely outcome will be that foreshadowed by the Budapest summit—a CSCE peacekeeping function based on a restricted mandate and few resources.

The Western European Union

The Western European Union (WEU) was formed in 1954 as a device to facilitate rearming West Germany and to bring it into NATO. The WEU remained moribund for 30 years, but in the early 1980s France began an effort to revive it as a European alternative to NATO.[28] In the Maastricht Treaty of 1992, the European Union decided to use the WEU as its nascent military arm. Currently there are 10 full members of the WEU: Belgium, France, Germany, Greece, Italy, Luxembourg, the Netherlands, Portugal, Spain and the UK. In addition, Iceland, Norway and Turkey hold associate status within the WEU, while Denmark and Ireland hold observer status. All these nations, except Ireland, are

---

[28] In 1973 French Foreign Minister Jobert had tried to revive the organization and met with a distinct lack of interest from his European colleagues.

also members of NATO. Debate rages over the issue of whether the WEU is a European organization working within the general framework of NATO or a free-standing organization that may co-operate with NATO when the occasion demands it.

During the early phases of the Yugoslav conflict, the French sought to activate the WEU for a collective intervention in the former Yugoslavia. Contingency planning envisaged up to 30 000 troops being dispatched. The plan was quashed when the UK objected, citing its experience in Northern Ireland.[29] None the less, the WEU entered the peacekeeping/peace-enforcing field in 1992 first through maritime surveillance operations in the Adriatic and later by participating in the UN-mandated blockade against the former Yugoslavia. The latter decision was made unanimously by the defence ministers of the WEU meeting in Rome on 20 November 1992.[30]

One advantage of the WEU is that France usually finds it easier to conduct multilateral military operations within the framework of the WEU rather than in NATO. Some also argue that the European nations should be better prepared and able to conduct collective military actions without the participation of the USA. The disadvantages of the WEU, compared with NATO, are that it lacks the integrated command structure of NATO and the powerful planning and logistic base that NATO can offer. To the extent that the WEU could operate with NATO, perhaps as a combined joint task force, some of those difficulties could be overcome.[31] It is unlikely that the WEU would be any more acceptable to Russia than would NATO as a peacekeeping or intervention force within the territory of the former Soviet Union. It is possible, however, that when fully developed the WEU could support UN missions not only in Eastern Europe and the Balkans but also in Africa and the Middle East. Such support could strengthen the reach of the United Nations if the WEU were to become a UN regional agency in accordance with Chapter VIII of the UN Charter. The WEU, almost automatically, will extend its membership into East-Central Europe if and when the European Union expands its membership, thus creating a connection between NATO and the new EU members.

The Commonwealth of Independent States

On 15 May 1992 several of the newly independent states of the former Soviet Union met at Tashkent and agreed to create a collective security arrangement. The signatory countries were Armenia, Kazakhstan, Russia, Tajikistan, Turkmenistan and Uzbekistan. Later, this role of the CIS was recognized by the

---

[29] Goodby, J. E., 'Peacekeeping in the New Europe', *Washington Quarterly*, spring 1992, pp. 153–71.

[30] For background on the sea patrols, see Fisher, M. and Oberdorfer, D., 'U.S., W. Europe set patrols in Adriatic', *Washington Post*, 11 July 1992. For the WEU decision, see Cowell, A., 'NATO and European warships blockade Yugoslavia', *New York Times,* 21 Nov. 1992, p. A3.

[31] Although the combined joint task force concept has not been fully developed, the WEU–NATO operations in the Adriatic appeared to be mutually supportive. On this point, see Riding, A., 'NATO agrees to use warships to enforce Yugoslav blockade', *New York Times*, 19 Nov. 1992, p. A1.

Helsinki Document 1992 and by President George Bush in a joint US–Russian declaration issued in Washington in June 1992.

Progress was slow in converting intentions into reality in terms of creating truly multilateral machinery. More importantly, CIS peacekeeping forces, dominated by Russia, lacked the quality of impartiality so necessary to peacekeeping when used in border regions of Russia. The problem was complicated by hesitations in withdrawing Russian troops based in the other states of the former Soviet Union. With no housing, no civilian employment for them and an inhospitable climate for Russian retirees in some of the new states, the withdrawals proceeded very slowly. In addition, Moscow declared itself the protector of ethnic Russians in the newly independent states, placing a new requirement on the Russian Army. This picture was further complicated by the political tendencies represented by Vladimir Zhirinovsky, which in effect advocated re-establishing the Russian empire.[32]

Russian military contingents still based in the newly independent states outside Russia have engaged in 'peacekeeping' activities, sometimes with a mandate, sometimes without. In Tajikistan the 201st Russian Motorized Rifle Division helped a Moscow-leaning faction take over the capital city of Dushanbe in December 1992. In Moldova 'peacekeeping' was being conducted in a unilateral fashion by the commander of Russia's 14th Army based in western Moldova, Lieutenant-General Alexander Lebed. On 28 February 1993 President Boris Yeltsin declared that Russia should be given 'special powers as guarantor of peace and security on the territory of the former Soviet Union',[33] and in his 1994 New Year's Day Address President Yeltsin pledged that he would defend Russians outside Russia, stating that 'on the basis of law and solidarity, we defend and will defend your and our common interests'.[34]

The experiences of the last three years suggest that peace-enforcing operations will be carried out by Russian troops in the smaller newly independent republics with little pretence that they are a multilateral CIS force. UN Secretary-General Boutros-Ghali even suggested, perhaps with this experience in mind, that UN peacekeeping operations might be taken over by major powers operating under a UN mandate.[35] The Security Council has, in fact, authorized the USA to intervene in Haiti but with the idea that the UN would take over after stability had been restored. The decision taken by the CSCE Budapest summit meeting in December 1994 appears to envisage only limited participation by Russian troops in the Nagorno-Karabakh operation, but the details remain to be worked out at this writing. This model for the future in the border regions of Russia would relieve some concerns about the impartiality of Russia.

---

[32] Kipp, J. W., 'The Zhirinovsky threat', *Foreign Affairs*, vol. 73, no. 3 (May/June 1994), pp. 72–86.

[33] Radio Free Europe/Radio Liberty (hereafter RFE/RL) *RFE/RL Daily Report*, 5 Mar. 1993.

[34] *RFE/RL Daily Report*, 3 Jan. 1993.

[35] Williams, D., 'Powers assert influence in peacekeeping roles', *Washington Post*, 30 July 1994, p. A12.

Another development of potentially great significance is the use of Russian forces in Chechnya. Being a constituent part of Russia, the question of international peacekeeping forces did not arise. However, in future situations, given the precedent of CSCE observers in Chechnya, the preventive diplomacy machinery of the CSCE might be called upon by minorities in Russia. This would be a major responsibility for the CSCE High Commissioner for Minorities.

Regional organizations outside Europe

African and Latin American nations have assigned responsibilities for collective security to organizations in which they participate. Unlike in Europe, however, hesitations about using these organizations spring both from the magnitude of the problems they face and from deep-seated concerns about the consequences of interventions in the internal affairs of their neighbours. Having defended their sovereignty fairly recently against preponderant outside powers, these nations seem unwilling to weaken the principle of non-intervention. In both Africa and Latin America the major regional organizations lack the tools for effective collective intervention. As one scholar notes, 'the absence of peacekeeping services and [effective] mediation organs is critical as far as institutional deficiencies of the OAU [Organization of African Unity] and OAS are concerned'.[36] East Asia has no organizations currently capable of collective military intervention, while political conflicts in the Middle East and South Asia have prevented regional organizations in those regions from taking effective actions.

Africa

The Organization of African Unity

The Organization of African Unity was founded on 25 May 1963, and currently has 52 members. Defence and security co-operation are listed as purposes of the OAU in Article 2 of its charter. OAU Charter Article 19 establishes a Commission of Mediation, Conciliation and Arbitration (CMCA) for peaceful dispute settlement, and Article 20 establishes a Specialized Commission for Defence.

A major obstacle to peacekeeping of the type being practised or envisaged in Europe and by the UN Security Council lies in the OAU's strong commitment to non-interference in the internal affairs of member states and the inviolability of borders. The principles outlined in Article 3 of the OAU Charter focus almost exclusively on the sovereign equality of members and non-interference in the internal affairs of member states.[37] The OAU takes these principles very seriously in light of the explosive conflicts that could result if nations interfered in the internal affairs of their neighbours, given the division of ethnic groups

[36] Imobighe, T., 'The OAU and OAS in regional conflict management: a comparative perspective', unpublished manuscript, United States Institute of Peace, Washington, DC, 1992, p. 373.
[37] For discussion of the Charter, see Naldi, G. J., *The Organization of African Unity: An Analysis of Its Role* (New York: Mansell Press, 1989), pp. 3–45.

between and among neighbouring states. The OAU quite deliberately endorsed all colonial borders rather than reopen tribal disputes. In 1977, for example, an OAU commission on the conflict between Ethiopia and Somalia reaffirmed the inviolability of frontiers inherited from the colonial era and condemned subversive activities on the part of neighbouring states or other states in the conflict.[38] The internal political and economic difficulties of its member states are another impediment to effective OAU action. The OAU has failed to make use of the CMCA for effective dispute resolution.[39] In part this stems from the fact that commission jurisdiction is optional, not compulsory.[40] Furthermore, public opinion cannot be brought to bear as the 'commission's reports can only be published with the consent of the parties'.[41] This also stems from the fact that, as Sam Amoo points out, the problem is not primarily institutional but political: 'the OAU as it is currently constructed was the only structure the African states could agree on. Consequently the talk of constitutional amendments and creating a regional security council (along the line of the UN Security Council) have always come to naught'.[42]

Nevertheless, mounting conflicts and the presence of literally millions of refugees on the continent led by 1979 to a proposal for the creation of a peacekeeping force. An OAU resolution that year approved, in principle, the establishment of a joint African defence force. Similarly, in 1981 the OAU Assembly affirmed the need for a peacekeeping force to be sent to Chad.[43] However, the attempt to organize this force was a failure. Garnering resources to support such resolutions has been a problem. One author notes that 'the OAU simply could not mobilize the necessary resources to monitor or supervise a number of cease-fires it was able to arrange'.[44]

In recent conflicts the OAU has been bypassed by other regional or international organizations. In Liberia the Economic Community of West African States, led by Nigeria, intervened in that nation's civil war in 1990 to separate the warring factions and restore a semblance of order. In Somalia the UN authorized intervention by outside forces to deliver urgently needed humanitarian aid after order in Somalia collapsed. France continues to conduct peacekeeping and humanitarian missions in francophone Africa. However, with a $65 million deficit owing to arrearages in OAU member's dues, the money needed to create these sorts of peacekeeping forces is lacking.[45] The Clinton Administration has proposed giving $5 million in aid to the OAU for conflict

[38] Rengger, H. J., *Treaties and Alliances of the World*, 5th edn (Longman Current Affairs: London, 1990), p. 390.

[39] Imobighe (note 36), p. 369.

[40] For a discussion of the CMCA and the OAU in general, see Amoo, S., 'Role of the OAU: past, present, and future', ed. D. R. Smock, *Making War and Waging Peace: Foreign Intervention in Africa* (United States Institute of Peace: Washington, DC, 1993), pp. 239–61.

[41] Amoo (note 40), p. 243.

[42] Amoo (note 40), p. 249.

[43] Rengger (note 38), p. 391.

[44] Imobighe (note 36), p. 370.

[45] Geekie, R., 'OAU to create conflict mechanism', *Africa Report*, vol. 38, no. 5 (Sep. 1993), p. 6.

prevention and peacekeeping activities.[46] While outside aid could bridge part of the gap, it is highly unlikely that the international community will give the OAU enough assistance to finance a force capable of carrying out a major peacekeeping or conflict resolution role. There is little prospect for any near-term enhancement of the effectiveness of the OAU in the field of conflict management.

The Economic Community of West African States

The Economic Community of West African States was established by the 1975 Treaty of Lagos and was intended to abolish trade barriers and promote economic co-operation among West African states. It now has 16 members. In 1978 ECOWAS took a political turn when it approved a general non–aggression protocol among member states and also reaffirmed the inviolability of member state borders. In 1981 ECOWAS heads of state signed a defence protocol that established a council of the ECOWAS heads of state and a commission of defence ministers and chiefs of staff.

The ECOWAS decision in 1990 to intervene in Liberia's civil war marked the first time that an African regional organization intervened militarily in the internal affairs of one of its members. The decision was prompted by the presence of thousands of foreigners trapped in Liberia who were being used as pawns in the conflict and by the 400 000 refugees who poured over the borders into neighbouring West African states. On 24 August 1990 the first ECOWAS contingent of 3000 soldiers, consisting of troops from Gambia, Ghana, Guinea, Nigeria and Sierra Leone (the ECOWAS Monitoring Group), landed in Monrovia. The main purpose of the group was, in the words of Ghanian Foreign Secretary Asamoah, to 'restore some normalcy so that things can function again, and also for the foreign nationals that want to leave, to be evacuated'.[47] Nigerian leadership was pivotal to provide the political will for the intervention. In November 1992 the United Nations imposed an arms embargo against the forces of the National Patriotic Front for Liberia, led by Charles Taylor. The Monitoring Group forces bogged down in fighting with the Liberian factions and made little progress towards a settlement.

After more than two years of negotiations, the main factions signed a peace accord on 25 July 1993. The diplomatic involvement of the United Nations along with pressure by the OAU proved important, and the UN further agreed to send a peacekeeping force to Liberia and to supervise disarmament.[48]

This operation demonstrated the dilemmas and possibilities of collective intervention and peace enforcement. First, the West African force never did obtain the cease-fire it had hoped for. In fact, Prince Johnson, who controlled Monrovia, encouraged the intervention to protect himself from his rival Charles

---

[46] 'US commitment to conflict resolution in Africa', *US Department of State Dispatch*, vol. 5, no. 15 (20 June 1994), p. 412.

[47] Novicki, M. A., 'A new role for ECOWAS', *Africa Report*, Nov./Dec. 1990, p. 17.

[48] Noble, K. B., 'After 13 years of a vicious war, Liberians dare to hope for peace', *New York Times*, 2 Aug. 1993, p. A2.

Taylor, who controlled the rest of the country. Fighting between the ECOWAS forces and Taylor's National Patriotic Forces of Liberia (NPFL) forces broke out almost immediately. Even with the cease-fire and the promise of elections, at the close of 1994 some 10 000 ECOWAS forces remained in Liberia.[49]

Second, the cost of the operation became a factor. The intervening states hoped for assistance from the West for the military action, but it was not forthcoming.[50] While the United States and others provided some small amounts of aid, the estimated $500 million cost of the operation was borne by ECOWAS. [51]

Finally, the question of impartiality arose. Soon after the intervention the ECOWAS force began to protect Liberian President Samuel Doe's tribe, the Krahns, and their allies, the Mandingo, from Taylor's forces. The Mandingo represent one of the largest ethnic groups in Guinea, one of the intervening powers.

A fair judgement at the close of 1994 is that while ECOWAS forces ultimately enjoyed some success in their intervention in Liberia this slow, grinding and expensive process may not be seen as a good example to emulate elsewhere.[52] The key to military success seemed to be the presence of Nigeria, willing to expend soldiers and treasure in the Liberia intervention, but the Nigerians also undercut the legitimacy of the role of ECOWAS owing to their dominance in the operation. The UN was somewhat effective since it could work with both ECOWAS and Taylor to broker an agreement acceptable to all. However, to do so the UN had to co-operate with the dominant regional power, Nigeria, which had its own political agenda in the conflict. The United States continues to explore the possibility of aiding ECOWAS in conflict resolution and preventive mediation.[53]

Latin America

The two paramount issues for collective security actions in the western hemisphere are the role of the USA in such efforts and the justifications for the violation of sovereignty.

The Treaty of Rio and the Organization of American States

The Treaty of Rio, or the 1947 Inter-American Treaty of Reciprocal Assistance, provides a strong basis for collective security operations in the Americas. Article 3 of the Treaty states that the signatories 'agree that an armed attack by any state against an American state shall be considered an attack against all the

[49] French, H. W., 'As war factions shatter, Liberia falls into chaos', *New York Times*, 22 Oct. 1994, p. 4.
[50] Noble, K. B., 'Civil war threatening to divide West African neighbors', *New York Times,* 29 Aug. 1990, p. A1.
[51] On costs see Shiner, C., 'A disarming start', *Africa Report*, May 1994, p. 64.
[52] Press, R., 'Support wavers for peacekeeping effort in Liberia', *Christian Science Monitor*, 1 Dec.1992, p. 4; and Shiner (note 51).
[53] See note 46, p. 412.

American states' and that signatories shall undertake collective defence measures as sanctioned by Article 51 of the UN Charter. The Treaty also calls for consultations and suspension of hostilities in the event of a conflict between members. It has been invoked in several disputes in Latin America, the last being the civil war in the Dominican Republic in 1965.

However, the use of the Rio Treaty for peacekeeping operations may be difficult. The preponderant role of the USA, coupled with the traditional fear among Latin American nations of US intervention in their affairs, make those nations reluctant to sanction the insertion of US forces in conflicts. In the face of a US claim that states could render assistance to other Treaty states under attack consistent with Treaty obligations, the Government of Mexico stated that 'consistent with the explicit text of the Treaty of Rio no state may claim the right to defense by forces of another American state, unless it was called for'.[54]

The Charter of the OAS is much more far-reaching than the Rio Treaty in that it encompasses economic and social concerns. With respect to collective security and peacekeeping, the OAS Charter calls for non-interference in the internal affairs of member states and supports collective security against aggression. The OAS Charter also includes provisions for an Inter-American Committee on Peaceful Settlement (IAPC); it has been ineffectual.

Political changes in Central and South America have led to changes in the OAS Charter. In 1985 the Charter was amended to allow for peacekeeping services to deal with regional crises.[55] On 4 June 1991 the OAS adopted the Santiago Commitment to Democracy and the Renewal of the Inter-American System. As part of the Santiago Commitment, OAS members declared 'Their decision to adopt efficacious, timely and expeditious procedures for the promotion and defense of representative democracy, in keeping with the Charter of the Organization of American States'.[56] The OAS General Assembly's Resolution on Representative Democracy of 5 June 1991 instructed the OAS Secretary-General 'to call for the immediate convocation of a meeting of the permanent council in case of any event giving rise to the sudden or irregular interruption of the democratic political institutional process or of the legitimate exercise of power by the democratically elected government in any of the Organization's member states'.[57]

One year later OAS delegates approved a document entitled *Cooperation for Security and Development in the Hemisphere: Regional Contributions to Global Security*. This document outlined goals and objectives regarding security issues.[58] The Nassau meeting that approved this document also formally created the Special Committee on Hemispheric Security. The committee's man-

---

[54] Statement quoted in Rengger (note 38), p. 433.

[55] Rengger (note 38), p. 436.

[56] Organization of American States (OAS), General Assembly, *The Santiago Commitment to Democracy and the Renewal of the Inter-American System*, 21st regular session, AF/doc.2734/91, 4 June 1991, Santiago, Chile.

[57] OAS, *Representative Democracy*, 21st regular session, AG/doc.2739/91, 6 June 1991, Santiago, Chile.

[58] See OAS document AG/RES 1179 (XXII-0/92), approved 23 May 1992.

date was extended in 1993 and it was specifically asked to examine a series of matters related to regional security, including the OAS–UN relationship and the improvement of conflict prevention and dispute settlement measures.[59]

With the end of the cold war the OAS in conjunction with the UN has also had an increased role in resolving regional conflicts. In 1990 the OAS, along with the UN, began overseeing the demobilization of Contra troops in Nicaragua.[60]

Haiti proved to be a difficult case for the OAS under the Santiago Commitment. The OAS imposed sanctions in 1991 following the coup and attempted to mediate between Jean Bertrand Aristide and the Haitian military, but to no avail. The OAS decided not to intervene, but to negotiate and let sanctions bite. In December 1992 UN Secretary-General Boutros-Ghali and then OAS Secretary-General João Baena Soares agreed to appoint former Argentine Foreign Minister Dante Caputo as their joint UN–OAS mediator for Haiti. The joint UN-OAS commission planned the deployment of human rights observers to Haiti in the spring of 1993.[61]

The UN, through Resolution 841 of 16 June 1993,[62] imposed a weapons and oil embargo against Haiti. Under this pressure, the OAS–UN mediation produced the Governor's Island accord on 3 July 1993, calling for Aristide's return by 30 October 1993. The Haitian military prevented this from occurring, and negotiations dragged into 1994, with the outflow of refugees becoming a flood by mid-year.

The OAS, however, lacked the political will for stronger measures and refused to consider the use of force in the situation, preferring to continue negotiations. An OAS spokesman stated, 'There is a lot of margin for political pressure and diplomacy, which he [the OAS Secretary-General] feels can still work. Under no circumstances does he feel we should use military force'.[63] The crisis atmosphere increased when Haiti expelled the UN–OAS human rights monitors in July 1994.[64]

In September 1994, under the threat of an imminent US invasion, Lieutenant-General Raoul Cedras agreed to step down from power under an agreement negotiated by former President Jimmy Carter, Senator Sam Nunn and former Chairman of the US Joint Chiefs of Staff General Colin Powell, US armed forces then occupied Haiti. OAS Secretary-General César Gaviria Trujillo, who

[59] See Vaky, V. P., 'The Organization of American States and multilateralism in the Americas', eds V. P. Vaky and H. Munoz, *The Future of the Organization of American States* (Twentieth Century Fund: New York, 1993), p. 21.

[60] See Christian, S., 'OAS goes in peace (that's what it came for)', *New York Times*, 16 July 1992, p. A4.

[61] Goshko, J., 'Monitors could be in Haiti by month's end', *Washington Post*, 22 Jan. 1993, p. A25; Preston, J., 'Haiti agrees to monitoring by U.N. and OAS', *Washington Post*, 10 Feb. 1993, p. A28.

[62] United Nations Security Council document S/RES/841 (1993), in UN Security Council document S/25957, 16 June 1993.

[63] French, H. W., 'U.S. hint of force to end Haiti crisis draws opposition', *New York Times*, 13 May 1994, p. A1.

[64] Farah, D., 'Haitians expelling U.N. rights team', *Washington Post*, 12 July 1994, p. A1.

succeeded Soares on 15 September 1994, expressed 'deep satisfaction over the agreement, which assures that political measures and diplomacy will prevail'.[65]

A lack of sufficient political will and doubts about legitimate grounds for intervention hamper the OAS. Robert Pastor has noted that the OAS has been ineffective because 'too often neither Latin America nor the United States wants to use it'.[66] The USA fears being outvoted in the OAS, while the Latin American nations fear the domestic repercussions of compromise with the United States in the OAS.

Other problems also inhibit the OAS's activity. As one report notes, 'no regional consensus yet exists on whether the OAS should develop some form of peacemaking or peacekeeping capacity, or whether it should continue to depend on the United Nations for all security related activity'.[67] Through 1994 OAS missions in peacekeeping have had the consent, if grudging, of all parties concerned. They have also been composed of monitoring missions of unarmed civilians. There is a traditional fear of US and regional hegemons taking advantage of peacekeeping, and it is unclear if the OAS charter would support such actions. The OAS has a relatively small budget of around \$35 million per year in country assessments. Funding for peacekeeping would have to come from unspecified special sources of funding.

Viron Vaky has summed up what he calls the OAS 'common denominator' on the topic of peacekeeping:

Diplomatic and economic sanctions may be recommended but the use of military force will not be considered;

OAS military contingents for protection as part of peacekeeping missions is a controversial subject, and probably not 'doable' now; and

It should be made clear that overthrowing a democratic government will not be cost-free, but there is not much agreement on how to determine what price aggression should pay.[68]

The US intervention in Haiti under a UN mandate suggests that regional organizations are not likely to be effective by themselves and need UN backing.

The Inter-American Defense Board

The Inter-American Defense Board (IADB) was established in 1942 to aid in hemispheric defence during World War II. The IADB currently consists of the USA, Mexico, all the Central American states except Belize, and all the countries of South America save Guyana and Suriname. It is charged with planning for the collective defence of the hemisphere and strengthening military cooperation among its member states. While the IADB may have a charter man-

[65] Brooke, J., 'Latin America breathes a half-sigh of relief over Haiti', *New York Times*, 20 Sep. 1994, p. A11.

[66] Pastor, R., 'Securing a democratic hemisphere', *Foreign Policy*, vol. 73 (winter 1988/89), p. 47.

[67] Inter-American Dialog, *Convergence and Community: The Americas in the 90s* (Inter-American Dialog: Washington, DC, 1992), p. 38.

[68] Vaky (note 59), p. 45.

date for a stronger role, it seems to lack the legitimacy necessary to do so. It has been ineffectual for two reasons. First, its intelligence units do not have access to classified materials, which substantially inhibits the ability of the IADB to plan. Second, and more important, the Latin American nations have traditionally not wanted the IADB to play a strong role.[69] The IADB planning and co-ordination for the removal of land mines in Nicaragua and eventually elsewhere in Central America could lead to greater IADB involvement in collective security operations in the post-cold war era.[70] The 23rd OAS General Assembly in Managua in 1993 did note that all OAS political organs may call on the IADB for 'technical–military advisory services and consultations'.[71] The future role of the IADB is currently under review by the OAS.

The Middle East and South Asia

Regional disputes in the Middle East and South Asia since decolonization have prevented the development of effective region-wide collective security organizations. The Arab states, however, have formed organizations that, in principle, could engage in collective security operations. The nations of South Asia have more recently also formed a regional organization to address the area's problems.

The League of Arab States (Arab League)

The Arab League was founded in 1945 and currently includes all the Arab states of the Middle East as well as the Palestine Liberation Organization (PLO). North African members of the League are Algeria, Egypt, Libya, Morocco and Tunisia. Other members of the League include Mauritania, Somalia and Sudan. The Constitution of the Arab League provides for periodic meetings of the Council, the supreme organ of the League. The Council is charged with promoting co-operation among Arab states, safeguarding members against aggression and preserving their independence, and arbitrating disputes between members. In 1950 several members of the League also formed a Collective Security Pact, calling for collective defence of members pursuant to obligations under the League Charter and Article 51 of the UN Charter.

Over the years the Arab League has been hamstrung by political divisions between members. Egypt and the more conservative Arab nations were at odds in the 1960s and again in the late 1970s following the 1979 Camp David Peace Accords with Israel.

The Persian Gulf War also severely divided the Arab League. Only 13 of the 21 members of the League attended an emergency session on the Gulf crisis

[69] See the discussion in Aldrich, H., 'Free for lunch?: the languid life of foreign attaches', *Washington Monthly*, Nov. 1982, pp. 33–37.
[70] See de Leon, F.V., 'The OAS and regional security', unpublished manuscript, US Institute of Peace, Washington, DC, 1993, p. 11.
[71] OAS document OEA/SER.P, AG/doc 3015/93 rev.1, 11 June 1993.

called by Egypt on 2 September 1990. The League was split between the conservative group of nations led by Egypt and Saudi Arabia, and the radical nations led by Iraq and several North African states.[72] Twelve member states sent forces in defence of Saudi Arabia, more for political reasons than for any collective security rationale under the Arab League.

More recently, the League has failed in its mediation attempts in Somalia and Yemen.[73] While the Arab League certainly has the resources and the charter mandate to be an active collective security organization, political divisions have denied the League the will and to a degree the legitimacy to take unified action through collective security.

The Co-operation Council for the Arab States of the Gulf

The Co-operation Council for the Arab States of the Gulf, or Gulf Co-operation Council (GCC), was formed on 25 May 1981, and currently consists of Bahrain, Kuwait, Oman, Qatar, Saudi Arabia and the United Arab Emirates. Its general objective is to promote economic and social co-operation among GCC members. Since its founding it has taken an active interest in promoting military co-operation among its members. It took a strong stand against Iranian expansion (indeed, fear of such expansion was one of the chief reasons for the creation of the GCC) and urged Iran to respect UN resolutions on freedom of navigation in the Persian Gulf as well as on the settlement of the conflict with Iraq. During the Gulf War there were proposals for a new Persian Gulf peacekeeping force composed of Egyptian, Saudi and Syrian troops.

The GCC seems to have the will, legitimacy and financial resources to engage in collective security operations. The GCC has done more than most regional organizations in the field of military co-operation and planning, but the small size of the GCC military forces, despite their possession of sophisticated military equipment, would make it difficult for them to engage in large-scale peacekeeping activities. The GCC can provide valuable diplomatic and military co-ordination mechanisms, however, including the facilitation of Western assistance should the need again arise.

The South Asian Association for Regional Cooperation

Consisting of Bangladesh, Bhutan, India, the Maldives, Nepal, Pakistan and Sri Lanka, the South Asian Association for Regional Cooperation (SAARC) was established in December 1985 to promote regional co-operation among the South Asian nations. The main purpose of the organization is to promote the agricultural and economic production of its members. Through the Islamabad Declaration of 1988 the organization called for increased vigilance against drug

---

[72] Clairborne, W., 'Arab League hardens stand on Iraq, seeks collective action on peace plans', *Washington Post*, 2 Sep. 1990, p. A34.
[73] See Wright, R., 'Yemen conflict seems to be settling into war of attrition, U.S. aides say', *Los Angeles Times*, 12 May 1994, p. A6.

trafficking, joint efforts against terrorism and an end to regional and global nuclear arms proliferation.[74] SAARC's Charter severely limits the role it could play in collective security, peacekeeping or peace-enforcement operations. The Charter provides for unanimity in decision making: 'bilateral and contentious' issues are excluded from its deliberations.[75] However, SAARC can offer opportunities for bilateral meetings between members on security issues.[76]

East Asia

There is no international organization in East Asia charged even in theory with peacekeeping responsibilities. Until recently the predominant form of international relations was essentially bilateral. There are, however, two multilateral organizations that might develop some security responsibilities.

The Association of South-East Asian Nations

The Association of South-East Asian Nations (ASEAN) was created in 1967 to promote regional reconciliation and manage intramural disputes following a period of tension between Indonesia and Malaysia.[77] It currently consists of Brunei Darussalam, Indonesia, Malaysia, the Philippines, Singapore and Thailand with Viet Nam scheduled to join the organization in 1995. Its purpose is to promote regional co-operation, chiefly in the economic sphere. The 1976 Treaty of Amity and Co-operation in South-East Asia and a Declaration of Concord stressed mutual respect for sovereignty and non-interference in the internal affairs of member states, and continuation of independent ASEAN military co-operation according to the individual needs and interests of ASEAN member states.[78] The ASEAN militaries do hold exercises among themselves and with outside countries on a regular basis.[79]

The Vietnamese invasion and occupation of Cambodia was a main concern of ASEAN, and it took a strong stand against foreign occupation of that country. It has taken an active role in promoting a peaceful solution to the conflict, both in pressing for Vietnamese withdrawal from Cambodia and in promoting co-operation among the resistance groups.[80] While ASEAN could not respond militarily, the invasion did bring the ASEAN states closer politically.[81] It has also concerned itself with the dispute over the Spratly Islands, attempting to mediate

[74] Rengger (note 38), p. 533.

[75] Rengger (note 38), p. 533.

[76] For an exhaustive discussion of SAARC and its future role see Mendis, V. L. B., *SAARC: Origins, Organization & Prospects* (Indian Ocean Centre for Peace Studies: Perth, Australia, 1991).

[77] Simon, S., The *Future of Asian-Pacific Security Collaboration* (Lexington Books: Lexington, Mass., 1988), p. 66.

[78] The documents are reprinted in Leifer, M., *ASEAN and the Security of South-East Asia* (Routledge Books: New York, 1989), pp. 165–74.

[79] Simon (note 77), pp. 80–86.

[80] See Jones, C., 'A fresh try at untangling Cambodia's political knot', *Christian Science Monitor*, 17 Feb. 1989, p. 3.

[81] See Leifer (note 78), chapter 4, and the ASEAN declaration *An Appeal for Kampuchean Independence*, of 21 Sep. 1983, reprinted in Leifer (note 78), pp. 187–88.

member claims and warily watching Chinese moves with respect to the islands.[82] As of the end of 1994 the dispute over the islands remained unresolved, with both China and Viet Nam awarding concessions to different US oil companies to explore disputed waters around the islands.[83]

On 25 July 1994 ASEAN broke new ground in the security area with the launching of the ASEAN Regional Forum (ARF) to discuss security issues in the region. The ARF consists of the 6 ASEAN nations, its 7 dialogue partners (Australia, Canada, the European Union, Japan, New Zealand, South Korea and the USA), its three observers (Laos, Papua New Guinea and Viet Nam), as well as China and Russia. The ARF plans to work on a consensual basis, with the modest short-term goal of simply getting the process of dialogue moving between so many nations with so many divergent interests.[84]

ASEAN has diplomatic solidarity, as it has seen the increased influence it can enjoy in world bodies such as the UN through united action; it is a valuable force for forging political discussions and consensus. As one analyst noted, 'getting the world to pay attention to Cambodia has been one of ASEAN's major accomplishments'.[85] The ASEAN countries could certainly afford to finance operations. However, given its make-up, ASEAN has difficulty translating this diplomatic unity into a system for collective military action. One reason for this is its lack of a military co-ordination mandate. Another is the divergent interests of its members in the security area.[86] This point means that both the political will and legitimacy to act are lacking beyond the initial stage of diplomatic co-ordination. The ARF represents a significant advance for ASEAN in the field of security discussions, but given its unwieldy size, lukewarm Chinese support and its approach of decision making by consensus, it is still a long way from being a meaningful organization for collective action in the security field.[87]

The Asia–Pacific Economic Cooperation forum

The Asia–Pacific Economic Cooperation (APEC) forum was founded in 1989 to promote Pacific regional co-operation. It includes, in addition to the ASEAN nations, Australia, Canada, Chile, China, Hong Kong, Japan, Mexico, New Zealand, Papua New Guinea, South Korea, Taiwan and the USA. Perspectives on the political role of APEC vary. A senior official at Japan's Ministry for International Trade and Industry noted: 'The important thing is that it is based

[82] Shenon, P., 'Asian nations hope to settle dispute over islands peacefully', *New York Times*, 23 July 1992, p. A9.

[83] Toft, S., 'China's army looms over Asia', *Christian Science Monitor*, 10 Aug. 1994, p. 20.

[84] See Ching, F, 'Discussing regional security: ASEAN moving cautiously to institute new Forum', *Far Eastern Economic Review*, 12 May 1994, p. 38; and Smith, C., 'A new beginning', *Far Eastern Economic Review*, 9 June 1994.

[85] Erlanger, S., 'For Asia, the strain is showing', *New York Times,* 16 July 1989, sec. IV, p. 2.

[86] For a discussion of individual ASEAN country interests in the regional context, see Tilman, R. O., *Southeast Asia and the Enemy Beyond: ASEAN Perceptions of External Threats* (Westview Press: Boulder, Colo., 1987)

[87] For a discussion of some of the activities the forum will likely undertake, see Branigan, W., 'East, West enter forum on security in South-East Asia', *Washington Post*, 26 July 1994, p. A14.

on economic reality, not politics. These relationships already exist'.[88] US officials have taken a different view. In a 1991 *Foreign Affairs* article, then US Secretary of State James Baker stated with respect to APEC that 'within this construct, new political and economic relationships offer additional support for a system of cooperative action by groups of Pacific nations to address both residual problems and emerging challenges'.[89] Discussions of political and security affairs take place at Post Ministerial Meetings; some hope that a security role may evolve from these discussions. The 1993 US National Security Strategy document cited these meetings as important for regional stability.[90]

APEC seems to be firmly moving towards being a strictly economic body, with regional meetings in 1993 and 1994 focused on trade issues and the possibility of a Pacific Free Trade Area in the 21st century. The membership and orientation of APEC will probably prevent it from engaging in collective security operations for some time to come. Furthermore, save Taiwan, all of the APEC nations are represented in the newly formed ARF, thus making that a natural venue for any political-security discussions or decision making.

V. A time for institution building

The experience of the past few years does not encourage hope for a vigorous role for regional organizations in maintaining international peace and security. Boutros-Ghali summed up the issue accurately. He stated, 'The capacity of regional organizations for peacemaking and peace-keeping varies considerably. None of them has yet developed a capacity which matches that of the United Nations, though some have accumulated important experience in the field and others are developing rapidly'.[91]

Among regional organizations, European regional institutions are the best suited to engage in collective military operations. NATO and to some extent the WEU can take advantage of well-developed logistical networks and four decades of defence co-operation among Western European nations. NACC and the PFP offer new opportunities for co-operation on an all-European basis. The CSCE process provides Europe with political legitimacy for seeking to enforce international norms in both interstate and intra-state affairs. Revisions of the CSCE consensus rule also mark a step forward by ending the threat that a single nation could block the rest of Europe from exercising preventive diplomacy. Early-warning mechanisms have strengthened the CSCE's preventive diplomacy role. The Budapest decision of December 1994 to prepare for a peacekeeping force in Nagorno-Karabakh is a potentially valuable precedent, although many steps that would make that a reality have yet to be taken.

[88] Sterngold, J., 'A wary step toward regional cooperation', *New York Times*, 17 Nov. 1991, section IV, p. 5.

[89] Baker, J. A., 'America in Asia', *Foreign Affairs*, vol. 70, no. 5 (winter 1991/92), p. 5.

[90] *National Security Strategy of the United States* (US Government Printing Office: Washington, DC, 1993), p. 19.

[91] *Supplement to An Agenda for Peace* (note 4), p. 21.

Outside Europe the regional organizations are not well suited to engage in collective security operations. Two principal sets of reasons account for this. The first set consists of practical difficulties, in that regional actors do not have the logistical capability for large-scale collective security operations even in their own regions, and many nations cannot support military forces beyond their own borders.

The second set is based on political problems. Many regional organizations, such as the Arab League and SAARC find themselves unable to rise to the challenge of collective operations for political reasons. Others, such as ASEAN, while developing new forums for political and diplomatic co-operation, still remain ambiguous about their security role. Many regional organizations have no charter mandate for security or peacekeeping in cases involving conflict internal to sovereign states and, in fact, usually have clauses in their charters prohibiting interference in the internal affairs of member states. Such is the problem faced by the OAU. Regional organizations may have a dominant member whose presence may be politically unacceptable to the target state of intervention but whose participation may be vital for financial or logistical reasons for the regional organization to undertake such a mission. The ECOWAS intervention in Liberia and the CIS intervention in Georgia illustrate cases where regional organizations did intervene in civil conflicts. However, a dominant power drove the agenda in both cases, and it may not be wise to endorse what amount to regional hegemonies and attempts by stronger powers using regional organizations to legitimize their sphere of influence policies. Of course, action through a regional organization could act as a modifying force on regional powers, but strong and united pressure by the smaller countries will be essential to accomplish this.

Given all these factors, it is not surprising that there has been an explosion of direct UN or UN-sanctioned peacekeeping activities. UN elements are currently deployed in Africa, East Asia, the Middle East, South Asia and in regions such as the Balkans and Central America that until recently had been off limits to UN forces. The UN has several factors working in its favour. First, since the end of the cold war the UN has functioned in many ways as a big power directorate. The USA sought and received UN sanction for its operations in the Persian Gulf, Somalia and Haiti. In recent years the Security Council has functioned without the use of the veto, thus permitting effective action even, to some extent, in controversial cases like the former Yugoslavia. In this way the UN effectively brings together Russia and the United States in the pursuit of operations which both great powers support.

Second, the United Nations is generally seen as impartial. It is therefore more acceptable to the regional actors. Third, the UN has access to funds and logistics that regional actors often lack. Despite being stretched to the breaking point, the UN still has potential access to funds and logistical resources from virtually every nation in the world. Most important in this regard, of course, is access to US, European, Middle Eastern and Asian sources of capital and access to US and European military logistics.

Regional organizations outside Europe can and do work with the UN to the best of their abilities on resolving conflicts in their regions. Boutros-Ghali in his *Supplement to An Agenda for Peace* recognized the broad and interlocking support mechanisms that have developed between the UN and regional organizations. The fact that states usually have dual membership in regional organizations and the United Nations makes this a natural development. This sort of co-operation will also prevent states from moving between regional organizations and the UN in order to avoid negotiations to resolve conflicts.[92] For the immediate future, UN operations, perhaps in conjunction with regional organizations, may be the best hope for collective security. Given their relative strengths and weaknesses, heavy reliance on regional organizations does not seem to be an option in the short term.

Outside of Europe, and even within Europe, there is little choice but to involve the UN in some capacity for the indefinite future for operations requiring the use of military forces sanctioned by a broad consensus of the major powers. Yet something akin to a revolution in thinking will be required to give the United Nations the kind of resources and expertise it really needs to manage and conduct international security operations. Failure to strengthen the UN will impose increased burdens on regional organizations that are not well placed to carry out collective security operations. It would mean forfeiting the capability to offer plausible means of preventive diplomacy, peacekeeping, protective security, peace enforcing or peace-building in many places around the world. In the immediate future the investment of necessary funds and requisite policy attention in the UN is imperative for the promotion of stability and security. In the long run, regional organizations may be able to take a more active role in regional collective security, but for the next several years the UN is the only international organization that is capable of dealing with regional conflicts in much of the world.

The UN is stretched to the limit, and perhaps beyond. It has entered a critical phase in its history in which new demands are being placed on it which it is ill prepared to handle. Like other international organizations it has encountered difficulties in adjusting to the post-cold war era and has become the butt of criticism, much of it amounting to scapegoating. It is clear that many regional conflicts can best be handled by the UN, acting as the agent for the Security Council, and thus for Russia and the USA. The two partners have much to gain from this, since neither Moscow nor Washington will wish to use their own forces if their basic interests are not directly affected. And yet it will not serve their interests to tolerate a proliferation of Cambodias, Rwandas and Somalias. A developing world full of humanitarian disasters and flouting of international norms will infect areas of greater interest to the United States and Russia sooner or later. The United Nations is ideally positioned to deal with such situations, at least in principle, while regional organizations generally are not.

[92] See Imobighe (note 36), p. 379.

There is no reason to think that other countries will pick up the burden if the UN's principal supporter during the cold war years, the United States, cuts its contribution. It would be tragic if just at the moment when the United Nations could begin to fulfil the hopes of its founders, hopes inspired by the US leaders of the World War II period first and foremost, the leading powers acted to shut down the United Nations except as an exercise in vacuous oratory. To cripple this instrument for world stability would be to ensure a more dangerous world and practically guarantee that burdens and more crises would be imposed on the United States. This would be a prescription for isolationism.

What is needed, instead of a retreat from responsibility, is an attack on the problems that plague the United Nations in order to strengthen the only peace-keeping organization that is broadly accepted around the globe. This is an area where the United States and Russia should co-operate in their own self-interest. More than financial support is involved, although that is also needed. Many of the ideas Boutros-Ghali proposed in his *Agenda for Peace* deserve a more serious hearing than they have yet received. National forces on 'stand-by' for UN missions, for example, could be an extremely useful tool in situations like Rwanda or Somalia. The United States and Russia should not have to become directly involved in most of these situations. Other nations can assume the burden. The idea of UN deterrent forces, such as those currently stationed in Macedonia, also deserves more attention.

Annual summit meetings of the heads of state and government of the UN Security Council could help the United Nations to correct its problems. Items for annual review would include: reforming the UN Secretariat to make it more responsive to current needs, placing UN finances on a more secure footing, improving UN performance in collective security operations and developing greater co-operation between the United Nations and regional organizations. US–Russian co-operation has opened the possibility that the United Nations can function as the founders of the organization envisaged some 50 years ago. For their own national interests and for the good of the international community they should strive to make this possibility a reality.

Appendix 10A. Supplement to An Agenda for Peace

SUPPLEMENT TO AN AGENDA FOR PEACE

Position Paper of the Secretary-General on the Occasion of the Fiftieth Anniversary of the United Nations

Report of the Secretary-General on the Work of the Organization
3 January 1995

I. Introduction

1. On 31 January 1992, the Security Council met for the first time at the level of heads of State or Government. The cold war had ended. It was a time of hope and change and of rising expectations for—and of—the United Nations. The members of the Council asked me to prepare an 'analysis and recommendations on ways of strengthening and making more efficient within the framework and provisions of the Charter the capacity of the United Nations for preventive diplomacy, for peacemaking and for peace-keeping' (see S/23500). Five months later, in June 1992, I submitted my report entitled 'An Agenda for Peace' (A/47/277-S/24111). It dealt with the three problems the Council had requested me to consider, to which I added the related concept of post-conflict peace-building. It also touched on peace enforcement.

2. In submitting my recommendations on how to improve the Organization's capacity to maintain peace and security, I said that the search for improved mechanisms and techniques would be of little significance unless the new spirit of commonality that had emerged, of which the Summit was such a clear manifestation, was 'propelled by the will to take the hard decisions demanded by this time of opportunity' (ibid., para. 6).

3. Subsequent discussion of 'An Agenda for Peace' in the General Assembly, in the Security Council and in Member States' parliaments established that there was general support for the recommendations I had put forward. That discussion, and the new process initiated in 1994 for the elaboration of 'An Agenda for Development' (see A/48/935), have also served to advance international consensus on the crucial importance of economic and social development as the most secure basis for lasting peace.

4. Since the Security Council Summit the pace has accelerated. There have been dramatic changes in both the volume and the nature of the United Nations activities in the field of peace and security. New and more comprehensive concepts to guide those activities, and their links with development work, are emerging. Old concepts are being modified. There have been successes and there have been failures. The Organization has attracted intense media interest, often laudatory, more often critical, and all too often focused on only one or two of the many peace-keeping operations in which it is engaged, overshadowing other major operations and its vast effort in the economic, social and other fields.

5. All this confirms that we are still in a time of transition. The end of the cold war was a major movement of tectonic plates and the after-shocks continue to be felt. But even if the ground beneath our feet has not yet settled, we still live in a new age that holds great promise for both peace and development.

6. Our ability to fulfil that promise depends on how well we can learn the lessons of the Organization's successes and failures in these first years of the post-cold-war age. Most of the ideas in 'An Agenda for Peace' have proved themselves. A few have not been taken up. The purpose of the present position paper, however, is not to revise 'An Agenda for Peace' nor to call into question structures and procedures that have been tested by time. Even less is it intended to be a comprehensive treatise on the matters it discusses. Its purpose is, rather, to highlight selectively certain areas where unforeseen, or only partly foreseen, difficulties have arisen and where there is a need for the Member States to take the 'hard decisions' I referred to two and a half years ago.

7. The Organization's half-century year will provide the international community an opportunity to address these issues, and the

related, major challenge of elaborating 'An Agenda for Development', and to indicate in a comprehensive way the direction the Member States want the Organization to take. The present position paper is offered as a contribution to the many debates I hope will take place during 1995 and perhaps beyond, inside and outside the intergovernmental bodies, about the current performance and future role of our Organization.

II. Quantitative and Qualitative Changes

8. It is indisputable that since the end of the cold war there has been a dramatic increase in the United Nations activities related to the maintenance of peace and security. The figures speak for themselves. The following table gives them for three dates: 31 January 1988 (when the cold war was already coming to an end); 31 January 1992 (the date of the first Security Council Summit); and today, on the eve of the fiftieth anniversary of the United Nations.

9. This increased volume of activity would have strained the Organization even if the nature of the activity had remained unchanged. It has not remained unchanged, however: there have been qualitative changes even more significant than the quantitative ones.

10. One is the fact that so many of today's conflicts are within States rather than between States. The end of the cold war removed constraints that had inhibited conflict in the former Soviet Union and elsewhere. As a result there has been a rash of wars within newly independent States, often of a religious or ethnic character and often involving unusual violence and cruelty. The end of the cold war seems also to have contributed to an outbreak of such wars in Africa. In addition, some of the proxy wars fuelled by the cold war within States remain unresolved. Interstate wars, by contrast, have become infrequent.

11. Of the five peace-keeping operations that existed in early 1988, four related to interstate wars and only one (20 per cent of the total) to an intra-state conflict. Of the 21 operations established since then, only 8 have related to inter-state wars, whereas 13 (62 per cent) have related to intra-state conflicts, though some of them, especially those in the former Yugoslavia, have some inter-state dimensions also. Of the 11 operations established since January 1992 all but 2 (82 per cent) relate to intra-state conflicts.

Table. Some statistics on United Nations activities related to peace and security, 1988 to 1994

	As at 31 January 1988	As at 31 January 1992	As at 16 December 1994
Security Council resolutions adopted in the preceding 12 months	15	53	78
Disputes and conflicts in which the United Nations was actively involved in preventive diplomacy or peacemaking in the preceding 12 months	11	13	28
Peace-keeping operations deployed			
Total	5	11	17
Classical	5	7	9
Multi-functional	–	4	8
Military personnel deployed	9570	11 495	73 393
Civilian police deployed	35	155	2130
International civilian personnel deployed	1516	2206	2260
Countries contributing military and police personnel	26	56	76

United Nations budget for peace-keeping operations (on an annual basis) (millions of United States dollars)	230.4	1689.6	3610.0[a]
Countries in which the United Nations had undertaken electoral activities in the preceding 12 months	–	6	21
Sanctions regimes imposed by the Security Council	1	2	7

[a] Projected

12. The new breed of intra-state conflicts have certain characteristics that present United Nations peace-keepers with challenges not encountered since the Congo operation of the early 1960s. They are usually fought not only by regular armies but also by militias and armed civilians with little discipline and with ill-defined chains of command. They are often guerrilla wars without clear front lines. Civilians are the main victims and often the main targets. Humanitarian emergencies are commonplace and the combatant authorities, in so far as they can be called authorities, lack the capacity to cope with them. The number of refugees registered with the Office of the United Nations High Commissioner for Refugees (UNHCR) has increased from 13 million at the end of 1987 to 26 million at the end of 1994. The number of internally displaced persons has increased even more dramatically.

13. Another feature of such conflicts is the collapse of state institutions, especially the police and judiciary, with resulting paralysis of governance, a breakdown of law and order, and general banditry and chaos. Not only are the functions of government suspended, its assets are destroyed or looted and experienced officials are killed or flee the country. This is rarely the case in inter-state wars. It means that international intervention must extend beyond military and humanitarian tasks and must include the promotion of national reconciliation and the re-establishment of effective government.

14. The latter are tasks that demand time and sensitivity. The United Nations is, for good reasons, reluctant to assume responsibility for maintaining law and order, nor can it impose a new political structure or new state institutions. It can only help the hostile factions to help themselves and begin to live together again. All too often it turns out that they do not yet want to be helped or to resolve their problems quickly.

15. Peace-keeping in such contexts is far more complex and more expensive than when its tasks were mainly to monitor cease-fires and control buffer zones with the consent of the States involved in the conflict. Peace-keeping today can involve constant danger.

16. I cannot praise too highly or adequately express my gratitude and admiration for the courage and sacrifice of United Nations personnel, military and civil, in this new era of challenge to peace and security. The conditions under which they serve are often extremely harsh. Many have given their lives. Many must persevere despite the loss of family members and friends.

17. It must also be recognized that the vast increase in field deployment has to be supported by an overburdened Headquarters staff that resource constraints have held at levels appropriate to an earlier, far less demanding, time.

18. A second qualitative change is the use of United Nations forces to protect humanitarian operations. Humanitarian agencies endeavour to provide succour to civilian victims of war wherever they may be. Too often the warring parties make it difficult or impossible for them to do so. This is sometimes because of the exigencies of war but more often because the relief of a particular population is contrary to the war aims of one or other of the parties. There is also a growing tendency for the combatants to divert relief supplies for their own purposes. Because the wars are intra-state conflicts, the humanitarian agencies often have to undertake their tasks in the chaotic and lawless conditions described above. In some, but not all, such cases the resulting horrors explode on to the world's television screens and create political pressure for the

United Nations to deploy troops to facilitate and protect the humanitarian operations. While such images can help build support for humanitarian action, such scenes also may create an emotional environment in which effective decision-making can be far more difficult.

19. This has led, in Bosnia and Herzegovina and in Somalia, to a new kind of United Nations operation. Even though the use of force is authorized under Chapter VII of the Charter, the United Nations remains neutral and impartial between the warring parties, without a mandate to stop the aggressor (if one can be identified) or impose a cessation of hostilities. Nor is this peace-keeping as practised hitherto, because the hostilities continue and there is often no agreement between the warring parties on which a peace-keeping mandate can be based. The 'safe areas' concept in Bosnia and Herzegovina is a similar case. It too gives the United Nations a humanitarian mandate under which the use of force is authorized, but for limited and local purposes and not to bring the war to an end.

20. A third change has been in the nature of United Nations operations in the field. During the cold war United Nations peace-keeping operations were largely military in character and were usually deployed after a cease-fire but before a settlement of the conflict in question had been negotiated. Indeed one of their main purposes was to create conditions in which negotiations for a settlement could take place. In the late 1980s a new kind of peace-keeping operation evolved. It was established after negotiations had succeeded, with the mandate of helping the parties implement the comprehensive settlement they had negotiated. Such operations have been deployed in Namibia, Angola, El Salvador, Cambodia and Mozambique. In most cases they have been conspicuously successful.

21. The negotiated settlements involved not only military arrangements but also a wide range of civilian matters. As a result, the United Nations found itself asked to undertake an unprecedented variety of functions: the supervision of cease-fires, the regroupment and demobilization of forces, their reintegration into civilian life and the destruction of their weapons; the design and implementation of de-mining programmes; the return of refugees and displaced persons; the provision of humanitarian assistance; the supervision of existing administrative structures; the establishment of new police forces; the verification

of respect for human rights; the design and supervision of constitutional, judicial and electoral reforms; the observation, supervision and even organization and conduct of elections; and the coordination of support for economic rehabilitation and reconstruction.

22. Fourthly, these multifunctional peace-keeping operations have highlighted the role the United Nations can play after a negotiated settlement has been implemented. It is now recognized that implementation of the settlement in the time prescribed may not be enough to guarantee that the conflict will not revive. Coordinated programmes are required, over a number of years and in various fields, to ensure that the original causes of war are eradicated. This involves the building up of national institutions, the promotion of human rights, the creation of civilian police forces and other actions in the political field. As I pointed out in 'An Agenda for Development' (A/48/935), only sustained efforts to resolve underlying socio-economic, cultural and humanitarian problems can place an achieved peace on a durable foundation.

III. Instruments for Peace and Security

23. The United Nations has developed a range of instruments for controlling and resolving conflicts between and within States. The most important of them are preventive diplomacy and peacemaking; peace-keeping; peace-building; disarmament; sanctions; and peace enforcement. The first three can be employed only with the consent of the parties to the conflict. Sanctions and enforcement, on the other hand, are coercive measures and thus, by definition, do not require the consent of the party concerned. Disarmament can take place on an agreed basis or in the context of coercive action under Chapter VII.

24. The United Nations does not have or claim a monopoly of any of these instruments. All can be, and most of them have been, employed by regional organizations, by ad hoc groups of States or by individual States, but the United Nations has unparalleled experience of them and it is to the United Nations that the international community has turned increasingly since the end of the cold war. The United Nations system is also better equipped than regional organizations or individual Member States to develop and apply the comprehensive, long-term approach needed to ensure the lasting resolution of conflicts.

25. Perceived shortcomings in the United Nations performance of the tasks entrusted to it have recently, however, seemed to incline Member States to look for other means, especially, but not exclusively, where the rapid deployment of large forces is required. It is thus necessary to find ways of enabling the United Nations to perform better the roles envisaged for it in the Charter.

A. Preventive diplomacy and peacemaking

26. It is evidently better to prevent conflicts through early warning, quiet diplomacy and, in some cases, preventive deployment than to have to undertake major politico-military efforts to resolve them after they have broken out. The Security Council's declaration of 31 January 1992 (S/23500) mandated me to give priority to preventive and peacemaking activities. I accordingly created a Department of Political Affairs to handle a range of political functions that had previously been performed in various parts of the Secretariat. That Department has since passed through successive phases of restructuring and is now organized to follow political developments worldwide, so that it can provide early warning of impending conflicts and analyse possibilities for preventive action by the United Nations, as well as for action to help resolve existing conflicts.

27. Experience has shown that the greatest obstacle to success in these endeavours is not, as is widely supposed, lack of information, analytical capacity or ideas for United Nations initiatives. Success is often blocked at the outset by the reluctance of one or other of the parties to accept United Nations help. This is as true of inter-state conflicts as it is of internal ones, even though United Nations action on the former is fully within the Charter, whereas in the latter case it must be reconciled with Article 2, paragraph 7.

28. Collectively Member States encourage the Secretary-General to play an active role in this field; individually they are often reluctant that he should do so when they are a party to the conflict. It is difficult to know how to overcome this reluctance. Clearly the United Nations cannot impose its preventive and peacemaking services on Member States who do not want them. Legally and politically their request for, or at least acquiescence in, United Nations action is a *sine qua non*. The solution can only be long-term. It may lie in creating a climate of opinion, or ethos, within the international community in which the norm would be for Member States to accept an offer of United Nations good offices.

29. There are also two practical problems that have emerged in this field. Given Member States' frequently expressed support for preventive diplomacy and peacemaking, I take this opportunity to recommend that early action be taken to resolve them.

30. The first is the difficulty of finding senior persons who have the diplomatic skills and who are willing to serve for a while as special representative or special envoy of the Secretary-General. As a result of the streamlining of the senior levels of the Secretariat, the extra capacity that was there in earlier years no longer exists.

31. The second problem relates to the establishment and financing of small field missions for preventive diplomacy and peacemaking. Accepted and well-tried procedures exist for such action in the case of peace-keeping operations. The same is required in the preventive and peacemaking field. Although special envoys can achieve much on a visiting basis, their capacity is greatly enhanced if continuity can be assured by the presence on the ground of a small support mission on a full-time basis. There is no clear view amongst Member States about whether legislative authority for such matters rests with the Security Council or the General Assembly, nor are existing budgetary procedures well-geared to meet this need.

32. Two solutions are possible. The first is to include in the regular budget a contingency provision, which might be in the range of $25 million per biennium, for such activities. The second would be to enlarge the existing provision for unforeseen and extraordinary activities and to make it available for all preventive and peacemaking activities, not just those related to international peace and security strictly defined.

B. Peace-keeping

33. The United Nations can be proud of the speed with which peace-keeping has evolved in response to the new political environment resulting from the end of the cold war, but the last few years have confirmed that respect for certain basic principles of peace-keeping are essential to its success. Three particularly important principles are the consent of the parties, impartiality and the non-use of force except in self-defence. Analysis of recent successes and failures shows that in all the

successes those principles were respected and in most of the less successful operations one or other of them was not.

34. There are three aspects of recent mandates that, in particular, have led peace-keeping operations to forfeit the consent of the parties, to behave in a way that was perceived to be partial and/or to use force other than in self-defence. These have been the tasks of protecting humanitarian operations during continuing warfare, protecting civilian populations in designated safe areas and pressing the parties to achieve national reconciliation at a pace faster than they were ready to accept. The cases of Somalia and Bosnia and Herzegovina are instructive in this respect.

35. In both cases, existing peace-keeping operations were given additional mandates that required the use of force and therefore could not be combined with existing mandates requiring the consent of the parties, impartiality and the non-use of force. It was also not possible for them to be executed without much stronger military capabilities than had been made available, as is the case in the former Yugoslavia. In reality, nothing is more dangerous for a peace-keeping operation than to ask it to use force when its existing composition, armament, logistic support and deployment deny it the capacity to do so. The logic of peace-keeping flows from political and military premises that are quite distinct from those of enforcement; and the dynamics of the latter are incompatible with the political process that peace-keeping is intended to facilitate. To blur the distinction between the two can undermine the viability of the peace-keeping operation and endanger its personnel.

36. International problems cannot be solved quickly or within a limited time. Conflicts the United Nations is asked to resolve usually have deep roots and have defied the peacemaking efforts of others. Their resolution requires patient diplomacy and the establishment of a political process that permits, over a period of time, the building of confidence and negotiated solutions to long-standing differences. Such processes often encounter frustrations and set-backs and almost invariably take longer than hoped. It is necessary to resist the temptation to use military power to speed them up. Peace-keeping and the use of force (other than in self-defence) should be seen as alternative techniques and not as adjacent points on a continuum, permitting easy transition from one to the other.

37. In peace-keeping, too, a number of practical difficulties have arisen during the last three years, especially relating to command and control, to the availability of troops and equipment, and to the information capacity of peace-keeping operations.

38. As regards command and control, it is useful to distinguish three levels of authority:

(a) Overall political direction, which belongs to the Security Council;

(b) Executive direction and command, for which the Secretary-General is responsible;

(c) Command in the field, which is entrusted by the Secretary-General to the chief of mission (special representative or force commander/chief military observer).

The distinctions between these three levels must be kept constantly in mind in order to avoid any confusion of functions and responsibilities. It is as inappropriate for a chief of mission to take upon himself the formulation of his/her mission's overall political objectives as it is for the Security Council or the Secretary-General in New York to decide on matters that require a detailed understanding of operational conditions in the field.

39. There has been an increasing tendency in recent years for the Security Council to micro-manage peace-keeping operations. Given the importance of the issues at stake and the volume of resources provided for peace-keeping operations, it is right and proper that the Council should wish to be closely consulted and informed. Procedures for ensuring this have been greatly improved. To assist the Security Council in being informed about the latest developments I have appointed one of my Special Advisers as my personal representative to the Council. As regards information, however, it has to be recognized that, in the inevitable fog and confusion of the near-war conditions in which peace-keepers often find themselves, as for example in Angola, Cambodia, Somalia and the former Yugoslavia, time is required to verify the accuracy of initial reports. Understandably, chiefs of mission have to be more restrained than the media in broadcasting facts that have not been fully substantiated.

40. Troop-contributing Governments, who are responsible to their parliaments and electorates for the safety of their troops, are also understandably anxious to be kept fully informed, especially when the operation concerned is in difficulty. I have endeavoured to meet their concerns by providing them with

regular briefings and by engaging them in dialogue about the conduct of the operation in question. Members of the Security Council have been included in such meetings and the Council has recently decided to formalize them. It is important that this should not lead to any blurring of the distinct levels of authority referred to above.

41. Another important principle is unity of command. The experience in Somalia has underlined again the necessity for a peace-keeping operation to function as an integrated whole. That necessity is all the more imperative when the mission is operating in dangerous conditions. There must be no opening for the parties to undermine its cohesion by singling out some contingents for favourable and others for unfavourable treatment. Nor must there be any attempt by troop-contributing Governments to provide guidance, let alone give orders, to their contingents on operational matters. To do so creates division within the force, adds to the difficulties already inherent in a multinational operation and increases the risk of casualties. It can also create the impression amongst the parties that the operation is serving the policy objectives of the contributing Governments rather than the collective will of the United Nations as formulated by the Security Council. Such impressions inevitably undermine an operation's legitimacy and effectiveness.

42. That said, commanders in the field are, as a matter of course, instructed to consult the commanders of national contingents and make sure that they understand the Security Council's overall approach, as well as the role assigned to their contingents. However, such consultations cannot be allowed to develop into negotiations between the commander in the field and the troop-contributing Governments, whose negotiating partner must always be the Secretariat in New York.

43. As regards the availability of troops and equipment, problems have become steadily more serious. Availability has palpably declined as measured against the Organization's requirements. A considerable effort has been made to expand and refine stand-by arrangements, but these provide no guarantee that troops will be provided for a specific operation. For example, when in May 1994 the Security Council decided to expand the United Nations Assistance Mission for Rwanda (UNAMIR), not one of the 19 Governments that at that time had undertaken to have troops on stand-by agreed to contribute.

44. In these circumstances, I have come to the conclusion that the United Nations does need to give serious thought to the idea of a rapid reaction force. Such a force would be the Security Council's strategic reserve for deployment when there was an emergency need for peace-keeping troops. It might comprise battalion-sized units from a number of countries. These units would be trained to the same standards, use the same operating procedures, be equipped with integrated communications equipment and take part in joint exercises at regular intervals. They would be stationed in their home countries but maintained at a high state of readiness. The value of this arrangement would of course depend on how far the Security Council could be sure that the force would actually be available in an emergency. This will be a complicated and expensive arrangement, but I believe that the time has come to undertake it.

45. Equipment and adequate training is another area of growing concern. The principle is that contributing Governments are to ensure that their troops arrive with all the equipment needed to be fully operational. Increasingly, however, Member States offer troops without the necessary equipment and training. In the absence of alternatives, the United Nations, under pressure, has to procure equipment on the market or through voluntary contributions from other Member States. Further time is required for the troops concerned to learn to operate the equipment, which they are often encountering for the first time. A number of measures can be envisaged to address this problem, for example, the establishment by the United Nations of a reserve stock of standard peace-keeping equipment, as has been frequently proposed, and partnerships between Governments that need equipment and those ready to provide it.

46. An additional lesson from recent experience is that peace-keeping operations, especially those operating in difficult circumstances, need an effective information capacity. This is to enable them to explain their mandate to the population and, by providing a credible and impartial source of information, to counter misinformation disseminated about them, even by the parties themselves. Radio is the most effective medium for this purpose. In all operations where an information capacity, including radio, has been provided, even if late in the day, it has been recognized to have made an invaluable contribution to the operation's success. I have instructed that in the

planning of future operations the possible need for an information capacity should be examined at an early stage and the necessary resources included in the proposed budget.

C. Post-conflict peace-building

47. The validity of the concept of post-conflict peace-building has received wide recognition. The measures it can use—and they are many—can also support preventive diplomacy. Demilitarization, the control of small arms, institutional reform, improved police and judicial systems, the monitoring of human rights, electoral reform and social and economic development can be as valuable in preventing conflict as in healing the wounds after conflict has occurred.

48. The implementation of post-conflict peace-building can, however, be complicated. It requires integrated action and delicate dealings between the United Nations and the parties to the conflict in respect of which peace-building activities are to be undertaken.

49. Two kinds of situation deserve examination. The first is when a comprehensive settlement has been negotiated, with long-term political, economic and social provisions to address the root causes of the conflict, and verification of its implementation is entrusted to a multifunctional peace-keeping operation. The second is when peace-building, whether preventive or post-conflict, is undertaken in relation to a potential or past conflict without any peace-keeping operation being deployed. In both situations the essential goal is the creation of structures for the institutionalization of peace.

50. The first situation is the easier to manage. The United Nations already has an entrée. The parties have accepted its peacemaking and peace-keeping role. The peace-keeping operation will already be mandated to launch various peace-building activities, especially the all-important reintegration of former combatants into productive civilian activities.

51. Even so, political elements who dislike the peace agreement concluded by their Government (and the United Nations verification provided for therein) may resent the United Nations presence and be waiting impatiently for it to leave. Their concerns may find an echo among Member States who fear that the United Nations is in danger of slipping into a role prejudicial to the sovereignty of the country in question and among others who may be uneasy about the resource implications of a long-term peace-building commitment.

52. The timing and modalities of the departure of the peace-keeping operation and the transfer of its peace-building functions to others must therefore be carefully managed in the fullest possible consultation with the Government concerned. The latter's wishes must be paramount; but the United Nations, having invested much effort in helping to end the conflict, can legitimately express views and offer advice about actions the Government could take to reduce the danger of losing what has been achieved. The timing and modalities also need to take into account any residual verification for which the United Nations remains responsible.

53. Most of the activities that together constitute peace-building fall within the mandates of the various programmes, funds, offices and agencies of the United Nations system with responsibilities in the economic, social, humanitarian and human rights fields. In a country ruined by war, resumption of such activities may initially have to be entrusted to, or at least coordinated by, a multifunctional peace-keeping operation, but as that operation succeeds in restoring normal conditions, the programmes, funds, offices and agencies can re-establish themselves and gradually take over responsibility from the peace-keepers, with the resident coordinator in due course assuming the coordination functions temporarily entrusted to the special representative of the Secretary-General.

54. It may also be necessary in such cases to arrange the transfer of decision-making responsibility from the Security Council, which will have authorized the mandate and deployment of the peace-keeping operation, to the General Assembly or other inter-governmental bodies with responsibility for the civilian peace-building activities that will continue. The timing of this transfer will be of special interest to certain Member States because of its financial implications. Each case has to be decided on its merits, the guiding principle being that institutional or budgetary considerations should not be allowed to imperil the continuity of the United Nations efforts in the field.

55. The more difficult situation is when post-conflict (or preventive) peace-building activities are seen to be necessary in a country where the United Nations does not already have a peacemaking or peace-keeping mandate. Who then will identify the need for such measures and propose them to the Government? If the measures are exclusively in the

economic, social and humanitarian fields, they are likely to fall within the purview of the resident coordinator. He or she could recommend them to the Government. Even if the resident coordinator has the capacity to monitor and analyse all the indicators of an impending political and security crisis, however, which is rarely the case, can he or she act without inviting the charge of exceeding his or her mandate by assuming political functions, especially if the proposed measures relate to areas such as security, the police or human rights?

56. In those circumstances, the early warning responsibility has to lie with United Nations Headquarters, using all the information available to it, including reports of the United Nations Development Programme (UNDP) resident coordinator and other United Nations personnel in the country concerned. When analysis of that information gives warning of impending crisis, the Secretary-General, acting on the basis of his general mandate for preventive diplomacy, peacemaking and peace-building, can take the initiative of sending a mission, with the Government's agreement, to discuss with it measures it could usefully take.

D. Disarmament

57. At their Summit on 31 January 1992, the members of the Security Council underscored their interest in and concern for disarmament, arms control and non-proliferation, with special reference to weapons of mass destruction. They committed themselves to taking concrete steps to enhance the effectiveness of the United Nations in those areas.

58. Considerable progress has been made since January 1992. The moratorium on nuclear testing continues to be largely observed. The Conference on Disarmament has finally decided to begin negotiations on a comprehensive test-ban treaty. The General Assembly has recommended the negotiation of a treaty to ban the production of fissile material. Efforts are under way to strengthen the Convention on the Prohibition of the Development, Production and Stockpiling of Bacteriological (Biological) and Toxin Weapons and on Their Destruction (resolution 2826 (XXVI), annex), ratified by 131 countries, through development of verification mechanisms. The Convention on the Prohibition of the Development, Production, Stockpiling and Use of Chemical Weapons and on Their Destruction,[1/] has been signed by 159 countries, but has not yet entered into force, pending ratification by the required 65 signatories. There have been some important accessions to the Treaty on the Non-Proliferation of Nuclear Weapons (resolution 2373 (XXII), annex).

59. I attach special importance to a successful conclusion of the forthcoming conference of the parties to the Non-Proliferation Treaty. It is also of great importance that the Chemical Weapons Convention enter into force as soon as possible. The momentum in all these areas needs to be maintained. Ways have to be found for reconciling transfer of technology with measures necessary to prevent its misuse for military purposes.

60. These issues are of paramount importance both to the security of humankind and to the release of economic, scientific and technological resources for peace and human progress. In the present paper, however, devoted as it is to the Organization's recent experience in handling specific conflicts, I wish to concentrate on what might be called 'micro-disarmament'. By this I mean practical disarmament in the context of the conflicts the United Nations is actually dealing with and of the weapons, most of them light weapons, that are actually killing people in the hundreds of thousands.

61. The contemporary significance of micro-disarmament is demonstrated by the enormous proliferation of automatic assault weapons, anti-personnel mines and the like. Competent authorities have estimated that billions of dollars are being spent yearly on light weapons, representing nearly one third of the world's total arms trade. Many of those weapons are being bought, from developed countries, by developing countries that can least afford to dissipate their precious and finite assets for such purposes, and the volume of the trade in light weapons is far more alarming than the monetary cost might lead one to suspect.

62. Micro-disarmament plays an important part in conjunction with all the other techniques discussed in the present paper. The assembly, control and disposal of weapons has been a central feature of most of the comprehensive peace settlements in which the United Nations has played a peace-keeping role. As a result, the Organization has an unrivalled experience in this field. Micro-disarmament is equally relevant to post-conflict peace-building: Nicaragua has shown what can be achieved through imaginative programmes to mop up large numbers of small arms circulating in a country emerging from a long civil

war. Disarmament can also follow enforcement action, as has been demonstrated in Iraq, where the United Nations Special Commission has played a pioneering role in practical disarmament, in this case involving weapons of mass destruction. All the sanctions regimes include an arms embargo and experience has confirmed the difficulty of monitoring cross-border arms flows into countries at war with their neighbours or within their own borders.

63. There are two categories of light weapons that merit special attention. The first is small arms, which are probably responsible for most of the deaths in current conflicts. The world is awash with them and traffic in them is very difficult to monitor, let alone intercept. The causes are many: the earlier supply of weapons to client States by the parties to the cold war, internal conflicts, competition for commercial markets, criminal activity and the collapse of governmental law and order functions (which both gives free rein to the criminals and creates a legitimate reason for ordinary citizens to acquire weapons for their own defence). A pilot advisory mission I dispatched to Mali in August 1994 at the request of that country's Government has confirmed the exceptional difficulty of controlling the illicit flow of small arms, a problem that can be effectively tackled only on a regional basis. It will take a long time to find effective solutions. I believe strongly that the search should begin now.

64. Secondly, there is the proliferation of anti-personnel mines. One of the positive developments in recent years has been the attention this problem has attracted. The international community has begun to address it. Current efforts in the context of the Convention on Prohibitions or Restrictions on the Use of Certain Conventional Weapons Which May Be Deemed to Be Excessively Injurious or to Have Indiscriminate Effects[2/] are giving priority to anti-personnel mines and the General Assembly's call for a moratorium on their export has won much support from manufacturing countries. In addition, the International Committee of the Red Cross (ICRC) is developing new protocols to the Convention. Meanwhile work continues to try to deal with the approximately 110 million land-mines that have already been laid. This is an issue that must continue to receive priority attention. The Register of Conventional Arms is important in these endeavours. It is essential that the Register be developed into a universal and non-discriminatory mechanism.

65. Progress since 1992 in the area of weapons of mass destruction and major weapons systems must be followed by parallel progress in conventional arms, particularly with respect to light weapons. It will take a long time to find effective solutions. I believe strongly that the search should begin now, and I intend to play my full part in this effort.

E. Sanctions

66. Under Article 41 of the Charter, the Security Council may call upon Member States to apply measures not involving the use of armed force in order to maintain or restore international peace and security. Such measures are commonly referred to as sanctions. This legal basis is recalled in order to underline that the purpose of sanctions is to modify the behaviour of a party that is threatening international peace and security and not to punish or otherwise exact retribution.

67. The Security Council's greatly increased use of this instrument has brought to light a number of difficulties, relating especially to the objectives of sanctions, the monitoring of their application and impact, and their unintended effects.

68. The objectives for which specific sanctions regimes were imposed have not always been clearly defined. Indeed they sometimes seem to change over time. This combination of imprecision and mutability makes it difficult for the Security Council to agree on when the objectives can be considered to have been achieved and sanctions can be lifted. While recognizing that the Council is a political body rather than a judicial organ, it is of great importance that when it decides to impose sanctions it should at the same time define objective criteria for determining that their purpose has been achieved. If general support for the use of sanctions as an effective instrument is to be maintained, care should be taken to avoid giving the impression that the purpose of imposing sanctions is punishment rather than the modification of political behaviour or that criteria are being changed in order to serve purposes other than those which motivated the original decision to impose sanctions.

69. Experience has been gained by the United Nations of how to monitor the application of sanctions and of the part regional organizations can in some cases play in this respect. However, the task is complicated by the reluctance of Governments, for reasons of sovereignty or economic self-

interest, to accept the deployment of international monitors or the international investigation of alleged violations by themselves or their nationals. Measuring the impact of sanctions is even more difficult because of the inherent complexity of such measurement and because of restrictions on access to the target country.

70. Sanctions, as is generally recognized, are a blunt instrument. They raise the ethical question of whether suffering inflicted on vulnerable groups in the target country is a legitimate means of exerting pressure on political leaders whose behaviour is unlikely to be affected by the plight of their subjects. Sanctions also always have unintended or unwanted effects. They can complicate the work of humanitarian agencies by denying them certain categories of supplies and by obliging them to go through arduous procedures to obtain the necessary exemptions. They can conflict with the development objectives of the Organization and do long-term damage to the productive capacity of the target country. They can have a severe effect on other countries that are neighbours or major economic partners of the target country. They can also defeat their own purpose by provoking a patriotic response against the international community, symbolized by the United Nations, and by rallying the population behind the leaders whose behaviour the sanctions are intended to modify.

71. To state these ethical and practical considerations is not to call in question the need for sanctions in certain cases, but it illustrates the need to consider ways of alleviating the effects described. Two possibilities are proposed for Member States' consideration.

72. The first is to ensure that, whenever sanctions are imposed, provision is made to facilitate the work of humanitarian agencies, work that will be all the more needed as a result of the impact of sanctions on vulnerable groups. It is necessary, for instance, to avoid banning imports that are required by local health industries and to devise a fast track for the processing of applications for exemptions for humanitarian activities.

73. Secondly, there is an urgent need for action to respond to the expectations raised by Article 50 of the Charter. Sanctions are a measure taken collectively by the United Nations to maintain or restore international peace and security. The costs involved in their application, like other such costs (e.g. for peacemaking and peace-keeping activities), should be borne equitably by all Member States and not exclusively by the few who have the misfortune to be neighbours or major economic partners of the target country.

74. In 'An Agenda for Peace' I proposed that States suffering collateral damage from the sanctions regimes should be entitled not only to consult the Security Council but also to have a realistic possibility of having their difficulties addressed. For that purpose I recommended that the Security Council devise a set of measures involving the international financial institutions and other components of the United Nations system that could be put in place to address the problem. In response, the Council asked me to seek the views of the heads of the international financial institutions. In their replies, the latter acknowledged the collateral effects of sanctions and expressed the desire to help countries in such situations, but they proposed that this should be done under existing mandates for the support of countries facing negative external shocks and consequent balance-of-payment difficulties. They did not agree that special provisions should be made.

75. In order to address all the above problems, I should like to go beyond the recommendation I made in 1992 and suggest the establishment of a mechanism to carry out the following five functions:

(a) To assess, at the request of the Security Council, and before sanctions are imposed, their potential impact on the target country and on third countries;

(b) To monitor application of the sanctions;

(c) To measure their effects in order to enable the Security Council to fine tune them with a view to maximizing their political impact and minimizing collateral damage;

(d) To ensure the delivery of humanitarian assistance to vulnerable groups;

(e) To explore ways of assisting Member States that are suffering collateral damage and to evaluate claims submitted by such States under Article 50.

76. Since the purpose of this mechanism would be to assist the Security Council, it would have to be located in the United Nations Secretariat. However, it should be empowered to utilize the expertise available throughout the United Nations system, in particular that of the Bretton Woods institutions. Member States will have to give the proposal their political support both at the United Nations and in the intergovernmental bodies

of the agencies concerned if it is to be implemented effectively.

F. Enforcement action

77. One of the achievements of the Charter of the United Nations was to empower the Organization to take enforcement action against those responsible for threats to the peace, breaches of the peace or acts of aggression. However, neither the Security Council nor the Secretary-General at present has the capacity to deploy, direct, command and control operations for this purpose, except perhaps on a very limited scale. I believe that it is desirable in the long term that the United Nations develop such a capacity, but it would be folly to attempt to do so at the present time when the Organization is resource-starved and hard pressed to handle the less demanding peacemaking and peace-keeping responsibilities entrusted to it.

78. In 1950, the Security Council authorized a group of willing Member States to undertake enforcement action in the Korean peninsula. It did so again in 1990 in response to aggression against Kuwait. More recently, the Council has authorized groups of Member States to undertake enforcement action, if necessary, to create conditions for humanitarian relief operations in Somalia and Rwanda and to facilitate the restoration of democracy in Haiti.

79. In Bosnia and Herzegovina, the Security Council has authorized Member States, acting nationally or through regional arrangements, to use force to ensure compliance with its ban on military flights in that country's air space, to support the United Nations forces in the former Yugoslavia in the performance of their mandate, including defence of personnel who may be under attack, and to deter attacks against the safe areas. The Member States concerned decided to entrust those tasks to the North Atlantic Treaty Organization (NATO). Much effort has been required between the Secretariat and NATO to work out procedures for the coordination of this unprecedented collaboration. This is not surprising given the two organizations' very different mandates and approaches to the maintenance of peace and security. Of greater concern, as already mentioned, are the consequences of using force, other than for self-defence, in a peace-keeping context.

80. The experience of the last few years has demonstrated both the value that can be gained and the difficulties that can arise when the Security Council entrusts enforcement tasks to groups of Member States. On the positive side, this arrangement provides the Organization with an enforcement capacity it would not otherwise have and is greatly preferable to the unilateral use of force by Member States without reference to the United Nations. On the other hand, the arrangement can have a negative impact on the Organization's stature and credibility. There is also the danger that the States concerned may claim international legitimacy and approval for forceful actions that were not in fact envisaged by the Security Council when it gave its authorization to them. Member States so authorized have in recent operations reported more fully and more regularly to the Security Council about their activities.

IV. Coordination

81. Just as the United Nations does not claim a monopoly of the instruments discussed above, neither can it alone apply them. All the efforts of the Security Council, the General Assembly and the Secretary-General to control and resolve conflicts need the cooperation and support of other players on the international stage: the Governments that constitute the United Nations membership, regional and non-governmental organizations, and the various funds, programmes, offices and agencies of the United Nations system itself. If United Nations efforts are to succeed, the roles of the various players need to be carefully coordinated in an integrated approach to human security.

82. Governments are central to all the activities discussed in the present position paper. It is they who authorize the activities and finance them. It is they who provide directly the vast majority of the personnel required, as well as most of the equipment. It is they who set the policies of the specialized agencies of the United Nations system and of the regional organizations. It is they whose continuing support, and, as necessary, intervention with the parties, is essential if the Secretary-General is to succeed in carrying out the mandates entrusted to him. It is they who are parties, or at least one of the parties, to each conflict the United Nations is trying to control and resolve.

83. A new trend in recent years has been the establishment of informal groups of Member States, created on an ad hoc basis to support the Secretary-General in the discharge of peacemaking and peace-keeping mandates

entrusted to him. They are normally referred to as 'Friends of the Secretary-General for . . .'. They have no formal mandate from the General Assembly or the Security Council and comprise States with a particular interest in the conflict in question. They have material and diplomatic resources that can be used to support the Secretary-General's efforts. Their value to him is as a sounding-board, as a source of ideas and comment and as a diplomatic instrument for bringing influence to bear on the parties.

84. This arrangement has been of value in a number of instances. It is nevertheless necessary to maintain a clear understanding of who is responsible for what. The Secretary-General has the mandate from the relevant intergovernmental body and must remain in the lead. The members of the 'Friends' group have agreed to support the Secretary-General at his request. If they take initiatives not requested by the Secretary-General, there is a risk of duplication or overlapping of efforts, which can be exploited by recalcitrant parties. Such initiatives can also raise questions in the intergovernmental body that expects the Secretary-General to retain responsibility for the mandate entrusted to him and to report to that body on his implementation of it.

85. As for regional organizations, Chapter VIII of the Charter defines the role they can play in the maintenance of peace and security. They have much to contribute. Since the Security Council Summit, the United Nations has extended considerably its experience of working with regional organizations in this field. On 1 August 1994, I convened a meeting in New York of the heads of a number of such organizations with which the United Nations had recently cooperated on the ground in peacemaking and peace-keeping. The meeting permitted a useful exchange of views and it is my intention to hold further meetings of this kind.

86. Cooperation between the United Nations and regional organizations takes a number of forms. At least five can be identified:

(a) Consultation: this has been well-established for some time. In some cases it is governed by formal agreements and reports are made to the General Assembly; in other cases it is less formal. The purpose is to exchange views on conflicts that both the United Nations and the regional organization may be trying to solve;

(b) Diplomatic support: the regional organization participates in the peacemaking activities of the United Nations and supports them by diplomatic initiatives (in a manner analogous to groups of 'Friends' as described above) and/or by providing technical input, as the Organization for Security and Cooperation in Europe (OSCE) does, for instance, on constitutional issues relating to Abkhazia. In the same way, the United Nations can support the regional organization in its efforts (as it does for OSCE over Nagorno-Karabakh);

(c) Operational support: the most developed example is the provision by NATO of air power to support the United Nations Protection Force (UNPROFOR) in the former Yugoslavia. For its part, the United Nations can provide technical advice to regional organizations that undertake peace-keeping operations of their own;

(d) Co-deployment: United Nations field missions have been deployed in conjunction with the Economic Community of West African States (ECOWAS) in Liberia and with the Commonwealth of Independent States (CIS) in Georgia. If those experiments succeed, they may herald a new division of labour between the United Nations and regional organizations, under which the regional organization carries the main burden but a small United Nations operation supports it and verifies that it is functioning in a manner consistent with positions adopted by the Security Council. The political, operational and financial aspects of the arrangement give rise to questions of some delicacy. Member States may wish at some stage to make an assessment, in the light of experience in Liberia and Georgia, of how this model might be followed in the future;

(e) Joint operations: the example is the United Nations Mission in Haiti, the staffing, direction and financing of which are shared between the United Nations and the Organization of American States (OAS). This arrangement has worked, and it too is a possible model for the future that will need careful assessment.

87. The capacity of regional organizations for peacemaking and peace-keeping varies considerably. None of them has yet developed a capacity which matches that of the United Nations, though some have accumulated important experience in the field and others are developing rapidly. The United Nations is ready to help them in this respect when requested to do so and when resources permit.

Given their varied capacity, the differences in their structures, mandates and decision-making processes and the variety of forms that cooperation with the United Nations is already taking, it would not be appropriate to try to establish a universal model for their relationship with the United Nations. Nevertheless it is possible to identify certain principles on which it should be based.

88. Such principles include:

(a) Agreed mechanisms for consultation should be established, but need not be formal;

(b) The primacy of the United Nations, as set out in the Charter, must be respected. In particular, regional organizations should not enter into arrangements that assume a level of United Nations support not yet submitted to or approved by its Member States. This is an area where close and early consultation is of great importance;

(c) The division of labour must be clearly defined and agreed in order to avoid overlap and institutional rivalry where the United Nations and a regional organization are both working on the same conflict. In such cases it is also particularly important to avoid a multiplicity of mediators;

(d) Consistency by members of regional organizations who are also Member States of the United Nations is needed in dealing with a common problem of interest to both organizations, for example, standards for peace-keeping operations.

89. Non-governmental organizations also play an important role in all United Nations activities discussed in the present paper. To date, 1003 non-governmental organizations have been granted consultative status with the United Nations and many of them have accredited representatives at United Nations Headquarters in New York and/or the United Nations Office at Geneva. The changed nature of United Nations operations in the field has brought non-governmental organizations into a closer relationship with the United Nations, especially in the provision of humanitarian relief in conflict situations and in post-conflict peace-building. It has been necessary to devise procedures that do not compromise their non-governmental status but do ensure that their efforts are properly coordinated with those of the United Nations and its programmes, funds, offices and agencies. Non-governmental organizations have also had great success in mobilizing public support and funds for humanitarian relief in countries affected by international or domestic conflict.

90. Within the United Nations system there are three levels at which coordination is required: within the United Nations Secretariat; between United Nations Headquarters and the head offices of other funds, programmes, offices and agencies of the United Nations system; and in the field.

91. The multifunctional nature of both peace-keeping and peace-building has made it necessary to improve coordination within the Secretariat, so that the relevant departments function as an integrated whole under my authority and control. Proposals the Secretary-General makes to the General Assembly or the Security Council on peace and security issues need to be based on coordinated inputs from the Departments of Political Affairs, Peace-keeping Operations, Humanitarian Affairs and Administration and Management and others. Guidance to the field must similarly be coordinated, in order to ensure that chiefs of missions do not receive conflicting instructions from different authorities within the Secretariat.

92. In an international bureaucracy interdepartmental cooperation and coordination come even less naturally than they do in a national environment. It has required some effort to ensure that the above objectives are met. I have entrusted the main responsibility in this regard to my Task Force on United Nations Operations and to interdepartmental groups at the working level on each major conflict where the organization is playing a peacemaking or peace-keeping role.

93. Improved coordination is equally necessary within the United Nations system as a whole. The responsibilities involved in multifunctional peace-keeping operations and in peace-building transcend the competence and expertise of any one department, programme, fund, office or agency of the United Nations. Short-term programmes are needed for ceasefires, demobilization, humanitarian relief and refugee return; but it is the longer-term programmes that help rebuild societies and put them back on the path of development. Short-term and long-term programmes need to be planned and implemented in a coordinated way if they are to contribute to the consolidation of peace and development. The mechanism for ensuring a more effective and equitable application of sanctions, which I have recommended earlier in the present position paper, will equally require close coordination between a large number of players on the United Nations stage.

94. Such coordination has to date proved difficult to achieve. Each of the agencies concerned has its own intergovernmental legislative body and its own mandate. In the past, there also has been insufficient interaction, in both directions, between those responsible in the Secretariat for designing and implementing peacemaking, peace-keeping and peace-building activities and the international financial institutions, who often have an all-important say in making sure that the necessary resources are available.

95. As regards coordination in the field, the current practice when a peace-keeping operation is deployed is to entrust this task to a special representative of the Secretary-General. Cambodia, El Salvador and Mozambique are successful examples, not least because of the cooperation extended to my Special Representatives by the various other components of the United Nations system.

96. For my part, I shall maintain my efforts in the Administrative Committee on Coordination and in my bilateral relations with the executive heads of the various funds, programmes, offices and agencies to achieve better coordination within the United Nations system in the context of peace and security. Governments of Member States can support those efforts. Many of the problems of coordination arise from the mandates decreed for the agencies by discrete intergovernmental bodies. As such, they defy the capacity for inter-Secretariat coordination. I accordingly recommend that Governments instruct their representatives in the various intergovernmental bodies to ensure that proper coordination is recognized to be an essential condition for the Organization's success and that it is not made hostage to inter-institutional rivalry and competition.

V. Financial Resources

97. None of the instruments discussed in the present paper can be used unless Governments provide the necessary financial resources. There is no other source of funds. The failure of Member States to pay their assessed contributions for activities they themselves have voted into being makes it impossible to carry out those activities to the standard expected. It also calls in question the credibility of those who have willed the ends but not the means—and who then criticize the United Nations for its failures. On 12 October 1994, I put to the Member States a package of proposals, ideas and questions on finance and budgetary procedures that I believe can contribute to a solution (see A/49/PV.28).

98. The financial crisis is particularly debilitating as regards peace-keeping. The shortage of funds, in particular for reconnaissance and planning, for the start-up of operations and for the recruitment and training of personnel imposes severe constraints on the Organization's ability to deploy, with the desired speed, newly approved operations. Peace-keeping is also afflicted by Member States' difficulties in providing troops, police and equipment on the scale required by the current volume of peace-keeping activity.

99. Meanwhile, there is continuing damage to the credibility of the Security Council and of the Organization as a whole when the Council adopts decisions that cannot be carried out because the necessary troops are not forthcoming. The continuing problems with regard to the safe areas in Bosnia and Herzegovina and the expansion of UNAMIR in response to genocide in Rwanda are cases in point. In the future it would be advisable to establish the availability of the necessary troops and equipment before it is decided to create a new peace-keeping operation or assign a new task to an existing one.

100. Peace-building is another activity that is critically dependent on Member States' readiness to make the necessary resources available. It can be a long-term process and expensive—except in comparison with the cost of peacemaking and peace-keeping if the conflict should recur. One lesson learned in recent years is that, in putting together the peace-building elements in a comprehensive settlement plan, the United Nations should consult the international financial institutions in good time to ensure that the cost of implementing the plan is taken into account in the design of the economic plans of the Government concerned. The problems in this area are aggravated by many donors' reluctance to finance crucial elements such as the conversion of guerrilla movements into political parties, the creation of new police forces or the provision of credit for the purchase of land in 'arms for land' programmes.

101. Compensation to Member States affected by sanctions on their neighbours or economic partners will also be possible only if the richer Member States recognize both the moral argument that such countries should not be expected to bear alone costs resulting from action collectively decided upon by the international community and the practical argu-

ment that such compensation is necessary to encourage those States to cooperate in applying decisions taken by the Security Council. I recognize that the sums involved will be large but I am convinced that they must be made available if the Council is to continue to rely on sanctions.

VI. Conclusion

102. The present position paper, submitted to the Member States at the opening of the United Nations fiftieth anniversary year, is intended to serve as a contribution to the continuing campaign to strengthen a common capacity to deal with threats to peace and security.

103. The times call for thinking afresh, for striving together and for creating new ways to overcome crises. This is because the different world that emerged when the cold war ceased is still a world not fully understood. The changed face of conflict today requires us to be perceptive, adaptive, creative and courageous, and to address simultaneously the immediate as well as the root causes of conflict, which all too often lie in the absence of economic opportunities and social inequities. Perhaps above all it requires a deeper commitment to cooperation and true multilateralism than humanity has ever achieved before.

104. This is why the pages of the present paper reiterate the need for hard decisions. As understanding grows of the challenges to peace and security, hard decisions, if postponed, will appear in retrospect as having been relatively easy when measured against the magnitude of tomorrow's troubles.

105. There is no reason for frustration or pessimism. More progress has been made in the past few years towards using the United Nations as it was designed to be used than many could ever have predicted. The call to decision should be a call to confidence and courage.

Notes

[1] *Official Records of the General Assembly, Forty-seventh Session, Supplement no. 27* (A/47/27), appendix I.
[2] See *The United Nations Disarmament Yearbook*, vol. 5, 1980 (United Nations publication, sales no. G.81.IX.4), appendix VII.

Source: UN document A/50/60 (S/1995/1), 3 Jan. 1995.

Appendix 10B. Code of Conduct on Politico-Military Aspects of Security

BUDAPEST DECISION V. CODE OF CONDUCT ON POLITICO-MILITARY ASPECTS OF SECURITY

Budapest, 6 December 1994

Preamble

The participating States of the Conference on Security and Co-operation in Europe (CSCE),

Recognizing the need to enhance security co-operation, including through the further encouragement of norms of responsible and co-operative behaviour in the field of security,

Confirming that nothing in this Code diminishes the validity and applicability of the purposes and principles of the Charter of the United Nations or of other provisions of international law,

Reaffirming the undiminished validity of the guiding principles and common values of the Helsinki Final Act, the Charter of Paris and the Helsinki Document 1992, embodying responsibilities of States towards each other and of governments towards their people, as well as the validity of other CSCE commitments,

Have adopted the following Code of Conduct on politico–military aspects of security:

I

1. The participating States emphasize that the full respect for all CSCE principles embodied in the Helsinki Final Act and the implementation in good faith of all commitments undertaken in the CSCE are of fundamental importance for stability and security, and consequently constitute a matter of direct and legitimate concern to all of them.

2. The participating States confirm the continuing validity of their comprehensive concept of security, as initiated in the Final Act, which relates the maintenance of peace to the respect for human rights and fundamental freedoms. It links economic and environmental co-operation with peaceful inter-State relations.

3. They remain convinced that security is indivisible and that the security of each of them is inseparably linked to the security of all others. They will not strengthen their security at the expense of the security of other States. They will pursue their own security interests in conformity with the common effort to strengthen security and stability in the CSCE area and beyond.

4. Reaffirming their respect for each other's sovereign equality and individuality as well as the rights inherent in and encompassed by its sovereignty, the participating States will base their mutual security relations upon a co-operative approach. They emphasize in this regard the key role of the CSCE. They will continue to develop complementary and mutually reinforcing institutions that include European and transatlantic organizations, multilateral and bilateral undertakings and various forms of regional and subregional co-operation. The participating States will co-operate in ensuring that all such security arrangements are in harmony with CSCE principles and commitments under this Code.

5. They are determined to act in solidarity if CSCE norms and commitments are violated and to facilitate concerted responses to security challenges that they may face as a result. They will consult promptly, in conformity with their CSCE responsibilities, with a participating State seeking assistance in realizing its individual or collective self-defence. They will consider jointly the nature of the threat and actions that may be required in defence of their common values.

II

6. The participating States will not support terrorist acts in any way and will take appropriate measures to prevent and combat terrorism in all its forms. They will co-operate fully in combating the threat of terrorist activities through implementation of international instruments and commitments they agree upon in this respect. They will, in particular, take steps to fulfil the requirements

of international agreements by which they are bound to prosecute or extradite terrorists.

III

7. The participating States recall that the principles of the Helsinki Final Act are all of primary significance and, accordingly, that they will be equally and unreservedly applied, each of them being interpreted taking into account the others.

8. The participating States will not provide assistance to or support States that are in violation of their obligation to refrain from the threat or use of force against the territorial integrity or political independence of any State, or in any other manner inconsistent with the Charter of the United Nations and with the Declaration on Principles Guiding Relations between Participating States contained in the Helsinki Final Act.

IV

9. The participating States reaffirm the inherent right, as recognized in the Charter of the United Nations, of individual and collective self-defence.

10. Each participating State, bearing in mind the legitimate security concerns of other States, is free to determine its security interests itself on the basis of sovereign equality and has the right freely to choose its own security arrangements, in accordance with international law and with commitments to CSCE principles and objectives.

11. The participating States each have the sovereign right to belong or not to belong to international organizations, and to be or not to be a party to bilateral or multilateral treaties, including treaties of alliance; they also have the right to neutrality. Each has the right to change its status in this respect, subject to relevant agreements and procedures. Each will respect the rights of all others in this regard.

12. Each participating State will maintain only such military capabilities as are commensurate with individual or collective legitimate security needs, taking into account its obligations under international law.

13. Each participating State will determine its military capabilities on the basis of national democratic procedures, bearing in mind the legitimate security concerns of other States as well as the need to contribute to international security and stability. No participating State will attempt to impose military domination over any other participating State.

14. A participating State may station its armed forces on the territory of another participating State in accordance with their freely negotiated agreement as well as in accordance with international law.

V

15. The participating States will implement in good faith each of their commitments in the field of arms control, disarmament and confidence- and security-building as an important element of their indivisible security.

16. With a view to enhancing security and stability in the CSCE area, the participating States reaffirm their commitment to pursue arms control, disarmament and confidence- and security-building measures.

VI

17. The participating States commit themselves to co-operate, including through development of sound economic and environmental conditions, to counter tensions that may lead to conflict. The sources of such tensions include violations of human rights and fundamental freedoms and of other commitments in the human dimension; manifestations of aggressive nationalism, racism, chauvinism, xenophobia and anti-semitism also endanger peace and security.

18. The participating States stress the importance both of early identification of potential conflicts and of their joint efforts in the field of conflict prevention, crisis management and peaceful settlement of disputes.

19. In the event of armed conflict, they will seek to facilitate the effective cessation of hostilities and seek to create conditions favourable to the political solution of the conflict. They will co-operate in support of humanitarian assistance to alleviate suffering among the civilian population, including facilitating the movement of personnel and resources dedicated to such tasks.

VII

20. The participating States consider the democratic political control of military, paramilitary and internal security forces as well as of intelligence services and the police to be an indispensable element of stability and security. They will further the integration of their armed forces with civil society as an important expression of democracy.

21. Each participating State will at all times provide for and maintain effective guidance to

and control of its military, paramilitary and security forces by constitutionally established authorities vested with democratic legitimacy. Each participating State will provide controls to ensure that such authorities fulfil their constitutional and legal responsibilities. They will clearly define the roles and missions of such forces and their obligation to act solely within the constitutional framework.

22. Each participating State will provide for its legislative approval of defence expenditures. Each participating State will, with due regard to national security requirements, exercise restraint in its military expenditures and provide for transparency and public access to information related to the armed forces.

23. Each participating State, while providing for the individual service member's exercise of his or her civil rights, will ensure that its armed forces as such are politically neutral.

24. Each participating State will provide and maintain measures to guard against accidental or unauthorized use of military means.

25. The participating States will not tolerate or support forces that are not accountable to or controlled by their constitutionally established authorities. If a participating State is unable to exercise its authority over such forces, it may seek consultations within the CSCE to consider steps to be taken.

26. Each participating State will ensure that in accordance with its international commitments its paramilitary forces refrain from the acquisition of combat mission capabilities in excess of those for which they were established.

27. Each participating State will ensure that the recruitment or call-up of personnel for service in its military, paramilitary and security forces is consistent with its obligations and commitments in respect of human rights and fundamental freedoms.

28. The participating States will reflect in their laws or other relevant documents the rights and duties of armed forces personnel. They will consider introducing exemptions from or alternatives to military service.

29. The participating States will make widely available in their respective countries the international humanitarian law of war. They will reflect, in accordance with national practice, their commitments in this field in their military training programmes and regulations.

30. Each participating State will instruct its armed forces personnel in international humanitarian law, rules, conventions and commitments governing armed conflict and will ensure that such personnel are aware that they are individually accountable under national and international law for their actions.

31. The participating States will ensure that armed forces personnel vested with command authority exercise it in accordance with relevant national as well as international law and are made aware that they can be held individually accountable under those laws for the unlawful exercise of such authority and that orders contrary to national and international law must not be given. The responsibility of superiors does not exempt subordinates from any of their individual responsibilities.

32. Each participating State will ensure that military, paramilitary and security forces personnel will be able to enjoy and exercise their human rights and fundamental freedoms as reflected in CSCE documents and international law, in conformity with relevant constitutional legal provisions and with the requirements of service.

33. Each participating State will provide appropriate legal and administrative procedures to protest the rights of all its forces personnel.

VIII

34. Each participating State will ensure that its armed forces are, in peace and in war, commanded, manned, trained and equipped in ways that are consistent with the provisions of international law and its respective obligations and commitments related to the use of armed forces in armed conflict, including as applicable the Hague Conventions of 1907 and 1954, the Geneva Conventions of 1949 and the 1977 Protocols Additional thereto, as well as the 1980 Convention on the Use of Certain Conventional Weapons.

35. Each participating State will ensure that its defence policy and doctrine are consistent with international law related to the use of armed forces, including in armed conflict, and the relevant commitments of this Code.

36. Each participating State will ensure that any decision to assign its armed forces to internal security missions is arrived at in conformity with constitutional procedures. Such decisions will prescribe the armed forces' missions, ensuring that they will be performed under the effective control of constitutionally established authorities and subject to the rule of law. If recourse to force cannot be avoided in performing internal security

missions, each participating State will ensure that its use must be commensurate with the needs for enforcement. The armed forces will take due care to avoid injury to civilians or their property.

37. The participating States will not use armed forces to limit the peaceful and lawful exercise of their human and civil rights by persons as individuals or as representatives of groups nor to deprive them of their national, religious, cultural, linguistic or ethnic identity.

IX

38. Each participating State is responsible for implementation of this Code. If requested, a participating State will provide appropriate clarification regarding its implementation of the Code. Appropriate CSCE bodies, mechanisms and procedures will be used to assess, review and improve if necessary the implementation of this Code.

X

39. The provisions adopted in this Code of Conduct are politically binding. Accordingly, this Code is not eligible for registration under Article 102 of the Charter of the United Nations. This Code will come into effect on 1 January 1995.

40. Nothing in this Code alters the nature and content of the commitments undertaken in other CSCE documents.

41. The participating States will seek to ensure that their relevant internal documents and procedures or, where appropriate, legal instruments reflect the commitments made in this Code.

42. The text of the Code will be published in each participating State, which will disseminate it and make it known as widely as possible.

Source: Section V of the Budapest Summit Declaration, Budapest, 6 Dec. 1994.

About the authors

James E. Goodby (USA) is Distinguished Service Professor of International Peace and Security at Carnegie Mellon University. During a 35-year career as a foreign service officer, he was head of the US delegation to the Stockholm Conference on Disarmament in Europe, Vice Chairman of the US delegation to the Strategic Arms Reduction Talks (START) and Ambassador to Finland. Since March 1993, as a consultant to the Department of State, he has served as Chief US Negotiator for the Safe and Secure Dismantlement of Nuclear Weapons and is responsible for negotiating agreements with Belarus, Kazakhstan, Russia and Ukraine, under which the USA provides equipment and technical services to these countries to assist them in dismantling weapons of mass destruction, preventing weapon proliferation and converting military facilities to civilian enterprises.

James Macintosh (Canada) is the principal researcher at Canadian Security Research where he specializes in arms control and security studies. He has done extensive contract research for Foreign Affairs and International Trade Canada and has worked on a variety of projects for different centres, foundations and agencies. He was Senior Research Associate at the York University Centre for International and Strategic Studies in Toronto, Canada, where he worked from September 1982 until August 1992. He holds a B.A. and M.A. in political science from York University.

John J. Maresca (USA) is the President of the Open Media Research Institute in Prague. He has been a Guest Scholar at the United States Institute of Peace in Washington, DC. He was formerly the US Ambassador to the CSCE, and has published a book (*To Helsinki*, 1985) on the negotiation of the Helsinki Final Act. He was sent as a Special Envoy to open US relations with the new states from the former USSR, and spent two years (1992–94) seeking to mediate the war over Nagorno-Karabakh.

M. Granger Morgan (USA) holds a Ph.D. in applied physics from the University of California, San Diego. Since 1977 he has been Head of the Department of Engineering and Public Policy at Carnegie Mellon University where he also oversees the Program on International Peace and Security.

Russell Leigh Moses (USA) is Assistant Professor of International Relations at the Johns Hopkins University, School of Advanced International Studies Center for Chinese and American Studies in Nanjing, China. He holds an M.A. and a Ph.D. in political science from the University of Pittsburgh. He is the author of *Freeing the Hostages: Re-examining US–Iranian Negotiations and Soviet Policy, 1979–1981* (1995) and is currently working on a study on the consequences of the withdrawal of politics and the primacy of economics in the post-cold war period.

William W. Newmann (USA) is a Ph.D. candidate at the Graduate School of Public and International Affairs at the University of Pittsburgh, and an Instructor of Political Science and Public Administration at Virginia Commonwealth University. He holds an M.A. and a B.A. in political science from Drew University and the University of Pennsylvania, respectively. His research focuses on US defence and foreign policy decision making.

Daniel B. O'Connor (USA) is completing his doctoral work at the School of International Service at the American University. He is writing a dissertation on military assistance decision making during the Reagan Administration. He is also a Presidential Management Intern at the National Aeronautics and Space Administration in Washington, DC.

Sergey Rogov (Russia) is Director of the Institute of USA and Canada (Moscow). He is the founding director of a new, independent institute focusing on arms control.

Mitchel B. Wallerstein (USA) holds a Ph.D. in political science from the Massachusetts Institute of Technology. He is currently Deputy Assistant Secretary of Defense for Counterproliferation Policy. Prior to joining the Department of Defense he was Deputy Executive Officer of the National Research Council (NRC). In 1987 and 1990 he was the Principal Staff Officer for two NRC reports on the subject of US export controls.

Phil Williams (UK) is Director of the Ridgway Center and Professor in the Graduate School of Public and International Affairs at the University of Pittsburgh. Prior to his current position, he was acting head of the International Security Program, Royal Institute of International Affairs, and senior lecturer in international relations, Department of Politics, University of Southampton. He is the author of several books and in the last two years, he has contributed articles in *Survival*, *The Washington Quarterly* and the *Bulletin of Narcotics* on issues related to transnational organized crime.

Index

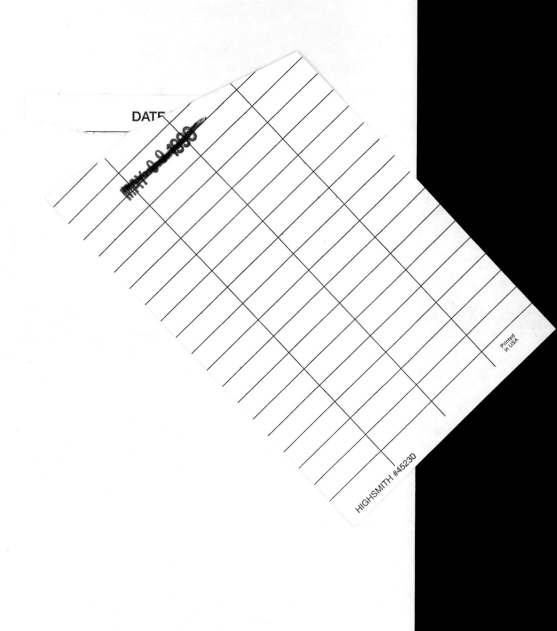

DATE

MAY 0 0 1998

HIGHSMITH #45230

Printed
in USA